FINANCIAL INTELLIGENCE, THE EXCHANGE OF INFORMATION AND TACKLING FINANCIAL CRIME IN THE UNITED KINGDOM

This book examines the international standards relating to information exchange, identifying its importance in relation to combatting money laundering, terrorist financing and fraud. Its timely publication follows the Financial Action Task Force (FATF) rating the UK's anti-money laundering and counterterrorism financing regimes as amongst the best in the world in its fourth Mutual Evaluation Report.

The book features an alternative review via three case studies – money laundering, terrorism financing and general fraud. These illustrate the importance of information exchange and highlight flaws in the UK's legal framework, challenging the conclusions of the FATF. Considering this comprehensive analysis, the book then provides recommendations for reform.

Financial Intelligence, the Exchange of Information and Tackling Financial Crime in the United Kingdom

A Critical Review

Nicholas Ryder

•HART•
OXFORD • LONDON • NEW YORK • NEW DELHI • SYDNEY

HART PUBLISHING
Bloomsbury Publishing Plc
Kemp House, Chawley Park, Cumnor Hill, Oxford, OX2 9PH, UK
1385 Broadway, New York, NY 10018, USA
Bloomsbury Publishing Ireland Limited, 29 Earlsfort Terrace, Dublin 2, D02 AY28, Ireland

HART PUBLISHING, the Hart/Stag logo, BLOOMSBURY and the Diana logo are trademarks of Bloomsbury Publishing Plc

First published in Great Britain 2026

A catalogue record for this book is available from the British Library.

Library of Congress Cataloging-in-Publication data

Names: Ryder, Nicholas author

Title: Financial intelligence, the exchange of information and tackling financial crime in the United Kingdom : a critical review / Nicholas Ryder.

Description: Oxford ; New York : Hart Publishing, 2026. | Includes bibliographical references and index. | Summary: "This book examines the international standards relating to information exchange, identifying its importance in relation to combatting money laundering, terrorist financing and fraud. Its timely publication follows the Financial Action Task Force (FATF) rating the UK's anti-money laundering and counter-terrorism financing regimes as amongst the best in the world in its fourth Mutual Evaluation Report. The book features an alternative review via four case studies that illustrate the importance of information exchange and highlight flaws in the UK's legal framework, challenging the conclusions of the FATF. Considering this comprehensive analysis, the monograph provides recommendations for reform"— Provided by publisher.

Identifiers: LCCN 2026002038 (print) | LCCN 2026002039 (ebook) | ISBN 9781509968909 hardback | ISBN 9781509968930 paperback | ISBN 9781509968923 Epub | ISBN 9781509968916 pdf

Subjects: LCSH: Commercial crimes—Law and legislation—Great Britain | Financial Action Task Force | Money laundering—Law and legislation—Great Britain | Money laundering—Prevention—Great Britain | Money laundering investigation—Great Britain | Terrorism—Finance—Law and legislation—Great Britain | Terrorism—Finance—Prevention—Government policy—Great Britain

Classification: LCC KD7990 .R93 2026 (print) | LCC KD7990 (ebook)

LC record available at https://lccn.loc.gov/2026002038

LC ebook record available at https://lccn.loc.gov/2026002039

ISBN: HB: 978-1-50996-890-9
ePDF: 978-1-50996-891-6
ePub: 978-1-50996-892-3

Typeset by Compuscript Ltd, Shannon

For product safety related questions contact productsafety@bloomsbury.com

To find out more about our authors and books visit www.hartpublishing.co.uk. Here you will find extracts, author information, details of forthcoming events and the option to sign up for our newsletters.

ACKNOWLEDGEMENTS

I would like to thank Verity Stuart, Kate Whetter and Sasha Jawed at Hart Publishing for all of their support.

My thanks also go to Dr Samantha Mapson and Dr Diana Johnson (University of the West of England), Dr Enrico Basile (Bocconi University), Dr Lorenzo Pasculli (University College London), Professor Umut Turksen (Exeter University), Petula Thomas-Jones (Cardiff University) and Thomas Burgess (Cardiff University) who reviewed early drafts of chapters.

The support from Cardiff University's School of Law and Politics through giving me a sabbatical greatly helped with the time I needed to finish this monograph. My colleagues Petula Thomas-Jones and Dr Henry Hillman also supported this through covering my other duties during my sabbatical.

And finally, this book is dedicated to my incredibly supportive niece Hannah, who has kept me equally grounded and challenged through the book-writing process, frequently reminding me of the double 'FF' in my title!

CONTENTS

TABLE OF LEGISLATION

United Nations

European Union

Financial Action Task Force

United Kingdom

TABLE OF LEGISLATION

United Nations

European Union

Financial Action Task Force

United Kingdom

1

Introduction

> A single financial institution has only a partial view of transactions and sees one small piece of what is often a large, complex puzzle. Criminals exploit this information gap by using multiple financial institutions within or across jurisdictions to layer their illicit financial flows. Without more accurate and consistent information, it becomes increasingly difficult for individual financial institutions to detect these activities. By using collaborative analytics, bringing data together, or developing other sharing initiatives in responsible ways, financial institutions seek to build a clearer picture of the puzzle, to better understand, assess, and mitigate money laundering and terrorist financing risks.[1]

I. Introduction

Financial crime poses a significant threat at global, regional and national levels, undermining economic stability, eroding public trust, facilitating corruption, organised crime and terrorism. In the United Kingdom (UK), the scale of the problem is stark. Financial crime is estimated to cost the country up to £350 billion annually.[2] Criminals exploit the financial system to move illicit funds rapidly across borders, making detection and disruption increasingly difficult. To counter this, robust and effective data-sharing mechanisms are essential for the UK to comply with the international standards of financial crime prevention and detection. By sharing financial and transactional data indicative of criminality, the private and public sectors can enhance risk detection and strengthen defences against money laundering, fraud and terrorist financing. Ultimately, such data-sharing initiatives are not just beneficial, they are essential to safeguard the integrity of financial systems and reducing the global footprint of financial crime. Therefore, this monograph examines the key aspects of financial crime in the UK through the lens of several important data-sharing legislative and policy developments.

[1] Financial Action Task Force (FATF), *Partnering in the Fight against Financial Crime – Data Protection, Technology and Private Sector Information Sharing* (FATF, 2022) at 3.

[2] M Button, B Hock and D Shepherd, *Economic Crime from Conception to Response* (Routledge, 2022) at 17.

II. Introducing Financial Crime

The term financial or economic crime is often used in common parlance and thus is one which we assume we know its meaning, despite the fact that there is 'no internationally accepted definition'.[3] As will be outlined in chapters four, five and six, definitions are abundant for money laundering, terrorist financing and fraud, but are vague for the collective expressions of both financial crime and white-collar crime. Any discussion must begin with the seminal definition of white-collar crime offered by Professor Edwin Sutherland.[4] He defined white-collar crime as 'a crime committed by a person of respectability and high social status in the course of his occupation'.[5] In his paper, Sutherland stated:

> The present-day white-collar criminals, who are more suave and deceptive than the 'robber barons', are represented … [by] many other merchant princes and captains of finance and industry, and by a host of lesser followers. Their criminality has been demonstrated again and again in the investigations of land offices, railways, insurance, munitions, banking, public utilities, stock exchanges, the oil industry, real estate, reorganisation committees, receiverships, bankruptcies, and politics.[6]

It has been suggested that the most important component of this definition is that white-collar crime is committed by people of a high social standing.[7] This was echoed by Kemper who noted that white-collar crime refers to 'illegal behaviour that takes advantage of positions of professional authority and power – or simply the opportunity structures available within business – for personal or corporate gain'.[8] Nevertheless, Sutherland's definition remains 'deeply contested'.[9] White-collar crime can be referred to as 'economic crime', which has been defined as involving

> money, finance or assets, the purpose of which is to unlawfully obtain a profit or advantage for the perpetrator or cause loss to others. This poses a threat to the UK's national security, economy and its institutions and causes serious harm to society and individuals.[10]

[3] International Monetary Fund, *Financial System Abuse, Financial Crime and Money Laundering – Background Paper* (International Monetary Fund, February 2001) at 5.

[4] E Sutherland, 'The White-Collar Criminal' (1940) *American Sociological Review* 5(1) 1–12 at 1.

[5] Sutherland, E. *White Collar Crime* (Dryden, 1949) at 9.

[6] See Sutherland (n 4) at 2.

[7] See M Benson and S Simpson, *White-Collar Crime: An Opportunity Perspective* (Routledge, 2009).

[8] M Kempa, 'Combating White-Collar Crime in Canada: Serving Victim Needs and Market Integrity' (2010) *Journal of Financial Crime* 17(2), 251–64, at 252.

[9] S Green, 'The Concept of White-Collar Crime in Law and Legal Theory' (2004) *Buffalo Criminal Law Review* 8(1), 1–34 at 3.

[10] HM Government, *Policy Paper Economic Crime and Corporate Transparency Act: Economic Crime in the UK* (HM Government, 2024) at 1. It is not the purpose of this book to offer an alternative definition of white-collar crime. For a more detailed discussion of alternative definitions, see G Gilbert, 'The Roots and Variant Definitions of the Concept of "White-Collar Crime"' in SR Van Slyke, ML Benson and FT Cullen (eds), The Oxford Handbook of White-Collar Crime (Oxford University Press, 2016) at 25–38.

Therefore, common types of financial crime include money laundering, terrorist financing, fraud, bribery and corruption and sanctions evasion. For the purpose of this monograph, the author focuses on money laundering, terrorist financing and fraud.

A. Money Laundering

The first financial crime to be considered is money laundering, which has been defined as the 'processing of criminal proceeds to disguise their illegal origin. This process is of critical importance, as it enables the criminal to enjoy these profits without jeopardizing their source'.[11] Furthermore, it has been defined by the United Nations Convention Against Illicit Traffic in Narcotic Drugs and Psychotropic Substances as

> the conversion or transfer of property, knowing that such property is derived from any offense(s), for the purpose of concealing or disguising the illicit origin of the property or of assisting any person who is involved in such offense(s) to evade the legal consequences of his actions.[12]

The objective of the process is to make the proceeds of crime appear to have been lawfully obtained. The process can be complicated, hard to detect and frequently involves numerous financial transactions in different countries.[13] The examination of money laundering is of critical importance because it enables criminal entities to enjoy a criminal lifestyle, which has been referred to as a 'champagne lifestyle'.[14] The traditional and contentious money laundering process involves three stages – placement, layering and integration.[15] At the placement stage the money launderer seeks to position the proceeds of the illegal activity in the financial system.[16] Here, the money launderer normally attempts to break up the profits into smaller amounts so as to avoid any cash or currency or suspicious transaction-reporting obligations. This technique is referred to as 'smurfing', or 'structured' payments.[17] The money launderer could target financial institutions and other professions including estate agents,[18]

[11] United Nations Office on Drugs and Crime, 'Money laundering' (n/d), available from /www.unodc.org/unodc/en/money-laundering/overview.html.

[12] United Nations Convention against Illicit Traffic in Narcotic Drugs and Psychotropic Substances (adopted 20 December 1988, entered into force 11 November 1990) 1582 UNTS 95, Article 3(1). Hereinafter, 'Vienna Convention'.

[13] T Edmonds, *Money Laundering Law, Briefing Paper no 2593* (House of Commons, 2018) at 10.

[14] See generally National Audit Office, *The Asset Recovery Agency* (National Audit Office, 2007) at 4.

[15] See M Levi and P Reuter, 'Money Laundering' (2006) *Crime and Justice* 34(1), 289–375, at 314.

[16] FATF, *Money Laundering and Terrorist Financing Typologies 2004-2005* (FATF, 2005) at 63.

[17] See generally S Welling, 'Smurfs, Money Laundering, and the Federal Criminal Law: The Crime of Structuring Transactions' (1989) *Florida Law Review* 41(2), 287–343, at 290–303.

[18] See FATF (n 16) at 73–74, 79, 80–81; FATF, *Guidance on Risk-Based Approach – Real Estate Sector* (FATF, 2022); I Zavoli C King, 'The Challenges of Implementing Anti-Money Laundering Regulation: An Empirical Analysis' (2021) *MLR* 84(4), 740–71 and B Unger and J Ferwerda, *Money Laundering in the Real Estate Sector – Suspicious Properties* (Edward Elgar, 2011).

accountants,[19] lawyers[20] and art dealers.[21] The second stage, or layering, involves a large number of financial transactions or conversions.[22] The purpose of this phase is to create as much distance between the initial placement of the proceeds of crime from their original source. It is during this stage that the money could be moved via the purchase of shares,[23] transferred to different countries via wire transfers[24] and internet payments systems,[25] thus making it increasingly difficult to detect. The final stage is integration, and it is at this point that the money reappears into the economy.[26]

It is impossible to determine the extent of money laundering and estimates vary. One of the most referred to estimates was published by the United Nations Office on Drugs and Crime (UNODC), which suggest that the annual amount of money laundered is between USD$800billion and USD$2trillion.[27] The International Monetary Fund estimated that the consensus range of laundered money could be between two and five per cent of the world's gross domestic product.[28] The calculation of money laundering is difficult to determine,[29] and it is hampered because there is 'no visible data'.[30] Indeed, the Financial Action Task Force (FATF) noted that the 'precise statistics are not available, and it is … impossible to produce a definitive estimate of the amount of money laundered'.[31] What cannot be disputed, is that money laundering is an enabler of significant harms that impacts society, the global

[19] See FATF, *Guidance on Risk-Based Approach – Accountants* (FATF, 2019).

[20] See FATF, *Money Laundering and Terrorist Financing Vulnerabilities of Legal Professionals* (FATF, 2013); K Benson, *Lawyers and the Proceeds of Crime – the Facilitation of Money Laundering and its Control* (Routledge, 2020); S Kebbell, *Anti-Money Laundering Compliance and the Legal Profession* (Routledge, 2022) and M Levi, 'Lawyers as Money Laundering Enablers? An Evolving and Contentious Relationship' (2022) *Global Crime* 23(2), 126–47.

[21] See FATF, *Money Laundering and Terrorist Financing in the Art and Antiquities Market* (FATF, 2023) and S Hufngael and C King, 'Anti-Money Laundering Regulation and the Art Market' (2020) *Legal Studies* 40(1), 131–50.

[22] FATF (n 16) at 63.

[23] See FATF, *Money Laundering and Terrorist Financing in the Securities Sector* (FATF, 2009).

[24] See FATF, *Guidance for a Risk-Based Approach – Money or Value Transfer Services* (FATF, 2016).

[25] FATF, *Money Laundering and Terrorist Financing Vulnerabilities of Commercial Websites and Internet Payment Systems* (FATF, 2008).

[26] FATF (n 16) at 63.

[27] House of Commons Treasury Committee, *Economic Crime Eleventh Report of Session 2021–22* (House of Commons Treasury Committee, 2022) at 38. Also see United Nations Office on Drugs and Crime (UNODC), *Estimating Illicit Financial Flows Resulting from Drug Trafficking and other Transnational Organized Crime* (UNODC, 2009).

[28] International Monetary Fund (IMF), 'Money Laundering: the Importance of International Countermeasures – Address by Michel Camdessus' (10 February 1998), available from https://www.imf.org/en/News/Articles/2015/09/28/04/53/sp021098. For a more detailed discussion of attempts to calculate the amount of money laundered, see J Walker and B Unger, 'Measuring Global Money Laundering: The Walker Gravity Model' (2009) *Review of Law and Economics* 5(2), 821–53.

[29] H Morais, 'Fighting International Crime and its Financing: The Importance of Following a Coherent Global Strategy Based on the Rule of Law' (2005) *Villanova Law Review* 50(3), 583–644, at 591.

[30] There are traditionally two approaches towards calculating the extent of money laundering. The first is based upon the assumption from macroeconomic data and secondly the financial information made available by anti-money laundering agencies. See J Harvey, 'Compliance and Reporting Issues Arising for Financial Institutions from Money Laundering Regulations: A Preliminary Cost Benefit Study' (2004) *Journal of Money Laundering Control* 7(4), 333–46, at 333.

[31] FATF, *Frequently Asked Questions – What is Money Laundering?* (n/d), available from www.fatf-gafi.org/en/pages/frequently-asked-questions.html#tabs-36503a8663-item-6ff811783c-tab.

economy and national security.[32] The scale of money laundering is aggravated by the increasingly global nature of the financial markets,[33] the link between money laundering and the sale of illegal narcotic substances[34] and the immeasurable number of money laundering mechanisms.[35] The relationship between money laundering and the manufacturing, distribution and sale of illegal narcotic substances is well documented, as is its association with the 'War on Drugs'.[36] This association was followed by President Ronald Regan in the 1980s,[37] but it did not prevent money laundering being referred to as the 'crime of the 1990s'.[38] As a result of the United States (US)-led 'War on Drugs', the international community implemented several legislative measures.[39] This included the Vienna Convention,[40] the UN Convention against Transnational Organised Crime,[41] and the UN Convention against Corruption.[42] Additionally, the European Union introduced a series of legislative measures including six Money Laundering Directives.[43] These legislative measures were supported by the soft law Recommendations of the FATF.[44]

[32] FATF, *Global Money Laundering Terrorist Financing Threat Assessment* (FATF, 2010) at 11.

[33] See, eg, Financial Conduct Authority, *Assessing and Reducing the Risk of Money Laundering Through the Markets* (Financial Conduct Authority, 2025).

[34] See, eg, FATF, *Money Laundering from Fentanyl and Synthetic Opioids* (FATF, 2022).

[35] See J Simser, 'Money Laundering: Emerging Threats and Trends' (2012) *Journal of Money Laundering Control* 16(1), 41–54.

[36] See A Amicelle, 'When Finance Met Security: Back to the War on Drugs and the Problem of Dirty Money' (2017) *Finance and Society* 3(2), 106–23.

[37] See, eg, B Bagley, 'US Foreign Policy and the War on Drugs: Analysis of a Policy Failure' (1988) *Journal of Interamerican Studies and World Affairs* 30(2-3), 189–212 and J Hawdon, 'The Role of Presidential Rhetoric in the Creation of a Moral Panic: Reagan, Bush, and the War on Drugs' (2001) *Deviant Behavior* 22(5), 419–45.

[38] See G Strafer, 'Money Laundering: The Crime of the '90s' (1989) *American Criminal Law Review* 27, 149–208.

[39] See generally N Ryder, *Money Laundering – an Endless Cycle? A Comparative Analysis of the Anti-Money Laundering Policies in the United States of America, the United Kingdom, Australia and Canada* (Routledge, 2012) at 8–39.

[40] See Vienna Convention (n 12).

[41] United Nations Convention against Transnational Organized Crime, GA Res 55/25, UN GAOR, 55th Sess, Supp No 49, Vol I, at 43, UN Doc A/55/49 (hereinafter 'Palermo Convention').

[42] United Nations General Assembly, United Nations Convention Against Corruption, A/58/422, 31 October 2003. Hereinafter 'UNCAC'.

[43] See Council Directive 91/308/EEC of 10 June 1991 on the prevention of the use of the financial system for the purpose of money laundering ('First Money Laundering Directive') [1991] OJ L166/77; Directive 2001/97/EC of the European Parliament and of the Council of 4 December 2001 amending Council Directive 91/308/EEC on prevention of the use of the financial system for the purpose of money laundering ('Second Money Laundering Directive') [2001] OJ L344/76; Directive 2005/60/EC of the European Parliament and of the Council of 26 October 2005 on the prevention of the use of the financial system for the purposes of money laundering and terrorist financing ('Third Money Laundering Directive') [2005] OJ L309/15; Directive (EU) 2015/849 of the European Parliament and of the Council of 20 May 2015 on the prevention of the use of the financial system for the purposes of money laundering or terrorist financing ('Fourth Money Laundering Directive') [2015] OJ L141/73; Directive (EU) 2018/843 of the European Parliament and of the Council of 30 May 2018 amending Directive (EU) 2015/849 on the prevention of the use of the financial system for the purposes of money laundering or terrorist financing ('Fifth Money Laundering Directive') [2018] OJ L156/43 and Directive (EU) 2018/1673 of the European Parliament and of the Council of 23 October 2018 on combating money laundering by criminal law ('Sixth Money Laundering Directive') [2018] OJ L284/22.

[44] See FATF, *FATF 40 Recommendations* (FATF, 1990); FATF, *FATF IX Special Recommendations* (Financial Action Task Force, 2001) and FATF, *International Standards on Combating Money Laundering and the Financing of Terrorism and Proliferation – The FATF Recommendations* (FATF, 2025).

B. Terrorist Financing

Terrorist financing, the second type of financial crime being considered in this book, is defined by the International Convention for the Suppression of the Financing of Terrorism as including 'assets of every kind, whether tangible or intangible, movable or immovable, however acquired, and legal documents or instruments in any form'.[45] Terrorist financing has also been referred to as 'reverse money laundering', which is a practice whereby 'clean' or 'legitimate' money is acquired and then funnelled to support acts of terrorism.[46] For the purposes of terrorist financing, terrorism in the UK is defined as the use or threat of action which involves serious violence against a person; serious damage to property; endangers a person's life; creates a serious risk to the health or safety of the public; or is designed to seriously interfere or disrupt an electronic system.[47] Prior to the Al-Qaeda terrorist attacks in the US on 11 September 2001 ('9/11'), the international community focused its financial crime efforts on addressing the threat of money laundering and it was not until two Al-Qaeda terrorist attacks in Kenya and Tanzania, that the United Nations introduced the International Convention.[48] However, the initial approach towards implementing the International Convention was lacklustre because terrorist financing was not considered a priority. Nevertheless, at the time of writing the International Convention has been signed by 188 different countries.[49] A direct consequence of 9/11 was a fundamental change in the international communities' attitudes towards addressing terrorist financing which resulted in the introduction of the Financial War on Terrorism.[50] However, this book argues that the legislative response was incorrectly based on the global anti-money laundering (AML) standards and strategy, which targets attempts by money launderers to conceal the profits of crime that contribute towards their so-called 'champagne lifestyle'. Terrorists and terrorist organisations tend not to generally make a profit to facilitate such a lifestyle, and their financing typologies differ from money launderers.[51]

[45] International Convention for the Suppression of the Financing of Terrorism (1999) Art 1, para 1 (hereinafter 'International Convention').

[46] For a more detailed discussion of this process, see S Cassella, 'Reverse Money Laundering' (2003) *Journal of Money Laundering Control*, 7(1), 92–94 at 92.

[47] Terrorism Act 2000, s 1.

[48] See, eg, J Mbaku, 'Counter-Terrorism Laws and Human Rights in African Countries' (2021) *Washington University Global Studies Law Review* 20, 863–1020, 907–15.

[49] International Monetary Fund, *International Cooperation in Combating the Financing of Terrorism. Good Practices to Enhance Effectiveness* (International Monetary Fund, 2022) at 153.

[50] See generally FATF, *The Financial War on Terrorism – A Guide by the Financial Action Task Force* (FATF, 2014) and N Ryder, *The Financial War on Terror: A Review of Counter-Terrorist Financing Strategies since 2001* (Routledge, 2015).

[51] For a contrasting view, see J Rosenthal, 'For-Profit Terrorism: The Rise of Armed Entrepreneurs' (2008) *Studies in Conflict & Terrorism* 31(6), 481–49.

C. Fraud

The international profile of fraud, the third type of financial crime examined in this book, has increased in part, to instances of fraud including the Bank of Credit and Commerce International,[52] Barings Bank,[53] Enron,[54] WorldCom,[55] Bernard Madoff,[56] Alan Stanford,[57] FTX,[58] Theranos[59] and its association with the 2007/2008 global financial crisis.[60] The UK has experienced large scale instances of fraud including, Polly Peck,[61] the Mirror Group Pension Scheme,[62] the Guinness share-trading fraud,[63] the collapse of Barlow Clowes,[64] the manipulation of the London Interbank Offered Rate/Foreign Exchange market[65] and fraud associated with the global pandemic.[66]

[52] J Kerry and H Brown, *The BCCI Affair A Report to the Committee on Foreign Relations United States Senate* (1992: 102d Congress 2d Session Senate Print 102–14).

[53] Board of Banking Standards, *Inquiry Report of the Board of Banking Standards Inquiry into the Circumstances of the Collapse of Barings Bank* (Board of Banking Standards, 1995).

[54] Permanent Subcommittee on Investigations of the Committee on Governmental Affairs, *The Role of the Board of Directors in Enron's Collapse* (Permanent Subcommittee on Investigations of the Committee on Governmental Affairs, 2002).

[55] D Beresford, N Katzenbach and C Rogers, *Report of Investigation by the Special Investigative Committee of the Board of Directors of WorldCom* (Securities and Exchange Commission, 2003).

[56] Securities and Exchange Commission Office of Investigations, *Investigation of Failure of the SEC to Uncover Bernard Madoff's Ponzi Scheme* (Securities and Exchange Commission Office of Investigations, 2009).

[57] Securities and Exchange Commission Office, *Investigation of the SEC's Response to Concerns Regarding Robert Allen Stanford's Alleged Ponzi Scheme* (Securities and Exchange Commission Office, 2010).

[58] United States Department of Justice, 'Samuel Bankman-Fried Sentenced to 25 Years for His Orchestration of Multiple Fraudulent Schemes' (28 March 2024), available at www.justice.gov/archives/opa/pr/samuel-bankman-fried-sentenced-25-years-his-orchestration-multiple-fraudulent-schemes.

[59] United States Department of Justice, 'Elizabeth Holmes Sentenced To More Than 11 Years For Defrauding Theranos Investors Of Hundreds Of Millions' (18 November 2022), available at www.justice.gov/usao-ndca/pr/elizabeth-holmes-sentenced-more-11-years-defrauding-theranos-investors-hundreds.

[60] See National Commission on the Causes of the Financial and Economic Crisis in the United States, *The Financial Crisis Inquiry Report* (National Commission on the Causes of the Financial and Economic Crisis in the United States, 2011). Also see D Johnson, *Competition Law and Financial Crime: A Comparative Analysis of International Responses to Market Manipulation* (Routledge, 2025).

[61] See generally T Pijper, 'The Collapse of Polly Peck International' in T Pijper (ed), 'Creative Accounting. Finance and Capital Markets Series' (Palgrave Macmillan, 1996) 141–59.

[62] See Department for Trade and Industry, *The Maxwell Report* (Department for Trade and Industry, 2001).

[63] See Department for Trade and Industry, *Guinness Plc* (Department for Trade and Industry, 1997).

[64] See Parliamentary Commissioners for Administration, *The Barlow Clowes Affair* (Parliamentary Commissioners for Administration, 1989).

[65] See generally HM Treasury Select Committee, *Fixing LIBOR: Some Preliminary Findings* (HM Treasury Select Committee, 2012).

[66] See National Audit Office, *Implementing Employment Support Schemes in Response to the COVID-19 Pandemic* (National Audit Office, 2020); Public Accounts Committee, *Covid-19: Bounce Back Loan Scheme* (Public Accounts Committee, 2020) and House of Commons Committee of Public Accounts, *Local Authority Administered COVID Support Schemes in England* (House of Commons Committee of Public Accounts, 2023).

The calculation of fraud, like money laundering, is fraught with methodological difficulties.[67] Indeed, the Fraud Review concluded that 'there are no reliable estimates of the cost of fraud'.[68] In 2023, the Office of National Statistics reported that fraud had become the most prevalent crime in the UK, accounting for over 40 per cent of reported crime.[69] In December 2024 it reported that there were 4.1 million reported instances of fraud, representing a 33 per cent increase from December 2023.[70] Therefore, the precise scale of fraud is considerable if unknown,[71] its under-reporting inhibits our understanding of the threat and there is a financial intelligence gap. Fraud is a threat to the UK economy,[72] it is the funding mechanism of choice for terrorists who have created a 'dossier' or 'black book' that advises them on what frauds go unreported and undetected.[73] Fraud poses a significant threat to UK businesses,[74] its citizens[75] and it is a mechanism that allows organised criminal gangs (OCGs) to benefit from significant financial gains. It has been estimated that that over 60 per cent of UK OCGs are involved in committing fraud.[76] Nonetheless, 86 per cent of fraud in the UK is not reported.[77]

III. International Legal Instruments – Data-Sharing

The monograph considers the international legal instruments and the international data-sharing standards for money laundering, terrorist financing and fraud. The

[67] Attorney General's Office, *Fraud Review – Final Report* (Attorney General's Office, 2006) at 7.

[68] ibid at 21.

[69] Office of National Statistics (ONS), 'Crime in England and Wales: Year Ending September 2024' (30 January 2025), available at www.ons.gov.uk/peoplepopulationandcommunity/crimeandjustice/bulletins/crimeinenglandandwales/yearendingseptember2024#fraud.

[70] ONS, 'Crime in England and Wales: Year Ending December 2024' (24 April 2025), available at www.ons.gov.uk/peoplepopulationandcommunity/crimeandjustice/bulletins/crimeinenglandandwales/yearendingdecember2024#:~:text=The%20Crime%20Survey%20for%20England%20and%20Wales%20(CSEW)%20estimated%209.6,ending%20(YE)%20December%202024.

[71] House of Lords Fraud Act 2006 and Digital Fraud Committee, *Fighting Fraud: Breaking the Chain* (House of Lords Fraud Act 2006 and Digital Fraud Committee, 2022) at 11.

[72] HM Government, *Fraud Strategy: Stopping Scams and Protecting the Public* (HM Government, 2023).

[73] N Ryder, 'To Report or not to Report? An Analysis of the Relationship between Defence against Terrorism Financing Suspicious Activity Reports and Fraud in the United Kingdom' in L de Koker and D Goldbarsht, *Financial Crime, Law and Governance – Navigating Challenges in Different Contexts* (Springer, 2024) 16920–2.

[74] National Crime Agency, 'Fraud' (n/d), available at www.nationalcrimeagency.gov.uk/what-we-do/crime-threats/fraud-and-economic-crime.

[75] International Public Sector Fraud Forum, *Guide to Understanding the Total Impact of Fraud* (Cabinet Office and Commonwealth Fraud Prevention Centre, 2020) 9–14.

[76] M Levi, 'Organised Fraud' in L Paoli (ed), *The Oxford Handbook of Organised Crime* (Oxford University Press, 2014) 460–81. It has been suggested that there are 4,772 OCGs and 59,000 known serious organised crimes suspected in the UK. See The Tony Blair Institute, *A New Approach to Serious and Organised Crime in the UK* (The Tony Blair Institute, 2024).

[77] See National Crime Agency (n 74).

Vienna Convention does not make any specific reference to customer due diligence (CDD) or data-sharing rules. However, it does lay the foundations for the global AML efforts. For example, Article 3 encourages countries to criminalise money laundering, which indirectly forces countries to adopt CDD measures to detect and prevent money laundering.[78] Article 5 suggests the adoption of mechanisms to trace, freeze, and confiscate proceeds of crime, thus requiring financial institutions to know their customers and to monitor transactions.[79] Article 7 promotes international cooperation in investigations, including sharing financial data across borders to track illicit funds.[80] Finally, Article 9 urges collaboration between law enforcement and financial institutions, which often includes data-sharing protocols and risk-based due diligence.[81] Therefore, the Vienna Convention does not define CDD procedures, but it has contributed towards the global AML frameworks including the FATF Recommendations,[82] the Basel Committee Guidelines focusing on banking supervision and customer identification[83] and the Wolfsberg Principles.[84]

Similarly, the Palermo Convention does not define CDD or include any data-sharing protocols, but it does establish key obligations that underpin those practices in the fight against organised crime and money laundering. For example, Article 7 applies to money laundering and advises countries to implement regulatory and supervisory regimes for financial institutions.[85] Thus, encouraging them to make use of customer identification, record-keeping, reporting of suspicious transactions and promoting cooperation with law enforcement agencies (LEAs) and financial intelligence units (FIUs). Article 9 includes measures against corruption that supports internal controls and compliance programmes in the private sector, which often include CDD procedures.[86] Article 10 applies to the liability of legal persons which aims to encourage accountability mechanisms for companies, which can include due diligence on clients and partners.[87] Similarly, Articles 12 to 14 relate to the confiscation and seizure of assets which requires mechanisms to trace and identify illicit assets, thus relying on financial data and customer profiling.[88] Penultimately, Article 18 focuses on mutual legal assistance that facilitates cross-border data-sharing for investigations, including financial records and

[78] See Vienna Convention (n 12) Art 3.
[79] ibid, Art 5.
[80] ibid, Art 7.
[81] ibid, Art 9.
[82] See generally N Mugarura, 'Customer Due Diligence (CDD) Mandate and the Propensity of its Application as a Global AML Paradigm' (2014) *Journal of Money Laundering Control* 17(1), 76–95.
[83] Basel Committee on Banking Supervision, *The Basel Framework* (Basel Committee on Banking Supervision, 2025).
[84] Wolfsberg Group, *Wolfsberg Anti-Money Laundering Principles for Private Banking* (Wolfsberg Group, 2012).
[85] See Palermo Convention (n 41) Art 7.
[86] ibid, Art 9.
[87] ibid, Art 10.
[88] ibid, Art 12.

customer information.[89] Finally, Article 27 on LEA cooperation promotes international collaboration, including the exchange of financial intelligence.[90]

The United Nations Convention Against Corruption does not use the 'customer due diligence', but like the Vienna and Palermo Conventions, its provisions lay a strong foundation for it. For example, Article 12 provides that states should promote transparency and accountability in private entities. This includes enhancing accounting and auditing standards, preventing corruption through internal controls and compliance programmes and encouraging cooperation between private sector and law enforcement.[91] Article 14 relates to measures to prevent money laundering that supports CDD by requiring financial institutions to identify customers, promoting record-keeping and suspicious transaction reporting and encouraging international cooperation on financial intelligence.[92] Similarly, Article 39 encourages cooperation between national authorities and the private sector by promoting information exchange between financial institutions and authorities, reporting mechanisms for suspicious activities and partnerships to detect and prevent corruption.[93] Article 40 states that bank secrecy laws should not hinder international cooperation or investigations, a key part for cross-border data-sharing. Finally, Articles 52–55 apply to asset recovery and promote the sharing of financial data across jurisdictions, tracing and recovering illicit assets and using CDD to identify beneficial ownership and prevent concealment.[94] Overall, the UN AML conventions function as a blueprint for national laws and international standards like the Recommendations. They do not specifically refer to CDD rules and data-sharing, but they require countries to build systems where CDD and data-sharing are essential tools to fight money laundering.

The first of three EU Money Laundering Directives (MLD) laid the foundation for CDD and data-sharing obligations.[95] While they were less prescriptive than later MLDs, they introduced several key principles. For example, the First MLD required customer identification and record-keeping for financial institutions; obliged entities to monitor transactions and report suspicious activity; introduced Know Your Customer principles and mandated retention of customer records for five years after the relationship ends.[96] The Second MLD expanded CDD obligations to include non-banking financial institutions (NBFIs), designated non-financial businesses and professions (DNFBPs), required reporting of suspicious transactions to FIUs and broadened the scope of predicate offences for money laundering.[97] The Third MLD introduced the risk-based approach (RBA)

[89] ibid, Art 18.
[90] ibid, Art 27.
[91] UNCAC (n 42) Art 12.
[92] ibid, Art 14.
[93] ibid, Art 39.
[94] ibid, Art 40.
[95] See Directive 91/308 (n 43).
[96] See above (n 43).
[97] ibid.

to CDD. Specifically, it required enhanced due diligence (EDD) for high-risk customers; it allowed simplified due diligence (SDD) for low-risk scenarios and mandated ongoing monitoring of customer relationships.[98] These MLDs did not explicitly regulate private-to-private data-sharing, they did promote the use of suspicious activity reports (SARs) to national FIUs; cooperation between financial institutions and authorities; cross-border information exchange for AML investigations and record-keeping obligations that enabled retrospective analysis and data-sharing with regulators.

Conversely, the next three MLDs delivered a stronger framework for combating financial crime, with increasingly detailed rules around CDD and data-sharing. The Fourth MLD introduced risk-based CDD; required the identification of beneficial owners of legal entities; mandated EDD for politically exposed persons (PEPs) and allowed SDD in low-risk cases.[99] The Fifth MLD expanded the CDD provisions to cover virtual currency exchanges and wallet providers; art dealers and prepaid card providers; required access to beneficial ownership registers and improved rules for anonymous transactions.[100] The Sixth MLD strengthened CDD by standardising identity verification across Member States; requiring exact matches to official documents; mandating verification of all nationalities held by a customer; and introduced regulatory technical standards for CDD.[101] Therefore, the fourth to sixth MLDs promoted the submission of SARs to FIUs; cross-border cooperation between Member States and FIUs and allowing access to beneficial ownership data for competent authorities. The Sixth MLD includes provisions for private entities to share personal data for AML/counter-terrorism financing (CTF) purposes under strict conditions; emphasis on harmonised definitions and predicate offences, improving legal clarity for data exchange and support for centralised supervision via the new EU Anti-Money Laundering Authority (AMLA).[102]

IV. International Standards – Data-Sharing

FATF Recommendations 2, 30, and 31 highlight the importance of national coordination and the operational capabilities of law enforcement in the fight against money laundering, terrorist financing, and proliferation financing.[103] Recommendation 2 emphasises the need for countries to establish strong frameworks for cooperation and coordination among key stakeholders, including

[98] ibid.
[99] ibid.
[100] ibid.
[101] ibid. Directive (EU) 2018/1673 (n 43).
[102] ibid.
[103] FATF, *International Standards on Combating Money Laundering and the Financing of Terrorism & Proliferation: The FATF Recommendations* (FATF, 2025) (hereinafter 'FATF Recommendations').

policymakers, financial intelligence units, regulators, and law enforcement, to ensure a unified and effective response.[104] Recommendation 30 underscores that law enforcement authorities should be empowered to conduct thorough investigations, especially those related to serious predicate offences, and must have the ability to identify, trace, and recover assets tied to criminal activities. It also stresses the necessity for adequate resources, training, and high integrity standards within investigative teams, along with support for international cooperation.[105] Complementing this, Recommendation 31 outlines the specific powers that these authorities must possess to carry out their duties successfully, such as accessing relevant records, conducting searches and seizures, interviewing witnesses, using advanced investigative techniques like undercover operations or digital forensics, and obtaining intelligence from FIUs, while maintaining operational secrecy to avoid tipping off suspects.[106]

FATF's Immediate Outcomes 1, 6, 7, and 9 reflect how effectively a country tackles money laundering and terrorist financing across different fronts.[107] Immediate Outcome 1 focuses on how well a country understands its money laundering and terrorist financing risks and whether it has developed responsive, coordinated strategies to address them using a RBA.[108] Immediate Outcome 6 assesses the use of financial intelligence by authorities, especially FIUs, in identifying illicit financial flows through SARs.[109] Immediate Outcome 7 highlights the importance of pursuing money laundering cases proactively, aiming for investigations and prosecutions that result in proportionate and dissuasive penalties. It also gauges whether authorities treat money laundering as a serious crime and target both domestic and international networks.[110] Lastly, Immediate Outcome 9 evaluates a country's capacity to identify and disrupt terrorist financing by investigating and prosecuting individuals or entities involved, applying swift and effective sanctions, and coordinating efforts using intelligence-led methods to dismantle financing channels that support terrorism.[111]

In its 2018 Mutual Evaluation Report (MER), the FATF concluded that the UK was 'compliant on 24 Recommendations and largely compliant on 15. The country remains partially compliant on 1 Recommendation'.[112] Specifically, the UK's

[104] ibid at 10–11.
[105] ibid at 24–25.
[106] ibid at 25.
[107] FATF, *Methodology for Assessing Technical Compliance with the FATF Recommendations and the Effectiveness of AML/CFT Systems* (FATF, 2023) (hereinafter 'FATF Methodology').
[108] ibid at 96.
[109] ibid at 113.
[110] ibid at 116.
[111] ibid at 121.
[112] FATF, 'United Kingdom' (n/d), available at www.fatf-gafi.org/en/countries/detail/united-kingdom.html#:~:text=Today%2C%20the%20United%20Kingdom%20is,partially%20compliant%20on%201%20Recommendation.

compliance with its Recommendations was rated as the best in the world.[113] One of the FATF's key findings was that 'co-operation and co-ordination between agencies on AML issues is a strength of the UK system'.[114] This will be examined in more detail in chapter three. Therefore, the UK was rated as being in full compliance with Recommendations 2, 30 and 31, which require national coordination and cooperation, including the exchange of information, between LEAs.[115] The UK was also considered to have moderate to high levels of effectiveness to Immediate Outcomes 1 and 6, concerning risk, policy and coordination, and financial intelligence, as well as Immediate Outcomes 7 and 9, concerning effective money laundering and terrorist financing investigations.[116]

V. Data-Sharing in Academic Literature

There is extensive literature on money laundering by Stessens;[117] Alldridge;[118] Gilmore;[119] Gallant;[120] Alexander;[121] Unger;[122] Booth et al;[123] Unger and Ferwerda;[124] Ryder;[125] Alldridge;[126] Benson;[127] Hatchard;[128] Dill[129] and Kebbell.[130] Collectively, these publications provide a detailed discussion of a wide range of issues associated with money laundering. However, there is little discussion of the

[113] FATF, *Anti-Money Laundering and Counter-Terrorist Financing Measures: United Kingdom Mutual Evaluation Report* (FATF, 2018) at 5 (hereinafter '2018 MER').

[114] ibid at 37.

[115] See FATF Recommendations (n 103).

[116] See FATF Methodology (n 107).

[117] G Stessens, *Money Laundering a New International Law Enforcement Model* (Cambridge University Press, 2000).

[118] P Alldridge, *Money Laundering Law: Forfeiture, Confiscation, Civil Recovery, Criminal Laundering and Taxation of the Proceeds of Crime* (Bloomsbury Publishing, 2003).

[119] W Gilmore, *Dirty Money – the Evaluation of International Measures to Counter Money Laundering and the Financing of Terrorism* (Council of Europe, 2004).

[120] M Gallant, *Money Laundering and the Proceeds of Crime* (Edward Elgar, 2005).

[121] R Alexander, *Insider Dealing and Money Laundering in the EU: Law and Regulation* (Ashgate, 2007).

[122] B Unger, *The Scale and Impacts of Money Laundering* (Edward Elgar, 2007).

[123] R Booth, S Farrell, G Bastable and N Yeo, *Money Laundering Law and Regulation* (Oxford University Press, 2010).

[124] B Unger, and J Ferwerda, *Money Laundering in the Real Estate Sector: Suspicious Properties* (Edward Elgar, 2011).

[125] N Ryder, *Money Laundering-an Endless Cycle? A Comparative Analysis of the Anti-money Laundering Policies in the United States of America, the United Kingdom, Australia and Canada* (Routledge, 2012).

[126] P Alldridge, *Impacts upon Substantive Laundering Law. What Went Wrong With Money Laundering Law?* (Palgrave, 2016).

[127] See Benson (n 20).

[128] J Hatchard, *Combating Money Laundering in Africa: Dealing with the Problem of PEPs* (Edward Elgar, 2020).

[129] A Dill, *Anti-Money Laundering Regulation and Compliance: Key Problems and Practice Areas* (Edward Elgar, 2021).

[130] See Kebbell (n 20).

use of financial intelligence and the subsequent exchange of information in the UK. Terrorist financing has attracted less commentary with the leading texts by Gurule;[131] Donoghue;[132] Bierseker and Eckert;[133] Vittori;[134] Ridley;[135] Freeman;[136] Ryder;[137] Basaranel and Turksen;[138] Azinge-Egbri[139] and Khah.[140] Several of these works focus on the impact of the terrorist attacks in September 2001, whilst others focus on the impact of the 'Financial War on Terrorism'. Some of the research refers to the use of financial intelligence and the exchange of information but the discussions on these topics are brief.

The leading publications on fraud include those by Doig;[141] Button and Gee;[142] Levi;[143] Krambia-Kapardis;[144] Manacorda and Grasso;[145] Doig and Levi;[146] Rotman[147] and Asher.[148] Tax evasion has attracted less commentary including work by Loutzenhiser and Feria;[149] Alldridge;[150] Turksen[151] and Bourton.[152] Authors have focused on bribery and corruption including Horder and Alldridge;[153]

[131] J Gurulé, *Unfunding Terror: The Legal Response to the Financing of Global Terrorism* (Edward Elgar, 2008).

[132] L Donohue, *The Cost of Counterterrorism: Power, Politics, and Liberty* (Cambridge University Press, 2008).

[133] T Biersteker, S Eckert and T Biersteker, *Countering the Financing of Terrorism* (Routledge, 2008).

[134] J Vittori, *The Evolution of Terrorism Resourcing* (Palgrave Macmillan, 2011).

[135] N Ridley, *Terrorist Financing: The Failure of Counter Measures* (Edward Elgar, 2012).

[136] M Freeman, *Financing Terrorism: Case Studies* (Routledge, 2016).

[137] See Ryder (n 50).

[138] B Başaranel and U Türkşen, *Counter-Terrorist Financing Law and Policy: An Analysis of Turkey* (Routledge, 2019).

[139] N Azinge-Egbiri, *Regulating and Combating Money Laundering and Terrorist Financing: The Law in Emerging Economies* (Routledge, 2021).

[140] Z Khah, *Counter-Terrorism Financing and Iran* (Routledge, 2023).

[141] A Doig, *Fraud* (Routledge, 2006).

[142] M Button, and J Gee, *Countering Fraud for Competitive Advantage: The Professional Approach to Reducing the Last Great* (Wiley, 2013).

[143] M Levi, *Regulating Fraud White-Collar Crime and the Criminal Process* (Routledge, 2013).

[144] M Krambia-Kapardis, *Corporate Fraud and Corruption: A Holistic Approach to Preventing Financial Crises* (Palgrave MacMillan, 2016).

[145] S Manacorda and C Grasso, *Fighting Fraud and Corruption at the World Bank: A Critical Analysis of the Sanctions* (Springer, 2018).

[146] A Doig, and M Levi, *Frauds and Financial Crimes: Trends, Strategic Responses, and Implementation Issues in England and Wales* (Routledge, 2023).

[147] M Rotman, *Regulating Fraud Across Borders: Internationalised Criminal Law Protection of Capital Markets* (Hart Publishing, 2021).

[148] J Ashser, *Fraud Markers, De-banking, and Financial Crime: A Legal Analysis of Counter-fraud Practices in the UK and Beyond* (Routledge, 2025).

[149] R de la Feria and G Loutzenhiser, *The Dynamics of Taxation: Essays in Honour of Judith Freedman* (Hart Publishing, 2020).

[150] P Alldridge, *Criminal Justice and Taxation* (Oxford University Press, 2017).

[151] U Turksen, *Countering Tax Crime in the European Union: Benchmarking the OECD's Ten Global Principles* (Hart Publishing, 2021).

[152] S Bourton, *Tax Evasion and the Law A Comparative Analysis of the UK and USA* (Routledge, 2024).

[153] J Horder and P Alldridge, *Modern Bribery Law: Comparative Perspectives* (Cambridge University Press, 2013).

Haywood;[154] Raphael;[155] Palmer;[156] Hock[157] and Pasculli.[158] Despite the merits of this literature, none make any reference to the use of financial intelligence and the exchange of information.

There is limited research that offers a commentary on the use of financial intelligence and the exchange of information towards tackling financial crime in the UK in light of the FATF Recommendations. There are two FATF MERs that have offered the most in-depth and comprehensive peer reviewed assessment on how UK law and policy align with its Recommendations. The 2018 MER rated the UK as having the best AML/CTF regime out of the 60 countries it has reviewed.[159] The Royal United Services Institute's report challenged the assumption that technical compliance equates to operational effectiveness, demonstrating that despite high FATF ratings the UK remained a staging ground for large-scale money laundering networks. The study referred to the disconnection between formal legal alignment and real-world outcomes, suggesting that MERs should include indicators on asset recovery rates, cross-border collaboration, and private-sector responsiveness.[160] Levi et al suggested that the absence of reliable, systematic data undermines any credible assessment of AML regimes. Here, the authors critique the FATF MERs for relying on ill-defined findings that are not based on current data, a problem that is compounded by the length of time between reports. The article concluded that until there is a more consistent, systematic data analysis that is enshrined in the MERs, decisions and ratings on the national effectiveness will continue to be rather ad hoc and politically motivated calling into question the process.[161] Bociga et al outline and discuss how each UK AML ecosystem handles different types of information. The authors develop a framework that covers a highly structured, mandatory information-sharing channel at one end and a more informal or trust based channel at the other end. The paper uncovered four interdependent drivers of successful information echange – strategic resources allocation, clear rules, culture shifts towards mutual trust and proactive state coordination. The authors concluded that these four factors constitute a state anchored model that can optimise intelligence-sharing.[162]

[154] P Heywood, *Routledge Handbook of Political Corruption* (Routledge, 2015).

[155] M Raphael, *Bribery: Law and Practice Paperback* (Oxford University Press, 2016).

[156] A Palmer, *Countering Economic Crime: A Comparative Analysis* (Routledge, 2017).

[157] B Hock, *Extraterritoriality and International Bribery: A Collective Action Perspective* (Routledge, 2022).

[158] See L Pasculli and N Ryder, *Corruption in the Global Era: Causes, Sources and Forms of Manifestation* (Routledge, 2019) and N Ryder and L Pasculli, *Corruption, Integrity and the Law: Global Regulatory Challenges* (Routledge, 2020).

[159] See FATF 2018 MER (n 113).

[160] Royal United Services Institute, *No Rest for the Wicked: Driving Change in the UK's Post-FATF Evaluation of the UK AML Regime* (Royal United Services Institute, 2019).

[161] M Levi, P Reuter, and T Halliday, 'Can the AML System Be Evaluated without Better Data?' (2018) *Crime, Law and Social Change* 69, 307–28.

[162] D Bociga, N Lord and E Bellotti, 'Dare to Share: Information and Intelligence Sharing within the UK's Anti-Money Laundering Regime' (2024) *Policing and Society* 35(6), 812–831.

Depsite the merits of this literature, neither considers the impact of the 2018 MER and there is limited discussion on terrorist financing and fraud. Therefore, this monograph delivers an original contribution to knowledge by providing a comprehensive, evidence-based framework to assesses the UK's compliance with the FATF Recommendations on CDD, the use of SARs and the related data-sharing mechanisms.

VI. Research Aims and Questions

This book critically examines the UK's compliance with international AML and CTF FATF standards, challenging the findings of the 2018 MER.[163] In its 2018 MER of the UK's compliance with its Recommendations, the FATF rated the UK's AML/CTF regime as the best in the world. The UK Government declared that there is 'no place for dirty money or the people that launder it' and that 'the UK has taken a leading role in the global fight against illicit finance'.[164] The UK was regarded as 'compliant' with all FATF recommendations relating to information exchange and moderate to high levels of effectiveness.[165] However, the general findings of the MER have been questioned by the Royal United Services Institute,[166] the House of Commons Foreign Affairs Committee,[167] HM Treasury Select Committee,[168] the Intelligence, Security Committee of Parliament[169] and Transparency International.[170] While the FATF highlighted strong inter-agency cooperation and legal compliance, this book, using a series of novel case studies, exposes deficiencies in the UK's financial intelligence framework, particularly in the domestic exchange of information. It argues that national coordination is flawed and under-explored in existing literature and by conducting an in-depth legal analysis that evaluates current data-sharing mechanisms through practical examples, the book reveals previously overlooked shortcomings and calls for reform in the UK's legal powers and gateways for financial information exchange. Therefore, the overarching aim of this book is to critically evaluate the adequacy and effectiveness of the UK's legal and institutional frameworks for the national

[163] FATF 2018 MER (n 113) at 3–4.

[164] ibid.

[165] ibid.

[166] T Keatinge, A Moiseienko, F Keen, D Artingstall and H Wood, *No Rest for the Wicked Driving Change in the UK's Post-FATF Evaluation AML Regime* (RUSI, 2019) at 2–3.

[167] See, eg, House of Commons Foreign Affairs Committee Moscow's Gold: Russian Corruption in the UK (House of Commons Foreign Affairs Committee, 2018).

[168] See House of Commons Treasury Committee, *Economic Crime – Anti-Money Laundering Supervision and Sanctions Implementation* (House of Commons Treasury Committee, 2019) and House of Commons Treasury Committee, *Economic Crime: Consumer View* (House of Commons Treasury Committee, 2019).

[169] House of Commons Intelligence Security Committee *Russia* (House of Commons Intelligence Security Committee, 2020).

[170] See House of Commons Treasury Committee (n 27) at 48.

exchange of financial intelligence among the public and private sectors, particularly in the context of money laundering, terrorist financing and fraud. Furthermore, the research aims to identify structural deficiencies considering the FATF 2018 MER and to propose reforms to improve information-sharing. The chapters of this book will also answer the following subsidiary research questions.

- To what extent does the FATF's compliance methodology fairly and effectively assess the use of SARs and exchange of financial intelligence exchange?
- How have the UK's MERs (2007 and 2018) influenced the evolution of its CDD and data-sharing frameworks under the FATF standards, and to what extent have these reforms effectively addressed sectoral inconsistencies, legislative deficiencies and operational gaps in the AML/CTF regime?
- How do inefficiencies in data-sharing, regulatory fragmentation, and limited reform responses impact the effectiveness of defence against money laundering (DAML) SARs and the broader UK AML regime in combating money laundering?
- How do inefficiencies in data-sharing and limited public-private collaboration impact the effectiveness of DAML SARs within the UK's AML regime, and to what extent has HM Government's response to the Law Commission's SARs review addressed these issues?
- To what extent do deficiencies in financial intelligence coordination and information exchange among UK CTF financing entities undermine compliance with FATF Recommendation 31 and hinder effective detection and prevention of terrorist financing considering legislative reforms and recent case studies?
- How does the complexity of the UK's legal framework for data-sharing affect the effectiveness of fraud prevention, and what legal and structural reforms are needed to improve coordination between public and private sector stakeholders?

VII. Methodology and Methods

This part of the chapter provides a brief outline and validation for the methodology and methods adopted for the book. Methodology refers to the overarching research strategy,[171] the theoretical and philosophical bases of which determine the conceptualisation of law, the nature of acceptable research questions and the data used to answer them.[172] The research methodology determines the appropriate methods, or techniques, used to obtain and analyse data, in accordance with the

[171] M Henn, M Weinstein and N Foard, *A Critical Introduction to Social Research* (Sage, 2009) at 10.
[172] D Watkins and M Burton (eds), *Research Methods in Law* (Routledge, 2013) at 2.

stated standards and values of the methodology.[173] Considering the research aims and questions, the research for this book was conducted using socio-legal methodology, supported by doctrinal analysis and the case study method. Socio-legal studies are an interdisciplinary research method in law that examine legal systems, rules, and institutions within their broader social context.[174] Rather than focusing solely on legal doctrine, this approach integrates insights from sociology, political science, economics, and other disciplines to explore how law operates in practice and affects society.[175] It often employs both qualitative and quantitative empirical methods to investigate how laws are applied, experienced, and enforced. The benefits of socio-legal research include a deeper contextual understanding of law, enhanced policy relevance, and the ability to critically assess legal systems and their social impacts.[176] Therefore, this research method strengthens the legitimacy and inclusiveness of legal systems by ensuring that law is not just a set of rules, but a dynamic institution embedded in society. The socio-legal approach is often complemented by the doctrinal approach.[177]

The doctrinal method is a traditional legal research approach that focuses on analysing authoritative legal sources such as statutes, case law, and regulations to determine what the law is on a given issue.[178] Often referred to as 'black-letter law', it involves systematic interpretation and synthesis of legal texts to clarify legal principles and construct coherent legal arguments.[179] This method offers several benefits: it provides clarity and certainty, ensures consistency and predictability in legal interpretation, and serves as an efficient tool for legal practitioners.[180] In law, the case study method analyses judicial decisions, statutes, or legal scenarios to understand legal principles, their interpretations, and applications. Case study research has been referred to as a 'strategy' of qualitative research,[181] and was

[173] See Henn et al (n 172).

[174] See generally D Harris, 'The Development of Socio-Legal Studies in the United Kingdom' (1983) *Legal Studies* 3(3), 315–33.

[175] See generally L Edelman and R Stryker, 'A Sociological Approach to Law and the Economy' in N Smelser and R Swedberg (eds), *The Handbook of Economic Sociology* (Sage, 2005) 527–52.

[176] See generally S Sood, 'Socio-Legal Approach to Research' (2023) *Journal of Legal Studies & Research* 9(5), 5–15; L Williams, 'Research Methods: Our Approach to Socio-Legal Research' in L William, S Corby, and B Pauksztat (eds), *Claiming Disability Discrimination Assessing Barriers to Justice* (Palgrave, 2025) 57–73 and L Webley, 'The Why and How of Conducting a Socio-Legal Empirical Research Project' in N Creutzfeld, M Mason and K McConnachie (eds), *Routledge Handbook of Socio-Legal Theory and Methods* (Routledge, 2015) 58–69.

[177] See P Bhat, 'Doctrinal Legal Research as a Means of Synthesizing Facts, Thoughts, and Legal Principles' in P Bhat, *Idea and Methods of Legal Research* (Oxford University Press, 2020) 143–68.

[178] See generally T Hutchinson and N Duncan, 'Defining and Describing What We Do: Doctrinal Legal Research' (2012) *Deakin Law Review* 17(1), 83–119.

[179] See generally J Vranken, 'Methodology of Legal Doctrinal Research' in M Van Hoecke (ed), *Methodologies of Legal Research. Which Kind of Method for What Kind of Discipline* (Hart Publishing, 1939) 111–21.

[180] See M Salter and J Mason, *Writing Law Dissertations: An Introduction and Guide to the Conduct of Legal Research* (Pearson, 2007).

[181] See J Creswell, *Research Design, Qualitative, Quantitative and Mixed Methods Approaches* (Sage, 2003) at 8–9.

defined by Yin as an empirical study that 'investigates a contemporary phenomenon in-depth within its real-life context, especially when the boundaries between the phenomenon and the context are not clearly evident'.[182] Argyrou stated that:

> The case study development offers an advantage to the legal researcher in answering questions of 'how' and 'why'. These are not legal questions per se, but they can be complementary to legal questions. In response to these questions, the legal researcher can use a contemporary set of real-life events data (collected through interviews, documents and observations), rather than legal arguments and theoretical.[183]

This method seeks to bridge the gap between legal theory and practical application, which enables a more in-depth understanding of how legal concepts work. Case studies allow legal scholars to explore how laws are interpreted, applied, and experienced in real-world contexts, which doctrinal methods might not be able to capture.[184] Schoch noted that the case study methodology is relevant across disciplines, including law and that case studies offer contextual depth, multiple data sources, and transferable insight.[185] Case studies offer depth, nuance, and are useful for exploring 'how' and 'why' questions in real-world settings where the boundaries between phenomenon and context are blurred.[186]

The UK faces an estimated £350billion annual cost from economic crime, with money laundering and fraud being major contributors. That scale demands innovative responses, including smarter data-sharing. Money laundering is ideal case study research on data-sharing and FATF compliance because it highlights the complexities of tackling transnational financial crime through collaborative efforts. Furthermore, it allows for analysis of how initiatives like the UK's Joint Money Laundering Task Force enhance detection while aligning with FATF standards on information-sharing and transparency. Terrorist financing often involves fraud, misuse of charities, abuse of financial systems and is associated with new forms of technology, making it an appropriate example of how data-sharing must bridge institutional silos. Furthermore, the FATF place CTF at the heart of its Recommendations contributing to a policy environment where data-sharing is essential. Terrorist financing typologies illustrate the need for effective data-sharing mechanisms to detect terrorist financing and intervene early. The sharing of data to prevent terrorism raises General Data Protection Regulation concerns, especially around profiling and consent. Therefore, this case study allows exploration of how the UK balances

[182] R Yin, *Case Study Research: Design and Methods* (Sage, 2014) at 16.
[183] A Argyrou, 'Making the Case for Case Studies in Empirical Legal Research' (2017) *Utrecht Law Review* 13(3), 95–113, at 100.
[184] ibid.
[185] K Schoch, 'Case Study Research' in GJ Burkholder et al (eds), *Research Design and Methods: An Applied Guide for the Scholar-Practitioner* (Sage, 2020) 245–58.
[186] K Robert, *Case Study Research and Applications: Design and Methods* (Sage, 2013).

civil liberties with proactive intelligence-sharing, particularly in light of initiatives like the National Crime Agency's (NCA) public-private partnerships.

Fraud makes a compelling case study because of the financial losses associated with it, its links to organised crime and terrorist financing. Addressing the threat requires increased collaboration between the public and private sector, thus illustrating the need for how data- sharing must overcome institutional silos and legal boundaries.

VIII. Structure of the Book

Chapter two identifies the importance of the FATF, briefly outlining its Recommendations before focusing on those that relate to the submission of a SAR and the exchange of information. The chapter proceeds by investigating the main features of the FATF MER, which assesses and monitors FATF members from different countries through peer reviews. The MER seeks to provide a comprehensive analysis and determination of how a country's AML/CTF regime complies with the FATF Recommendations. The onus of compliance is to demonstrate that they are compliant with the Recommendations and the chapter explores the components used by FATF to determine the levels of compliance with its Recommendations – effectiveness and technical compliance. Furthermore, the chapter critically reviews the FATF methodology that it used to determine a country's level of compliance. Chapter three appraises the UK's response to the 2007 MER by identifying and reviewing the related data-sharing legislative and policy developments since the UK's 2007 MER. The legislative measures included the introduction of a comprehensive AML/CTF legislative framework that exceeded the international standards. Chapter four focuses on money laundering and uses case studies to illustrate the weaknesses in financial intelligence and subsequent exchange of information. This includes the legal profession, the financial services sector and AML supervisory agencies. Chapter five focuses on the use of financial intelligence and exchange of information in terrorist financing. This chapter presents evidence that illustrates weaknesses in the exchange of information via three studies that focus on the terrorist attacks in London (July 2005), Manchester (May 2017), and London (June 2017). Conversely, the chapter identifies three further case studies that have illustrated examples of best practice where data-sharing mechanisms have resulted in the convictions of terrorist financiers. As outlined in chapters four and five, the UK has a strong history of utilising financial intelligence as part of its broader financial crime strategy, a point clearly illustrated by the AML/CTF reporting provisions. However, chapter six presents evidence that the reporting of fraud can be contrasted with both money laundering and terrorist financing. The chapter highlights the deficiencies in the reporting of fraud by five case studies that focus on Action Fraud, The Police, Social Media Platforms and the Telecommunications Sector and the Bounce Back Loan Scheme. The chapter concludes that there are inherent flaws in the UK's ability to obtain and exchange information to detect fraud. Considering this assessment, the chapter will make several recommendations aimed at improving the reporting of fraud. Chapter seven summarises the findings of this book in relation to the research questions and concludes by making recommendations to reform current legislation and data-sharing mechanisms in the UK.

2

The Financial Action Task Force, its Recommendations and Methodology

> In the past decade the FATF seems to have lost its way, as it struggles to determine what all this investment in laws, new agencies and awareness-raising is trying to achieve, beyond the elusive notion of effectiveness.[1]

I. Introduction

This chapter begins by highlighting the importance of the role of the Financial Action Task Force (FATF) in addressing financial crime, before focusing on its Recommendations and Immediate Outcomes (IOC), relating to customer due diligence (CDD), the use of Suspicious Activity Reports (SARs) and the related data-sharing mechanisms. The chapter begins by providing an historical overview of the FATF that identifies its initial focus on money laundering, before extending its remit to include terrorist financing following the Al-Qaeda terrorist attacks in September 2001 (9/11), before briefly discussing the expansion of the Recommendations to include countering proliferation financing (CPF). The chapter then moves on to identify and appraise the FATF methodology used for conducting the periodical Mutual Evaluation Reports (MERs). Here, the chapter investigates the main features of the MER, which are 'in-depth country reports analysing the implementation and effectiveness of measures to combat money laundering and terrorist financing'.[2] The MER provides a comprehensive analysis and determination of how a country's anti-money laundering and counter-terrorist financing (AML/CTF) regime complies with the Recommendations. Therefore, the chapter explores the components used by FATF to determine the levels of compliance with its Recommendations – effectiveness and technical compliance. The chapter questions the suitability of the regime, particularly in light of the 2018 United Kingdom (UK) MER, where FATF rated the UK's

[1] T Keatinge, 'What's the Point of the Financial Action Task Force Standards?' (7 August 2024), availableatwww.rusi.org/explore-our-research/publications/commentary/whats-point-financial-action-task-force-standards.

[2] Financial Action Task Force (FATF), 'Mutual Evaluations' (n/d), available at www.fatf-gafi.org/en/topics/mutual-evaluations.html.

AML/CTF regime as the best in the world.[3] The penultimate part of the chapter focuses on Recommendations that deal with CDD, the use of SARs and data-sharing. Specifically, it considers Recommendations 2, 30 and 31 and Immediate Outcomes 1, 6, 7 and 9. Therefore, the subsidiary research question answered here is 'to what extent does the FATF MER methodology provide an accurate and objective assessment of a country's AML/CTF regime, particularly regarding financial intelligence and the exchange of information'?

II. The Financial Action Task Force

The FATF has been described as the 'single most important international body in terms of the formulation of anti-money laundering policy'.[4] The FATF was created in July 1989 and influenced by 'the General Assembly of the UN's adoption in 1988 of a universal pledge to put a halt to money laundering'.[5] The main objective of the FATF is to protect the global financial system from being used for illicit purposes including money laundering, terrorist financing, and the financing of weapons of mass destruction.[6] In order to meet achieve this objective, the FATF working with other international stakeholders undertakes a wide range of tasks which includes:

- identifying and analysing money laundering, terrorist financing and other threats to the integrity of the financial system, including the methods and trends involved;
- developing and refining the international standards for combating money laundering and the financing of terrorism and proliferation to ensure that they are up-to-date and effective;
- assessing and monitoring its Members, through 'peer reviews' or MER and follow-up processes, to determine the degree of technical compliance, implementation and effectiveness of systems to combat money laundering and the financing of terrorism and proliferation; refining the standard assessment methodology and common procedures for conducting mutual evaluations and evaluation follow-up;

[3] FATF, *Anti-Money Laundering and Counter-Terrorist Financing Measures: United Kingdom Mutual Evaluation Report* (FATF, 2018) (hereinafter 'FATF 2018 MER'). For a more detailed analysis and commentary see chapters three to six.

[4] W Gilmore, *Dirty Money – the Evaluation of International Measures to Counter Money Laundering and the Financing of Terrorism* (Council of Europe, 2004) at 89.

[5] J Johnson, 'Is the Global Financial System AML/CTF Prepared?' (2008) *Journal of Financial Crime* 15(1), 7–21, at 8. Also see G7 Information Centre, 'Economic Declaration' (16 July 1989), available at https://g7.utoronto.ca/summit/1989paris/communique/index.html.

[6] FATF, 'Mandate of the FATF' (n/d), available at www.fatf-gafi.org/en/the-fatf/mandate-of-the-fatf.html.

- identifying and engaging with high-risk, non-cooperative jurisdictions and those with strategic deficiencies in their national regimes, and coordinating action to protect the integrity of the financial system against the threat posed by them;
- promoting full and effective implementation of the FATF Recommendations by all countries through the global network of FATF-style regional bodies (FSRBs) and international organisations;
- responding as necessary to significant new and emerging threats and risks to the integrity of the financial system consistent with the needs identified by the international community;
- assisting jurisdictions in implementing financial provisions of the United Nations Security Council Resolutions (UNSCR) on terrorism and non-proliferation, assessing the degree of implementation and the effectiveness of these measures in accordance with the FATF mutual evaluation and follow-up process, and preparing guidance as needed to facilitate implementation of relevant international obligations in a manner compatible with the FATF standards;
- maintaining engagement with other international organisations and bodies to increase the outreach of the activities and objectives of the FATF;
- engaging and consulting with the private sector and civil society on matters related to the overall work of the FATF; and
- undertaking any new tasks agreed by its Members in the course of its activities and within the framework of this Mandate; and taking on these new tasks only where it has a particular additional contribution to make while avoiding duplication of existing efforts elsewhere.[7]

The FATF achieves these objectives by setting international standards or 'Recommendations' and the promotion of effective implementation of legal, regulatory, and operational measures to combat these threats.[8] The FATF's membership criteria includes a commitment to its Recommendations, a willingness to undertake mutual evaluations and participation in the FATF process.[9] There are 40 FATF members, including 38 countries and two regional organisations (the Gulf Cooperation Council and the European Commission) and 31 international and regional organisations, which are 'Associate Members' or 'Observers'.[10] The FATF is not a law enforcement agency, it is not a law-making body but an international policy-making body.[11]

[7] See ibid.

[8] FATF, 'What We Do' (n/d), available at www.fatf-gafi.org/en/the-fatf/what-we-do.html.

[9] FATF, 'Membership Process and Criteria' (n/d), available at www.fatf-gafi.org/en/the-fatf/membership-process-criteria.html.

[10] FATF, 'Frequently Asked Questions' (n/d), available at www.fatf-gafi.org/en/pages/frequently-asked-questions.html#tabs-36503a8663-item-cacccf71cf-tab.

[11] ibid.

The FATF Recommendations seek to provide a comprehensive framework for countries to combat money laundering,[12] and their remit is regularly updated.[13] For example, the scope of the Recommendations were extended to include terrorist financing in response to 9/11.[14] In light of the evolution of money laundering techniques, the FATF revised its Recommendations in 2003.[15] Further amendments were made in 2012, when the FATF incorporated the 'Special Recommendations' into the 40 Recommendations and the scope was extended to include the financing of weapons of mass destruction.[16] The remit of the Recommendations were further broadened to include the regulation and supervision of the activities and service providers related to cryptoassets.[17] The FATF reinforced the global beneficial ownership rules in its Recommendations to stop criminals from hiding their illicit activities and dirty money behind secret corporate structures.[18]

The importance of the Recommendations is illustrated by UNSCR 1617 which strongly urges 'all Member States to implement the comprehensive, international standards embodied in the FATF Forty Recommendations on Money Laundering'.[19] This was also referred to in UNSCR 2368,[20] UNSCR 2462,[21] UNSCR 2610,[22] UNSCR 2664[23] and UNSCR 2734,[24] which all reiterate the necessity of all countries to fully implement the Recommendations. The significance of the Recommendations is illustrated by over 200 jurisdictions committing

[12] FATF, 'History of the FATF' (n/d), available at www.fatf-gafi.org/en/the-fatf/history-of-the-fatf.html#:~:text=In%20April%201990%2C%20less%20than,Special%20Recommendations%20on%20terrorist%20financing.

[13] FATF, *Financial Action Task Force on Money Laundering: Report 1990 –1991* (FATF, 1991).

[14] These were referred to as the 'Special Recommendations'. See FATF, *FATF IX Special Recommendations* (FATF, 2001). In October 2004, the FATF published a Ninth Special Recommendation on terrorist financing, and the recommendations were referred to as the 40+9 Recommendations.

[15] FATF, *The 40 Recommendations* (FATF, 2003).

[16] FATF, *The FATF Recommendations* (FATF, 2012).

[17] See FATF, *History of the FATF* (n 12).

[18] FATF, *Beneficial Ownership of Legal Persons* (FATF, 2022). At the time of writing, the most recent update to the Recommendations was published in June 2025. See FATF, *International Standards on Combating Money Laundering and the Financing of Terrorism and Proliferation – The FATF Recommendations* (FATF, 2025) (hereinafter 'FATF Recommendations 2025').

[19] United Nations Security Council Resolution (UNSCR) 1617 (2005) S/RES/1617 (2005), adopted by the Security Council at its 5244th meeting on 29th July 2005. Also see Resolution 60/288 of the UN General Assembly (20 September 2006) which provides 'to encourage states to implement the comprehensive international standards embodied in the Forty Recommendations on Money Laundering and the Nine Special Recommendations on Terrorist Financing of the Financial Action Task Force'.

[20] UNSCR 2368 (20 July 2017) UN DOC S/RES/2368, available at https://main.un.org/securitycouncil/en/s/res/2368-%282017%29.

[21] UNSCR 2462 (28 March 2019) UN Doc S/RES/2462, available at https://main.un.org/securitycouncil/en/content/sres24622019.

[22] UNSCR 2610 (17 December 2021) UN DOC S/RES/2610, available at https://main.un.org/securitycouncil/en/content/sres26102021.

[23] UNSCR 2664 (9 December 2022) UN DOC S/RES/2664, available at https://main.un.org/securitycouncil/en/content/sres2664-2022.

[24] UNSCR 2734 (10 June 2024) UN DOC S/RES/2734, available at https://main.un.org/securitycouncil/en/content/res-2734-2024.

to adopting the FATF Standards.[25] Additionally, the Recommendations have influenced the evolution of the European Union's (EU) Money Laundering Directives (MLDs). For example, the First MLD was heavily modelled on the 40 Recommendations;[26] the adoption of the risk based approach (RBA) was entrenched in the Fourth MLD;[27] the development of the FATF's ambition to improve levels of transparency resulted in the EU mandating the public registers of beneficial ownership in the Fifth MLD and inclusion of cryptocurrencies within the scope of Recommendations was reciprocated here.[28] Therefore, the Recommendations are the cornerstone of international efforts to combat money laundering and terrorist financing, shaping both UN and EU frameworks. Several UNSCRs have embedded the Recommendations, advising Member States to adopt robust financial controls aligned with the Recommendations. Similarly, the EU's MLDs have evolved in close coordination with the Recommendations by incorporating its RBA, beneficial ownership transparency, and the regulation of cryptocurrencies.[29]

Members of the FATF are committed to implementing the Recommendations and have agreed to be subject to multilateral surveillance, peer review and the publication of the Non-Cooperative Countries and Territories (NCCT) or Black list.[30] Members have their implementation of the Recommendations monitored by MERs which assess how well countries implement the measures to combat money laundering, terrorist financing and proliferation financing.[31] The MER has two key parts – effectiveness and technical compliance.[32] In order to encourage compliance with the Recommendations, the FATF was reliant on a system of 'coercion'.[33] This was illustrated by the publication of the NCCT list which contained countries that did not meet the international standards.[34] By 'June 2000 this process

[25] FATF, *Countries* (n/d), available at www.fatf-gafi.org/en/countries.html#:~:text=Over%20200%20jurisdictions%20around%20the,of%20FSRBs%20and%20FATF%20memberships.

[26] See Council Directive 91/308/EEC of 10 June 1991 on the prevention of the use of the financial system for the purpose of money laundering ('First Money Laundering Directive') [1991] OJ L166/77.

[27] See Directive (EU) 2015/849 of the European Parliament and of the Council of 20 May 2015 on the prevention of the use of the financial system for the purposes of money laundering or terrorist financing ('Fourth Money Laundering Directive') [2015] OJ L141/7.

[28] Directive (EU) 2018/843 of the European Parliament and of the Council of 30 May 2018 amending Directive (EU) 2015/849 on the prevention of the use of the financial system for the purposes of money laundering or terrorist financing (Fifth Money Laundering Directive) [2018] OJ L156/43.

[29] For a more detailed discussion of the influence of the Recommendations on the EU, see I de Oliveira, 'The Governance of the Financial Action Task Force: An Analysis of Power and Influence throughout the Years' (2018) *Crime, Law and Social Change* 69(2), 153–72.

[30] For a more detailed discussion, see JC Sharman, *The Money Laundry: Regulating Criminal Finance in the Global Economy* (Cornell University Press, 2011) 99–130.

[31] FATF, Mutual Evaluations (n 2). Also see R Sansonetti, 'The Mutual Evaluation Process: A Methodology of Increasing Importance at International Level' (2000) *Journal of Financial Crime* 7(3), 218–26.

[32] ibid.

[33] R Hulsse, 'Creating Demand for Global Governance: The Making of a Global Money-Laundering Problem' (2007) *Global Society* 21(2), 155–78, at 167.

[34] B Zagaris, *International White-Collar Crime – Cases and Materials* (Cambridge University Press, 2010) 60–63.

had resulted in the creation of a blacklist of … jurisdictions where serious problems had been identified',[35] which has been labelled as 'disturbing and [it] suggests a policy redolent of extraterritorial bullying'.[36] The NCCT list was criticised by the International Monetary Fund and World Bank, which resulted in a change of policy by the FATF,[37] which feared it might lose its authority as the global AML agency.[38] Demetis took the view that 'no G7 country has ever been blacklisted, for whatever reason, despite the fact that a large amount of laundered money goes through the US and the UK'.[39] This is surprising as London has often been referred to as the 'money laundering capital of the world'.[40]

The early use of the NCCT list was a form of coercion to improve the international adoption of the FATF Recommendations. While the FATF lacked formal legal authority, inclusion on the NCCT list triggered reputational damage,[41] financial isolation[42] and economic downturn.[43] The original NCCT list was not associated with a specific Recommendation yet it served as a compliance assessment against the Recommendations. The current process is managed by the International Co-operation Review Group and is linked more directly to Recommendations.[44] For example, Recommendation 19 urges countries to apply enhanced due diligence (EDD) and countermeasures to jurisdictions identified by FATF as high-risk and non-cooperative.[45] This informal pressure created powerful incentives for rapid reform, with most countries attempting to quickly align with FATF Recommendations to maintain access to global financial markets. As of 13 June 2025, the countries on the blacklist are the Democratic People's Republic

[35] See Gilmore (n 4) at 147.

[36] T Doyle, 'Cleaning Up Anti-Money Laundering Strategies: Current FATF Tactics Needlessly Violate International Law' (2002) *Houston Journal of International Law* 24, 279–313, at 282.

[37] See Hulsse (n 33).

[38] P Alldridge, 'Money Laundering and Globalisation' (2009) *Journal of Law and Society* 35(4), 437–63, at 444.

[39] D Demetis, *Technology and Anti-Money Laundering: A Systems Theory and Risk-Based Approach* (Edward Elgar, 2010) at 20.

[40] See J Heathershaw, A Cooley, T Mayne, C Michel, T Prelec, J Sharman and R Soares de Oliveira, *The UK's Kleptocracy Problem: How Servicing Post-Soviet Elites Weakens the Rule of Law* (Chatham House, 2021).

[41] See K Eggenberger, 'When is Blacklisting Effective? Stigma, Sanctions and Legitimacy: The Reputational and Financial Costs of being Blacklisted' (2018) *Review of International Political Economy* 25(4), 483–504.

[42] See, eg, L De Koker, J Howell and N Morris, 'Economic Consequences of Grey Listing by the Financial Action Task Force (2023) *Risks* 11(5), 81; L De Koker, 'FATF Grey Listing: Time to Revisit the Approach' (2024) *Journal of Money Laundering Control* 27(4), 621–24 and H Khouny and H Drissi, 'Addressing the Challenges of Weak AML Measures in Developing Countries: Key Concerns of FATF and Consequences of Grey Listing' (2025) *Multidisciplinary Science Journal* 7(3), 20251502025150, https://doi.org/10.31893/multiscience.2025150.

[43] M Kida and S Paetzold, *The Impact of Gray-Listing on Capital Flows: An Analysis using Machine Learning* (International Monetary Fund, 2021) at 5.

[44] FATF, 'High-Risk and other Monitored Jurisdictions' (n/d), available at www.fatf-gafi.org/en/publications/High-risk-and-other-monitored-jurisdictions/More-on-high-risk-and-non-cooperative-jurisdictions.html.

[45] See FATF Recommendations 2025 (n 18) at 72.

of Korea, Iran and Myanmar.[46] The NCCT initiative illustrated FATF's strategic use of soft power to enforce compliance through visibility and peer pressure. Consequently, the FATF has moved away from using the NCCT list to identify 'high-risk and other monitored jurisdictions' or the 'Grey list'.[47]

The 'jurisdictions under increased monitoring' identifies countries with strategic weaknesses in their AML and CTF frameworks, which are formally committed to resolving them.[48] Once a country is assessed via an MER, it agrees to an action plan outlining specific reform.[49] As of June 2025, the following countries are on the Grey list: Algeria; Angola; Bolivia; Bulgaria; Burkina Faso; Cameroon; Côte d'Ivoire; Democratic Republic of Congo; Haiti; Kenya; Lao; People's Democratic Republic; Lebanon; Monaco; Mozambique; Namibia; Nepal; Nigeria; South Africa; South Sudan; Syria; Venezuela; Vietnam; Virgin Islands (UK) and Yemen. High-risk jurisdictions are the Democratic People's Republic of Korea; Iran and Myanmar. FATF then places the country under increased monitoring, requiring regular progress updates and maintaining public listings that are updated three times a year.[50] If a country is placed on the Grey list it signals to the global financial community that EDD is warranted when dealing with entities from that jurisdiction. Indeed, the UK's Money Laundering Regulations mandates that the regulated sector must apply EDD and enhanced ongoing monitoring in situations presenting a high risk of money laundering or terrorist financing. This includes relationships with individuals or entities from high-risk third countries.[51] Removal from the list occurs only after FATF confirms that the agreed reforms have been effectively implemented. The Black and Grey lists identify countries with shortcomings in AML and CTF systems but differ in intensity and global response. Countries associated with the Black list have critical deficiencies and are non-cooperative, prompting FATF to recommend strong countermeasures, including sanctions and financial isolation. Conversely, the Grey list identifies jurisdictions that pose an elevated risk, yet the list members are actively cooperating with the FATF to improve. These countries face reputational challenges and EDD but remain engaged in reform.

The EU maintains its own list of high-risk third countries with AML and CTF deficiencies.[52] While aligned with the FATF Grey and Black lists, the EU conducts independent assessments and can include or exclude jurisdictions accordingly.

[46] See FATF, 'High-Risk and other Monitored Jurisdictions' (n/d), available at www.fatf-gafi.org/en/publications/High-risk-and-other-monitored-jurisdictions/More-on-high-risk-and-non-cooperative-jurisdictions.htmlFATF.

[47] ibid.

[48] See FATF, 'Black and Grey Lists' (n/d), available from www.fatf-gafi.org/en/countries/black-and-grey-lists.html.

[49] See FATF, 'High-Risk and other Monitored Jurisdictions' (n 46).

[50] ibid.

[51] The Money Laundering, Terrorist Financing and Transfer of Funds (Information on the Payer) Regulations 2017 (SI 2017/692), Regulation 33.

[52] Directive (EU) 2015/849 of the European Parliament and of the Council of 20 May 2015 on the prevention of the use of the financial system for the purposes of money laundering or terrorist financing [2015] OJ L141/73–117, Art 9.

This list is compiled and regularly updated by the European Commission, which assesses jurisdictions based on a detailed methodology that considers international standards, such as the FATF Recommendations.[53] Countries identified are subject to EDD under EU law,[54] meaning financial institutions must apply stricter checks when dealing with entities from these jurisdictions. The listing process involves priority setting, assessment, formal listing, and ongoing monitoring and updates published through delegated regulations.[55] This process involves technical reviews, consultations with key EU bodies including the European Banking Authority and Europol and may include bilateral dialogues and on-site visits. The EU applies a rigorous methodology that evaluates both technical compliance and the practical effectiveness of their AML/CTF frameworks.[56]

III. Methodology

The FATF has adopted a structured methodology to determine the level of compliance by countries towards implementing the Recommendations. The FATF Methodology outlines how countries are evaluated for AML, CTF and proliferation financing.[57] The assessment is based on two core pillars – technical compliance and effectiveness. The FATF stated that the technical compliance assessment 'addresses the specific requirements of the FATF Recommendations, principally as they relate to the relevant legal and institutional framework of the country and the powers and procedures of the competent authorities'.[58] The technical compliance pillar of the methodology evaluates whether a country has the necessary legal, regulatory, and institutional frameworks to meet the Recommendations.[59] Here, the technical compliance evaluates whether a country has established an adequate legal, regulatory, and institutional framework in line with the FATF Recommendations. For example, this includes assessing whether appropriate laws and regulations are in place, whether key institutions such as financial intelligence units (FIUs) and law enforcement agencies (LEAs) are functioning, and whether operational measures such as CDD, record keeping and submitting SARs are being implemented.[60] Each

[53] ibid.

[54] Directive (EU) 2018/843 of the European Parliament and of the Council of 30 May 2018 amending Directive (EU) 2015/849 on the prevention of the use of the financial system for the purposes of money laundering or terrorist financing [2018] OJ L156/43, Art 18.

[55] See generally K Rose, 'De-Risking or Re-Contracting: The Risk Dilemma of EU Money Laundering Regulation' (2020) *The Journal of Risk Finance* 21(4), 445–58.

[56] See European Commission, 'Anti-Money Laundering and Countering the Financing of Terrorism at International Level' (n/d), available at https://finance.ec.europa.eu/financial-crime/anti-money-laundering-and-countering-financing-terrorism-international-level_en.

[57] FATF, *Methodology for Assessing Technical Compliance with the FATF Recommendations and the Effectiveness of AML/CFT/CPF Systems* (FATF, 2025).

[58] ibid at 6.

[59] ibid at 16.

[60] ibid at 28–120.

Recommendation receives one of four ratings: Compliant, Largely Compliant, Partially Compliant, or Non-Compliant.[61] The technical compliance forms one half of the FATF evaluation process, the other comprising effectiveness, which measures how well these frameworks are working in practice.

In terms of the effectiveness, FATF

> seeks to assess the adequacy of the implementation of the FATF Recommendations and identifies the extent to which a country achieves a defined set of outcomes that are central to a robust AML/CFT/CPF system. The focus of the effectiveness assessment is therefore on the extent to which the legal and institutional framework is producing the expected results.[62]

Therefore, the effectiveness pillar evaluates how well a country's AML, CTF and CPF system works in practice. The FATF stated that the assessment of effectiveness is intended to 'improve the FATF's focus on outcomes … identify the extent to which the national AML/CFT/CPF system is achieving the objectives of the FATF Standards and identify any systemic weaknesses; and … enable countries to prioritise measures to improve their system'.[63] Therefore, the FATF has defined effectiveness as 'the extent to which the defined outcomes are achieved'.[64] In order to determine effectiveness, the FATF has adopted an approach that focuses on 'hierarchy of defined outcomes'.[65] The FATF stated that

> at the highest level, the objective in implementing AML/CFT/CPF measures is that financial systems and the broader economy are protected from the threats of money laundering and the financing of terrorism and proliferation, thereby strengthening financial sector integrity and contributing to safety and security.[66]

The purpose of the high-level objective is to protect financial systems and the broader economy from money laundering, terrorist financing, and proliferation financing. FATF focuses on the 11 Immediate Outcomes, which provide a structured view of how well a country's AML/CFT/CPF measures operate as a system. Each of the Immediate Outcomes is rated as either High Effectiveness; Substantial Effectiveness; Moderate Effectiveness; or Low Effectiveness and reflect how well the country achieves the intended results in each area.

The FATF methodology combines technical compliance with effectiveness in an attempt to ensure that countries do not 'tick boxes' but actually reduce financial crime.[67] A key part of the FATF methodology is the adoption of the RBA which

[61] ibid at 17.
[62] ibid at 6.
[63] ibid at 19.
[64] ibid.
[65] ibid.
[66] ibid.
[67] For a more detailed discussion, see R Pol, 'Anti-Money Laundering Effectiveness: Assessing Outcomes or Ticking Boxes?' (2018) *Journal of Money Laundering Control* 21(2), 215–30; M Killick and D Parody, 'Implementing AML/CFT Measures that Address the Risks and not Tick Boxes' (2007) *Journal of Financial Regulation and Compliance* 15(2), 210–16.

encourages jurisdictions to tailor their AML, CTF and CPF measures to specific risk profiles, promoting proportionality and efficient use of resources.[68] The global standardisation of the Recommendations seeks to provide a consistent framework used by FATF, regional bodies, the International Monetary Fund, and World Bank to enable comparability across jurisdictions.[69] The methodology recognises the importance of the prioritisation of sector-weighting on high-risk areas such as cryptocurrencies, offshore finance and trade-based money laundering.[70] The 2022 update to the methodology-integrated CPF reflects evolving global threats and also evaluates the unintended consequences and whether AML/CTF measures inadvertently cause financial exclusion or de-risking.[71] The FATF's 2025 methodology seeks to address concerns about regulatory burden and financial exclusion by placing greater emphasis on proportionality and simplified measures within its RBA.[72] Under the revised Recommendations, countries are required to allow and encourage simplified AML/CTF measures in lower-risk scenarios, making it easier for under-resourced regulators to tailor obligations without compromising security.[73] Supervisors are also expected to assess whether financial institutions are implementing proportionate controls, rather than defaulting to over-compliance due to a limited understanding of risk. This shift helps reduce the pressure on regulators to issue exhaustive guidance and instead promotes flexible, context-sensitive supervision.

FATF's technical compliance methodology has faced notable criticism for prioritising the existence of formal laws and institutions over their real-world functionality, leading to 'box-ticking'. This has caused financial exclusion where strict CDD requirements often limit access for low-income individuals and small businesses. Developing countries struggle to meet this requirement because they often lack the resources to implement the AML/CTF measures. However, they still face the same evaluative standards and reputational risks as wealthier nations. Evaluations conducted by peer reviewers have also been accused of inconsistency and subjectivity, raising concerns about transparency and fairness. Furthermore, the technical framework has been slow to adapt to emerging financial threats such as cryptoassets and decentralised platforms, with outdated standards. Therefore, there is an increasing recognition that strong technical compliance scores do not always translate into effective action.

The FATF effectiveness part of the assessment seeks to surpass the legal frameworks, but it does often fall short in capturing real-world impact. For example,

[68] See FATF, 'The FATF Recommendations' (n/d), available from www.fatf-gafi.org/en/topics/fatf-recommendations.html#:~:text=The%20cornerstone%20of%20the%20FATF,in%20the%20highest%20risk%20areas.

[69] ibid.

[70] See FATF, *Methodology for Assessing Technical Compliance with the FATF Recommendations* (n 57).

[71] ibid.

[72] ibid.

[73] See FATF, 'FATF Updates Standards and Consults on Guidance to Better Promote Financial Inclusion' (25 February 2025), available at www.fatf-gafi.org/en/publications/Fatfrecommendations/update-standards-promote-financial-conclusion-feb-2025.html.

some evaluations focus on outputs such as the number of investigations rather than outcomes such as successful prosecutions or asset recovery. This could incentivise superficial rather than meaningful enforcement. Additionally, the peer-review process used to assess effectiveness has been criticised for inconsistency and lack of transparency, with some countries alleging that political or economic biases influence scoring.[74] Developing nations face challenges due to limited resources, making it difficult to meet FATF's expectations for effectiveness despite having strong technical compliance.[75] Moreover, FATF has been slow to adapt its effectiveness metrics to emerging threats like cryptoassets and decentralised finance, leaving gaps in its ability to assess modern financial ecosystems. Lastly, there's a perceived accountability gap: when FATF standards are misapplied or abused, there's little recourse or corrective mechanism, raising questions about governance and legitimacy. Another criticism is that compliance does place a heavy burden on supervisors and several jurisdictions must issue detailed guidance on simplified measures and prove their effectiveness, that is challenging for under-resourced regulators.[76] Additionally, that inconsistent application is influenced by the flexibility in interpretation may lead to uneven assessments across countries and evaluators, especially in politically sensitive contexts. Finally, the 'evaluation cycle pressure' demands more frequent and intensive preparation, which may strain national authorities and institutions.[77]

The FATF methodology is designed to assess how effectively countries combat money laundering, terrorist financing, and proliferation financing. It consists of two pillars: technical compliance with the FATF Recommendations, and the effectiveness of a country's measures in practice. Recent updates reflect a shift toward real-world impact, prioritising operational evidence over formal regulations, integrating proliferation financing evaluations throughout, and offering more flexibility through risk-based assessments. While these changes promote proportionality and inclusion, they also introduce complexities such as inconsistencies in interpreting risk justifications.

IV. Mutual Evaluation Process and Reports

The FATF mutual evaluation process is a comprehensive peer-review mechanism used to assess how effectively countries implement measures to combat money

[74] See generally C Littrell, 'Economic and Demographic Biases in FATF Mutual Evaluation Results' in D Goldbarsht and L de Koker (eds), *Financial Crime and the Law: Identifying and Mitigating Risks* (Springer, 2024) 191–224.

[75] See generally N Jensen and C Png, 'Implementation of the FATF 40+ 9 Recommendations: A Perspective from Developing Countries' (2011) *Journal of Money Laundering Control* 14(2), 110–20.

[76] T Keatinge, S Reimer and I Chase, 'Good Intentions: The FATF Faces Its Own Unintended Consequences' (5 August 2021), available at www.rusi.org/explore-our-research/publications/commentary/good-intentions-fatf-faces-its-own-unintended-consequences.

[77] See I Chakrabarty, 'The Financial Action Task Force Entrapped within Hypocrisy and Rhetoric: Using India as a Case Study' (2023) *Asia Pacific Law Review* 31(2), 402–27.

laundering, terrorist financing, and proliferation financing.[78] They are designed to ensure global consistency in applying the Recommendations and to promote continuous improvement in national frameworks.[79] The mutual evaluation process can take over 18 months. The process begins with the training of assessors or experts from FATF Members and regional bodies which receive instruction on FATF Recommendations, while representatives from the country being assessed are trained on what they will need to submit and demonstrate. Assessors are then selected based on their expertise, though the assessed country has no input in the selection. The evaluation starts with a technical compliance review, where assessors examine whether the country's laws and regulations align with FATF standards. Subsequently, a scoping exercise assists assessors in determining which areas to prioritise during their on-site visit, considering factors like risk, economic structure, political stability, and institutional maturity. During the visit, the country provides data on how well its AML/CTF systems perform across 11 thematic areas. Following this, assessors draft a report detailing technical and effectiveness findings, invite feedback from the assessed country, and consult independent reviewers – although assessors retain full control over ratings and content. The report is then presented at a FATF Plenary, where members, excluding the assessed country, discuss and vote on the findings. If approved, the report undergoes a final technical quality check before being published, typically within two months. In the final stage, the country enters a follow-up process, which may range from regular reporting to public warnings depending on how well it addresses identified deficiencies.[80]

Therefore, the MER is a comprehensive document that summarises results of the peer-reviewed assessment of a country's AML, CTF and CPF mechanisms. The reports serve as both an analytical tool and a benchmark for gauging national compliance with the Recommendations and the country's legislative and institutional frameworks are in line with FATF standards, providing ratings for each recommendation that range from 'Compliant' to 'Non-Compliant'. Meanwhile, the effectiveness component examines the practical impact of these measures across 11 Immediate Outcomes, such as risk understanding, intelligence collection, supervisory oversight, investigation capacity, and international cooperation. Each outcome is rated on a scale from 'High' to 'Low Effectiveness' based on evidence gathered during on-site visits and stakeholder consultations. Additionally, the MER includes key findings that summarise the strengths and vulnerabilities in implementing the financial integrity measures. It also outlines priority actions and strategic recommendations aimed at closing critical gaps in performance. The MER provides a contextual analysis that aims to help interpret the results

[78] FATF, 'Mutual Evaluation' (n/d), available at www.fatf-gafi.org/en/publications/Mutualevaluations/More-about-mutual-evaluations.html#:~:text=FATF%20mutual%20evaluations%20are%20in,risks%20it%20is%20exposed%20to.

[79] ibid.

[80] ibid.

within the country's broader risk environment, financial sector composition, and institutional capacity. The MER acts as a diagnostic and a catalyst, encouraging jurisdictions to pursue reforms, uphold international commitments, and maintain credibility within the global financial system.

The MER offers several benefits, including strengthening a country's AML/CTF regime,[81] enhancing its reputation and international standing,[82] and promoting financial transparency and stability.[83] It also provides a framework for continuous improvement and capacity-building within the country's financial system. However, the use of MERs by FATF has been questioned. For instance, Pisa concluded that the FATF measurement of effectiveness is flawed due to its inconsistent approach.[84] He noted that the FATF assessors inexplicably place an emphasis on certain risks but not others,[85] which are inconsistent with that of other countries, in turn raising reservations as to the FATF's globally respected status. Nance concluded that the MER process is often misunderstood and rather than being coercive, it operates through diagnostic monitoring and iterative learning.[86] Furthermore, Littrell identified the disproportionately negative ratings for poorer, Black-majority, and small island states, while white-majority new world countries tend to receive more favourable assessments.[87] Chakrabarty concluded that there is potential for hypocrisy and rhetoric in the FATF's approach, using India as a case study.[88] Thus, raising concerns about legitimacy and fairness in the evaluations. Conversely, Makgothu emphasises that the FATF's function and its major achievements in developing a uniform international framework cannot be overstated.[89] Nanyun and Nasiri identified the positive influence of MERs in harmonising legislation, enhancing enforcement, and legitimising FATF's processes. It credits MERs with advancing peer pressure mechanisms that encourage compliance and reform among Member States.[90] However, the peer reviews are not always impartial or consistent in their assessments.[91] The World Bank utilised the FATF's Recommendations to

[81] I Chase, J van der Valk and T Keatinge, *Assessing the Financial Action Task Force's Impact on Digital Financial Inclusion* (Royal United Services Institute, 2021).

[82] See Littrell (n 74).

[83] ibid.

[84] See M Pisa, *Does the Financial Action Task Force (FATF) Help or Hinder Financial Inclusion? A Study of FATF Mutual Evaluation Reports* (Center for Global Development, 2019) at 18.

[85] ibid.

[86] See M Nance, 'Re-Thinking FATF: An Experimentalist Interpretation of the Financial Action Task Force' (2018) *Crime, Law and Social Change* 69, 131–52.

[87] See Littrell (n 74).

[88] See Chakrabarty (n 77).

[89] T Makgothu, 'Building Legislative Frameworks: Domestication of the Financial Action Task Force' (2020) *European Journal of Law Reform* 22(2) 209, 210.

[90] NM Nanyun and A Nasiri, (2021). 'Role of FATF on Financial Systems of Countries: Successes and Challenges, (2021) *Journal of Money Laundering Control* 24(2), 234–45.

[91] S Deshmukh, 'Universal Procedures? An Analysis of Text (Dis)similarities in FATF Mutual Evaluation Reports' (2025) *Journal of Economic Criminology* 8, available at https://doi.org/10.1016/j.jeconc.2025.100152.

develop a financial inclusion product risk assessment tool, further improving FATF's image, in particular in third world countries.[92]

V. The FATF Recommendations

The 40 Recommendations were originally published by FATF in 1990 and they were devised to combat money laundering and protect the integrity of the global financial systems.[93] The Recommendations included measures that criminalise money laundering, confiscate the proceeds of crime, prevent the use of shell banks and measures to ensure transparency in financial transactions and ownership structures.[94] The Recommendations provided that financial institutions are required to conduct CDD to identify and verity customers; maintain transaction records for at least five years; report unusual or suspicious activity to its FIU and implement AML compliance programmes and staff training.[95] The Recommendations suggested that the AML obligations should be extended to other professions including the legal profession, accountants, real estate agents, dealers in precious metals and stones and trust and company service providers.[96] The FATF Recommendations emphasise the promotion of mutual legal assistance, information-sharing between countries, extradition agreements and collaborative investigations.[97] Other Recommendations related to the creation of an FIU, the imposition of sanctions for non-compliance and preventing criminals from owning or controlling financial institutions.[98]

The original Recommendations had a transformative impact on global efforts to combat money laundering. They established the first comprehensive international AML framework, prompting countries to criminalise money laundering, regulate financial institutions, and enhance international cooperation. The Recommendations became the blueprint for national legislation and regulatory systems, leading to the creation of FIUs and the adoption of CDD and the submission of SARs. They have influenced the development of FATF-style regional bodies and were integrated into broader financial governance structures, laying the foundation for subsequent expansions into CTF proliferation financing.

[92] K Celik, 'Impact of the FATF Recommendations and their Implementation on Financial Inclusion' (World Bank Group, 2021) at 25, available at https://documents1.worldbank.org/curated/en/597781637558061429/pdf/Impact-of-the-FATF-Recommendations-and-their-Implementation-on-Financial-Inclusion-Insights-from-Mutual-Evaluations-and-National-Risk-Assessments.pdf?_gl=1*v1093y*_gcl_au*NjI3NzkxMTYzLjE3MjM2NjI4NTI.

[93] FATF, *The Forty Recommendations* (FATF, 1990).

[94] ibid.

[95] ibid.

[96] ibid.

[97] ibid.

[98] ibid. For a more detailed discussion of the 40 Recommendations, see C Rose, *International Anti-Corruption Norms: Their Creation and Influence on Domestic Legal Systems* (Oxford University Press, 2015) 177–216.

Terrorist financing did not fall within the scope of the 40 Recommendations and it was not until 9/11 that it was brought within the remit of the FATF.[99] In October 2001, the then G7 Finance Ministers released an 'Action Plan to Combat the Financing of Terrorism', focusing on immediate actions to disrupt terrorist funding and structural changes to prevent future misuse of the financial system.[100] The key parts of the Action Plan were the freezing of terrorist assets, the creation of FIUs in all countries, increased international cooperation and information-sharing.[101] A progress report was published in February 2002 that outlined the actions taken to implement the Action Plan, highlighting measures undertaken to freeze assets, improve information-sharing, and enhance their national frameworks for combating terrorist financing.[102] Consequently, FATF published 'Eight Special Recommendations' on 30 October 2001.[103] The Special Recommendations referred to the need for countries to ratify and implement UNSCR 1373, criminalising the financing of terrorism, permitting the freezing and confiscation of terrorist assets, reporting suspicious transactions that relate to terrorism, the promotion of international cooperation to tackle terrorist financing, alternative remittance systems, wire transfers and non-profit organisations.[104] A ninth Special Recommendation was added in October 2004.[105] Of particular relevance here is Special Recommendation four, which refers to the reporting of suspected instances of terrorist financing.[106] This Recommendation requires financial institutions and other bodies, which are subject to AML reporting obligations, to report, to competent authorities, any suspicious activity where they believe funds are to be used for acts of terrorism or by terrorist organisations.[107] The Special Recommendations expanded the scope of the Recommendations to include CTF measures which prompted countries to criminalise terrorist financing, freeze the assets of designated individuals and entities, and improve international cooperation and information-sharing. They also led to stricter controls on alternative remittance systems, wire transfers, and the regulation of non-profit organisations. The Recommendations were instrumental in shaping the 2003 Recommendations, which saw the merging of the AML and CTF standards into a unified framework.

[99] For an interesting discussion of the Recommendations of the FATF, see J Jeremie, 'Known Risk in a World of Unknown Threats: The Character and Implications of Risk in the Context of Economically Motivated Crime' (2012) *Company Lawyer* 33(8), 231–34.

[100] G7 Research Group, 'Statement of the G7 Finance Ministers and Central Bank Governors', (6 October 2001), available at https://g7.utoronto.ca/finance/fm100601.htm#:~:text=We%2C%20the%20G7%20Finance%20Ministers,financing%2C%20including%20through%20increased%20transparency.

[101] ibid.

[102] United States Department of Treasury, *Action Plan: Progress Report on Combating the Financing of Terrorism* (United States Department of Treasury, 2002).

[103] See FATF, *FATF IX Special Recommendations* (n 14).

[104] ibid.

[105] ibid.

[106] ibid.

[107] ibid.

In February 2012, the FATF published its amended set of Recommendations which 'fully integrate CTF and AML controls, introducing new measures to counter the financing of the proliferation of weapons of mass destruction, and they will better address the laundering of the proceeds of corruption and tax crimes'.[108] The then President of the FATF stated that the:

> Adoption of the revised Recommendations demonstrates countries' shared commitment to fight money laundering, terrorist financing and the financing of the proliferation of weapons of mass destruction. The revised Recommendations include requirements for stronger safeguards in the financial sector, strengthened law enforcement tools and improved international cooperation.[109]

The amendments to the FATF's 40+9 Recommendations introduced enhancements to the global AML and CTF efforts. Important changes included the implementation of targeted financial sanctions to combat the financing of weapons of mass destruction and enhanced transparency to prevent the hiding of assets behind legal entities. The revised standards strengthened requirements for a politically exposed person and expanded the predicate offences to include tax crimes. Furthermore, an enhanced RBA allowed countries and financial institutions to allocate resources more efficiently by concentrating on higher-risk areas. The amendments also aimed to promote more effective international cooperation through improved information exchange, joint investigations, and asset tracking and confiscation. The 2012 amendments provided FATF with a single and unified framework set of Recommendations.

The 2025 Recommendations introduced several updates aimed at enhancing financial inclusion while maintaining AML/CTF standards.[110] The key themes of the updated Recommendations were the replacement of the term 'commensurate' with 'proportionate' across its standards to clarify that AML/CTF measures should match the level of risk identified.[111] Specifically, countries are now required to allow and encourage simplified CDD where risks are lower.[112] Finally, the changes aim to reduce barriers for underserved populations, especially

[108] FATF, 'FATF Steps Up the Fight against Money Laundering and Terrorist Financing' (16 February 2012), available at www.fatf-gafi.org/content/dam/fatf-gafi/recommendations/FATF%20Recommendations%202012.pdf.coredownload.inline.pdf. For a more detailed discussion see G Sutton, 'The New FATF Standards' (2012) *George Mason Journal of International Commercial Law*, 4, 68–136.

[109] See FATF, 'FATF Steps Up the Fight' (n 108) 121.

[110] For a more detailed discussion of the link between the FATF Recommendations and Financial Inclusion, see L De Koker, 'Aligning Anti-Money Laundering, Combating of Financing of Terror and Financial Inclusion: Questions to Consider when FATF Standards are Clarified' (2011) *Journal of Financial Crime* 18(4), 361–86; A Shehu, 'Promoting Financial Inclusion for Effective Anti-Money Laundering and Counter Financing of Terrorism (AML/CFT)' (2012) *Crime, Law and Social Change* 57(3), 305–23 and R Stanley, and RP Buckley, 'Protecting the West, Excluding the Rest: The Impact of the AML/CTF Regime on Financial Inclusion in the Pacific and Potential Responses' (2016) *Melbourne Journal of International Law* 17(1), 83–106.

[111] See FATF Recommendations 2025 n 18 at 8, 10, 19 and 24–26.

[112] ibid at 10.

the 1.4billion people globally without access to banking services.[113] Overall, the Recommendations have had a profound and wide-ranging impact on global financial systems, regulatory frameworks, and efforts to combat financial crime.[114] The Recommendations are the international benchmark for AML/CTF and combating proliferation financing.[115] Consequently, countries have aligned their laws and regulations with the Recommendations, creating a more uniform global approach to financial crime prevention.[116] Numerous countries have introduced, revised and updated legislation to comply with the Recommendations.[117] Conversely, countries that fail to meet the Recommendations risk being placed on the 'Grey' or 'Black' lists, which has led to reduced foreign investment, increased transaction scrutiny and reputational damage and economic isolation.[118] It has been suggested that the Recommendations have fostered cross-border collaboration, enabling better information-sharing and mutual legal assistance between jurisdictions.[119] Ultimately, the FATF Recommendations have not only elevated global compliance standards but also incentivised greater transparency and accountability across both public and private sectors.

VI. Information-Sharing Recommendations

One of the most important mechanisms to tackle money laundering, terrorist financing and other types of financial crime is information-sharing 'concerning financial activity with possible links to crime and terrorism is shared in a timely and effective manner between and with both public and private sector'.[120] The

[113] ibid at 8, 10, 19 and 24–26 and World Economic Forum, 'Why Financial Inclusion is the Key to a Thriving Digital Economy' (29 July 2024), available from www.weforum.org/stories/2024/07/why-financial-inclusion-is-the-key-to-a-thriving-digital-economy/.

[114] See generally E Mekpor, A Aboagye and J Welbeck, 'The Determinants of Anti-Money Laundering Compliance Among the Financial Action Task Force (FATF) Member States' (2018) *Journal of Financial Regulation and Compliance* 26(3), 442–59; WN Shahin, E El-Achkar and R Shehab, 'The Monetary Impact of Regulating Banking and Financial Sectors by FATF on Non-Cooperative Countries and Territories' (2012) *Journal of Banking Regulation* 13(1), 63–72; D Goldbarsht and H Harris, 'Enhancing Integrity in the Implementation of FATF Recommendations: Robust Governance Frameworks to Combat Financial Crime in an Age of Intergovernmental Rulemaking' in *Financial Crime, Law and Governance: Navigating Challenges in Different Contexts* (Springer, 2024) 141–67.

[115] See Nanyun and Nasiri (n 90) and L De Koker, 'The 2012 Revised FATF Recommendations: Assessing and Mitigating Mobile Money Integrity Risks within the New Standards Framework' (2012) *Washington Journal of Law, Technology & Arts* 8(3), 165.

[116] See Rose (n 98).

[117] ibid.

[118] See Keatinge et al (n 76).

[119] See D Artingstall, 'Asking the Right Questions: Effective Information Sharing in the FATF Context' (13 June 2016), available at www.rusi.org/explore-our-research/publications/commentary/asking-right-questions-effective-information-sharing-fatf-context; FATF, *Private Sector Information Sharing* (FATF, 2017).

[120] FATF, 'FATF Guidance – Private Sector Information Sharing' (n/d), available at www.fatf-gafi.org/en/publications/Fatfgeneral/Guidance-information-sharing.html.

FATF stated that 'information sharing can allow financial institutions, supervisory and law authorities to make better use of available resources and exploit new technologies and business models to develop innovative techniques to tackle money laundering and terrorist financing'.[121] As outlined above, the FATF seeks to promote effective information-sharing in its efforts to improve and coordinate global efforts against money laundering, terrorist financing and proliferation financing. Specifically, these objectives aim to improve transparency across the financial system, enhance cooperation between the public and private sector, support accurate risk assessment and to facilitate enforcement and supervisory actions. FATF has consolidated its information-sharing requirements from its Recommendations, impacting seven Immediate Outcomes in its effectiveness methodology. The Guidance covers public–private sector sharing and governments should aim to share information with financial institutions to detect and prevent money laundering and terrorist financing.[122] Financial institutions should be able to share information across their own entities and institutions that are not part of the same group should be allowed to share relevant information, with data protection safeguards in place. The Recommendations and guidance provide that LEAs, regulators and FIUs should collaborate and exchange data in an effective and efficient manner and that data-sharing mechanisms must be subjected to respect data protection laws and include safeguards to prevent misuse or breaches. The Guidance outlines how the Recommendations seek to support and encourage responsible data-sharing to combat financial crime and emphasises that over half of the Recommendations include information-sharing.[123] The Guidance aims to improve the effectiveness of the AML and CTF efforts by improving how financial institutions share information. Importantly, the Guidance focuses on the legal and operational barriers and identifies a number of challenges including data protection laws that restrict cross-border sharing, the lack of clarity on what information can be shared legally and technological limitations and inconsistent internal policies.[124] The Guidance explains how the Recommendations apply to private sector information-sharing and specifically highlights information-sharing within financial groups, the sharing of information on suspicions that funds are the proceeds of crime or related to terrorist financing within the financial group, the confidentiality of SARs and tipping-off and how it interacts with group-wide sharing.[125] This Guidance is a strategic blueprint for financial institutions navigating the complex intersection of compliance, privacy, and global cooperation.

In July 2022, the FATF published its *Partnering in the Fight Against Financial Crime: Data Protection, Technology and Private Sector Information Sharing*.[126]

[121] ibid.
[122] FATF, *Private Sector Information Sharing* (n 119).
[123] ibid.
[124] ibid at 4.
[125] ibid at 7–17.
[126] FATF, *Partnering in the Fight Against Financial Crime: Data Protection, Technology and Private Sector Information Sharing* (FATF, 2022).

This report aims to help jurisdictions responsibly enhance, design and implement information collaboration initiatives among private sector entities, in accordance with data protection and privacy rules, so that the risks associated with increased sharing of personal data are appropriately taken into account.[127] Criminals often exploit gaps in financial oversight by using multiple institutions across jurisdictions to obscure illicit funds, making it difficult for any one institution to detect suspicious activities.[128] To tackle this, financial institutions are increasingly turning to collaborative data-sharing initiatives to build a clearer picture of financial transactions and better combat money laundering and terrorist financing.[129] The report provides guidance for jurisdictions to responsibly design and implement such collaborative efforts, ensuring compliance with data protection and privacy rules. It outlines global regulatory requirements, real-world case studies from FATF Members, and offers non-binding recommendations to help countries foster effective private sector information-sharing within legal frameworks. The publication highlights the limitations of siloed financial institutions, which often see only fragments of illicit activity, and advocates for responsible data-pooling to build a clearer picture of criminal networks. Crucially, it emphasises the need to balance enhanced information-sharing with strict adherence to data protection and privacy regulations. The FATF demonstrates that such collaboration is feasible within legal frameworks, offering non-binding recommendations to help jurisdictions design effective, privacy-conscious initiatives.

A. Recommendation 2

The FATF Recommendation 2 urges countries to establish national cooperation and coordination mechanisms to effectively combat money laundering, terrorist financing, and proliferation financing. It emphasises that both high-level policy-makers and operational authorities should collaborate to develop and implement AML and CTF strategies. This includes creating inter-agency frameworks that allow for timely information exchange, aligning efforts across ministries, law enforcement, FIUs, and other relevant bodies. Importantly, the recommendation also calls for ensuring that such coordination respects data protection, privacy, and other legal norms. The Recommendation provides:

> Countries should have national AML/CFT/CPF policies, informed by the risks1 identified, which should be regularly reviewed, and should designate an authority or have a coordination or other mechanism that is responsible for such policies. Countries should ensure that policy-makers, the financial intelligence unit (FIU),

[127] ibid.

[128] See M Tiwari, A Gepp and K Kumar, 'A Review of Money Laundering Literature: The State of Research in Key Areas' (2020) *Pacific Accounting Review* 32(2), 271–303.

[129] See FATF, *Partnering in the Fight Against Financial Crime* (n 126).

> law enforcement authorities, supervisors and other relevant competent authorities, at the policymaking and operational levels, have effective mechanisms in place which enable them to cooperate, and, where appropriate, coordinate and exchange information domestically with each other concerning the development and implementation of policies and activities to combat money laundering, terrorist financing and the financing of proliferation of weapons of mass destruction. This should include cooperation and coordination between relevant authorities to ensure the compatibility of AML/CFT/CPF requirements with Data Protection and Privacy rules and other similar provisions.[130]

The interpretative guidance from the FATF states that countries should set up appropriate frameworks that enable different government bodies to work together effectively in tackling money laundering, terrorist financing and proliferation financing. These frameworks can be unified or tailored separately for each risk area. A designated authority, or a dedicated mechanism, should take charge of guiding national policy and coordinating efforts across relevant agencies. Participating agencies may vary by country but generally include central government departments such as finance, justice, foreign affairs, LEAs, FIU, intelligence services, tax and customs authorities, financial regulators, company and beneficial ownership registries, and others as applicable. To make this collaboration function smoothly, nations should establish operational systems that support coordination and swift information-sharing for AML, CTF, and CPF. This could involve clarifying each authority's role and data needs, using standardised formats and secure channels to exchange information, and building practical tools such as joint teams or shared databases.[131]

FATF Recommendation 2 emphasises the importance of coordinated domestic efforts in combating money laundering, terrorist financing, and proliferation financing by requiring countries to establish mechanisms for effective collaboration among relevant authorities. Its intent is to ensure that FIUs, law enforcement, regulators, and policymakers work together at both strategic and operational levels to develop coherent responses to emerging risks. When properly implemented, this Recommendation strengthens national AML/CTF/CPF frameworks through aligned policies, shared intelligence, and streamlined enforcement. However, its effectiveness depends heavily on institutional maturity, legal clarity, and political will, which can vary widely across jurisdictions. Challenges such as siloed operations, ambiguous roles, and data privacy concerns can hinder its practical application. Despite these hurdles, Recommendation 2 serves as a foundational pillar of financial integrity by encouraging countries to build inclusive, responsive, and coordinated systems that reflect real-world complexity and evolving threat landscapes.

[130] See FATF, *The FATF Recommendations* (n 16) at 10–11.
[131] FATF Recommendations 2025 (n 18) at 37.

B. Recommendation 30

Recommendation 30 outlines the responsibilities of law enforcement and investigative authorities in combating money laundering, terrorist financing and related crimes. It requires countries to designate competent authorities with the power to investigate money laundering and terrorist financing offences, trace illicit assets, and initiate actions to freeze or seize property suspected of being criminal proceeds. These authorities must be equipped with sufficient financial, human, and technical resources, and staffed by professionals with high integrity and confidentiality standards. The Recommendation also encourages the use of specialised multidisciplinary teams and international cooperation to enhance the effectiveness of financial and asset investigations. The Recommendation provides:

> Countries should ensure that designated law enforcement authorities have responsibility for money laundering and terrorist financing investigations within the framework of national AML/CFT policies. At least in all cases related to major proceeds-generating offences, these designated law enforcement authorities should develop a pro-active parallel financial investigation when pursuing money laundering, associated predicate offences and terrorist financing. This should include cases where the associated predicate offence occurs outside their jurisdictions. Countries should ensure that competent authorities have responsibility for expeditiously identifying, tracing and initiating actions to freeze and seize property that is, or may become, subject to confiscation, or is suspected of being proceeds of crime. Countries should also make use, when necessary, of permanent or temporary multi-disciplinary groups specialised in financial or asset investigations. Countries should ensure that, when necessary, cooperative investigations with appropriate competent authorities in other countries take place.'[132]

FATF Recommendation 30 calls for countries to designate specialised law enforcement and competent authorities responsible for conducting financial investigations into money laundering, terrorist financing and predicate offences. These investigations aim to uncover criminal networks, trace illicit assets, and produce evidence for prosecution. Authorities should be empowered to freeze or seize property linked to criminal activity and collaborate through parallel investigations alongside traditional criminal inquiries. To support effective investigations, countries are encouraged to adopt legal measures that enable controlled operations, such as covert investigations, by postponing arrests or seizures when necessary. The Recommendation also applies to non-LEAs tasked with financial investigations, including anti-corruption enforcement bodies. These authorities must be adequately resourced and staffed with professionals who uphold confidentiality, integrity, and specialised skills. Multidisciplinary teams should be considered to enhance investigative capacity.[133]

[132] See FATF, *The FATF Recommendations* (n 16) at 23–24.
[133] ibid at 107–108.

Recommendation 30 focuses on the responsibilities and capabilities of LEAs and investigative authorities in combating money laundering, terrorist financing and proliferation financing. It requires countries to ensure that designated authorities are empowered to conduct financial crime investigations, trace illicit assets, and initiate confiscation procedures. The strength of Recommendation 30 lies in its emphasis on operational capacity and resource adequacy. It mandates that LEAs have the authority to investigate money laundering and terrorist financing cases, including those linked to predicate offences, and that they are equipped with sufficient resources. This includes access to specialised units, multidisciplinary teams, and cooperation mechanisms, both domestically and internationally. The Recommendation also encourages the use of asset tracking and freezing tools, which are essential for disrupting criminal networks and recovering proceeds of crime. However, implementation varies widely across jurisdictions. In some countries, LEAs lack the necessary training, technology, or legal authority to pursue complex financial investigations. Fragmented institutional frameworks or overlapping mandates can lead to inefficiencies or turf conflicts. Additionally, political interference or weak judicial systems may undermine the independence and effectiveness of investigative bodies. In essence, Recommendation 30 is a cornerstone of enforcement capability within the FATF framework. It seeks to bridge the gap between regulatory compliance and real-world disruption of financial crime. Its success depends not only on legal provisions but also on institutional strength, inter-agency coordination, and sustained investment in investigative capacity. When fully realised, it empowers countries to move beyond detection and toward meaningful deterrence and asset recovery.

C. Recommendation 31

FATF Recommendation 31 outlines the powers and responsibilities of law enforcement and investigative authorities in tackling money laundering terrorist financing and related offences. It requires countries to ensure that competent authorities can access all necessary documents and information for investigations and prosecutions. These authorities should be empowered to use a wide range of investigative tools, such as search and seizure, witness interviews, undercover operations, intercepting communications, and accessing computer systems. They must also be able to identify account holders and trace assets without alerting suspects. Additionally, authorities should have mechanisms to request relevant data from FIUs to support their investigations. When conducting investigations of money laundering, associated predicate offences and terrorist financing, competent authorities should be able to obtain access to all necessary documents and information for use in those investigations, and in prosecutions and related actions. This should include powers to use compulsory measures for the production of records held by financial institutions, designated non-financial businesses and professions and other natural or legal persons, for the search of persons and premises, for taking witness statements, and for the seizure and obtaining of evidence. Countries should ensure that competent authorities conducting investigations are able to use a wide range of investigative techniques suitable for the investigation of money laundering, associated predicate offences and terrorist financing. These investigative techniques include undercover operations, intercepting communications, accessing computer systems and controlled delivery. In addition, countries should have effective mechanisms in place to identify, in a timely manner, whether natural or legal persons hold or control accounts. They should also have mechanisms to ensure that competent authorities have a process to identify assets without prior notification to the owner. When conducting investigations, competent authorities should be able to ask for all relevant information held by the FIU.[134] A key part of Recommendation 31 is that it encourages collaboration with the FIU to access relevant intelligence, reinforcing the importance of cooperation.

D. Immediate Outcomes

The FATF Immediate Outcomes are a set of 11 key performance benchmarks used to evaluate the practical effectiveness of a country's AML/CTF and CPF systems. Rather than focusing solely on legal frameworks, these outcomes assess how well these measures work in practice across several areas. The first outcome ensures that countries understand their money laundering and terrorist financing risks and coordinate responses appropriately. The second evaluates their capacity to engage in meaningful international cooperation with foreign counterparts. The third focuses on how effectively authorities supervise financial institutions and designated non-financial businesses using a RBA. The fourth gauges the use of preventive measures like CDD and SAR. The fifth assesses the transparency of legal persons and arrangements, particularly through access to beneficial ownership information. The sixth examines how authorities use financial intelligence to detect and investigate illicit activity. The seventh and eighth outcomes measure how successfully money laundering offences are prosecuted and how criminal assets are confiscated. Outcomes nine and 10 focus on terrorist financing, while the 11th outcome evaluates the implementation of proliferation financing sanctions, ensuring entities involved in weapons of mass destruction do not gain access to funds in violation of UNSCRs. These Immediate Outcomes collectively form the cornerstone of the FATF's effectiveness assessment, shifting the focus from formal compliance to tangible, real-world impact. Of relevance here are Immediate Outcomes 1, 6, 7 and 9.

i. Immediate Outcome 1

Immediate Outcome 1 focuses on whether a country understands its money laundering and terrorist financing risks and has developed effective policies and coordination

[134] ibid at 25.

mechanisms to address them. It evaluates how well national authorities identify, assess, and communicate these risks across relevant agencies and sectors. This includes the existence of a robust national risk assessment, the integration of risk findings into AML/CTF strategies, and the extent to which public and private stakeholders are aligned in their understanding and response. The outcome also considers whether policies are proportionate to the risks and whether coordination among agencies leads to meaningful action. In short, it's about ensuring that a country's AML/CTF efforts are grounded in a clear, shared understanding of its unique risk landscape.

ii. Immediate Outcome 6

Immediate Outcome 6 of the FATF methodology assesses how effectively a country uses financial intelligence to combat money laundering, terrorist financing and proliferation financing. It focuses on whether competent authorities, such as the FIU, LEAs and supervisory bodies, can access and analyse financial data, including transaction reports, account information, and other sources. The objective is to ensure that this intelligence is not just collected but actively used to identify suspicious activity, support investigations, and generate actionable leads. Authorities should be able to integrate financial intelligence with other data sources to build comprehensive cases and disrupt illicit networks. In essence, this outcome measures whether financial intelligence is a central and effective tool in the country's AML/CTF and CPF arsenal.

iii. Immediate Outcome 7

Immediate Outcome 7 of the FATF methodology focuses on the investigation and prosecution of money laundering offences. It assesses whether a country's law enforcement and judicial authorities are effectively identifying, investigating, and prosecuting money laundering cases in a way that is proportionate, dissuasive, and consistent with the risks faced. This outcome looks at whether authorities pursue money laundering as a stand-alone crime, not just as an add-on to other offences, and whether they target both simple and complex cases, including those involving foreign predicate offences or professional money launderers. It also considers the use of parallel financial investigations, the quality of case-building, and the application of appropriate sanctions. The goal is to ensure that money laundering is treated as a serious criminal threat and that enforcement efforts result in meaningful deterrence and disruption of illicit financial flows.

iv. Immediate Outcome 9

Immediate Outcome 9 of the FATF methodology focuses on the investigation and prosecution of terrorist financing offences. It assesses whether a country's authorities are effectively identifying, investigating, and prosecuting individuals or entities involved in financing terrorism. The goal is to ensure that terrorist financing cases are pursued with appropriate urgency and that sanctions imposed are proportionate, dissuasive, and consistent with the severity of the offence. This outcome also examines whether countries treat terrorist financing, and whether they apply a RBA to prioritising cases. Authorities should be able to detect both domestic and international terrorist financing activity, including low-level or indirect support, and demonstrate that their legal and operational frameworks lead to meaningful enforcement outcomes.

VII. Conclusion

The chapter identified the historical background of the FATF, briefly outlining its Recommendations before specifically focusing on those that relate to the submission of a SAR and the exchange of information (Recommendations 2, 30 and 31 and Immediate Outcomes 1, 6, 7 and 9). The chapter investigated the main features of the FATF MER, which seeks to provide a comprehensive analysis and determination of how a country's AML/CTF regime complies with the FATF Recommendations. The onus of compliance is on the country to demonstrate that they are compliant with the Recommendations. The chapter explored the components used by FATF to determine the levels of compliance with its Recommendations – effectiveness and technical compliance. The chapter critically reviewed the FATF Methodology that it used to determine a country's level of compliance and concluded that the FATF methodology does offer a robust framework for evaluating countries' AML, CTF and CPF systems. The methodology attempts to balance the technical compliance, namely whether the law and regulations align with the Recommendations, with effectiveness, which are the measures covered by the 11 Immediate Outcomes. Such as an approach ensures that countries are not merely implementing legislation but are implementing them to mitigate financial crime risks. The methodology's emphasis on risk-based assessments does allow for tailored evaluations, though critics argue that effectiveness scoring can be subjective and resource-intensive. The FATF methodology has disproportionately impacted countries in the Global South due to its resource-intensive compliance requirements and political bias. Developing nations struggle to meet the technical and effectiveness standards set by the FATF, not because of unwillingness, but due to limited institutional capacity, financial constraints, and differing legal frameworks. The methodology's emphasis on uniform benchmarks overlooks contextual realities, such as informal economies or alternative financial systems common in these regions. Placement on the FATF's 'Grey list' triggers economic consequences such as reduced foreign investment and increased scrutiny from international banks, further straining these economies. This creates a cycle where countries are penalised for systemic challenges rather than actual risk levels, reinforcing global financial inequalities. Overall, the FATF methodology represents a significant evolution in global financial oversight, shifting the focus from formal compliance to functional performance.

3

The United Kingdom's Fourth Mutual Evaluation Report – An Alternative View

> The UK has taken a leading role in the global fight against illicit finance. I'm delighted with today's report which shows our efforts are being recognised, and sends a strong message to criminals that we will come for them, their assets and their money.*

I. Introduction

The United Kingdom (UK) is an integral member in the international efforts to tackle financial crime since the creation of the Financial Action Task Force (FATF) and introduction of the first anti-money laundering convention by the United Nations (UN). In fact, the UK introduced legislation to tackle money laundering and terrorist financing before the creation of the FATF, the introduction of the UN Convention Against Illicit Traffic in Narcotic Drugs and Psychotropic Substances and the International Convention for the Suppression of Terrorist Financing (hereinafter 'Vienna Convention').[1] Subsequently, the UK has implemented all of the international anti-money laundering (AML), counter-terrorist financing (CTF) mechanisms, it has chaired the FATF and held its presidency twice.[2] The UK's levels of compliance with the FATF Recommendations are assessed via Mutual Evaluation Reports (MERs), the first was in 2007,[3] the second in 2018,[4] and a third is due to take place in 2027–2028.[5] In its 2007 MER, the FATF concluded that

* HM Government, 'UK Takes Top Spot in Fight against Dirty Money' (7 December 2018), available at www.gov.uk/government/news/uk-takes-top-spot-in-fight-against-dirty-money#:~:text=FATF%20%2C%20the%20global%20standard%2Dsetter%20for%20anti%2Dmoney,its%20use%20of%20financial%20sanctions%20against%20terrorists.

[1] For a more detailed discussion see chapters four and five.

[2] See Financial Action Task Force (FATF), *FATF Annual Report 1993-1994* (FATF, 1994).

[3] FATF, *Third Mutual Evaluation Report Anti-Money Laundering and Counter Terrorist Financing The United Kingdom and of Great Britain and Northern Ireland* (FATF, 2007) (hereinafter 'FATF 2007 MER').

[4] FATF, *Anti-Money Laundering and Counter-Terrorist Financing Measures: United Kingdom Mutual Evaluation Report* (FATF, 2018) (hereinafter 'FATF 2018 MER').

[5] K Westmore, *Conference Report UK FATF Mutual Evaluation Taskforce First Meeting Report* (Royal United Services Institute, 2025) at 1.

the UK had a comprehensive legal framework to tackle money laundering and terrorist financing; wide-ranging powers to recover the proceeds of crime; mechanisms to freeze and seize terrorist-related assets; an effective financial intelligence unit (UKFIU); the financial regulator had extensive powers to monitor and ensure compliance by the firms it regulates and the designated non-financial business and professions (DNFBPs) as defined by the FATF were covered.[6] However, the MER identified deficiencies in the implementation of the financial intelligence and data-sharing Recommendations.

The 2018 MER noted that the UK continued to face substantial financial crime risks and this is 'reflected in the country's strong … AML/CFT policies, strategies and proactive initiatives'.[7] In particular, the FATF concluded that the UK aggressively pursues money laundering and terrorist financing prosecutions; law enforcement agencies (LEAs) have a wide range of powers to obtain beneficial ownership and other information; the UK is a global leader in promoting corporate transparency, DNFBPs are subjected to broad AML and CTF requirements[8] and the 'UK has … taken a leading role in designating terrorists at the UN and EU level'.[9] Therefore, the FATF concluded that the 'UK's overall AML/CTF regime is effective in many respects'.[10] However, the MER identified a similar weakness to those raised in 2007, including the investigation of suspicious transactions, the UKFIU lacked sufficient resources and the suspicious activity reporting (SAR) regime needed to be modernised and reformed.[11]

Following the publication of the 2018 MER, HM Government (HMG) stated, 'the findings of the MER showed that the UK has the strongest overall AML/CTF regime'.[12] Keatinge et al noted that that 'in PR terms at least, the government's efforts seem to have paid off'.[13] The HM Treasury Select Committee warned that 'while the latest evaluation [by FATF] is positive, the Government should not be complacent'.[14] Transparency International commended the efforts of HMG

[6] FATF, 'Mutual Evaluation of United Kingdom of Great Britain and Northern Ireland' (n/d), available at www.fatf-gafi.org/en/publications/Mutualevaluations/Mutualevaluationofunitedkingdomofgreatbritainandnorthernireland.html#:~:text=Download-,Mutual%20evaluation%20of%20United%20Kingdom%20of%20Great%20Britain%20and%20Northern,by%20the%20firms%20it%20regulations.

[7] FATF, 'The United Kingdom's Measures to Combat Money Laundering and Terrorist Financing' (n/d), available at www.fatf-gafi.org/en/publications/Mutualevaluations/Mer-united-kingdom-2018.html.

[8] FATF 2018 MER (n 4).

[9] FATF, 'The UK's Measures' (n 7).

[10] FATF 2018 MER (n 4).

[11] ibid.

[12] HM Government, 'UK Takes Top Spot in Fight against Dirty Money' (7 December 2018), available at www.gov.uk/government/news/uk-takes-top-spot-in-fight-against-dirty-money#:~:text=FATF%20%2C%20the%20global%20standard%2Dsetter%20for%20anti%2Dmoney,its%20use%20of%20financial%20sanctions%20against%20terrorists.

[13] T Keatinge, A Moiseienko, F Keen, D Artingstall and H Wood, *No Rest for the Wicked Driving Change in the UK's Post-FATF Evaluation AML Regime* (Royal United Services Institute, 2019) at iii.

[14] House of Commons Treasury Committee, *Economic Crime Eleventh Report of Session 2021–22* (House of Commons Treasury Committee, 2022) at 76.

but warned that 'these measures must now be properly resourced and enforced with criminal sanctions if the UK is to meet the scale of the problem of dirty money.[15] It is interesting to note that several Select Committee investigations have continued to highlight the UK's strong association with financial crime since the publication of the 2018 MER.[16] It is against this background, that this chapter reviews the findings of the 2007 and 2018 MERs and concentrates on the financial intelligence and exchange of information, Recommendations and Immediate Outcomes. The first part of the chapter illustrates how the UK has adhered to, implemented and frequently exceeded the international AML/CTF laws and standards. The next part focuses on the financial intelligence and exchange of information findings of the 2007 MER, identifying areas in further need of reform and appraises the legislative response. The chapter then moves on to the financial intelligence and exchange of information findings of the 2018 MER and then appraises the legislative and policy response by HMG. The penultimate part of the chapter introduces the cases studies that serve to challenge the financial intelligence and exchange of information conclusions of the 2018 MER. Therefore, the subsidiary research question that this chapter answers is how successfully has the UK implemented and responded to international AML and CTF standards, as reflected in the financial intelligence and information exchange findings of the 2007 and 2018 MERs?

II. Implementation of International Standards

The UK's commitment to the international AML/CTF standards can be traced back to its role as a founding Member of the FATF, through its responses to the 2007 and 2018 MER, the implementation of the three UN AML Conventions and the European Union (EU) Money Laundering Directives (MLD). The UK signed and ratified the Vienna Convention by the Criminal Justice (International Co-operation) Act 1990 and it has been positively considered by the judiciary.[17] Furthermore, the UK has signed and ratified the UN Conventions against

[15] Transparency International, 'UK's "£100 billion" Dirty Money Problem Must be Confronted Following International Review' (7 December 2018), available from https://archive.transparency.org.uk/uk-s-100-billion-dirty-money-problem-must-be-confronted-following-international-review.

[16] See, eg, House of Commons Foreign Affairs Committee, *Moscow's Gold: Russian Corruption in the UK* (House of Commons Foreign Affairs Committee, 2018); House of Commons Treasury Committee *Economic Crime – Anti-Money Laundering Supervision and Sanctions Implementation* (House of Commons Treasury Committee, 2019); House of Commons Intelligence Security Committee, *Russia* (House of Commons Intelligence Security Committee, 2020); House of Commons Treasury Committee, *Economic Crime: Consumer View* (House of Commons Treasury Committee, 2019) and House of Commons Treasury Committee, *Economic Crime* (House of Commons Treasury Committee, 2022).

[17] Criminal Justice (International Co-operation) Act (1990), ss 12–24. See, eg, *R v Montila* [2005] 1 All ER 113; *R v Rezvi* [2002] 1 All ER 801; *Crown Prosecution Service v Richards* [2006] EWCA Civ 849; *Lodhi v Governor of Brixton Prison (No 2)* [2002] EWHC 2029 (Admin); and *R v Hussain* [2002] EWCA Crim 6.

Transnational Organised Crime ('hereinafter 'Palermo Convention')[18] and the Convention against Corruption (UNCAC).[19] The UK ratified the Council of Europe Convention on Laundering, Search, Seizure and Confiscation of the Proceed of Crime in September 1992.[20] The UK implemented five MLDs before leaving the EU in January 2020,[21] and in several circumstances, the UK measures have gone beyond the requirements of the MLDs. Within the context of EU financial crime laws this is referred to as gold plating, where a Member State goes beyond the minimum requirements of the MLD while implementing it into national law.[22]

The UK is a full member of all the major international bodies that set AML/CTF standards. It was a founding member of FATF and continues to sit on its Steering Group and plenary, helping draft and update the Recommendations. Through the UKFIU, hosted by the National Crime Agency (NCA), the UK is also a member of the Egmont Group of FIUs, which facilitates secure information-sharing on cross-border money-laundering and terrorist-financing cases.[23] In the private-sector, UK-based banks and financial institutions participate in the Wolfsberg Group's correspondent-banking and risk-management working groups, while regulators and industry bodies engage in Basel Committee and G7 anti-money-laundering fora to shape global supervisory practices.[24] Together, these memberships ensure the UK both adopts and helps refine the world's leading AML/CTF standards.

The UK's CTF legislation predates the introduction of the International Convention and it has significant experience of tackling terrorism.[25] In fact, its

[18] United Nations Convention against Transnational Organized Crime, GA Res 55/25, UN GAOR, 55th Sess, Supp No 49, Vol I, at 43, UN Doc A/55/49. See FATF 2007 MER (n 3) at 250. Also see Serious Organised Crime and Police Act 2005, s 95.

[19] United Nations, 'Conference of the States Parties to the United Nations Convention against Corruption' (20 March 2019), available at https://assets.publishing.service.gov.uk/government/uploads/system/uploads/attachment_data/file/802272/Executive_Summary_of_the_United_Kingdom_-_Review_cycle_2__Chapter_II_and_V_.pdf.

[20] ETS No 141.

[21] See European Union (Withdrawal) Act 2018 and the Sanctions and Anti-Money Laundering Act 2018. The five MLDs were implemented by Money Laundering Regulations 1993 (SI 1993/1933); Money Laundering Regulations 2003 (SI 2003/3075); Money Laundering Regulations 2007 (SI 2007/2157); Money Laundering, Terrorist Financing and Transfer of Funds (Information on the Payer) Regulations 2017 (SI 2017/692) and Money Laundering and Terrorist Financing (Amendment) Regulations 2019 (SI 2019/1511).

[22] See generally E Herlin-Karnell, 'The Robustness of EU Financial Crimes Legislation: A Critical Review of the EU and UK Anti-Fraud and Money Laundering Scheme' (2017) *European Business Law Review* 28(4), 427–46.

[23] See FATF 2007 MER (n 3) at 85.

[24] See Bank of International Settlements, 'Basel Committee Membership' (14 May 2024), available from www.bis.org/bcbs/membership.htm and Organization for Economic Cooperation and Development, 'United Kingdom' (n/d), available at www.oecd.org/en/countries/united-kingdom.html#:~:text=The%20United%20Kingdom%20was%20one,one%20of%2038%20OECD%20Members.

[25] For a general discussion, see JG DeLeeuw and WA Pridemore, 'The Threat from Within: A Conjunctive Analysis of Domestic Terrorism Incidents in the United States, United Kingdom, and Ireland' (2018) *Perspectives on Terrorism* 12(4), 26–54.

counter-terrorist legislation can be traced back to the late nineteenth century.[26] As a consequence of the rise of domestic terrorism, the UK enacted the Northern Ireland (Emergency Provisions) Act 1973 and the Prevention of Terrorism (Temporary Provisions) Act 1974. These were amended by the Prevention of Terrorism (Temporary Provisions) Act 1989 which criminalised contributions towards acts of terrorism,[27] contributions to resources of proscribed organisations,[28] assisting in retention or control of terrorist funds,[29] disclosure of information about terrorist funds,[30] penalties and forfeiture.[31] These measures were largely ineffective and a review concluded that the scope of its terrorist financing provisions should be extended.[32] Consequently, the Terrorism Act 2000 introduced a series of criminal offences relating to terrorist financing.[33]

The UK responded to the Al-Qaeda terrorist attacks in September 2001 (9/11) by implementing the Anti-Terrorism, Crime and Security Act 2001 which contained measures that permitted the seizure of terrorist cash anywhere in the UK,[34] freezing of funds at the start of a terrorist-related investigation,[35] examining accounts that might be used to support acts of terrorism,[36] imposed CTF reporting obligations[37] and allowed HM Treasury to freeze the accounts of people where they have reasonable grounds to suspect they pose a threat to the UK.[38] Thus, implementing United Nations Security Council Resolution (UNSCR) 1373.[39] Additionally, the UK has introduced the Counter-Terrorism Act 2008,[40] the Criminal Finances Act 2017,[41] the Sanctions and Anti-Money Laundering

[26] L Donohue, *The Cost of Counterterrorism – Power, Politics and Liberty* (Cambridge University Press, 2008) at 129. However, it is important to note that several laws were introduced in the nineteenth century to address the threat of Fenian groups and the Irish nationalist movements including the Explosives Act 1883, the Prevention of Crimes Act 1871 and the Arms (Ireland) Act 1881. For a more detailed discussion, see L Jarvis and M Lister, *Anti-terrorism, Citizenship and Security* (Manchester University Press, 2015) 13–38 and C Walker, 'Anti-Terrorism Laws: The United Kingdom's Unfinished History' in A Silke (ed), *In Routledge Handbook of Terrorism and Counterterrorism* (Routledge, 2018) 406–15.

[27] Prevention of Terrorism (Temporary Provisions) Act 1989, s 9.

[28] ibid s 10.

[29] ibid s 11.

[30] ibid s 12.

[31] ibid s 13. See generally Lord Colville of Culross, *Review of the Operation of the Prevention of Terrorism (Temporary Provisions) Act 1984* (Cm 264, 1987) and B Dickson, 'The Prevention of Terrorism (Temporary Provisions) Act 1989' (1989) *Northern Ireland Legal Quarterly* 40(3), 250–67.

[32] Home Office, *Legislation against Terrorism – A Consultation Paper* (Home Office, 1998) at para 6.14.

[33] Terrorism Act 2000, ss 15–20.

[34] Anti-Terrorism, Crime and Security Act 2001, sch 1, pt 2, para 2.

[35] ibid pt 2, ss 4–16.

[36] ibid sch 2, pt 1, para 1.

[37] ibid ss 17–19.

[38] ibid s 4.

[39] The Terrorism (United Nations Measures) Order 2001 (SI 2001/3365).

[40] This Act expanded powers for forfeiture of terrorist property, introduced notification requirements for convicted individuals, and strengthened financial intelligence-sharing.

[41] This Act strengthened law enforcement's ability to seize suspicious assets, introduced Unexplained Wealth Orders, and expanded powers to civilian financial investigators.

Act 2018[42] and the Counter-Terrorism and Border Security Act 2019.[43] Therefore, the UK has maintained a comprehensive and internationally aligned AML/CTF system. However, while the 2007 and 2018 evaluations have praised the UK's effectiveness, both highlighted the need for improvements in the use of financial intelligence and exchange of information.

III. 2007 Mutual Evaluation Report

This subsection of the chapter provides an overview of the findings and conclusions of the 2007 MER and focuses on the financial intelligence and exchange of information Recommendations. The 2007 MER concluded that the money laundering and terrorist financing offences are broad and the number of prosecutions is increasing. Furthermore, the UK has comprehensive powers to restrain, confiscate, and recover proceeds of crime, and to freeze and seize terrorist-related assets.[44] Furthermore, the MER concluded that the then city regulator, the Financial Services Authority (FSA), had extensive powers to monitor and ensure compliance by the firms it regulated. The MER noted that all FATF-defined DNFBPs are currently covered, with strong oversight of casinos, lawyers, and most accountants, while gaps in monitoring real estate and company service providers are set to be addressed under the third MLD. Interestingly, the MER concluded that 'overall, the UKFIU, housed within the then Serious Organised Crime Agency, is now an effective FIU'.[45] However, the FATF did identify deficiencies for customer due diligence (CDD) which lie in the fact that certain requirements, such as beneficial ownership, are not laid out in law or regulations.[46] In order to address this, the UK introduced the Money Laundering Regulations to implement and comply with the Third MLD.[47] The next part of the chapter identifies the FATF Recommendations, the ratings, and examines the UK's response, identifying concerns regarding the information exchange.

A. Recommendation 5

The 2007 MER rated the UK 'Partially Compliant' with Recommendation 5, citing several CDD deficiencies. For example, Joint Money Laundering Steering Group Guidance did not require verifying agents' authority or identifying and confirming

[42] This law provided the framework for autonomous UK sanctions post-Brexit, including asset freezes targeting terrorist groups like ISIL and Al-Qaeda.

[43] This Act updated offences related to online content and travel, indirectly supporting financial disruption efforts.

[44] See FATF 2007 MER (n 3) at 4.

[45] ibid at 6.

[46] ibid at 9.

[47] See above, n 21. See Directive 2005/60/EC of the European Parliament and of the Council of 26 October 2005 on the prevention of the use of the financial system for the purpose of money laundering and terrorist financing [2005] OJ L309/15.

beneficial owners, nor did it mandate collecting purpose-of-business-relationship information.[48] Ongoing monitoring obligations applied only in high-risk scenarios, with no general duty to review or update CDD records or to step up measures when risk increased. Simplified CDD exemptions were broad and could be used without formal risk assessments, even where money laundering was suspected. Finally, there was no enforceable obligation to terminate relationships or conduct enhanced due diligence when CDD remained incomplete, and many guidance provisions carried no regulatory weight for Money Services Businesses or unsupervised sectors.[49]

The FATF urged the UK to legislate a comprehensive CDD regime that mandates verifying beneficial owners and authorised representatives at onboarding, documenting a relationship's purpose and nature, and making ongoing due diligence compulsory, especially when suspicion of money laundering or terrorist financing arises. Any simplified CDD must be backed by documented low-risk assessments. Legally binding rules should require terminating relationships if CDD remains incomplete, extending CDD to existing clients based on material risk, and ensuring regular updates of all CDD records.[50]

The UK response was the introduction of the Money Laundering Regulations 2007,[51] which aligned the UK with the Third MLD.[52] Specifically, the Money Laundering Regulations strengthened the identification and verification of customers and beneficial owners; introduced clearer rules for ongoing monitoring and enhanced due diligence and applied CDD obligations to a broader range of sectors, including legal professionals, estate agents, and high-value dealers.[53] The FATF published its 'Follow-Up Report' to the 2007 MER in 2009 and acknowledged that the UK had made 'substantial progress' in addressing the weaknesses, particularly regarding Recommendation 5.[54] Therefore, the FATF removed the UK from the regular follow-up process and was satisfied that it had reached levels effectively equivalent to 'Compliant or Largely Compliant'.[55]

B. Recommendation 26

Recommendation 26 provides that countries should establish an FIU that receives and requests SARs and relevant information concerning potential

[48] See FATF 2007 MER (n 3) at 127. Also see Joint Money Laundering Steering Group, *Prevention of Money Laundering/Combating the Financing of Terrorism – Guidance for UK Financial Service Sector Part 1* (Joint Money Laundering Steering Group, 2006) and see Joint Money Laundering Steering Group, *Prevention of Money Laundering/Combating the Financing of Terrorism – Guidance for UK Financial Service Sector Part II – Sectorial Guidance* (Joint Money Laundering Steering Group, 2006).

[49] See FATF 2007 MER (n 3) at 127.

[50] ibid at 289–90.

[51] See above, n 21.

[52] Directive 2005/60 (n 47).

[53] See above, n 21.

[54] FATF, *Mutual Evaluation Fourth Follow-Up Report: Anti-Money Laundering and Combating the Financing of Terrorism – The United Kingdom* (FATF, 2009) (hereinafter '*4th Follow-Up Report*') at 4.

[55] ibid.

money laundering or terrorist financing. Furthermore, the FIU should be able to conduct analysis and ensure appropriate dissemination of this data. In order to perform this function, the FIU must have access to financial, administrative, and law enforcement information necessary to carry out its responsibilities, particularly in analysing SARs.[56] The FATF concluded that the UK FIU 'substantially meets the criteria of Recommendation 26 and appears to be a generally effective FIU'.[57] However, FATF recommended that the UKFIU should increase its 'analytical capabilities … to maintain its role as the national center for receiving, analysing and disseminating SARS … in this respect, the UK FIU should continue to increase its staff'.[58] The MER rated the UK as 'Largely Compliant' with Recommendation 26 but noted three specific concerns. Firstly, the effectiveness and workability of the consent process at that time.[59] Secondly, the UKFIU did not conduct sufficient pro-active analysis on SARs and that they were often over reliant on individual LEAs to undertake their own analysis. This has the potential to hamper the UKFIU's analytical functions and its ability to provide advice and to develop its expertise about money laundering and terrorist financing typologies. Finally, the MER noted that the UKFIU did not publish SARs statistics, typologies and trends.[60]

In response to the 2007 MER, the UK introduced the Money Laundering Regulations to implement the Third MLD which extended the range of regulated entities and enhancing requirements for CDD, Politically Exposed Persons (PEPs), correspondent banking and shell bank controls. HMG elevated sector-specific guidance into law, endorsing the Joint Money Laundering Steering Group's rules for financial firms, HM Revenue & Customs' (HMRC) guidance for money service businesses and trust and company service providers, and professional bodies' frameworks for accountants and notaries. Following these reforms, the FATF recognised the UK's substantial progress, removing it from regular follow-up and shifting to a biennial reporting cycle effective from 2011.[61]

C. Recommendation 27

Recommendation 27 provides that countries assign money laundering and terrorist financing investigations to designated LEAs and strengthen efforts by employing advanced investigative methods such as undercover operations and controlled deliveries. They are also encouraged to form specialised groups focused on asset investigation and collaborate with international authorities to

[56] FATF, *FATF 40 Recommendations* (FATF, 2004) at 10–11.
[57] See FATF 2007 MER (n 3)at 88.
[58] ibid.
[59] See generally The Law Commission, *Anti-Money Laundering: The SARS Regime Consultation Paper* (Law Commission, 2018) at 7–10; 153–58 and 175–87.
[60] See FATF 2007 MER (n 3) at 88–89.
[61] FATF, *4th Follow-Up Report* (n 54).

enhance the effectiveness of these investigations.[62] The MER noted that the UK was 'Compliant' with Recommendation 27.[63] In response to Recommendation 27 on terrorist asset-freezing, the UK strengthened its domestic regime by enacting the Counter-Terrorism Act 2008, which extended HM Treasury's powers to designate individuals and organisations and to freeze their assets in accordance with UNSCRs and FATF standards.[64] These amendments streamlined the listing and de-listing process for terrorist entities, introduced both targeted and broad-based financial sanction measures, and provided clear legal mechanisms for UK authorities to identify, seize, and immobilise suspect funds and economic resources.

D. Recommendation 28

Here, competent authorities must have the ability to access and gather relevant documents and information when investigating money laundering and its related offences. This includes the authority to enforce mandatory production of records from financial institutions and individuals, as well as to conduct searches of people and premises, and seize evidence needed for legal proceedings.[65] The MER concluded that the UK demonstrated a strong and proactive stance in tackling both predicate offences and the financial aspects of crime and terrorism. Multiple competent authorities are designated to investigate and prosecute money laundering, while the National Terrorist Financial Investigation Unit (NTFIU) pursues terrorist financing in coordination with broader terrorism probes. Agencies are well-structured, adequately resourced, and uphold high standards of integrity and confidentiality. Rigorous training in AML and CTF – particularly financial investigations – is not only common but mandatory. UK authorities also possess extensive powers to obtain and seize evidence, including key financial records.[66]

E. Recommendation 29

Supervisory bodies must be equipped with sufficient authority to oversee financial institutions' adherence to AML and CTF regulations. This includes the power to carry out inspections, demand access to relevant data and records, and impose appropriate administrative penalties when institutions fail to meet compliance

[62] See *FATF 40 Recommendations* (n 56) at 11.

[63] See FATF 2007 MER (n 3) at 101.

[64] Counter-Terrorism Act 2008, sch 7. The Terrorist Asset-Freezing etc. Act 2010 amended the Counter-Terrorism Act 2008 and extended HM Treasury's powers to designate individuals and organisations. See the Terrorist Asset-Freezing etc. Act (2010), s 2(1)(a) and (b). Also see *HM Treasury v Ahmed (A v HM Treasury)* [2010] UKSC 2.

[65] See *FATF 40 Recommendations* (n 56) at 88.

[66] See FATF 2007 MER (n 3) at 101.

standards.[67] The MER concluded that the UK was 'Largely Compliant' and noted that those entities who are not regulated by the FSA should be brought within the then regulatory regime.[68]

F. Recommendation 30

Recommendation 30 provides that 'countries should provide their competent authorities involved in combating money laundering and terrorist financing with adequate financial, human and technical resources. Countries should have in place processes to ensure that the staff of those authorities are of high integrity'.[69] The FATF rated the UK 'Largely Compliant' and identified weaknesses regarding how HMRC allocates its resources to large MSBs and not smaller MSBs where the money laundering and terrorist financing could be higher. Furthermore, the UKFIU should increase resources in order to meet commitments made under HMG reviews.[70]

G. Recommendation 31

Recommendation 31 provided that

> countries should ensure that policymakers, the FIU, law enforcement and supervisors have effective mechanisms in place which enable them to co-operate, and where appropriate coordinate domestically with each other concerning the development and implementation of policies and activities to combat money laundering and terrorist financing.[71]

Here, the MER concluded that the UK maintains strong internal collaboration among policymakers, the UKFIU, LEAs, supervisors, and other authorities involved in combating money laundering and terrorist financing. Operational cooperation between agencies is notably effective, supported by a well-established network of interdepartmental and interagency communication.[72] Therefore, the UK was rated 'Compliant'.

H. Recommendation 32

Under Recommendation 32, countries are expected to enable their competent authorities to assess the effectiveness of their AML and CTF frameworks by

[67] See ibid at 11.
[68] See ibid at 198–99.
[69] See *FATF 40 Recommendations* (n 56) at 11.
[70] See FATF 2007 MER (n 3) at 282.
[71] See *FATF 40 Recommendations* (n 56) at 11.
[72] See FATF 2007 MER (n 3) at 284.

maintaining comprehensive statistical records. These should cover key metrics such as the number of SARs received and shared, investigations, prosecutions, money laundering and terrorist financing convictions, assets frozen, seized, or confiscated, and data on mutual legal assistance and other forms of international cooperation.[73] The MER concluded that the UK was 'Largely Compliant' with this Recommendation but did note that there were no statistics on the breakdown of the offences concerned for money laundering of terrorist financing, nor on the number granted and refused, or the time required to respond. Furthermore, the MER noted that there were no comprehensive statistics for CTF convictions, the UKFIU does not have precise figures on the number of SARs analysed and disseminated and the UK does not maintain comprehensive statistics on cross-border disclosures concerning suspected instances of money laundering and terrorist financing.[74]

I. Mutual Evaluation Follow-Up Report

In October 2009, the FATF published its Follow-Up Report assessing the UK's response to its 2007 MER.[75] This review revisited the deficiencies identified in the 2007 MER and re-measured the effectiveness of the legislative, regulatory, and supervisory changes the UK had implemented. Here, the FATF concluded that the UK had taken substantial and effective steps to address the shortcomings highlighted in 2007. Consequently, the UK was removed from the FATF's regular follow-up process and transitioned to a biennial reporting cycle. This change reflected the FATF's confidence that the UK's AML/CTF regime had improved and it required less oversight. A key part of the Follow-Up Report was Recommendation 5 (CDD), where the UK was rated 'Partially Compliant' in 2007.

Following the 2007 MER, the UK responded with a number of legislative and policy measures to address the shortcomings identified by FATF. The Money Laundering Regulations 2007 improved the CDD obligations and improved scrutiny of PEPs, beneficial ownership transparency and high-risk transactions.[76] In conjunction, updated guidelines were published by the Joint Money Laundering Steering Groupand the Counter-Terrorism Act 2008 reinforced the UK's CTF efforts.[77] The FATF 2009 Follow-Up Report assessed the UK's progress in addressing deficiencies identified in the MER.[78] The original evaluation had placed the

[73] See *FATF 40 Recommendations* (n 56) at 11.
[74] See FATF 2007 MER (n 3) at 282.
[75] FATF, *4th Follow-Up Report* (n 54).
[76] See above, n 21.
[77] See Joint Money Laundering Steering Group (n 48). Also see M Goldby, 'The Impact of Schedule 7 of the Counter-Terrorism Act 2008 on Banks and their Customers' (2010) *Journal of Money Laundering Control* 13(4), 351–71.
[78] FATF, *4th Follow-Up Report* (n 54).

UK under the regular follow-up process, due to its 'Partial Compliance' with Recommendation 5.

IV. 2018 Mutual Evaluation Report

The 2018 MER assessed the effectiveness of the UK's measures and their alignment with FATF Recommendations. As the world's largest provider of financial services, the UK processes a vast volume of global transactions making it vulnerable to financial crime.[79] Nonetheless, the 2018 MER concluded that the UK continues to demonstrate a strong awareness of these risks and has implemented robust national policies, strategies, and proactive initiatives to mitigate them.[80] The UK actively investigates and prosecutes financial crimes, securing approximately 1,400 money laundering convictions annually.[81] LEAs benefit from a wide range of investigative powers and data-sharing partnerships that enable them to access beneficial ownership information and leverage it in investigations.[82] However, the MER noted that the UKFIU required more resources, and reforms are needed to modernise the SARs regime. Therefore, little progress has been made from the findings of the 2007 MER. Nonetheless, the UK continues to lead in global corporate transparency and uses the outcomes of its risk assessments to enhance corporate reporting and registration practices.[83] All financial institutions and designated non-financial businesses including lawyers, accountants, and real estate professionals must comply with comprehensive AML/CTF obligations.[84] Supervisors conduct extensive outreach and implement controls to prevent criminals or their associates from gaining professional credentials or access to financial institutions. However, oversight intensity remains uneven across sectors, and the UK needs to ensure its supervision aligns with its elevated risk profile. The UK has shown high effectiveness in investigation and prosecution in terrorist financing cases and continues to play a key role in terrorist designations.[85] Additionally, the UK promotes international implementation of targeted financial sanctions related to proliferation and demonstrates strong domestic compliance. While the UK's AML/CTF regime is highly effective in many areas, improvement is needed in supervisory practices and the handling of SARs.[86] The next part of the chapter identifies the FATF Recommendations, the ratings and examines the UK's response, identifying concerns regarding the information exchange.

[79] FATF 2018 MER (n 4).
[80] However, for a contrasting view see chapter seven.
[81] FATF 2018 MER (n 4).
[82] ibid.
[83] ibid.
[84] For a more detailed discussion and analysis of the legal profession see section IV.F.
[85] FATF 2018 MER (n 4).
[86] ibid.

A. Recommendation 2

Recommendation 2 provides that countries should create national AML, CTF and countering proliferation financing (CPF) policies that are guided by risks and subjected to regular review.[87] Countries are expected to assign responsibility for these policies to a designated authority. In order to ensure the coordinated and effective implementation, policymakers, the UKFIU, LEAs, supervisory bodies, and other competent authorities should have robust systems for cooperation, coordination, and domestic information exchange. This collaboration should also extend to ensuring that the AML and CTF reporting obligations are fully compatible with Data Protection laws.[88]

The UK was 'Compliant' with Recommendation 2. Specifically, the MER concluded that essential ministerial-level bodies remain active, several national mechanisms for cooperation and coordination have evolved since the 2007 MER. This includes the Strategic Defence and Security Review[89] and the AML/CTF Action Plan.[90] Policy updates are facilitated through the Money Laundering Advisory Committee, the Money Laundering Working Group, and Ministerial oversight committees.[91] The Strategic Defence and Security Review and its associated CONTEST strategy inform resource allocation for counter-terrorism efforts, including CTF, while the CTF Strategy is reviewed annually by the Home Office.[92] Responsibility for addressing domestic terrorism threats in Northern Ireland lies with the Secretary of State for Northern Ireland, with regional input channelled through dedicated Ministerial oversight mechanisms.[93]

Criterion 2.2 outlines how HM Treasury and the Home Office share responsibility for the development and implementation of the AML/CTF policy.[94] Under Criterion 2.3, strategic AML leadership is provided by the ministerial-level Criminal Finances Board, supported by the official-level Money Laundering Working Group. Operational coordination is managed by the National Strategic Tasking and Coordination Group, comprising the NCA, police forces, HMRC, security services, and Border Force. This group oversees the Money Laundering Strategic Action Plan and the Criminal Finance Threat Group, which addresses ML risks identified in the Strategic Action Plan. The CTF strategy is led by the

[87] ibid.

[88] Financial Action Task Force, *International Standards on Combating Money Laundering and the Financing of Terrorism and Proliferation – The FATF Recommendations* (FATF, 2025) at 10–11.

[89] HM Government, *National Security Strategy and Strategic Defence and Security Review 2015 A Secure and Prosperous United Kingdom* (HM Government, 2015).

[90] Home Office and HM Treasury, *Action Plan for Anti-Money Laundering and Counter-Terrorist Finance* (Home Office and HM Treasury, 2016).

[91] FATF 2018 MER (n 4).

[92] ibid.

[93] ibid at 175–76.

[94] ibid.

Home Office as part of the broader counter-terrorism CONTEST strategy. In parallel with the CFB, CTF efforts are coordinated by the ministerial-level Terror Finance Board, chaired by the Minister for Security and supported by officials from law enforcement, intelligence services, relevant ministries, and charity regulators. The Board sets strategic direction, reviews and approves the CTF strategy, and ensures its implementation. Policy and operational coordination on domestic terrorism and organised crime in Northern Ireland is facilitated through entities such as the Strategic Oversight Group, Operational Coordination Group, and Tackling Paramilitaries Taskforce.[95] Additionally, the HMG has published the Economic Crime Plan 2019–22,[96] the Economic Crime Plan 2,[97] the Fraud Strategy,[98] its response to the Law Commission Review on SARs,[99] its response to the anti-money laundering review (AMLA)[100] and its fourth AML/CTF National Risk Assessment (NRA).[101]

Therefore, HMG's strategy towards tackling financial crime appears to be coordinated and multifaceted. Operational coordination is managed through the National Strategic Tasking and Coordination Group, which integrates agencies like the NCA, HMRC, and Border Force. These bodies oversee key initiatives such as the Money Laundering Strategic Action Plan and the Criminal Finance Threat Group. Tailored approaches for Northern Ireland involve the Strategic Oversight Group and the Tackling Paramilitaries Taskforce. The Home Office leads counter-terrorist finance efforts under the broader CONTEST strategy. Meanwhile, HMG has continued to demonstrate its commitment to reform and transparency by publishing Economic Crime Plans 1 and 2, a national Fraud Strategy, and responses to key reviews, the Law Commission. While comprehensive, this approach faces challenges from potential fragmentation, limited private sector integration, and the need for clearer outcome metrics to evaluate effectiveness.

B. Recommendation 30

Under Recommendation 30, countries are expected to ensure that LEAs are tasked with investigating money laundering and terrorist financing in alignment with

[95] FATF 2018 MER (n 4) at 175–76.

[96] HM Government and UK Finance, *Economic Crime Plan 2019-22* (HM Government and UK Finance, 2019).

[97] HM Government and UK Finance, *Economic Crime Plan 2 2023-26* (HM Government and UK Finance, 2023).

[98] Home Office, *Fraud Strategy: Stopping Scams and Protecting the Public* (Home Office, 2023).

[99] HM Government, *Response to Law Commission Review of the SARs Regime* (HM Government, 2024).

[100] See HM Treasury, *Reform of the Anti-Money Laundering and Counter Terrorism Financing Supervisory Regime Consultation* (HM Treasury, 2023) and HM Treasury, *Improving the Effectiveness of the Money Laundering Regulations Consultation Response* (HM Treasury, 2024).

[101] Home Office and HM Treasury, *National Risk Assessment of Money Laundering and Terrorist Financing 2025* (Home Office and HM Treasury, 2025).

national AML/CTF frameworks.[102] In cases involving major proceeds-generating offences, these authorities should proactively conduct parallel financial investigations, addressing both the underlying crimes and associated laundering or financing activities. Competent authorities must also be responsible for swiftly identifying, tracing, and initiating actions to freeze and confiscate criminal assets or their equivalent value.[103] Where appropriate, countries should deploy permanent or temporary multidisciplinary teams with expertise in financial and asset investigations. Furthermore, effective international cooperation should be guaranteed through joint investigations with relevant authorities in other jurisdictions when necessary.[104]

The MER rated the UK as 'Compliant' with the requirements set out under Recommendation 30. Under Criterion 30.1, investigative responsibility for money laundering and most associated predicate offences lies with the Police and the NCA, who are supported by Regional Organised Crime Units, the Scottish Crime Campus, the Economic Crime Unit of the Police Service of Northern Ireland, and the Joint Agency Task Force.[105] Tax-related offences and their associated money laundering are investigated by HMRC, while the Serious Fraud Office (SFO) handles complex fraud and corruption cases. Terrorist financing investigations are conducted by the NTFIU, supported regional Counter-Terrorism Units. In Northern Ireland, these cases fall under the Crime Operations Department of the Police.[106]

Criterion 30.2 provides that all LEAs that are responsible for investigating predicate offences have the authority to conduct parallel financial investigations into associated money laundering and terrorist financing offences, regardless of where the initial offence occurred. They may also transfer cases when appropriate. Under Criterion 30.3, designated entities including the Police, NCA, HMRC, SFO, and accredited financial investigators are empowered to identify, trace, freeze, and seize criminal assets. Dedicated Asset Confiscation Enforcement teams support these agencies in executing confiscation orders.[107] Criterion 30.4 confirms that Recommendation 30 applies to all relevant investigative authorities, and the UK Secretary of State may issue directives authorising specific individuals or groups to exercise financial investigation powers. Under Criterion 30.5, although the UK lacks a standalone anti-corruption enforcement body, the SFO investigates significant or complex corruption cases, while the Police manage other cases. Both agencies are equipped to pursue linked AML/CTF offences and apply relevant asset recovery powers. Overall, all criteria are satisfied, and Recommendation 30 is assessed as compliant.[108]

[102] FATF 2018 MER (n 4).
[103] ibid.
[104] FATF, *International Standards* (n 88) at 24–25.
[105] FATF 2018 MER (n 4).
[106] ibid at 225.
[107] ibid.
[108] ibid at 225.

C. Immediate Outcome 1

Immediate Outcome 1 evaluates how effectively a country identifies, assesses, and responds to money laundering, terrorist financing, and proliferation financing risks. It examines the depth of national risk understanding, the proportionality of policies developed in response, and the extent of coordination among public authorities. To score highly, countries must demonstrate strong inter-agency collaboration, targeted strategies based on risk assessments, and tangible actions aligned with those risks. While most FATF member countries perform relatively well in this area, regional members show mixed results, often struggling with limited policy implementation and weak coordination efforts.[109]

In the UK, national and sector-specific AML and CTF policies, strategies, and actions are directly informed by its NRA. A review of the main strategic documents, such as the National Security Strategy and the Strategic Defence and Security Review illustrate the UK's commitment to tackling identified vulnerabilities.[110] The FATF took the view that collaboration was an important part of the UK's adherence with Immediate Outcome 1. For instance, the relevant authorities contributed towards the 2015 and 2017 NRAs, the HMG launched its AML/CTF, the permanent establishment of the Joint Money Laundering Intelligence Taskforce (JMLIT) to strengthen public–private information exchange, the creation of the Office for Professional Body Anti-Money Laundering Supervision (OPBAS) to improve oversight of legal and accounting professionals, and ongoing reforms to the SARs.[111] The FATF noted that the Criminal Finances Act 2017 has broadened the powers of LEAs to investigate, prosecute, and recover assets, and the 2017 Money Laundering Regulations strengthened supervisory standards by mandating criminal-record checks for key trust roles.[112] In response to the growing financial crime risks from cryptocurrencies, the UK has extended its AML/CTF obligations into that sector.[113] However, FATF did note that although these initiatives leverage both qualitative insights and quantitative data, their impact could be improved by consistent national statistics on investigations, prosecutions, convictions, asset confiscations, and international cooperation.[114]

[109] FATF, *Report on the State of Effectiveness and Compliance with the FATF Standards* (FATF, 2022) at 12.

[110] See HM Government, *National Security Strategy 2025: Security for the British People in a Dangerous World* (HM Government, 2025) and HM Government, *The Strategic Defence Review 2025 – Making Britain Safer: Secure at Home, Strong Abroad* (HM Government, 2025).

[111] OPBAS. For a more detailed analysis of these two bodies see chapter four at VIII and IX.

[112] See chapter four.

[113] For a more detailed discussion about the regulation of cryptocurrencies in the UK, see H Hillman, 'Pass or Play: Should Regulators Address the Money Laundering Risks Posed by Cryptocurrencies Themselves or Await Legislative Reform?' (2024) *Journal of Business Law* 4, 301–28.

[114] FATF 2018 MER (n 4) at 35–36.

D. Immediate Outcome 6

Immediate Outcome 6 assesses how effectively a country uses financial intelligence to combat money laundering, terrorist financing, and proliferation financing. It emphasises the importance of timely access to financial data by authorities such as FIUs and LEAs, and how well that data is integrated with other sources to identify and dismantle criminal networks. For a country to be rated effective, it must demonstrate routine use of financial intelligence in investigations, strong collaboration among agencies, and concrete results like prosecutions or asset recoveries. Common challenges include disjointed data systems, weak feedback between FIUs and law enforcement, and insufficient use of suspicious transaction reports.[115]

The FATF noted that competent authorities across the UK are able to and regularly access and leverage a wide range of financial intelligence to investigate money laundering and terrorist financing. The MER noted that JMLIT has consistently delivered strong results. However, the long-standing resource and analytical constraints on the UKFIU has been identified by the MER as an area in need of improvement. Despite a high volume of quality SARs from financial institutions, under-reporting persists in higher-risk sectors such as trust and company service providers, lawyers and accountants, underscoring the need for comprehensive SAR regime reform.[116] The MER noted that inter-agency cooperation on AML/CTF is a strength, reflecting progress since the 2007 MER.[117]

E. Immediate Outcome 7

Immediate Outcome 7 assesses how effectively a country investigates and prosecutes money laundering offences. It focuses on whether LEAs pursue money laundering cases that reflect the country's risk profile, including complex and large-scale operations, and whether they apply appropriate sanctions upon conviction. To be rated effective, countries must demonstrate that money laundering offences are regularly identified and prosecuted, with convictions leading to proportionate penalties. Immediate Outcome 7 also considers whether authorities target both standalone money laundering offences and those linked to predicate offences, and whether they pursue cases involving professional enablers and legal persons.[118] The MER noted that the UK continues to maintain a sustained, high-volume enforcement effort against money laundering, pursuing more than 2,000 prosecutions and securing roughly 1,400 convictions each year in cases. The FATF

[115] ibid at 36.
[116] FATF 2018 MER (n 4) at 6.
[117] ibid.
[118] ibid at 36.

noted that LEAs are equipped with powerful investigative tools and streamlined information-sharing frameworks.[119]

F. Immediate Outcome 9

Immediate Outcome 9 evaluates how effectively a country investigates and prosecutes terrorist financing. Here, FATF focuses on whether a country's authorities pursue terrorist financing investigation cases that associate with the country's risk profile, apply proportionate and dissuasive sanctions, and integrate financial investigations into broader counter-terrorism strategies.[120] To be rated effective, countries must demonstrate that the terrorist financing offences are consistently identified, prosecuted, and sanctioned, with efforts targeting both individuals and networks. Furthermore, Immediate Outcome 9 considers the use of alternative measures including regulatory or administrative actions where criminal prosecution is not possible and evaluates the level of international cooperation in disrupting terrorist financing activities.[121] The FATF concluded that the UK pursues terrorist-financing investigations as a key part of its broader counter-terrorism operations. Case studies demonstrated that authorities tackle a wide array of terrorist financing schemes, embedding these probes firmly within the national counter-terrorism strategy.[122] The MER noted that coordination across jurisdictions, regions and sectors is robust, and relationships between terrorist financing units, financial institutions and the non-profit sector are particularly effective.[123]

The MER noted that the UK has a comprehensive toolkit that supports terrorist financing investigations including asset freezing, seizure and confiscation; withdrawal of lawful benefits; movement and activity restriction orders; and powers to block or seize bank account funds.[124] In Northern Ireland, LEAs have continued to adapt to its unique landscape by prosecuting suspected terrorist financing activity under alternative offences,[125] often those linked to organised

[119] FATF 2018 MER (n 4) at 7. For a contrasting view of the information- sharing frameworks, see chapters four, five and six.

[120] ibid.

[121] ibid at 42.

[122] For a contrasting view, see N Ryder, 'To Report or Not to Report? An Analysis of the Relationship between Defence against Terrorism Financing Suspicious Activity Reports and Fraud in the United Kingdom' in L de Koker and D Goldbarsht, *Financial Crime, Law and Governance – Navigating Challenges in Different Contexts* (Springer, 2024) 169–202.

[123] For a more detailed discussion on the link between terrorist financing and charities, see FATF, *Best Practices – Combating the Abuse of Non-Profit Organisations* (FATF, 2015) and FATF, *Terrorist Financing* (FATF, 2008) and C Walker, 'Terrorism Financing and the Governance of Charities' in C King, C Walker. and J Gurule, *The Palgrave Handbook of Criminal and Terrorism Financing Law* (Springer, 2018) 1085–1115.

[124] For a more detailed discussion, see chapter five at II.

[125] See J John and M Garrod, 'Legacies of the Troubles: The Links between Organized Crime and Terrorism in Northern Ireland' (2022) *Studies in Conflict & Terrorism* 45(5-6), 389–428.

crime,[126] to secure effective outcomes.[127] However, the MER failed to include here a discussion and review of the embarrassment of the data-sharing mechanisms that exist to tackle terrorist financing. A review of the terrorist financing data-sharing mechanisms in chapter five illustrates several deficiencies that challenge the rating provided by the FATF for Immediate Outcome 9.[128]

G. FATF Follow-Up Report

The FATF published its Follow-Up Report and Technical Compliance Re-Rating in May 2022 which examined the UK's progress in addressing the deficiencies identified and how it has implemented any new requirements introduced since the MER.[129] Here, the FATF concluded that the UK has made progress towards improving its AML/CTF regime and it is 'Compliant' on 24 Recommendations and 'Largely Compliant' on 15. Specifically, the FATF noted improvements in the UK's risk-based approach, enhancement of CDD and correspondent banking requirements and the extension of targeted financial sanctions for terrorism and proliferation financing. Furthermore, the UK strengthened its regulation of non-profit organisations, improved transparency of legal persons and has implemented new wire-transfer rules in line with international standards. Overall, FATF concluded that this reflected the UK's robust legal framework, risk-based supervisory and enforcement mechanisms, and enhanced regulatory coordination across government agencies.[130] However, for Recommendation 29 (FIU), the UK was rated 'Partially Compliant'. Here, the FATF noted that the remaining technical compliance challenges were resource constraints within the UKFIU, the need for further refinement of regulatory oversight over certain DNFBPs, where Recommendation 22 (CDD) and Recommendation 23 (other measures) are rated largely compliant but could be strengthened. The FATF encouraged the UK Government to continue to provide investment in supervisory capacity and interagency information-sharing to achieve full compliance.

V. Government Response

Following the publication of the 2018 MER, HMG stated that FATF awarded the UK its highest possible rating for measures such as combating terrorist financing

[126] For a more detailed discussion, see R Basra and PR Neumann, 'Criminal Pasts, Terrorist Futures: European Jihadists and the New Crime-Terror Nexus' (2016) *Perspectives on Terrorism* 10(6), 25–40 and S Hutchinson and P O'Malley, 'A Crime–Terror Nexus? Thinking on Some of the Links between Terrorism and Criminality' (2007) *Studies in Conflict Terrorism* 30(12), 1095–1107.

[127] FATF 2018 MER (n 4) at 8.

[128] For a more detailed discussion, see chapter five at V.

[129] FATF, *Follow Up Report and Technical Compliance Re-Rating* (FATF, 2022).

[130] ibid.

and enforcing financial sanctions. Among 60 jurisdictions assessed, this accolade cements the UK's position as a world leader with one of the toughest AML regimes ever evaluated.[131] In particular, it highlighted its best practices as identified by the 2018 MER that included how the UK has aggressively investigated and prosecuted money laundering, the introduction of Unexplained Wealth Orders, how it has used all means at its disposal to disrupt terrorist financing, the prevention of the misuse of companies and trusts, acting as a global leader by adopting a public register of company beneficial ownership and a register of trusts with tax consequences and worked with international partners to tackle illicit finance, through a strong legal framework and a liaison network spanning over 160 jurisdictions.[132] John Glen MP, the then Economic Secretary to the Treasury and City Minister, said that the MER confirmed that the UK's AML/CTF regime is among the strongest globally.[133] Ben Wallace MP, the then Minister for Security and Economic Crime, added that the MER confirms the UK's leadership in combating illicit finance and that HMG will deploy every available power and tactic and work with collaboratively with partners to tackle money laundering.[134]

Conversely, the Royal United Services Institute stated that between 2015 and 2018, the UK rolled out an extensive suite of new AML strategies, initiatives, and organisational structures, an effort widely perceived as preparation for its decennial FATF evaluation in December 2018.[135] Transparency International UK noted that the MER measured legislation and not implementation.[136] Similarly, the Treasury Select Committee noted the results of the MER were positive, HMG should not be complacent, the threat of money had not receded and that its response to the MER was 'slow and inadequate'.[137]

VI. Conclusion

The UK has been at the forefront of the global efforts to address money laundering and terrorist financing. Since the creation of the FATF in 1989, the UK has implemented every major international AML and CTF standard, it has chaired the FATF on two occasions, undergone two MERS and a third is due to take place in 2027–28. The 2007 MER praised the UK's AML/CTF legal frameworks but identified a number of shortcomings relating to CDD and the UKFIU. The 2018 MER commended the UK for its world-leading AML/CTF measures, yet many of the weaknesses identified in 2007 persisted: the under resourcing of the UKFIU

[131] See HM Government (n 12).
[132] ibid.
[133] ibid.
[134] ibid.
[135] See Keatinge et al (n 13) at iii.
[136] House of Commons Treasury Committee (n 14) at 48.
[137] ibid at 49.

and deficiencies in the SARs regime. As a global financial centre, the UK has faced scrutiny over its AML/CTF regimes and this chapter examines how it has implemented the FATF Recommendations. It has focused on the findings of the 2007 and 2018 MER illustrating how it has complied with the CDD, SAR and related data-sharing Recommendations. Therefore, the subsidiary research questions this chapter answers are how successfully has the UK implemented and responded to the FATF standards as reflected in the related conclusions of the 2007 and 2018 MER? To answer this question the chapter outlined the UK's adoption of the FATF Recommendations, it investigated the 2007 MER and Follow-Up Report before analysing the 2018 MER. The penultimate part of the chapter briefly outlined the HMG's response to the MERs.

The 2007 and 2018 MERs highlighted consistent deficiencies in the UK's CDD, SARs regime and related data-sharing mechanisms. The FATF noted that the implementation of the Third MLD via the 2007 Money Laundering Regulations address these shortcomings. The implementation of the Regulations could be regarded as a turning point in the UK's AML/CTF framework because they directly addressed the weaknesses highlighted in the 2007 MER. The scope of the Regulations was extended to include a broader range of professions including estate agents, accountants and high-value dealers. By the time the FATF published the Follow-Up Report to the 2018 MER in 2022, the UK was rated as 'Largely Compliant' with the CDD Recommendation, largely reflecting the positive impact of the implementation of the Fourth and Fifth MLD. Nonetheless, both follow up reports highlighted ongoing resource and capacity restraints on the UKFIU. For instance, the 2009 Follow-Up Report noted that the UKFIU continued to see an increase in the number of SARs submitted and that it lacked an effective IT system to turn the financial data into strategic intelligence. Similarly, the 2022 Follow-Up Report also noted that the UKFIU continues to struggle with the number of SARs submitted by reporting entities. Consequently, FATF recommended that the UKFIU should be better resourced. The 2009 Follow-Up Report recommended that the UK should improve the levels of cooperation between the UKFIU and LEAs and the creation of the National Economic Crime Centre and JMLIT had improved levels of cooperation. However, FATF did recommend that JMLIT should be underpinned by a statutory framework. Across both MERs and follow up reports, the FATF acknowledged that the UK had made improvements to its CDD rules, but that there were still areas for improvement.

The 2018 MER rated the UK's AML/CTF regime as the best in the world.[138] One of the FATF's key findings was that 'Co-operation and co-ordination between agencies on AML/CTF issues is a strength of the UK system and a significant improvement since the UK's last evaluation'.[139] The UK was rated 'Compliant' with Recommendations 2, 30 and 31, which require national coordination and

[138] FATF 2018 MER (n 4).
[139] ibid at 37.

cooperation, including the exchange of information, between LEAs.[140] The UK was also considered to have moderate to high levels of effectiveness in regards to Immediate Outcomes 1 and 6, concerning risk, policy and coordination, and financial intelligence, as well as Immediate Outcomes 7 and 9, concerning effective money laundering and terrorism financing investigations.[141] Therefore, according to the FATF, the UK has successfully implemented and responded to the FATF standards. The next three chapters, however, present evidence that questions and challenges the findings of the FATF MER that apply to financial intelligence and the exchange of information by presenting novel case studies on money laundering, terrorist financing and fraud. The case studies will serve to demonstrate inherent flaws in the UK's ability to ensure the exchange of information between LEAs to detect and address financial crimes. The case studies for chapter four on money laundering focus on the legal profession, the financial services sector and the AML supervisory agencies. The terrorist financing case studies in chapter five focus on the terrorist attacks in London 2005, Manchester 2017, London 2017 and the convictions of Amal El-Wahabi and Oghenochuko Ojiri. Chapter six on fraud focuses on Action Fraud, the police, social media and the telecommunications sector.

[140] ibid at 176, 225 and 226.
[141] ibid at 38, 58, 71 and 104.

4

Money Laundering

Clean money is worth more than dirty money.[1]

I. Introduction

The United Kingdom (UK) is vulnerable to a wide range of financial crimes, terrorist activity and serious organised crime.[2] The risks at a national and international level are becoming more complex, as organised criminal gangs (OCGs) and terrorist groups continue to adapt to law-enforcement responses to avoid detection. The foundation of the efforts to prevent money laundering are the customer due diligence (CDD) rules, defence against money laundering suspicious activity reports (DAML SARs) and the related data-sharing mechanisms. DAML SARs are submitted to the UK Financial Intelligence Unit (UKFIU), the National Crime Agency (NCA), by virtue of the Proceeds of Crime Act 2002 (POCA). Regrettably, the current complicated system is considered deficient by stakeholders, from SAR submitters and analysts, especially owing to its inability to cope with the large volumes of SARs.[3] For example, as illustrated in Table 1, there has been a 262.43 per cent increase in the number of SARs submitted to the UKFIU from 2009–2010 to 2024–2025.[4] The chapter begins by defining money laundering, outlining its stages and identifying its extent. The second part identifies the legislative framework that applies to the submission of DAML SARs, focusing on the CDD aspects of the Money Laundering Regulations and POCA. The next section presents three studies to appraise the CDD rules, DAML SARs and related data-sharing mechanisms in light of the conclusions of the 2018 Financial Action Task Force Mutual Evaluation Report (2018 FATF MER). The fourth section summarises the key findings and outlines reforms aimed at addressing the deficiencies of CDD, DAML SARs and the data-sharing mechanisms. Therefore, the subsidiary research questions this chapter answers are to what extent do the CDD and DAML SARs, supported by the existing legislative framework and

[1] P Alldridge, *Money Laundering Law: Forfeiture, Confiscation, Civil Recovery, Criminal Laundering and Taxation of the Proceeds of Crime* (Bloomsbury Publishing, 2003) at 1.

[2] See HM Treasury and Home Office, *National, Risk Assessment of Money Laundering and Terrorist Financing 2025* (HM Treasury and Home Office, 2025).

[3] See generally Law Commission, *Anti-Money Laundering: The SARs Regime Consultation Paper* (Law Commission, 2018) ('2018 Report') and Law Commission, *Anti-Money Laundering: The SARs Regime* (Law Commission, 2019) ('2019 Report').

[4] See below Table 1 below at section V.

financial-intelligence led data-sharing mechanisms, effectively detect and prevent money laundering, and what reforms, guided by the 2018 FATF MER are necessary to address their identified deficiencies.

II. Money Laundering

Money laundering is the illegal process or act by which individuals or groups attempt to disguise, hide or distance themselves from their illegal activities.[5] Transparency International described money laundering as 'the process of concealing the origin, ownership or destination of illegally or dishonestly-obtained money by hiding it within legitimate economic activities in order to make it appear legal'.[6] The process can be complicated, hard to detect and involves numerous financial transactions, often in different countries.[7] Therefore, the money laundering process is of critical importance because it enables criminal entities to enjoy a so-called criminal lifestyle.[8]

The traditional and contentious money laundering process involves three stages – placement, layering and integration. At the placement stage the money launderer seeks to position the proceeds of the illegal activity in the financial system.[9] Here, the money launderer normally attempts to break up the profits into smaller amounts so as to avoid any cash, currency or suspicious transaction reporting obligations. This technique is referred to as 'smurfing', or 'structured' payments.[10] The money launderer could target financial institutions and other professions including estate agents,[11] accountants,[12] lawyers,[13] and art dealers.[14] The second stage, or layering, involves a large number of financial transactions or

[5] See generally J Ferwerda, 'Definitions of Money Laundering in Practice' in B Unger, J Ferweda, M van den Broek and I Deleanu (eds), *The Economic and Legal Effectiveness of the European Union's Anti-Money Laundering Policy* (Edward Elgar, 2014) at 87–96.

[6] Transparency International UK, *Paradise Lost: Ending the UK's Role as a Safe Haven for Corrupt Individuals, their Allies and Assets* (Transparency International UK, 2016) at 4.

[7] T Edmonds, *Money Laundering Law, Briefing Paper no 2593* (House of Commons, 2018) at 10.

[8] See generally National Audit Office, *The Asset Recovery Agency* (National Audit Office, 2007).

[9] Financial Action Task Force (FATF), *Money Laundering and Terrorist Financing Typologies 2004-2005* (FATF, 2005 at 63.

[10] See generally S Welling, 'Smurfs, Money Laundering, and the Federal Criminal Law: The Crime of Structuring Transactions' (1989) *Florida Law Review* 41(2), 287–343.

[11] See FATF, *Money Laundering and Terrorist Financing Typologies* (n 9) at 73–74, 79, 80–81; FATF, *Guidance on Risk-Based Approach – Real Estate Sector* (FATF, 2022); I Zavoli and C King, 'The Challenges of Implementing Anti-Money Laundering Regulation: An Empirical Analysis' (2021) *MLR* 84(4), 740–71 and B Unger and J Ferwerda, *Money Laundering in the Real Estate Sector – Suspicious Properties* (Edward Elgar, 2011).

[12] FATF, *Guidance on Risk-Based Approach – Accountants* (FATF, 2019).

[13] See FATF, *Money Laundering and Terrorist Financing Vulnerabilities of Legal Professionals* (FATF, 2013); K Benson, *Lawyers and the Proceeds of Crime – the Facilitation of Money Laundering and its Control* (Routledge, 2020); S Kebbell, *Anti-Money Laundering Compliance and the Legal Profession* (Routledge, 2022) and M Levi, 'Lawyers as Money Laundering Enablers? An Evolving and Contentious Relationship' (2022) *Global Crime* 23(2), 126–47.

[14] FATF, *Money Laundering and Terrorist Financing in the Art and Antiquities Market* (FATF, 2023) and S Hufngael and C King, 'Anti-Money Laundering Regulation and the Art Market' (2020) *Legal Studies* 40(1), 131–50.

conversions.[15] The purpose of this phase is to create as much distance between the initial placement of the proceeds of crime from their original source. It is during this stage that the money could be moved via the purchase of shares,[16] transferred to different countries via wire transfers,[17] and internet payments systems,[18] thus making it increasingly difficult to detect. The final stage is integration, and it is at this stage that the money reappears into the economy.[19]

It is impossible to determine the extent of money laundering and estimates vary widely. For example, the United Nations Office on Drugs and Crime (UNODC), suggest that the annual amount of money laundered is between USD$800billion and USD$2trillion.[20] The International Monetary Fund (IMF) estimated that the consensus range of laundered money could be between two and five per cent of the world's gross domestic product.[21] The calculation is hampered because there is 'no visible data on the amount of money laundered'.[22] Indeed, the FATF noted that without 'precise statistics … it is … impossible to produce a definitive estimate of the amount of money laundered'.[23] Therefore, estimates must be treated with caution.[24] The scale of money laundering is aggravated by the global nature of the financial markets,[25] the immeasurable number of money laundering mechanisms[26] and the link between money laundering and the sale of illegal narcotic substances.[27] This symbiotic relationship was cemented by the instigation

[15] See FATF, *Money Laundering and Terrorist Financing Typologies* (n 9) at 63.

[16] FATF, *Money Laundering and Terrorist Financing in the Securities Sector* (FATF, 2009).

[17] FATF, *Guidance for a Risk-Based Approach – Money or Value Transfer Services* (FATF, 2016).

[18] FATF, *Money Laundering and Terrorist Financing Vulnerabilities of Commercial Websites and Internet Payment Systems* (FATF, 2008).

[19] See FATF, *Money Laundering and Terrorist Financing Typologies* (n 9)at 63.

[20] House of Commons Treasury Committee, *Economic Crime Eleventh Report of Session 2021–22* (House of Commons Treasury Committee, 2022) at 38. Also see United Nations Office on Drugs and Crime (UNODC), *Estimating Illicit Financial Flows Resulting from Drug Trafficking and other Transnational Organized Crime* (UNODC, 2009).

[21] International Monetary Fund, 'Money Laundering: The Importance of International Countermeasures – Address by Michel Camdessus' (10 February 1998), available at www.imf.org/en/News/Articles/2015/09/28/04/53/sp021098. For a more detailed discussion of attempts to calculate the amount of money laundered, see J Walker, 'Estimates of the Extent of Money Laundering in and through Australia', paper prepared for the Australian Transaction Reports and Analysis Centre, John Walker Consulting Services, Queanbeyan, Australia (September 1995) and J Walker and B Unger, 'Measuring Global Money Laundering: The Walker Gravity Model' (2009) *Review of Law and Economics* 5(2), 821–853.

[22] There are traditionally two approaches towards calculating the extent of money laundering. The first is based upon assumption from macro-economic data and secondly the financial information made available by AML agencies. See J Harvey, 'Compliance and Reporting Issues Arising for Financial Institutions from Money Laundering Regulations: A Preliminary Cost Benefit Study' (2004) *Journal of Money Laundering Control* 7(4), 333–46, at 333.

[23] FATF, 'Frequently asked Questions – What is Money Laundering?' (n/d), available at www.fatf-gafi.org/en/pages/frequently-asked-questions.html#tabs-36503a8663-item-6ff811783c-tab.

[24] See, eg, M Levi, 'Following the Criminal and Terrorist Money Trails' in P van Duyne, K Von Lampe and J Newell, *Criminal Finances and Organising Crime in Europe* (Wolf Legal Publishers, 2003) 105–22.

[25] See, eg, Financial Conduct Authority (FCA), *Assessing and Reducing the Risk of Money Laundering Through the Markets* (FCA, 2025).

[26] See, eg, example J Simser, 'Money Laundering: Emerging Threats and Trends' (2012) *Journal of Money Laundering Control* 16(1), 41–54.

[27] See, eg, FATF, *Money Laundering from Fentanyl and Synthetic Opioids* (FATF, 2022).

of the 'War on Drugs'[28] and the introduction of anti-money laundering (AML) measures by the United Nations,[29] the European Union (EU) and FATF.[30]

The most commonly used mechanism to combat money laundering are the CDD obligations, the use of DAML SARs and sharing of data.[31] These mechanisms aim to provide the UKFIU and Law Enforcement Agencies (LEAs) with important financial intelligence which might not otherwise be visible. One of the FATF's key findings in the 2018 MER was that 'co-operation and co-ordination between agencies on AML issues is a strength of the UK system'.[32] The UK was rated 'Compliant' with Recommendations 2, 30 and 31, which require national coordination and cooperation, including the exchange of information, between LEAs.[33] The UK was also considered to have 'Moderate' to 'High' levels of effectiveness to Immediate Outcomes 1 and 6, concerning risk, policy and coordination, and financial intelligence, as well as Immediate Outcomes 7 and 9, concerning effective money laundering and terrorist financing investigations. This chapter challenges these conclusions by using three case studies that demonstrate shortcomings in the UK's CDD mechanisms, the use of DAML SARs and in the ability to ensure the exchange of information.[34]

III. Customer Due Diligence

The CDD rules are contained in the Money Laundering Regulations 2017 and supported by POCA.[35] Part 7 of POCA establishes the core money-laundering offences of concealing, disguising, converting, transferring or removing criminal property and overlays them with reporting duties for regulated firms and individuals in scope of the Money Laundering Regulations.[36] The Regulations adopt and layer in a risk-based framework for prevention, mandating CDD and ongoing monitoring as primary defences against the laundering of illicit funds and the financing of terrorism. A member of the regulated sector is required to conduct CDD when a new business relationship is established, where there is suspected money laundering or terrorist financing, there is doubt surrounding

[28] See generally P Alldridge, 'Money Laundering and Globalization' (2008) *Journal of Law and Society* 35(4), 437–63.

[29] See chapter two.

[30] See FATF, *FATF 40 Recommendations* (FATF, 2003) and FATF, *FATF IX Special Recommendations* (FATF, 2001).

[31] See chapter one at sections III and IV.

[32] FATF, *Anti-Money Laundering and Counter-Terrorist Financing Measures United Kingdom Mutual Evaluation Report* (FATF, 2018) ('FATF 2018 MER') at 37.

[33] FATF, *International Standards on Combating Money Laundering and the Financing of Terrorism & Proliferation: The FATF Recommendations* (FATF, 2025).

[34] See, eg, U Turksen and E Erken, *Anti-Money Laundering and the Law: Comparative Approaches to Countering Predicate Crimes* (Routledge, 2024).

[35] The Money Laundering, Terrorist Financing and Transfer of Funds (Information on the Payer) Regulations 2017 (SI 2017/692) (hereinafter 'the MLRs').

[36] Proceeds of Crime Act 2002 (POCA), ss 327–29.

the adequacy or veracity of earlier customer information and where the occasional transaction is above the €15 000 threshold (or €10 000 for high-value dealers).[37] These can be described as trigger points to ensure that the customer identity and transaction purpose are scrutinised both at onboarding and at important stages thereafter.

The CDD process comprises three levels. Firstly, simplified due diligence (SDD) applies to low-risk customers and involves only basic identity checks. Secondly, the standard due diligence that covers most customers, requiring full identity verification (name, address, date of birth), a clear understanding of the business relationship and ongoing transaction monitoring. Finally, enhanced due diligence (EDD) is reserved for high-risk situations, such as politically exposed persons, clients from high-risk jurisdictions or unusually large transactions, and demands in-depth background checks, verification of funds and wealth sources, and continuous, more frequent oversight.[38] Separately, POCA imposes statutory obligations to report suspicions of money laundering via DAML SARs,[39] with tipping-off offences for disclosing that a SAR is being considered or has been made.[40]

DAML SARs have faced persistent challenges, despite a plethora of reforms. One of the main criticisms is how difficult it is to navigate for reporters, especially those in the private sector. The quality of DAML SARs remains a longstanding concern, with many reports generally lacking actionable intelligence or sufficient detail. Although legislative changes, such as raising the de minimis threshold, have aimed to reduce unnecessary reporting, confusion still exists around when a DAML is required.[41] Additionally, the burden on LEAs and the UKFIU remains high, with processing delays and inconsistent outcomes contributing to frustration among stakeholders. These inefficiencies are identified and appraised in the next section.

IV. Defence against Money Laundering Suspicious Activity Reports

This subsection of the chapter identifies the mandatory reporting requirements and the number of DAML SARs submitted to the UKFIU. The first AML reporting requirements were contained in the Drug Trafficking Offences Act 1986.[42] It is interesting to note that before this Act, the reporting system was informal and based

[37] See generally HM Government, 'Your Responsibilities under Money Laundering Supervision' (23 May 2025), available at www.gov.uk/guidance/money-laundering-regulations-your-responsibilities.

[38] See generally N Mugarura, 'Customer Due Diligence (CDD) Mandate and the Propensity of its Application as a Global AML Paradigm Available to Purchase' (2014) *Journal of Money Laundering Control* 17(1), 76–95.

[39] POCA ss 330–31.

[40] ibid s 333.

[41] ibid s 339A.

[42] Drug Trafficking Offences Act 1986, s 24(3).

around personal relationships and trust.[43] These were amended by the Criminal Justice Act 1993,[44] which implemented the First Money Laundering Directive (MLD),[45] and introduced the concept of mandatory reporting.[46] The reporting requirements have since been amended by POCA 2002 and the Money Laundering Regulations.

The offence of money laundering is contained within Part 7 of POCA and it applies to money laundering activities on or after 23 February 2003.[47] The Act contains three principal offences. Firstly, concealing, disguising, converting, transferring or removing criminal property from the jurisdiction.[48] Secondly, entering into or becoming concerned in an arrangement knowing or suspecting it to facilitate the acquisition, retention, use or control of criminal property on behalf of another person.[49] Thirdly, acquiring, using or possessing criminal property.[50] It is also an offence to be part of a conspiracy, to attempt to commit, or to counsel, aid, abet or procure any of the above. All three offences can be committed by any person, irrespective of the fact that they work within the regulated sector or undertake a relevant business. Of particular relevance here is the failing to disclose suspicions or knowledge of money laundering.[51] A person does not commit an offence under section 327 if, 'he makes an authorised disclosure under section 338 and (if the disclosure is made before he does the act mentioned in subsection (1)) he has the appropriate consent'.[52] This is known as the consent defence and relates to consent given to the defendant that he can proceed on the basis of the authorised disclosure.[53] An authorised disclosure is 'a disclosure to a constable, a customs officer or a nominated officer by the alleged offender that property is criminal property',[54] with the defence also applying to situations whether the defendant intended to make a disclosure but had a reasonable excuse for not doing so: the reasonable excuse defence. Furthermore, a person does not commit an offence if

> (a) he knows or believes on reasonable grounds, that the relevant criminal conduct occurred in a particular country or territory outside the United Kingdom, and (b) the relevant criminal conduct – (i) was not, at the time it occurred, unlawful under the criminal law then applying in that country or territory, and (ii) is not of a description prescribed by an order made by the Secretary of State.[55]

[43] M Levi and L Gelemerova, 'The Anti-Money Laundering Architecture of the United Kingdom' in B Vogel and J Maillart, *National and International Anti-Money Laundering Law Developing the Architecture of Criminal Justice, Regulation and Data Protection* (Intersentia, 2020) 641–792 at 642.

[44] Criminal Justice Act 1993, s 18.

[45] Directive 91/308/EEC on the Prevention of the Use of the Financial System to Launder Money [1993] OJ L166/ 27.

[46] See generally M Kemal, 'Anti-Money Laundering Regulations and its Effectiveness' (2014) *Journal of Money Laundering Control* 17(4), 416–27.

[47] R Forston, 'Money Laundering Offences under POCA 2002' in W Blair and R Brent (eds), *Banks and Financial Crime – The International Law of Tainted Money* (Oxford University Press, 2010) at 157.

[48] POCA s 327.

[49] ibid s 328.

[50] ibid s 329.

[51] ibid s 330.

[52] ibid s 327(2).

[53] See *Hosni Tayeb v HSBC Bank Plc* [2004] EWHC 1529.

[54] POCA s 338(1).

[55] ibid s 327(2A).

Finally and applying only to deposit-taking institutions, a body does not commit an offence if 'a) it does the act in operating an account maintained with it, and b) the value of the criminal property concerned is less than the threshold amount determined under s. 339A for the act'.[56]

Additionally, section 329 provides the adequate consideration defence. This covers those people who have accepted dirty money for ordinary consumable goods and/or services. In such cases, the person receiving the money is not obliged to question the source of it.[57] It can also be relied upon by professional advisors who have received money for or on account of costs (unless it is a gross overpayment of the services given), but will not apply if the defendant knows or suspects that the payment will help another to carry out criminal conduct. If this is the case the person is treated as not having paid proper consideration.[58] Employees working within the regulated sector may also have a defence if they can prove that they have received inadequate training from their employers on matters of money laundering and/or their requirements to disclose.[59]

DAML SARs have been subjected to criticism due to their inefficiency and lack of clarity, often overwhelming the UKFIU with low-quality or overly cautious submissions. The threshold for suspicion is vague, leading to inconsistent reporting thus potentially undermining their effectiveness in targeting serious financial crime. The next section of the chapter appraises DAML SARs.

V. Defensive SARs Reporting

The defensive reporting of SARs occurs when a regulated firm submits a DAML SAR to protect itself from regulatory criticism or legal liability rather than because of a genuine suspicion of money laundering. In practice, this means filing reports 'just in case' to avoid potential scrutiny, even when the underlying suspicion is weak or speculative. The Law Commission noted that individuals in the regulated sector often engage in defensive reporting out of fear of personal criminal liability if they fail to report a transaction that later proves illicit.[60] Reporting entitles and their employees face several factors that feed defensive reporting. The expansive definition of 'criminal property' under POCA leaves room for interpretation, prompting firms to err on the side of reporting to avoid ambiguity.[61] Compliance

[56] ibid s 327(2C).

[57] ibid s 329(2)(c). Adequate consideration is defined by POCA as 'a person acquires property for inadequate consideration if the value of the consideration is significantly less that the value of the property'. Therefore, adequate consideration could equate to the market value of the goods, depending on condition, eg new or second-hand. See ibid s 329(3)(a).

[58] Crown Prosecution Service, 'Proceeds of Crime Act 2002 Part 7 – Money Laundering Offences', available at www.cps.gov.uk/prosecution-guidance/money-laundering-offences.

[59] POCA, s 330.

[60] See Law Commission 2018 Report (n 3). Also see Home Office and HM Treasury, *Joint Home Office and HM Treasury Action Plan for Anti-Money Laundering and Counter-Terrorist Finance* (Home Office and HM Treasury, 2016) at 39.

[61] POCA, s 340. See also Z Hamin, W Rosalili, W Rosli, N Omar, A Armadajaya and P Mahmud, 'Configuring Criminal Proceeds in Money Laundering Cases in the UK' (2014) *Journal of Money*

officers can face fines or even prosecution for failing to file a SAR if suspicious activity is later uncovered, which can incentivise over-reporting as a protective measure.[62] The regulated sector and Designated Non-Financial Businesses and Professions are required to report any allegations of money laundering to the UKFIU.[63] The Regulations apply to a wide range of financial institutions, including credit institutions, financial institutions, auditors, insolvency practitioners, external accountants, tax advisors, independent legal professionals, trust or company service providers, estate agents, high-value dealers and casinos.[64]

If a reporting entity suspects that it is being used for the purposes of money laundering, it is required to notify its Money Laundering Reporting Officer (MLRO), who must then compile an DAML SAR and file it with the UKFIU, which determines if further action is necessary. DAML SARs act as a 'warning' or 'alert' system to LEAs and act as a 'vital source of intelligence not only on economic crime but on a wide range of criminal activity'.[65] For example, DAML SARs have been used to find sex offenders, murder suspects, human trafficking victims and detecting fraud committed by OCGs.[66] Therefore, the regime provides the 'most significant intelligence available'.[67] A DAML SAR can be 'used multiple times by different users for different purposes'.[68] For example, 'the information within a SAR may inform HM Revenue & Customs about taxation, local police about fraud or theft'.[69] Nonetheless, the SARs regime does have 'other impacts [that] cannot be ignored'.[70] For example, UK Finance reported that there were 48.1billion payment transactions in 2023,[71] all of which need to be monitored for money laundering.[72] Indeed, the Law Commission reported that UK financial institutions 'investigate approximately 20 million alerts which are produced by automated response systems calibrated to flag unusual activity'.[73] The alerts when combined with defensive reporting,[74] increased compliance costs and the low reporting threshold have resulted in an increase

Laundering Control 17(4), 374–84 and R Fortson, 'Money Laundering Offences under POCA 2002' in W Blair, R Brent and T Grant (eds), *Banks and Financial Crime: The International Law of Tainted Money* (Oxford University Press, 2017).

[62] See Kebbell (n 13) at 890.

[63] The National Crime Agency (NCA) was established by virtue of the Crime and Courts Act 2013, s 1.

[64] See POCO, sch 9 and the MLRs, reg 12.

[65] NCA, 'Suspicious Activity Reports' (n/d), available at https://www.nationalcrimeagency.gov.uk/what-we-do/crime-threats/money-laundering-and-illicit-finance/suspicious-activity-reports.

[66] ibid.

[67] NCA, *SARs in Action – Issue 1* (NCA, 2019) at 4.

[68] NCA, 'Suspicious Activity Reports' (n 65).

[69] ibid.

[70] Law Commission 2018 Report (n 3) at 59.

[71] UK Finance, *UK Payment Market Summary* (UK Finance, 2024) at 6.

[72] Law Commission 2018 Report (n 3) at 59.

[73] ibid.

[74] See A Leong, 'Chasing Dirty Money: Domestic and International Measures against Money Laundering' (2007) *Journal of Money Laundering Control* 10(2), 140–56, at 142 and M Goldby, 'Anti-Money Laundering Reporting Requirements Imposed by English Law: Measuring Effectiveness and Gauging the Need for Reform' (2013) *Journal of Business Law* 4, 367–97 at 368.

in the submission of DAML SARs to the UKFIU.[75] In his evidence to the HM Treasury Select Committee, Graeme Biggar, the then Director-General at the National Economic Crime Centre (NECC), stated: '20 years ago, we got 20,000 suspicious activity reports in … this is year, we will [receive] … three quarters of a million … the sheer volume coming through is really significant and very hard to deal with'.[76] The trend remained upwards, as Table 1 demonstrates:

Table 1 Number of SARs Submitted to either UKFIU (2010–2023)

YEAR	NUMBER OF SARS SUBMITTED
APRIL 2009 – MARCH 2010	240,582[77]
APRIL 2010 – MARCH 2011	247,601[78]
APRIL 2011 – MARCH 2012	278,665[79]
APRIL 2012 – MARCH 2013	316,527[80]
APRIL 2013 – MARCH 2014	354,186[81]
APRIL 2014 – MARCH 2015	381,882[82]
APRIL 2016 – MARCH 2017	634,113[83]
APRIL 2017 – MARCH 2018	463,938[84]
APRIL 2019 – MARCH 2019	478,437[85]
APRIL 2019 – MARCH 2020	573,085[86]
APRIL 2020 – MARCH 2021	742,317[87]
APRIL 2021 – MARCH 2022	901,255[88]
APRIL 2022 – MARCH 2023	859,905[89]
2023–2024	872,048[90]

The surge in DAML SARs submitted to the UKFIU illustrates an escalation in defensive reporting, where firms file DAML SARs not necessarily due to genuine

[75] See Law Commission 2018 Report (n 3) at 59 and 68.

[76] Treasury Committee, 'Oral Evidence: Economic Crime, HC 917' (Monday 25 January 2021, Graeme Bigger), available at committees.parliament.uk/oralevidence/1571/pdf/.

[77] Serious Organised Crime Agency (SOCA), *The Suspicious Activity Reports Regime Annual Report 2010* (SOCA, 2010) at 4.

[78] SOCA, *The Suspicious Activity Reports Regime Annual Report 2011* (SOCA, 2011) at 10.

[79] SOCA, *The Suspicious Activity Reports Regime Annual Report 2012* (SOCA, 2012) at 12.

[80] National Crime Agency (NCA), *The Suspicious Activity Reports Regime Annual Report 2013* (NCA, 2013) at 6.

[81] NCA, *The Suspicious Activity Reports Regime Annual Report 2014* (NCA, 2014) at 7.

[82] NCA, *The Suspicious Activity Reports Regime Annual Report 2015* (NCA, 2015) at 7.

[83] NCA, *SARs Annual Report 2017* (NCA, 2017) at 6. There was no report for 2015–2016.

[84] NCA, *SARs Annual Report 2018* (NCA, 2018) at 3.

[85] NCA, *SARs Annual Report 2019* (NCA, 2019) at 4.

[86] NCA, *SARs Annual Report 2020* (NCA, 2020) at 4.

[87] NCA, *Suspicious Activity Report 2022* (NCA, 2023) at 4.

[88] ibid.

[89] ibid.

[90] NCA, *Suspicious Activity Report 2024* (NCA, 2025) at 3.

suspicion, but to protect themselves from regulatory scrutiny. This practice, driven by fear of non-compliance penalties and vague legal thresholds, often results in low-quality reports that overwhelm the system without adding meaningful intelligence. The next subsection explores how this climate of caution is amplified by the Financial Conduct Authority's (FCA) increasingly assertive enforcement activity. With a strategic focus on impactful deterrence, the FCA's stance has created a 'fear factor' among regulated entities, prompting over-reporting and risk-averse behaviour that may hinder rather than help effective financial crime prevention.

A. Fear Factor

Failure to comply with the AML reporting obligations and the penalties and consequences that can be inflicted has created a 'fear factor', which in turn has prompted an increase in the number of DAML SARs submitted to the UKFIU. Indeed, the Law Commission observed that 'reporters and nominated officers told us that their fears of individual criminal liability often overrode rational judgement in deciding whether or not to make a disclosure'.[91] The fear factor is driven by an enforcement strategy adopted by the FCA and its predecessor the Financial Services Authority (FSA).[92] The regulator has a wide range of enforcement powers (criminal, civil and regulatory) which can be used against firms and individuals who do not achieve the regulatory standards.[93] Specifically, the regulator can impose financial penalties,[94] prohibit individuals from undertaking regulated activities,[95] public censure[96] and prosecution.[97] The FCA has favoured imposing financial penalties on the regulated sector and individuals as opposed to criminal prosecutions.[98] Further examples of fines imposed by the FCA are outlined in Table 2.

Table 2 Fines Imposed by the FSA/FCA between 2013–2024

Year	Company	Amount (£)
2013	Prudential Assurance Company Ltd[99]	474.23million
2014	HSBC[100]	1.47billion

(continued)

[91] Law Commission 2019 Report (n 3) at 91.

[92] See generally T McDermott, 'Enforcement and Credible Deterrence in the FCA' (18 June 2013), available at www.fca.org.uk/publication/news/enforcement-credible-deterrence-speech.pdf.

[93] FCA, 'Enforcement' (21 April 2016), available at www.fca.org.uk/news/news-stories/2016-fines.

[94] Financial Services and Markets Act 2000, s 206(1).

[95] ibid s 56.

[96] ibid s 87M.

[97] ibid s 402.

[98] Financial Services Authority (FSA), 'Delivering Credible Deterrence' (27 April 2009), available at www.fsa.gov.uk/library/communication/speeches/2009/0427_mc.shtml.

[99] Financial Conduct Authority (FCA), '2013 Fines', available at www.fca.org.uk/news/news-stories/2013-fines.

[100] FCA, '2014 Fines', available at www.fca.org.uk/news/news-stories/2014-fines.

Table 2 ***(Continued)***

Year	Company	Amount (£)
2015	Barclays Bank Plc[101]	905,219,078
2016	Millburn Insurance Company Ltd[102]	22.2million
2017	Merrill Lynch International[103]	229.5million
2018	Santander UK Plc[104]	60.47million
2019	Goldman Sachs[105]	392.3million
2020	Commerzbank AG[106]	192.57million
2021	HSBC Bank[107]	63.9million
2021	NatWest Bank[108]	264.8million
2021	Sunrise Brokers LLP[109]	642,000
2021	Santander UK Plc[110]	107.7million
2022	Gatehouse Bank Plc[111]	1.5million
2022	Ghana International Bank Plc[112]	5.8million
2022	Al Rayan Bank Plc[113]	4.02million
2023	Guaranty Trust Bank (UK) Ltd[114]	7.67million

(continued)

[101] FCA, '2015 Fines', available at www.fca.org.uk/news/news-stories/2015-fines.
[102] FCA, '2016 Fines', available at www.fca.org.uk/news/news-stories/2016-fines.
[103] FCA, '2017 Fines', available at www.fca.org.uk/news/news-stories/2017-fines.
[104] FCA, '2018 Fines', available at www.fca.org.uk/news/news-stories/2018-fines.
[105] FCA, '2019 Fines', available at www.fca.org.uk/news/news-stories/2019-fines.
[106] FCA, '2020 Fines', available at www.fca.org.uk/news/news-stories/2020-fines.
[107] FCA, 'FCA Fines HSBC Bank plc £63.9 million for Deficient Transaction Monitoring Controls' (17 December 2021), available at www.fca.org.uk/news/press-releases/fca-fines-hsbc-bank-plc-deficient-transaction-monitoring-controls.
[108] FCA, 'NatWest Fined £264.8 million for Anti-Money Laundering Failures' (17 December 2021), available at www.fca.org.uk/news/press-releases/natwest-fined-264.8million-anti-money-laundering-failures#:~:text=NatWest%20fined%20%C2%A3264.8%20million%20for%20anti%2Dmoney%20laundering%20failures%20%7C%20FCA.
[109] FCA, 'FCA Fines Sunrise Brokers LLP £642,400 for Serious Financial Crime Control Failings in Relation to Cum-ex Trading' (12 November 2021), available at ca.org.uk/news/press-releases/sunrise-brokers-llp-fine-serious-financial-crime-control-failings.
[110] FCA, 'FCA Fines Santander UK £107.7 million for Repeated Anti-Money Laundering Failures' (9 December 2022), available at www.fca.org.uk/news/press-releases/fca-fines-santander-uk-repeated-anti-money-laundering-failures.
[111] FCA, 'FCA Fines Gatehouse Bank £1.5 million for Poor Anti-Money Laundering Checks' (14 October 2022), available at www.fca.org.uk/news/press-releases/fca-fines-gatehouse-bank-1.5m-poor-anti-money-laundering-checks.
[112] FCA, 'FCA Fines Ghana International Bank Plc £5.8m for Failings in its Anti-Money Laundering Controls' (23 June 2022), available at www.fca.org.uk/news/press-releases/fca-fines-ghana-international-bank-5.8m-failings-aml-controls.
[113] FCA, 'FCA Penalises Al Rayan Bank PLC for Anti-Money Laundering Failures' (11 January 2023), available at www.fca.org.uk/news/press-releases/fca-penalises-al-rayan-bank-plc-anti-money-laundering-failures.
[114] FCA, 'FCA Fines Guaranty Trust Bank (UK) Limited £7.6 million for Further Failures in its Anti-Money Laundering Systems and Controls' (10 January 2023), available at www.fca.org.uk/news/press-releases/fca-fines-guaranty-trust-bank-uk-limited-ps76-million-further-failures-its-anti-money-laundering.

Table 2 ***(Continued)***

Year	Company	Amount (£)
2024	Metro Bank Plc[115]	16.67m
2025	Monzo[116]	21million
2025	Barclays Bank UK Plc and Barclays Bank Plc[117]	42million

However, where the financial penalty is imposed on the individual, frequently an MLRO, it can have 'longer-lasting consequences … [and have a] greater deterrent effect'.[118] Financial penalties have been imposed 'regardless of whether the breach has resulted in actual harm to customers'.[119] For example, Michael Wheelhouse the MLRO of Sindicatum Holdings Limited was fined £17,500 for 'not having adequate AML systems and controls in place for verifying and recording clients' identities'.[120] In May 2010, Alpari (UK) Ltd was fined £140,000 for failing to have adequate AML systems and controls and £14,000 on its former MLRO, Sudipto Chattopadhyay, who failed to widen the firm's AML compliance levels after its customers increased from 400 to 11,000.[121] Habib Bank AG Zurich was fined £525,000 and its MLRO, Syed Itrat Hussainn, £17,500 for a 'failure to take reasonable care to establish and maintain adequate anti-money laundering systems and controls'.[122] In 2016, the FCA fined Sonali Bank (UK) Limited £3.25m, its MLRO Stephen Smith, £17,900 and prohibited him from 'performing the MLRO or compliance oversight functions at regulated firms'.[123] More recently, the FCA imposed a financial penalty of £632,594 on David Brian Price (former executive director and MLRO).[124]

[115] FCA, 'FCA Fines Metro Bank £16m for Financial Crime Failings' (12 November 2024), available at www.fca.org.uk/news/press-releases/fca-fines-metro-bank-16m-financial-crime-failings.

[116] FCA, 'FCA Fines Monzo £21m for Failings in Financial Crime Controls' (8 July 2025), available at www.fca.org.uk/news/press-releases/fca-fines-monzo-21m-failings-financial-crime-controls.

[117] FCA, 'FCA Fines Barclays £42 million for Poor Handling of Financial Crime Risks' (17 July 2025), available at www.fca.org.uk/news/press-releases/fca-fines-barclays-42-million-poor-handling-financial-crime-risks.

[118] See R Peat and I Mason, 'Credible Deterrence in Action: The FSA Brings a Series of Cases against Traders' (2009) *Company Lawyer* 30(9), 278–79, at 278.

[119] See A Lewis, R Pretorius and E Radmore, 'Outsourcing in the Financial Services Sector' (2013) *Compliance Officer Bulletin* 106, 1–34, at 3.

[120] FSA, 'FSA Fines Firm and MLRO for Money Laundering Controls Failings' (29 October 2009), available at www.fsa.gov.uk/pages/library/communication/pr/2008/125.shtml.

[121] FSA, 'FSA Fines Alpari and its Former Money Laundering Reporting Officer, Sudipto Chattopadhyay for Anti-Money Laundering Failings' (5 May 2010), available at www.fsa.gov.uk/pages/library/communication/pr/2010/077.shtml.

[122] FSA, 'FSA Fines Habib Bank AG Zurich £525,000 and Money Laundering Reporting Officer £17,500 for Anti-Money Laundering Control Failings' (15 May 2012), available at www.fsa.gov.uk/library/communication/pr/2012/055.shtml.

[123] FCA, 'FCA Imposes Penalties on Sonali Bank (UK) Limited and its Former Money Laundering Reporting Officer for Serious Anti-Money Laundering Systems Failings' (12 October 2016), availableatwww.fca.org.uk/news/press-releases/fca-imposes-penalties-sonali-bank-uk-limited-money-laundering.

[124] FCA, 'Two Individuals Face Bans and £1.3m Fine for Pension Transfer Advice Failings' (1 September 2023), available at www.fca.org.uk/news/press-releases/two-individuals-face-bans-and-1m-fine-pension-transfer-advice-failings.

The threat of personal liability has contributed towards an increase in the submission of DAML SARs and MLROs have erred on the side of over-reporting. The FCA's Decision Procedure and Penalties Manual outlines the factors it considers when fining individuals and when these are applied to MLROs, the FCA has transformed what was once a firm-level risk into personal liability for senior compliance officers.[125] Therefore, the FCA has increasingly imposed sanctions directly on MLROs shifting from firm-level to personal accountability by levying fines and bans intended to deter negligence and strengthen AML controls.

B. Increased Compliance Costs

Defensive reporting is a costly consequence of regulatory pressure, particularly as reporting entities seek to protect themselves from potential enforcement action. In an environment where the threshold for suspicion is low and unclear and the consequences of under-reporting are severe; institutions err on the side of caution which has resulted in a large volume of DAML SARS being submitted to the UKFIU. This risk-averse approach inflates compliance costs as firms invest heavily in staff training. Rather than enhancing the quality of financial crime detection, this trend diverts resources toward process and protection, undermining the efficiency and effectiveness of AML efforts.[126] In 2004, the British Bankers Association, now UK Finance, claimed that its members spent £250million per year to comply with the reporting obligations.[127] In 2013 KPMG reported that the regulated sector's estimated compliance costs had increased by 53 per cent.[128] In June 2021, LexisNexis Risk Solutions reported that annual AML compliance costs in the UK was £28.7billion and this would increase to £30billion by 2023.[129] In 2024, PWC noted that financial institutions had reported a 65 per cent increase in AML/counter-terrorist financing (CTF) compliance costs.[130] The Institute of Economic Affairs reported that the figure was £34billion.[131] The cost of AML compliance in the UK has increased, with reporting entities collectively spending over £35billion a year. It has been suggested that on average, firms now invest over

[125] The factors include the nature, seriousness, and duration of the breach; benefits gained or losses avoided; impact on consumers, market orderliness, and financial-crime risks; level of cooperation and remedial action taken; and an individual's disciplinary history and compliance-culture track record. See FCA, *The Decision Procedure and Penalties Manual* (FCA, 2025) at DEPP 6.

[126] Home Office, *Report on the Operation in 2004 of the Terrorism Act 2000* (Home Office, 2004) at 19–20.

[127] ibid.

[128] KPMG, 'Global Anti-Money Laundering Survey' (2014), available at www.kpmg.com/KY/en/IssuesAndInsights/ArticlesPublications/PublishingImages/global-anti-money-laundering-survey-v3.pdf.

[129] LexisNexis Risk Solutions, *Cutting the Costs of AML Compliance* (LexisNexis Risk Solutions, 2021).

[130] PwC, *PwC EMEA AML Survey 2024 – UK Insights into Effectiveness* (PwC, 2024) at 2.

[131] Institute of Economic Affairs, *Debanked – The Economic and Social Consequences of Anti-Money Laundering Regulation* (Institute of Economic Affairs, 2024) at 6.

£21,000 every year just to meet AML requirements.[132] The largest financial institutions allocate between £300million annually to AML programmes,[133] with the average AML compliance costing £186.5million.[134]

In 2004 HM Treasury asserted that one of the important aims of its then AML policy was to ensure that compliance costs were proportionate.[135] The evidence suggests that this is not the case. HM Government 'recognises that requirements under the Money Laundering Regulations … [can] create costs and burdens which can be significant'.[136] In 2024, HM Treasury published a consultation paper aimed at improving the effectiveness of the Regulations.[137] The consultation paper, which forms part of the Economic Crime Plan II and builds on the 2022 Review of the UK's AML and CTF Regime, seeks to improve the Regulations by closing loopholes and minimising burdens. The consultation concentrated on four themes – making CDD more proportionate and effective; strengthening system co-ordination; providing clarity on the scope of the Regulations and reforming requirements for Trust Registration Service.[138] In conjunction with the consultation paper, HM Treasury commissioned a survey on the costs of compliance with the Money Laundering Regulations. In July 2025, HM Treasury published its response to the consultation paper which contained measures to close loopholes, improve risk-based CDD, improve coordination among AML agencies and LEAs, clarify scope and registration duties (including for crypto-asset service providers), and enhance the accuracy and timeliness of trust beneficial-ownership data through Trust Registration Service improvements. Specifically, the response included measures aimed at proportionate CDD thresholds, simplified processes for low-risk clients, reinforced information-sharing protocols, refined definitions to remove ambiguity, digital registration levers for Small and Medium-Sized Enterprises (SMEs), automated trustee reminders and verification steps, and technical amendments to align with sanction regimes and FATF standards.[139] The response proposes clearer thresholds for both SDD and EDD, ensuring that firms concentrate resources on higher-risk transactions and relationships. The response illustrates the commitment to joint guidance, co-developed with supervisors and law enforcement, to promote a consistent, risk-based approach across sectors. The UK is 'Largely Compliant' according to the rating provided by FATF Recommendation 10 on CDD, but by tightening thresholds, clarifying beneficial ownership requirements,

[132] LexisNexis Risk Solutions, *True Costs of Financial Crime Compliance* (LexisNexis Risk Solutions, 2024) at 3.

[133] LexisNexis Risk Solutions, *Cutting the Costs* (n 129) at 3.

[134] ibid.

[135] HM Treasury, *Anti-Money Laundering Strategy* (HM Treasury, 2004) at 25.

[136] HM Treasury, *Review of the UK's AML/CFT Regulatory and Supervisory Regime* (HM Treasury, 2022) at 19.

[137] HM Treasury, *Improving the Effectiveness of the Money Laundering Regulations Consultation* (HM Treasury, 2024).

[138] This is part of a wider programme aimed at reducing money laundering as outlined in the Economic Crime Plan 2023–2026. See HM Government and UK Finance, *Economic Crime Plan 2 2023–2026* (HM Government and UK Finance, 2023).

[139] HM Treasury, *Improving the Effectiveness of the Money Laundering Regulations Consultation Response* (HM Treasury, 2025).

and reinforcing EDD on higher-risk relationships, the proposed changes could improve the UK's rating. If enacted and enforced, they could elevate the UK's standing to 'Compliant' with Recommendation 10.

C. Interpretation of Suspicion

The interpretation of suspicion in the context of money laundering reporting is a challenge for the regulated sector. The legal threshold provides a low bar and it intended to promote vigilance; it creates ambiguity for compliance professionals who must decide whether a transaction warrants the submission of a DAML SAR. The lack of clear guidance can lead to over-reporting to the UKFIU which burdens them with poor intelligence but also inflates compliance costs and diverts resources from more targeted financial crime prevention efforts. The uncertainty of the definition of the concept of suspicion has been 'recognised to be a problem for some time'.[140] The Law Commission added that 'a majority of stakeholders expressed the view that suspicion remains ill-defined, unclear and inconsistently applied'.[141] There is no UK statutory definition of suspicion, none is provided by the FATF Recommendations or any of the MLDs and it has been left 'to the courts to interpret this and other suspicion-based tests'.[142] The interpretation of suspicion in *R v Da Silva* has been commonly used by the judiciary and is regarded as a 'guiding principle by those with reporting obligations'.[143] Here, the Court of Appeal deliberated the interpretation of suspicion under the Criminal Justice Act 1988.[144] The Court noted that:

> What then does the word 'suspecting' mean in its particular context in the 1988 Act? It seems to us that the essential element in the word 'suspect' and its affiliates, in this context, is that the defendant must think that there is a possibility, which is more than fanciful, that the relevant facts exist. A vague feeling of unease would not suffice. But the statute does not require the suspicion to be 'clear' or 'firmly grounded and targeted on specific facts' or based upon 'reasonable grounds'.[145]

Furthermore, Lord Hope in *R v Sail (Abdulrahman)* stated:

> … the assumption is that the person has a suspicion, otherwise he would not be thinking of doing what the statute contemplates. The objective test is introduced in the interest of fairness, to ensure that the suspicion has a reasonable basis for it. The subjective

[140] See Law Commission 2018 Report (n 3) at 72. Also see S Lander, *Review of the Suspicious Activity Reports Regime* (Serious Organised Crime Agency, 2006) at 53–54.

[141] ibid at 63. Also see *Joint Home Office and HM Treasury Action Plan* (n 60) at 39.

[142] See Law Commission 2018 Report (n 3) at 71.

[143] *R v Da Silva* [2006] EWCA Crim 1654, [2007] 1 WLR 303. The House of Lords recommended that as a general principle, the meaning of an ordinary word of the English language is not a question of law. See *Brutus v Cozens* (1972) 56 Cr App R 799 at 804. Here, the House of Lords endorsed a general principle of statutory interpretation in criminal law that the meaning of an ordinary word of the English language is not a question of law.

[144] Criminal Justice Act 1988, s 93A(1)(a).

[145] *R v Da Silva* [2006] EWCA Crim 1654, [2006] 2 Cr App R 35.

> test – actual suspicion – is not enough. The objective test – that there were reasonable grounds for it – must be satisfied too.[146]

Moreover, according to the Court of Appeal in *K v National Westminster Bank, HMRC, SOCA*,[147] the interpretation of suspicion is the same in civil law as it is in criminal law. Applying case law, we therefore have what is often referred to as the 'more than fanciful possibility test'.[148] In *Hussien v Chong Fook Kam*, the Court offered the 'ordinary meaning' of suspicion as 'a state of conjecture or surmise where proof is lacking: I suspect but I cannot prove'.[149] The Law Commission concluded that the threshold of suspicion has contributed towards the submission of a large number of DAML SARS.[150] Specifically, the Law Commission noted that the money laundering offences under POCA 2002 create a 'low threshold for criminality', which means that once a reporter has the 'suspicion that property is criminal in origin, they are at risk of committing an offence'.[151] In the context of money laundering, suspicion is a state of mind that is more than a human or idle curiosity. The term involves a genuine consideration that there is a possibility, beyond a mere possibility, that illicit activities are taking place.

DAML SARs serve as a vital tool in combating money laundering. However, this section has demonstrated that their effectiveness is compromised. Defensive reporting has inundated the UKFIU with low-quality reports, making it more challenging to identify genuine threats. In an effort to ensure compliance and avoid penalties, reporting entities frequently submit DAML SARs without sufficient scrutiny, prioritising quantity over quality. As shown in Table 1 above, the number of submissions continues to rise, exacerbating the issue of data saturation and limiting the UKFIU's ability to extract actionable intelligence. The deliberately low threshold for suspicion is intended to encourage reporting, yet it often leads to ambiguity. The legal test, which requires suspicion to be 'more than fanciful' but not necessarily certain, creates inconsistencies in reporting. Some institutions err on the side of caution, submitting reports unnecessarily, while others hesitate due to uncertainty. As a result, despite the crucial role of DAML SARs, their impact is diminished by defensive reporting, excessive submissions, and the lack of a clear definition of suspicion. To enhance their effectiveness, regulatory authorities must provide clearer guidance, establish improved mechanisms for filtering relevant

[146] *R v Sail (Abdulrahman)* [2006] UKHL 18, para 52.

[147] *K v National Westminster Bank, HMRC, SOCA* [2006] EWCA Civ 1039.

[148] Financial Services Commission, *Guidance Notes – Systems of Control to Prevent the Financial System from being Used for Money Laundering or Terrorist Financing Activities* (Financial Services Commission, 2011) at 8.1.

[149] *Hussien v Chong Fook Kam* [1970] AC 942, [1970] 2 WLR 441.

[150] See Law Commission 2018 Report (n 3) at 91.

[151] ibid. Also see The Joint Money Laundering Steering Group, *Prevention of Money Laundering/Combating Terrorist Financing – Guidance for the UK Financial Sector* (Joint Money Laundering Steering Group, 2023) at 6.11 ff.

reports, and expand data-sharing opportunities to strengthen the fight against financial crime.

VI. Case Studies

This part of the chapter examines four case studies (the legal profession, financial institutions, AML supervisory agencies and public-private partnerships) to discover challenges in applying CDD rules, conducting risk assessment, the internal reporting of suspicious activity and the exchange of data among supervisory bodies. Understanding these obstacles is crucial for designing targeted reforms and enhancing collaboration among the stakeholders charged with tackling illicit finance.

A. The Legal Profession

This case study is based on 18 instances where firms and/or individuals within the legal profession have failed to follow and implement the AML rules. Of these 18 cases, 13 involved failures to conduct AML risk assessments, three related to breaches of the CDD rules and three where the firm did not verify the source of funds. The total amount of fines levied was £1.045million, averaging £61,473 per case. This section begins by outlining the rationale for selecting the legal profession, before briefly outlining the facts of each case and then providing an overall commentary on the findings of the case study. In particular, the case study identifies common deficiencies that were previously identified by the 2007 and 2018 MERs, thus challenging ratings provided by FATF.

The legal profession provides an interesting opportunity to assess the application of the CDD rules and wider AML reporting obligations because they play an important role in a wide range of financial matters that could be exploited to launder the proceeds of crime.[152] The profession deals with financial transactions that allows them access to confidential financial details that could indicate money laundering risks.[153] Additionally, the legal profession is bound by client confidentiality rules that can limit its ability to submit DAML SARs to the UKFIU. Lawyers may hesitate to file a DAML SARs due to concerns about damaging client relationships or misinterpreting legitimate transactions as suspicious and could be referred to as 'reluctant partners' in the battle against money laundering.[154] Understandably, the legal profession

[152] See NCA, *National Strategic Assessment Serious and Organised Crime* (NCA, 2018) at 39.

[153] See S Schneider, 'Testing the Limits of Solicitor-Client Privilege: Lawyers, Money Laundering, and Suspicious Transaction Reporting' (2006) *Journal of Money Laundering Control* 9(1), 27–47.

[154] See generally Solicitors Regulatory Authority (SRA), 'SRA Code of Conduct for Solicitors, RELs, RFLs and RSLs' (n/d) para 6.3, available www.sra.org.uk/solicitors/standards-regulations/code-conduct-solicitors/; and SRA, 'SRA Code of Conduct for Firms' (n/d), available at www.sra.org.uk/

has submitted a very small number of DAML SARs to the UKFIU. Between April 2022 and March 2024, 859,905 SARs were submitted to the UKFIU,[155] and of these, only 2,526 were from independent legal professionals, 0.29 per cent of the total.[156] Additionally, law firms have not been subjected to the same level of scrutiny or levels of enforcement when compared to financial institutions.[157] The following 17 enforcement actions reveal critical gaps in how legal professionals conduct CDD and risk assessments, setting the stage for a comprehensive analysis of these systemic shortcomings.

i. Duffield Harrison LLP

Duffield Harrison LLP was fined £25,000 by the Solicitors Regulation Authority (SRA) for failing to conduct adequate client risk assessments, policies, controls and procedures, and maintaining proper records.[158] The SRA concluded that the firm did not have a documented AML risk assessment (between June 2017 and December 2019);[159] the firm had failed to create compliant AML policies and it failed to carry out adequate risk assessments for client matters.[160]

ii. Tyndallwoods Solicitors Ltd

Tyndallwoods was fined £27,000 for not having the appropriate AML measures in place over a seven-year period.[161] Here, the SRA determined that the firm did not have 'the required risk assessment and policies, controls and procedures documents' between 2017 and 2024.[162] Consequently, the SRA concluded that the 'conduct showed a disregard for statutory and regulatory obligations and had the

solicitors/standards-regulations/code-conduct-firms/. See also K Helgesson and U Mörth, 'Client Privilege, Compliance and the Rule of Law: Swedish Lawyers and Money Laundering Prevention' (2018) *Crime, Law and Social Change* 69(2), 227–48. A similar point has been made for financial institutions. See G Favarel-Garrigues, T Godefroy and P Lascoumes, 'Reluctant Partners? Banks in the Fight Against Money Laundering and Terrorism Financing in France' (2011) 42 *Security Dialogue* 179, 189.

[155] NCA (n 90) at 7.

[156] ibid.

[157] See generally Benson (n 13) and Kebbell (n 13). For a discussion on financial institutions, see E Takáts, 'A Theory of "Crying Wolf": The Economics of Money Laundering Enforcement' (2011) *The Journal of Law, Economics, & Organization* 27(1), 32–78.

[158] SRA, 'Duffield Harrison LLP' (28 January 2025), available at www.sra.org.uk/consumers/register/organisation/?sraNumber=383068.

[159] See MLRs at reg 18.

[160] J Hyde, 'Four More Firms Hit with SRA Fines for AML Failings' (4 February 2025), available at www.lawgazette.co.uk/news/four-more-firms-hit-with-sra-fines-for-aml-failings/5122240.article.

[161] SRA, 'Tyndallwoods Solicitors Limited' (2 December 2024), available at www.sra.org.uk/consumers/solicitor-check/598368/.

[162] J Hyde, 'Birmingham Firm Fined More than £27,000 for AML Failings' (7 January 2025), available at www.lawgazette.co.uk/news/birmingham-firm-fined-more-than-27000-for-aml-failings/5121938.article.

potential to cause harm, by facilitating dubious transactions that could have led to money laundering'.[163]

iii. Burch Phillips & Co

Burch Phillips & Co was fined £3,740 following an investigation by the SRA,[164] which concluded that the firm had failed to conduct client and matter risk assessments and it did not maintain AML policies, controls, and procedures between August 2018 and August 2024.[165]

iv. Commercial Law Practice

Commercial Law Practice was fined £11,579 by the SRA for breaching the AML rules.[166] Here, the SRA concluded that after conducting a desk-based review, several client files lacked proper risk assessments, the firm had failed to conduct adequate client and matter risk assessments (between October 2011 and March 2024) and it neglected to ascertain the extent of CDD measures (October 2011 and June 2017).[167]

v. Tolhurst Fisher LLP

Tolhurst Fisher LLP paid a fine of £120,000 for AML breaches.[168] The SRA noted that several client files did not contain any risk assessment and no source of funds check had been undertaken.[169] Approximately 70 per cent of the firm's work fell within the scope of the Regulations and focused on conveyancing, which is at high risk of money laundering.[170] The firm admitted that over a decade it had failed

[163] SRA, 'Burch Phillips & Co' (14 January 2025), available at www.sra.org.uk/consumers/solicitor-check/652439/.

[164] ibid.

[165] See MLRs at regs 19 and 28.

[166] SRA, 'Commercial Law Practice' (4 December 2025), available at www.sra.org.uk/consumers/solicitor-check/446707/.

[167] The Money Laundering Regulations 2007 (SI 2007/2157), Regulation 7 and 28.

[168] SRA, 'Tolhurst Fisher LLP' (14 August 2024), available at https://guidance.sra.org.uk/consumers/solicitor-check/463244/.

[169] J Hyde, 'SDT Fines Firm £120k for 15-year Breaches of AML Regulations' (19 May 2025), available at www.lawgazette.co.uk/news/sdt-fines-firm-120k-for-15-year-breaches-of-aml-regulations/5123326.article. The SRA concluded that the firm breached the MLRs.

[170] See SRA, 'OPBAS Confirms that Conveyancing Work is High-Risk' (12 December 2024), available at www.sra.org.uk/sra/news/sra-update-134-opbas-conveyancing/#:~:text=Sector%2Dwide%20impact,through%20robust%20systems%20and%20processes; SRA, 'Annual Report by the Money Laundering Reporting Officer (MLRO) for the Year Ended 5 April 2024' (5 June 2024), available at www.sra.org.uk/globalassets/documents/sra/board-meetings/2024/july/annex-1---mlro-annual-report-ye-april-2024.pdf?version=4a13a7; SRA, 'Risk Assessment Sectoral Risk Assessment – Anti-Money Laundering and Terrorist Financing' (5 March 2025), available at sra.org.uk/pdfcentre/?type=Id&data=697721737; and FCA, *Anti-Money Laundering Supervision by the Legal and Accountancy Professional Body Supervisors: Progress and Themes from our 2023/2024 Supervisory Work* (Financial Conduct Authority, 2024).

to implement the necessary safeguards that were not reviewed or updated, thus breaching Regulation 20.[171]

vi. Batchelor Sharp

Batchelor Sharp was fined £23,035.50 by the SRA for several AML compliance breaches.[172] Following an investigation, the SRA determined that several client files lacked proper risk assessments, and the firm admitted it had not completed any risk assessments prior to March 2023. The SRA concluded that this breach persisted longer than reasonable, demonstrating a pattern of non-compliance.

vii. Simpson Thacher & Bartlett

Simpson Thacher & Bartlett was fined £300,000 for breaches of AML regulations after the SRA concluded that the firm had failed to conduct a firm-wide risk assessment between June 2017 and March 2020. The fine was approved by the Solicitors Disciplinary Tribunal,[173] marking one of the largest penalties for AML compliance failures for the legal profession.

viii. Clyde & Co

Clyde & Co has been fined £500,000 by the Solicitors Disciplinary Tribunal (SDT) for failing to carry out CDD on a corporate client for over four years. The firm admitted to not conducting adequate monitoring or obtaining sufficient due diligence material.[174]

ix. Holden Smith Law

Holden Smith Law Ltd has been fined £36,622 by the SRA for AML failures over a five-year period.[175] The firm failed to conduct client and matter risk assessments over a five-year period, which exposed potential risks by facilitating dubious transactions. The SRA's investigation found that none of the files reviewed contained the required risk assessments, constituting a breach.

[171] See above MLRs at Regulation 20.

[172] SRA, 'Batchelor Sharp' (29 February 2024), available at www.sra.org.uk/consumers/solicitor-check/046711/#:~:text=Batchelor%20Sharp%20was%20directed%20to,for%20longer%20than%20was%20reasonable.

[173] See Solicitors Disciplinary Tribunal (SDT), 'Case No 12639-2024, *Solicitors Regulation Authority Ltd v Simpson Thacher & Bartlett*' (12 March 2025), available at https://solicitorstribunal.org.uk/case/12639/.

[174] J Hyde and B Castro, 'Clyde & Co Fined £500,000 after Admitting Due Diligence Failure' (11 January 2024), available at www.lawgazette.co.uk/news/clyde-fined-500000-after-admitting-due-diligence-failure/5118383.article.

[175] J Hyde, 'Yorkshire Firm Fined £36,000 over Money Laundering Failings' (22 April 2025), available at www.lawgazette.co.uk/news/yorkshire-firm-fined-36000-over-money-laundering-failings/5123049.article.

x. *Burrows*

Burrows was fined £12,989.68 by the SRA for AML compliance failures.[176] The SRA concluded that the firm did not undertake risk assessments and failed to implement compliant policies, controls, and procedures over a five-year period. The SRA's investigation revealed that Burrows failed to carry out client and matter risk assessments on five sampled files, violating the Money Laundering Regulations 2017. The regulator noted that the firm's pattern of non-compliance persisted for nearly six years, heightening the risk of money laundering.

xi. *Fitzpatrick & Co*

Fitzpatrick & Co was fined of £2,376 issued by the SRA. The firm, led by Kolawole Babatunde Idowu, was found to have seven property sales that HM Land Registry initially refused to register due to concerns about identification and verification documents. Additionally, the SRA identified two payments totalling £34,000 that did not relate to an underlying legal transaction, further breaching compliance rules. The regulator categorised the misconduct as 'more serious', with a medium impact/risk of harm.[177]

xii. *Ashfords LLP*

Ashfords LLP was fined £101,357 by the SRA for AML compliance failures.[178] The breaches related to conveyancing transactions, where the firm failed to properly verify the ultimate beneficial owner and source of funds. One transaction involved a UK-registered charity, where the firm did not obtain sufficient documentation regarding a trustee loaning funds for the purchase. Another transaction revealed a potential link to a sanctioned entity, which was only discovered during a retrospective search.

xiii. *Steinbergs Solicitors*

Steinbergs Solicitors was fined £3,778 by the SRA for AML failures.[179] The firm was found to have lacked a firm-wide risk assessment, violating the Money Laundering

[176] Law Society Gazette, 'Revealed: Fines Mount Up as SRA Cracks Down on AML Breaches' (n/d), available at www.lawgazette.co.uk/news/revealed-fines-mount-up-as-sra-cracks-down-on-aml-breaches/5118978.article.

[177] E Tawfick, 'SRA Imposes Fines Exceeding £55,000 for Anti-Money Laundering Breaches' (25 April 2024), available at https://todaysfamilylawyer.co.uk/sra-imposes-fines-exceeding-55000-for-anti-money-laundering-breaches/.

[178] SRA, 'Ashfords LLP' (15 December 2023), available at www.sra.org.uk/consumers/solicitor-check/508761/.

[179] SRA, 'Steinbergs Solicitors' (14 January 2025), available at www.sra.org.uk/consumers/solicitor-check/079406/#:~:text=Steinbergs%20Solicitors%20will%20pay%20a,and%20Disciplinary%20Procedure%20Rules%3B%20and.

Regulations 2017.[180] Additionally, Steinbergs failed to establish and maintain adequate policies, controls, and procedures to mitigate money laundering risks, further breaching Regulation 19.[181]

xiv. Dentons

Dentons faced allegations of breaching AML regulations between 2013 and 2017. The SDT dismissed the charges determining that its failure to conduct adequate AML checks was inadvertent and did not amount to professional misconduct. The SRA appealed and the High Court overturned the SDT's ruling, agreeing with the SRA that Dentons had indeed failed to comply with AML regulations.[182]

xv. Gordons Partnership

Gordons Partnership was fined £77,784 for failing to comply with the Money Laundering Regulations.[183] The firm did not complete appropriate client and matter risk assessments on six files, it failed to maintain fully compliant policies, controls, and procedures, and did not conduct an independent audit[184] strategy, drawing comparison to the case discussed in the next study.

xvi. Amphlett Lissimore Bagshaws LLP

Amphlett Lissimore Bagshaws LLP was fined £114,006 by the SRA on 28 July 2025 for AML failings. The firm failed to maintain fully compliant policies, controls and procedures from December 2019 to March 2024 and neglected to conduct required client and matter risk assessments between December 2019 and January 2024.[185]

xvii. Taylor Vinters LLP

Taylor Vinters LLP was fined £172,934 by the SRA in July 2025 after it failed to identify that it was acting for a non-domestic politically exposed person (PEP) in a 2017 UK residential property purchase and provided another law firm with

[180] The SRA concluded that the firm breached Regulation 18 of the MLRs.

[181] The SRA concluded that the firm breached Regulation 19 of the MLRs.

[182] *Solicitors Regulation Authority Limited v Dentons UK and Middle East LLP* [2025] EWHC 535 (Admin).

[183] J Hyde, 'Compliance Officers Overwhelmed as SRA Dishes out £77K Fine' (4 June 2025), available at www.lawgazette.co.uk/news/compliance-officers-overwhelmed-as-sra-dishes-out-77k-fine/5123465.article.

[184] SRA, 'Gordons Partnership' (27 May 2025), available at www.sra.org.uk/consumers/register/organisation/?sraNumber=800769.

[185] SRA, 'Amphlett Lissimore Bagshaws LLP' (28 July 2025), available at www.sra.org.uk/consumers/solicitor-check/554555/.

inaccurate assurances that the buyer was not a PEP.[186] The Money Laundering Regulations 2007 stipulate that firms should have obtained senior management approval, verified the source of the PEP's wealth and funds, and conducted enhanced ongoing monitoring, but it did not identify the client as a PEP until two months after completion, thereby breaching Regulation 14(4).[187]

xviii. Taylor Fordyce

Rory Peter Heddle Fordyce, a director and compliance officer at Winchester-based firm Taylor Fordyce, was fined £32,500 by the SDT for several AML breaches. Between 2013 and 2015, he failed to conduct proper AML checks on Anar Mahmudov, the son of Azerbaijan's former national security minister, receiving two high-value transfers of £1.1 million and nearly £1.95 million into the firm's client account without verifying the source of wealth. He also admitted using that client account as his personal banking facility, with over £638,000 of personal payments passing through over eight years.[188]

xix. J R Jones Solicitors

J R Jones Solicitors agreed a regulatory settlement with the SRA after admitting several AML failures. Over a six-year period the firm failed to apply CDD, it did not undertake client and matter risk assessments and failed to implement compliant AML policies, controls and procedures to mitigate money-laundering risks. Under Rule 3.1(b) of the SRA Regulatory and Disciplinary Procedures Rules the firm agreed to pay a financial penalty of £10,719 and investigation costs of £600.[189]

xx. Richard Kanani & Co Ltd

Richard Kanani & Co Ltd entered into a regulatory settlement with the SRA and agreed to pay a £2,137 fine for AML failures. Here, the SRA concluded that the firm had failed to document client and matter risk assessments as required, meaning the firm could not demonstrate that it had applied risk-sensitive CDD

[186] J Hyde, 'Firm Fined £173,000 for Inadequate Checks on Foreign Client' (25 July 2025), available at www.lawgazette.co.uk/news/firm-fined-173000-for-inadequate-checks-on-foreign-client/5124022.article.

[187] SRA, 'Taylor Vinters LLP' (24 July 2025), available at www.sra.org.uk/consumers/solicitor-check/560892/.

[188] SRA, '*Solicitors Regulation Authority Ltd v Rory Peter Heddle Fordyce*' (25 July 2025), available at https://solicitorstribunal.org.uk/case/12560/.

[189] SRA, 'J R Jones Solicitors' (10 July 2025), available at www.sra.org.uk/consumers/solicitor-check/192990/#:~:text=J%20R%20Jones%20Solicitors%20will%20pay,and%20Disciplinary%20Procedures%20rules%3B%20and.

at the start and throughout matters.[190] Although the firm held a compliant risk assessment template, it was not consistently used, resulting in breaches of the SRA Principles 2019 and SRA Code of Conduct for Firms 2019.[191]

This case study illustrates a pattern of non-compliance within the legal profession regarding AML reporting obligations. With 18 documented breaches, 13 failures to conduct the appropriate risk assessments, the legal profession are either unaware of or insufficiently committed to the AML regulatory frameworks. The cumulative fines of over £1 million reflect the importance of these breaches, yet the average penalty suggests that enforcement lacks the deterrent power necessary to improve levels of compliance. The case study challenges the competence of the application of the AML Regulations, especially in light of the deficiencies previously highlighted regarding the legal profession by the 2007 and 2018 MERs. This recurrence illustrates that the legal profession has not improved its levels of compliance, the low rate of DAML SARs submitted to the UKFIU raises questions about the sector's willingness and capacity to tackle money laundering. The key role of the legal profession in facilitating multifaceted financial transactions places them in a unique position that allows them to act as gatekeepers. The case study suggests there is a failure to fully embrace this role and there is a lack of thorough examination and enforcement when compared to financial institutions, further exacerbating the problem. If the legal profession continues to operate in this manner, with limited accountability, it undermines the integrity of the UK's AML framework and the overall rating of the 2018 MER.

The 2007 MER concluded that the application of the then AML regime did not consistently apply to all members of the legal profession. For example, while the legal profession fell within the scope of the Money Laundering Regulations, barristers, notaries and other independent legal practitioners often fell outside AML requirements. Furthermore, trust and company service providers operated under minimal or no AML obligations, thus creating loopholes in the system. The MER also noted that the supervision of the legal sector was fragmented across several bodies, each applying its own standards and enforcement strategies. There was no single organisation that coordinated inspections, issued guidance or imposed sanctions, which undermined the overall effectiveness. Furthermore, the CDD procedures within the legal profession were inadequate, especially for high-value or complex transactions involving offshore entities and discretionary trusts. The AML practices lacked standardised risk-assessment frameworks, and EDD was seldom applied. This uneven approach made it challenging for supervisors to measure and determine whether firms were verifying client identities or assessing transaction risks. The 2007 MER noted that the submission of DAML SARs by the legal professionals was notably low, raising concerns that AML obligations were being sidelined due to client

[190] See MLRs at Regulations 28(12)(a)(ii) and 28(13).

[191] SRA, 'Richard Kanani & Co Ltd' (18 July 2025), available at www.sra.org.uk/consumers/solicitor-check/614526/.

confidentiality. The MER noted that the application of the risk-based approach (RBA) for the legal profession was inconsistently implemented and smaller firms applied a 'one-size-fits-all' approach as opposed to tailoring controls, as required by the RBA. Without clear internal policies for categorising clients by risk level, firms struggled to allocate resources effectively to their highest-risk areas. Record-keeping and audit trails were also inconsistent across the profession with the documentation of CDD checks, risk assessments and internal audit reviews often being incomplete.

The 2018 MER highlighted the uneven supervision of lawyers and other independent legal professionals. Although the 2017 Money Laundering Regulations brought all legal professionals into scope, addressing the anomaly identified in the 2007 MER, oversight of the profession varied. Some bodies applied a light touch or focused on lower-risk practices, leaving higher-risk areas insufficiently monitored and creating loopholes. The MER noted that legal professionals continued to submit DAML SARs at a much lower rate than financial institutions and other regulated entities. The legal profession continues to prioritise client confidentiality over reporting duties, and existing guidance did not clearly delineate when a report was required. The application of the RBA was once again inconsistently applied, with small firms lacking the resources or expertise to undertake the required risk assessments. Deficiencies in CDD and record-keeping were another concern raised by the MER.

The case study identifies weaknesses in how the legal profession applies its AML reporting obligations. In several instances, deficiencies have emerged in executing risk assessments, fulfilling CDD obligations and verifying client funds. The inadequacies have resulted in an increase of disciplinary actions by the SRA. Internal risk assessments are essential for detecting suspicious activities and mitigating money laundering risks because they enable law firms to evaluate client relationships and transactions while maintaining legal standards. The case study illustrated that lapses in conducting proper risk assessments could be associated to limited awareness, inadequate AML policies and procedures, negligence, or resource constraints. As a result, the SRA has intensified inspections and imposed higher financial penalties on firms that fail to meet the AML standards.[192] These activities are supported by the Economic Crime and Corporate Transparency Act 2023 which empowers the SRA to impose unlimited fines for breaches related to money laundering.[193] The case study has illustrated persistent weakness in the application of the CDD for the legal profession since the 2007 MER.[194] This failure challenges the 2018 MER's[195]

[192] See SRA, 'Anti-Money Laundering Annual Report 2023–24' (SRA, 2024); SRA, 'Report Shows More AML Action Driving Improvements' (31 October 2024), available at www.sra.org.uk/sra/news/press/2024-press-releases/aml-action-improvements/.

[193] Economic Crime and Corporate Transparency Act 2023, s 207.

[194] FATF, *Third Mutual Evaluation Report Anti-Money Laundering and Counter Terrorist Financing The United Kingdom and of Great Britain and Northern Ireland* (FATF, 2007) (hereinafter '2007 MER').

[195] FATF 2018 MER (n 32).

'Partially Compliant' and the 'Largely Compliant' rating achieved in the 2022 FATF Follow-Up Report.[196] As this case study demonstrates inconsistent levels of implementation and regulation, it undermines the effectiveness of the FATF MER process when there are inconsistencies regarding the supervision and enforcement of the legal profession by the SRA.

VII. Financial Services Sector

The second case study is based on 17 instances where financial institutions have failed to follow and implement the AML rules. Of these 17, ten involved CDD, two involved internal reporting deficiencies, two related to risk assessments, one involved the automated transaction monitoring system, one involved inadequate staff training and financial crime risk management. The total amount of fines levied was £853.1million, averaging £50.1million per case. This section begins by outlining the rationale for selecting the financial services sector, before discussing each case and then providing an overall commentary on the findings of the case study. Like the first case study, this identifies common deficiencies that were previously identified by the 2007 and 2018 MERs, thus challenging ratings provided by FATF.

Financial institutions are vulnerable to money laundering and they submit the largest number of DAML SARs to the UKFIU.[197] The sector handles millions of transactions each day ranging from cash deposits and if only a small fraction appears suspicious, the sheer volume ensures a high number of alerts.[198] Large financial institutions bolster this reporting through sophisticated transaction-monitoring systems powered by rule-based engines and machine-learning algorithms.[199] Historical scandals have shown instances where banks failed to report suspicious activity or were even complicit in money laundering.[200] Therefore, financial institutions are critical gatekeepers in detecting and preventing money laundering, making them an ideal case study.

A. Metro Bank Plc

In 2024 Metro Bank Plc was fined £16.675million for failing to have the appropriate AML systems and controls to oversee 60million transactions valued at over

[196] FATF, *Follow Up Report and Technical Compliance Re-Rating* (FATF, 2022).

[197] See NCA (n 90) at 8.

[198] See generally Bank of England, 'Payment and Settlement Statistics' (n/d), available from www.bankofengland.co.uk/payment-and-settlement/payment-and-settlement-statistics.

[199] See B Oztas, et al 'Transaction Monitoring in Anti-Money Laundering: A Qualitative Analysis and Points of View from Industry' (2024) *Future Generation Computer Systems* 159, 161–71; and D Chau, and M van Dijck Nemcsik, *Anti-Money Laundering Transaction Monitoring Systems Implementation: Finding Anomalies* (John Wiley & Sons, 2020).

[200] See generally S Toms, 'Financial Scandals: A Historical Overview' (2019) *Accounting and Business Research* 49(5), 477–99 and P Yeoh, 'Banks' Vulnerabilities to Money Laundering Activities' (2020) *Journal of Money Laundering Control* 23(1), 122–35.

£51billion for money laundering risks.[201] Metro Bank Plc employed an automated monitoring customer transaction system to detect financial crime. However, there was an error in how data was fed into the system, 'meaning that transactions taking place on the same day an account was opened, and any further transactions until the account record was updated, were not monitored'.[202] The FCA noted that 'staff did raise concerns about some transaction data not being monitored … but these did not result in the issue being identified and fixed'.[203]

B. Santander UK Plc

Santander UK Plc was fined £107.7million after the FCA identified severe and constant loopholes in its AML controls.[204] Over five years Santander UK Plc did not adequately supervise and manage its AML systems which limited the 'account oversight of more than 560,000 business customers'.[205] The FCA concluded that the bank had weak systems to authenticate the information provided by its customers about their business affairs and it had neglected to adequately 'monitor the money customers had told them would be going through their accounts compared with what actually was being deposited'.[206] The FCA, said

> Santander's poor management of their AML systems and their inadequate attempts to address the problems created a prolonged and severe risk of money laundering and financial crime … there were also examples of the bank failing to promptly deal with 'red flags' associated with suspicious activity, such as automated monitoring alerts.[207]

These weaknesses resulted in £298million passing through the bank before it closed the accounts.

C. Commerzbank London

In July 2020, Commerzbank AG (London Branch) was fined £37.8million for failing to implement satisfactory AML systems and controls.[208] During a five-year

[201] FCA, 'FCA Fines Metro Bank £16m for Financial Crime Failings' (12 November 2024), available at www.fca.org.uk/news/press-releases/fca-fines-metro-bank-16m-financial-crime-failings.

[202] ibid.

[203] ibid.

[204] Santander qualified for a 30% discount, without this, the financial penalty would have been £153.9million. See FCA, 'FCA Fines Santander UK £107.7 million for Repeated Anti-Money Laundering Failures' (9 December 2022), available at www.fca.org.uk/news/press-releases/fca-fines-santander-uk-repeated-anti-money-laundering-failuresFCA fines Santander UK £107.7 million.

[205] ibid.

[206] ibid.

[207] ibid.

[208] FCA, 'FCA Fines Commerzbank London £37,805,400 over Anti-Money Laundering Failures' (17 June 2020), available at www.fca.org.uk/news/press-releases/fca-fines-commerzbank-london-37805400-over-anti-money-laundering-failures.

period, Commerzbank AG, was alerted to a series of AML weaknesses by the FCA on three occasions but did not take any remedial action. The FCA published specific guidance on how the regulated sector could limit their exposure to financial crime risks and took enforcement action against several firms.[209] Nonetheless, the weaknesses continued and the FCA determined three weaknesses. Firstly, that Commerzbank London had failed to 'conduct timely periodic due diligence on its clients'.[210] Secondly, Commerzbank AG had failed to address weaknesses in its 'automated tool for monitoring money laundering risk on transactions for clients'.[211] Here, the FCA noted that Commerzbank London had acknowledged that '40 high-risk countries' and '1,110 high-risk clients' were not added to its transaction monitoring system.[212] Finally, the FCA concluded that Commerzbank London 'failed to have adequate policies and procedures in place when undertaking customer due diligence on clients'.[213]

D. Standard Chartered Bank

The FCA fined Standard Chartered Bank £102.1million for AML failures in two high-risk areas of its business, UK Wholesale Bank Correspondent Banking and its branches in the United Arab Emirates (UAE).[214] The FCA identified 'serious and sustained' faults in the bank's AML controls, including its CDD and continuing monitoring. Here, the FCA concluded that Standard Chartered Bank 'failed to establish and maintain risk-sensitive policies and procedures, and failed to ensure its UAE branches applied UK equivalent AML and counter-terrorist financing controls'.[215] The Money Laundering Regulations compel Standard Chartered Bank to require its global branches and subsidiaries to apply the same CDD and continuous monitoring as those in the UK.[216,217]

[209] ibid.
[210] ibid.
[211] ibid.
[212] ibid.
[213] ibid.
[214] FCA, 'FCA Fines Standard Chartered Bank £102.2 million for Poor AML Controls' (9 April 2019), available at www.fca.org.uk/news/press-releases/fca-fines-standard-chartered-bank-102-2-million-poor-aml-controls.
[215] ibid. The FCA identified three examples including a person opening an account with 3million UAE Dirham in cash in a suitcase, failing to gather adequate information on a customer who was exporting a product which could have a military application and not reviewing 'due diligence on a customer despite repeated red flags such as a blocked transaction from another bank indicating a link to a sanctioned entity'.
[216] The Money Laundering Regulations 2007, Regulation 15.
[217] FCA (n 214).

E. Standard Bank

In January 2014 the FCA fined Standard Bank £7.6million because it had 'failed to take reasonable care to ensure that all aspects of its AML policies were applied appropriately and consistently'.[218] Here, Standard Bank did not regularly perform EDD measures before starting business relationships with corporate customers who had an association with PEPs. Moreover, the FCA determined that the bank did not consistently maintain the 'appropriate level of ongoing monitoring for existing business relationships by keeping customer due diligence up to date'.[219]

F. Sonali Bank

Sonali Bank was fined £3.25million after the FCA identified 'serious and systematic weaknesses [that] affected almost all levels of its AML control'.[220] Here, the bank did not comply with its obligations towards 'CDD, the identification and treatment of politically exposed persons, transaction and customer monitoring and making suspicious activity reports'.[221]

G. Al Rayan Bank

Al Rayan Bank allowed money to pass through UK bank accounts without undertaking the required CDD assessments. The FCA concluded that Al Rayan Bank had failed to sufficiently ascertain and determine its customers' Source of Wealth and Source of Funds to determine that there was no connection to financial crime.[222] The deficiencies worsened due to inadequate staff training that contributed towards a higher financial crime risk.[223] The FCA concluded that the bank had 'failed to manage the risk that it might be used to facilitate money-laundering'.[224] Consequently, Al Rayan Bank was fined £4.023million.[225]

[218] FCA, 'Standard Bank PLC Fined £7.6m for Failures in its Anti-Money Laundering Controls' (23 January 2014), available at www.fca.org.uk/news/standard-bank-plc-fined-for-failures-in-its-antimoney-laundering-controls.

[219] ibid.

[220] See FCA (n 123).

[221] ibid.

[222] FCA, 'FCA Penalises Al Rayan Bank PLC for Anti-Money Laundering Failures' (11 January 2023), available at www.fca.org.uk/news/press-releases/fca-penalises-al-rayan-bank-plc-anti-money-laundering-failures.

[223] ibid.

[224] ibid.

[225] ibid.

H. Guaranty Trust Bank Plc

Guaranty Trust Bank Plc was fined £7.671million for AML failings that adversely affected customers who were based in jurisdictions with a higher risk of financial crime, namely PEPs.[226] Between 2014 and 2019, the bank failed to carry out satisfactory customer risk assessments, which were underlined to the bank by both internal and external bodies, including the FCA. However, the bank failed any remedial steps. The FCA concluded that Guaranty Trust Bank Plc, did not 'develop a plan that was capable of addressing its AML weaknesses, exposing it and the broader market to financial crime risks for a prolonged period'.[227]

I. HSBC Bank Plc

HSBC Bank Plc was fined £63.9 million for inadequate transaction monitoring controls and for failings in its AML procedures.[228] HSBC Bank Plc used an automated transaction process as part of monitoring transactions to detect financial crime, which the FCA concluded was flawed. Specifically, the FCA concluded that the bank failed to consider whether the scenarios used to identify indicators of money laundering or terrorist financing adequately covered all relevant risks. Additionally, HSBC did not appropriately test or update the parameters within its transaction-monitoring systems, nor did it verify the accuracy and completeness of the data being fed into and held within those monitoring systems.[229]

J. Deutsche Bank

In 2017, Deutsche Bank was fined £163m for failing to maintain an adequate AML control system between 2012 and 2015.[230] Following an investigation the FCA highlighted a series of data-sharing shortcomings including inadequate performance of CDD; inconsistent customer and country risk rating methods; deficient AML procedures and policies; weak AML IT infrastructure and no automatic AML system for detecting suspicious activity. Deutsche Bank did not obtain sufficient

[226] FCA, 'FCA Fines Guaranty Trust Bank (UK) Limited £7.6 million for Further Failures in its Anti-Money Laundering Systems and Controls' (10 January 2023), available at www.fca.org.uk/news/press-releases/fca-fines-guaranty-trust-bank-uk-limited-ps76-million-further-failures-its-anti-money-laundering.

[227] ibid.

[228] FCA, 'FCA Fines HSBC Bank plc £63.9 million for Deficient Transaction Monitoring Controls' (17 December 2021), available at www.fca.org.uk/news/press-releases/fca-fines-hsbc-bank-plc-deficient-transaction-monitoring-controls.

[229] ibid.

[230] FCA, 'FCA Fines Deutsche Bank £163 million for Serious Anti-Money Laundering Controls Failings' (31 January 2017), available at www.fca.org.uk/news/press-releases/fca-fines-deutsche-bank-163-million-anti-money-laundering-controls-failure.

information about its customers to enhance its risk assessment processes and underpin its transaction monitoring. Consequently, Deutsche Bank's Russia-based subsidiary executed approximately 2,500 mirror trades between 2012 and 2014,[231] which were used to transfer $6billion from Russia, via Deutsche Bank in the UK, to accounts in several countries including Cyprus, Estonia and Latvia. The mirror trades were received by DB Moscow, which executed both sides at the same time. The FCA noted that

> customers on the Moscow and London sides of the mirror trades were connected to each other and the volume and value of the securities was the same on both sides … [the trades resulted in the] conversion of Roubles into US Dollars … is highly suggestive of financial crime.[232]

The FCA concluded that Deutsche Bank failed to adequately manage the creation of new customer relationships which were used by 'unidentified customers to transfer approximately $10 billion, of unknown origin, from Russia to offshore bank accounts in a manner that is highly suggestive of financial crime'.[233]

K. National Westminster Bank Plc

In December 2021, National Westminster Bank Plc became the first bank to be convicted of failing to comply with the Money Laundering Regulations and fined £264,772.6million.[234] Here, NatWest failed to adequately monitor the financial activities of Fowler Oldfield, a jewellery business between 2012 and 2016. When Fowler Oldfield initially became a customer, National Westminster Bank Plc understood that it would not accept cash deposits.[235] Nonetheless, Fowler Oldfield deposited approximately £365m with National Westminster Bank Plc, around £265m was in cash.[236] Several employees of the bank reported their suspicions or 'red flags' to colleagues who were responsible for investigating suspected instances of money laundering. Staff raised concerns about the 'significant amounts of Scottish bank notes deposited throughout England, deposits of notes carrying a prominent musty smell, and individuals acting suspiciously

[231] A mirror trade is defined as 'trades or transactions involving securities used for currency conversion for illegitimate or no apparent business purpose'. See FATF, *Guidance for a Risk-Based Approach – Securities Sector* (FATF, 2018) at 54.

[232] FCA (n 230).

[233] ibid.

[234] NatWest admitted it had breached Regulations 8(1), 8(3) and 14(1) of the MLRs.

[235] For a more detailed discussion of the historical relationship between Fowler Oldfield and NatWest, see V Barnes and F De Pascalis, 'R. v NatWest (2021): Another Turning Point in the Regulation of Big Banks?' (2023) *Company Lawyer*, 44(5), 143–1513.

[236] In March 2025 the Crown Prosecution Service announced that four people were sentenced in relation to a £266 million money laundering operation that was linked to Fowler Oldfield. See Crown Prosecution Service, 'Four People Jailed for One of the Largest Money Laundering Cases in the UK' (7 March 2025), available at www.cps.gov.uk/cps/news/four-people-jailed-one-largest-money-laundering-cases-uk.

when depositing cash in NatWest branches'.[237] Furthermore, the problems were exacerbated by the bank's transaction monitoring system mistakenly designating some cash deposits as cheque deposits. Here, the FCA concluded that because 'cheques carry a lower money laundering risk than cash, this was a significant gap in the bank's monitoring of a large number of customers depositing cash'.[238] In sentencing, Mrs Justice Cockerill stated, 'it must be borne in mind that although in no way complicit in the money laundering which took place, the Bank was functionally vital. Without the Bank – and without the Bank's failures – the money could not be effectively laundered'.[239] The FCA stated that 'NatWest is responsible for a catalogue of failures in the way it monitored and scrutinised transactions that were self-evidently suspicious … these failures created an open door for money laundering'.[240]

L. Gatehouse Bank Plc

In October 2022, Gatehouse Bank Plc was fined £1.584million by the FCA for serious weaknesses in its AML controls and systems.[241] Gatehouse Bank Plc did not undertake sufficient assessments on its customers and it neglected to undertake the appropriate safeguarding checks of its customers who were classified as PEPs. The FCA identified one example where Gatehouse Bank Plc accepted deposits over a two-year period of $62million without investigating the funds for financial crime threats. The FCA concluded that this highlighted the problems associated with inadequate AML systems and controls.

M. Ghana International Bank

Ghana International Bank Plc was fined £5.829million for weak AML controls over its correspondent banking activities.[242] Between 2012 and 2016 Ghana International Bank failed to undertake the required checks 'when it established relationships with the overseas banks and failed to demonstrate it had assessed

[237] FCA, 'NatWest Fined £264.8 million for Anti-Money Laundering Failures' (17 December 2021), available at www.fca.org.uk/news/press-releases/natwest-fined-264.8million-anti-money-laundering-failures#:~:text=NatWest%20fined%20%C2%A3264.8%20million%20for%20anti%2Dmoney%20laundering%20failures%20%7C%20FCA.

[238] ibid.

[239] ibid.

[240] ibid.

[241] FCA, 'FCA Fines Gatehouse Bank £1.5 million for Poor Anti-Money Laundering Checks' (14 October 2022), available at www.fca.org.uk/news/press-releases/fca-fines-gatehouse-bank-1.5m-poor-anti-money-laundering-checks.

[242] FCA, 'FCA Fines Ghana International Bank Plc £5.8m for Failings in its Anti-Money Laundering Controls' (23 June 2022), available at www.fca.org.uk/news/press-releases/fca-fines-ghana-international-bank-5.8m-failings-aml-controls.

those banks' AML controls'.[243] Importantly the bank did not carry out reviews of the 'information it held on the banks it had a relationship with, failed to give staff adequate training on how to scrutinise transactions properly and did not establish appropriate policies and procedures for staff'.[244] The FCA noted that Ghana International Bank was unable to 'to identify and assess the risks posed by its correspondent bank customers and properly scrutinise transactions worth £9.5billion processed on their behalf during the relevant period'.[245]

N. Canara Bank

In June 2016, Canara Bank was fined £896,100 for not maintaining its AML systems.[246] Between 2012 and 2016 Canara Bank

> failed to maintain adequate systems and controls to manage the risk of money laundering. These failures were systemic and affected almost all levels of its business and governance structure including senior management, governance/ Oversight, money laundering reporting function and weak AML systems and controls.[247]

O. EFG Private Bank Ltd

In 2014 EFG Private Bank Ltd was fined £4.2million for not adequately establishing and sustaining an effective AML control for high-risk customers.[248] By 2011 approximately a quarter of EFG Private Bank Ltd customers were determined to present 'a higher risk of money laundering of reputational risk … [of these] 94 were held by politically exposed persons'.[249] Following an investigation, the FSA raised concerns about deficiencies in the firm's AML record-keeping obligations and that EFG Private Bank Ltd had failed to monitor its higher-risk accounts. The FCA concluded that the bank had 'manifestly failed to ensure that it was addressing its AML risks. Its poor implementation of its agreed policies risked the bank handling the proceeds of crime'.[250]

[243] ibid.
[244] ibid.
[245] ibid.
[246] FCA, 'FCA Fines and Imposes a Restriction on Canara Bank for Anti-Money Laundering Systems Failings' (6 June 2016), available at www.fca.org.uk/news/press-releases/fca-fines-and-imposes-restriction-canara-bank-anti-money-laundering-systems-failings.
[247] ibid.
[248] FCA, 'FCA Fines EFG Private Bank £4.2m for Failures in its Anti-Money Laundering Controls' (24 April 2013), available at www.fca.org.uk/news/press-releases/fca-fines-efg-private-bank-%C2%A342m-failures-its-anti-money-laundering-controls.
[249] ibid.
[250] ibid.

P. Monzo Bank Ltd

Monzo Bank Ltd was fined £21million for inadequate anti-financial crime systems and controls and for persistently breaching a requirement preventing it from opening accounts for high-risk customers.[251] Due to its customer base increasing from 600,000 to 5.5million, the bank's financial crime controls did not keep pace. In particular, Monzo failed to design, implement and maintain adequate customer onboarding, customer risk assessment and transaction monitoring systems to mitigate the risk of financial crime. These systemic failings resulted in the FCA requiring a comprehensive, independent review of the bank's financial crime framework in 2020. Furthermore, Monzo was required not to open new accounts for high-risk customers, which it repeatedly failed to comply with.

Q. Barclays Bank UK Plc and Barclays Bank Plc

The FCA fined Barclays Bank UK Plc and Barclays Bank Plc £42 million for separate instances of failings in its financial crime risk management – one relating to WealthTek and one relating to Stunt & Co.[252] In the first case, the bank failed to ascertain it had obtained enough information to understand the money laundering risks before opening a client account for WealthTek. The FCA stated that 'one simple check it could have done was to look at the Financial Services Register before opening the account. Had it done so, it would have seen that WealthTek was not permitted by the FCA to hold client money'.[253] Consequently, there was an increased risk of misappropriation of client money or money laundering. In the second case, the FCA fined Barclays Bank Plc £39.3million for failing to adequately manage money laundering risks associated with providing banking services to Stunt & Co. Here, Barclays did not obtain enough information at the start of the business relationship or undertake ongoing monitoring. A year into the relationship, Stunt & Co received £46.8million from Fowler Oldfield, a multimillion-pound money laundering operation. Barclays did not consider the money laundering risks associated with the firm even after receiving information from an LEA about suspected money laundering through Fowler Oldfield, and after learning that the police had raided both firms. Barclays only conducted a review of its exposure to Fowler Oldfield through its customers, including Stunt & Co, after it learned of the FCA's decision to prosecute NatWest over their relationship with Fowler

[251] FCA, 'FCA Fines Monzo £21m for Failings in Financial Crime Controls' (8 July 2025), available at www.fca.org.uk/news/press-releases/fca-fines-monzo-21m-failings-financial-crime-controls.

[252] FCA, 'FCA Fines Barclays £42 million for Poor Handling of Financial Crime Risks' (16 July 2025), available at www.fca.org.uk/news/press-releases/fca-fines-barclays-42-million-poor-handling-financial-crime-risks.

[253] ibid.

Oldfield. By providing banking services to Stunt & Co, Barclays facilitated the movement of funds linked to financial crime.

The second case study underscores the critical importance of the financial services sector as a focal point for AML scrutiny. Financial institutions process millions of daily transactions and generate more DAML SARs than any other industry, making them indispensable gatekeepers in the fight against money laundering. Historical data and high-profile scandals have illustrated weaknesses within financial institutions and other regulated entities can allow money laundering, even when transaction-monitoring systems are in place. Across the 17 enforcement actions examined, CDD failures dominated, accounting for ten. Two cases involved breakdowns in internal reporting obligations, while another two exposed shortcomings in risk assessments. Separate instances revealed failures in automated transaction-monitoring systems and deficiencies in staff training and financial crime risk management. Collectively, regulators imposed £853.1million in fines, averaging £50.1 million per breach, signifying the severe financial and reputational costs of weak AML controls. This case study reiterates deficiencies FATF identified in its 2007 and 2018 MER, notably inconsistent application of CDD measures, lapses in internal escalation and reporting, and flaws in automated alert mechanisms and risk-based policies. The 2007 MER noted that some financial institutions failed to consistently apply CDD measures, leading FATF to rate Recommendation 5 as 'Partially Compliant'.[254] A concern highlighted by the MER was the inconsistent application of the RBA approach towards CDD. While FATF had, since 2003, encouraged EDD in higher-risk situations, such as with politically exposed persons and correspondent banking, and allowed SDD for genuinely lower-risk entities like listed public companies, UK financial institutions often blurred these distinctions. Simplified measures were over-used, and enhanced checks under-applied, undermining the targeting of resources where they were most needed. To remedy these deficiencies, the FATF's follow-up procedures required the UK to bring its CDD regime to a level equivalent to a 'Compliant' or 'Largely Compliant' rating. Authorities were urged to issue clearer guidance on risk-based CDD application, conduct targeted inspections of banks' CDD practices, and strengthen industry training and internal controls so that financial institutions could embed a genuinely risk-sensitive culture across their operations. The 2018 MER found that despite the robust legal framework, there was an inconsistent implementation across the financial sector. Larger financial institutions demonstrated strong CDD practices, but smaller banks, money service businesses, and certain non-bank financial institutions exhibited gaps.[255]

It is interesting to note the connection between the conviction of NatWest Bank Plc, the fine imposed on Barclays in July 2025 and the Bradford-based gold

[254] See chapter three.
[255] ibid.

dealer Fowler Oldfield, which channelled over £365million through NatWest accounts, despite the bank's own rules against accepting cash dealings with Fowler Oldfield. Despite rating Fowler Oldfield as a risk customer, NatWest downgraded its rating in 2013 only for it to be re-elevated in 2016. Nonetheless, staff at NatWest branches processed deposits of up to £1.8million in one day without activating the EDD procedures that should have applied. It is important to note that Fowler Oldfield did not directly bank with Barclays, but the FCA concluded that the bank's transaction monitoring system failed to identify suspicious transactions associated with the same network of cash couriers. The FCA noted that the patterns of frequent high-value cash flows through intermediary firms was unflagged by Barclays, illustrating how weaknesses at one financial institution can expose others when an investigation widens. The Criminal Finances Act 2017 introduced new information-sharing mechanisms that allowed financial institutions and members of the regulated sector to voluntary exchange information on suspected money laundering with each other or the UKFIU. However, this mechanism is voluntary and ineffective to address the threat of money laundering. Making the information-sharing mechanisms mandatory and automatic could improve the UK's defences against money laundering.

These recurring failings challenge the compliance ratings awarded by FATF, suggesting that a robust legal framework and strong enforcement are insufficient. The persistence of these weaknesses illustrates the need for financial institutions to reinforce their CDD frameworks with clearer guidance, improved internal reporting systems and regularly calibrate automated systems to evolving money laundering. This case study demonstrates that financial institutions remain vulnerable to money laundering when legal obligations are not translated and consistently implemented. To protect the integrity of the financial system, firms must move beyond tick-box compliance and move towards an intelligence-driven approach that involves robust governance, continuous training, and proactive supervisory engagement.

VIII. Anti-Money Laundering Supervisory Authorities and Data-Sharing

The third case study focuses on the anti-money laundering supervisory authorities (AMLSA), which oversee compliance across a wide range of sectors. Their objective is to ensure that over '90,000 businesses maintain strong and proportionate controls and supporting them to remain responsive to the latest risks in their sector'.[256] The AMLSA include the FCA, HM Revenue & Customs (HMRC) and the Gambling Commission. The FCA is responsible for setting and enforcing

[256] HM Treasury, *Policy Paper: Anti-Money Laundering and Counter-Terrorist Financing: Supervision Report: 2023-24* (HM Treasury, 2025).

AML rules for financial services firms, they conduct risk assessments, oversee the regulated sector and take enforcement action against non-compliance.[257] HMRC oversees AML compliance for certain sectors, including trust and company service providers, and monitors for tax evasion and money laundering.[258] The Gambling Commission regulates and supervises AML compliance within the gambling industry.[259] Each of these bodies have the legal authority and enforcement power to impose financial penalties and other sanctions for firms for failing to comply.[260] The UK has adopted a slightly different approach to other jurisdictions which have used the single agency approach such as Canada (The Financial Transactions and Reports Analysis Centre of Canada),[261] France (The Autorité de Contrôle Prudentiel et de Résolution),[262] Australia (Australian Transaction Reports and Analysis Centre)[263] and the EU (EU AML Authority).[264]

These are sector-specific regulators for legal and accountancy professionals and are overseen by the Office for Professional Body Anti-Money Laundering Supervision (OPBAS), which operates under the remit of the FCA. OPBAS was established in January 2018 as part of reforms to strengthen the AML supervisory framework.[265] HM Treasury stated that OPBAS will 'work across the UK's anti-money laundering supervisory regime to improve standards and ensure supervisors and law enforcement work together more effectively'.[266] OPBAS has published a dedicated Sourcebook and regular guidance notes to promote a consistent, risk-based approach to AML supervision across those sectors.[267] The Office is fully funded by levies imposed on the supervisors it oversees, with those costs passed on to the firms under each professional body supervisor's (PBS)

[257] See generally *Financial Conduct Authority Handbook – Money Laundering and Terrorist Financing* (Financial Conduct Authority, 2025) at ch 3.

[258] See HM Treasury (n 256).

[259] See generally, Gambling Commission, 'Anti-Money Laundering' (n/d), available at www.gambling-commission.gov.uk/licensees-and-businesses/aml.

[260] See Financial Services and Markets Act 2000, s 206(1); the Money Laundering Regulations 2017, Regulation 76 and Gambling Act 2005, s 121.

[261] See Simser (n 26).

[262] See Favarel-Garrigues et al (n 154).

[263] See P Latimer, 'Australia: Australian Transaction Reports and Analysis Centre (austrac)' (1995) *Journal of Financial Crime*, 3(3), 306–307 and N Jensen, 'Creating an Environment in Australia Hostile to Money Laundering and Terrorism Financing: A Changing Role for AUSTRAC' (2008) *Macquarie Journal of Business Law* 5, 93–111.

[264] See S Tosza and O Voordeckers, 'An Anti-Money Laundering Authority for the European Union: A New Center of Gravity in AML Enforcement' (2024) *ERA Forum* 25(3), 405–24 and G Schiavo, 'The Single Supervisory Mechanism (SSM) and the EU Anti-Money Laundering Framework Compared: Governance, Rules, Challenges and Opportunities' (2022) *Journal of Banking Regulation* 23(1), 91–105.

[265] HM Treasury, 'UK Establishes New Money Laundering Watchdog' (21 December 2017), available at www.gov.uk/government/news/uk-establishes-new-money-laundering-watchdog.

[266] ibid.

[267] Office for Professional Body Anti-Money Laundering Supervision and Financial Conduct Authority (OPBAS), *Sourcebook for Professional Body Anti-Money Laundering Supervisors* (OPBAS and FCA), 2023).

remit.[268] OPBAS oversees 25 PBS in the legal and accountancy sectors, ensuring they apply effective AML supervision.

The PBS include the Institute of Chartered Accountants in England and Wales (ICAEW), the Law Society/Solicitors Regulation Authority, the Association of Chartered Certified Accountants, the Institute of Chartered Accountants of Scotland, the Bar Standards Board and OPBAS.[269] The PBS undertake an important role in managing AML compliance within their sectors, ensuring that professionals adhere to the Money Laundering Regulations 2017. Specifically, the PBS are responsible for monitoring compliance with AML regulations among their members; providing guidance and support to firms; facilitating collaboration between statutory supervisors, law enforcement agencies, and other PBS; undertaking risk-based supervision and ensuring professional and ethical standards are upheld within the industry.[270]

OPBAS facilitates collaboration and information-sharing between PBS, statutory supervisors such as the FCA and HMRC, and law enforcement agencies to improve sector-wide intelligence and risk awareness.[271] The OPBAS Sourcebook provided that information and intelligence-sharing is important to reduce money laundering within a structured framework for exchanging AML intelligence.[272] To achieve this objective, OPBAS works closely with professional bodies and other stakeholders to ensure that information flows are joined up and effective. Key to that effort is the legal, accountancy and devolved-nations Intelligence and Security Exchange Working Groups (ISEWGs), set up jointly with the NECC to enable both tactical and strategic sharing.[273] PBS are expected to maintain dedicated processes and staffed functions for collecting, analysing and triaging information on suspicious activity. They should participate in national and cross-sector intelligence networks or forums to share emerging typologies and red-flag indicators. All incoming and outgoing intelligence requests, responses and any follow-up actions need to be logged in a centralised system, and data protection and confidentiality measures must be embedded throughout every information-sharing channel.[274]

Since its creation, OPBAS has been subjected to criticism. For example, Wood suggested that OPBAS has 'not been able to deal with the fundamental problem with our AML supervision system, which is that it is fragmented and broken'.[275] This was echoed by Transparency International which stated that the UK's AML

[268] HM Treasury, *Post-implementation Review of the Oversight of Professional Body Anti-Money Laundering and Counter Terrorist Financing Supervision Regulations 2017* (HM Treasury, 2022) at 3.

[269] FCA, 'Office for Professional Body Anti-Money Laundering Supervision (OPBAS)' (23 January 2018), available at www.fca.org.uk/about/how-we-operate/who-work-with/opbas.

[270] ibid.

[271] See OPBAS (n 267) at 2.22.

[272] ibid.

[273] ibid at 2.24.

[274] ibid at 6.2–6.3.

[275] H Wood, Treasury Committee, Oral Evidence: Economic Crime, HC 145, Thursday 8 July 2021, available at https://committees.parliament.uk/oralevidence/2532/pdf/.

supervision system remains 'highly fragmented'.[276] Westmore identified four problems with OPBAS: under-resourcing; conflicted governance structures; fragmented, inconsistent risk-based approaches; and inconsistent enforcement.[277] Spotlight on Corruption stated that the current system is fragmented supervision across multiple bodies, chronically high non-compliance rates (around 30 per cent for English solicitors and over 50 per cent for Scottish firms), inconsistent sanctioning powers, reluctance to pursue large law firms through disciplinary tribunals, and reliance on self-declarations to identify regulated work.[278]

Each of the statutory supervisors maintain comprehensive datasets on the entities they oversee. For instance, the FCA holds data on the 42,000 firms it regulates. HMRC holds transactional data, client details and compliance documentation on money service businesses, high-value dealers, estate agents, trust and company service providers, certain accountancy firms and art market participants. The Gambling Commission retains licensing information, compliance records, transactional logs and customer identification data for gambling operators; and PBS record AML compliance checks, client risk assessments and business declarations for their members.[279] All of these data sources can be harnessed to build strategic intelligence, drive operational investigations and provide evidentiary support in court to secure criminal convictions when required. Bociga et al concluded that 'in the AML regime, no single entity or node possesses all the necessary information to combat money laundering activities, making collaboration and information sharing essential for developing AML strategies'.[280]

Sectoral silos mean that PBS often restrict information flows to their own memberships, applying inconsistent AML reporting formats and timetables. DAML SARs, client risk assessments and enforcement outcomes remain confined within individual PBS rather than feeding into a unified national picture, leaving gaps in the overall understanding of professional-services-facilitated laundering.[281] Outside the SARs regime, there is no formalised, cross-sector channel for the timely exchange of intelligence between PBS and the UKFIU or regional organised crime units. This limits the ability of LEAs to link suspicious

[276] Transparency International, Treasury Committee, Oral evidence: Economic crime, HC 145, Thursday 8 July 2021, available at https://committees.parliament.uk/oralevidence/2532/pdf/.

[277] K Westmore, 'Policy Briefs – Anti-Money Laundering Supervision of the Professions in the UK: Four Key Challenges and How to Address Them' (24 October 2023), available at www.rusi.org/explore-our-research/publications/policy-briefs/anti-money-laundering-supervision-professions-uk-four-key-challenges-and-how-address-them.

[278] H Taylor, *Broken Record: Latest Round of Legal Sector AML Reports Shows it is Time for Reform* (Spotlight on Corruption, 2025). Also see House of Commons Treasury Committee, *Economic Crime – Anti-Money Laundering Supervision and Sanctions Implementation Twenty-Seventh Report of Session 2017–19* (House of Commons Treasury Committee, 2019) at 13.

[279] D Bociga, N Lord, and E Bellotti, 'Dare to Share: Information and Intelligence Sharing within the UK's Anti-Money Laundering Regime' (2024) *Policing and Society* 35(6), 812–31, at 819–20.

[280] ibid at 820.

[281] H Wood, D Artingstall, H Campbell and A Moiseienko, *Known Unknowns: Plugging the UK's Intelligence Gaps on Money Laundering Involving Professional Services Providers* (Royal United Services Institute (RUSI), 2018).

patterns across different professional sectors and slows the progress of operational investigations.[282] Although OPBAS was created to improve consistency across PBS, it lacks the statutory authority to compel the real-time transfer of AML data. Instead, it relies on annually published, high-level reports from each PBS, which are frequently aggregated or redacted to protect professional or client confidentiality. This inadequate oversight power prevents OPBAS from obtaining the detailed intelligence needed to spot emerging laundering trends.[283]

The AML supervisory framework is fragmented and deficient in information-sharing. While OPBAS was created to complement supervisory approaches, varying levels of effectiveness across the PBS under the Money Laundering Regulations 2017 have undermined the regime. Data silos, legal constraints, and limited trust hinders collaboration and intelligence-sharing between PBS, statutory supervisors and LEAs. The commitments set out in the Economic Crime Plan II is recognition of these deficiencies, but the persistence of fragmentation suggests a more centralised, streamlined model is still needed. In the next part of the case study, the weaknesses in the data-sharing mechanisms and reporting channels among statutory AML agencies are identified, illustrating the inconsistent application of the FATF Standards.

A. HMRC and the FCA

This subsection of the case study illustrates deficiencies in the data-sharing mechanisms between the AMLSA. In February 2015, a whistle-blower stated that HSBC bank had assisted wealthy clients to evade paying tax.[284] The International Consortium of Investigative Journalists reported that HSBC Private Bank (Suisse) had continued to offer services to customers linked to allegations of bribery, arms trafficking and the sale of conflict diamonds. Furthermore, it was reported that the bank continued to work for people and institutions that are closely associated with the regimes of Hosni Mubarak, Ben Ali and Bashar al-Assad. There were suggestions that clients in jurisdictions benefited from HSBC tax advice and services, leading to tax avoidance and evasion. It was suggested that HSBC was more than a passive recipient of funds, it established the accounts and also assured its clients that details of accounts held would not be disclosed to national authorities.[285] In fact, HSBC advised its customers on how to avoid the European Savings Tax Directive,[286] and even supplied anonymous credit cards so that the funds could

[282] ibid.
[283] See Wood et al (n 281).
[284] International Consortium of Investigative Journalists, 'Banking Giant HSBC Sheltered Murky Cash Linked to Dictators and Arms Dealers' (International Consortium for Investigative Journalists, 8 February 2015), available at www.icij.org/investigations/swiss-leaks/banking-giant-hsbc-sheltered-murky-cash-linked-dictators-and-arms-dealers.
[285] ibid.
[286] Council Directive 2003/48/EC of 3 June 2003 on Taxation of Savings Income in the Form of Interest Payments [2003] OJ L157/38.

be withdrawn without exposure.[287] It was determined that of the leaked accounts held by 106,000 clients in 203 countries, approximately 7,000 clients were based in the UK and of those, over 1,000 had not paid the correct amount of tax.[288] HMRC's response to the HSBC scandal was 'seriously legally flawed'.[289] Only one prosecution has been brought against a UK client and no criminal prosecution has been brought against the bank itself for assisting banking customers with tax evasion and money laundering offences.[290] This approach can be contrasted with the enforcement approach adopted in the United States of America and France, which reached a Deferred Prosecution Agreement with, and imposed significant penalties on the bank.[291] The important issues here was sharing information. Lin Homer, then Chief Executive of HMRC, noted that HMRC could not pursue action against the bank as HMRC was not responsible for investigating allegations of money laundering and was prohibited from sharing information with other LEAs unless used to aid the enforcement of taxation.[292] Indeed, to protect taxpayer confidentiality, the Treaty providing for the exchange of information in tax matters between France and the UK provides that any information received:

> shall be disclosed only to persons or authorities concerned with the assessment or collection of, the enforcement or prosecution in respect of, or the determination of appeals in relation to, the taxes referred to in paragraph 1 … such persons or authorities shall use the information only for such purposes.[293]

However, the Treaty is modelled on the Organisation for Economic Co-operation and Development's Tax Convention on Income and on Capital, which provides that the Convention 'allows the sharing of tax information by the tax authorities of the receiving State with other LEAs and judicial authorities in that State on certain high priority matters'.[294] Accordingly, information can be exchanged with other LEAs in accordance with the Convention when two conditions are met: the laws of both countries must permit the use of the information for other purposes

[287] BBC News, 'HSBC Bank "Helped Clients Dodge Millions in Tax"' (10 February 2015), available at www.bbc.co.uk/news/business-31248913.

[288] ibid.

[289] O Bowcott, 'HSBC Should Face UK Criminal Charges, Says Former Public Prosecutor' (22 February 2015), available at www.theguardian.com/politics/2015/feb/22/hsbc-uk-criminal-charges-former-public-prosecutor-hmrc.

[290] *R v Shanly*, The Times, 5 July 2012 (Wood Green Crown Court).

[291] United States Department of Justice, 'Justice Department Announces Deferred Prosecution Agreement with HSBC Private Bank (Suisse) SA' (10 December 2019), available at www.justice.gov/opa/pr/justice-department-announces-deferred-prosecution-agreement-hsbc-private-bank-suisse-sa.

[292] See Public Accounts Committee, *Oral Evidence: Tax Avoidance and Evasion: HSBC* (23 March 2015, HC 2014-15 1095-I) and Public Accounts Committee, *Oral Evidence: Increasing the Effectiveness of Tax Collection: A Stocktake of Progress Since 2010* (11 February 2015, HC 2014–15, 974-I).

[293] Convention between the Government of the United Kingdom of Great Britain and Northern Ireland and the Government of the French Republic for the Avoidance of Double Taxation and the Prevention of Fiscal Evasion with Respect to Taxes on Income and on Capital Gains with Protocol (Signed June 19 2008, entered into force December 18 2009) 2011 UKTS 005, Art 27(2).

[294] Organisation for Economic Co-operation and Development (OECD), *OECD Agreement on Exchange of Information in Tax Matters* (OECD, 2002) at para 12.3.

and the supplying state must authorise such use.[295] HMRC claimed that it asked the French authorities for permission to share the data with other LEAs in 2010; a claim that was disputed in France.[296] The activities of HSBC (Suisse) were only revealed to the FCA and other LEAs in 2015, following the dissemination of the information in the media.[297] Following this, HMRC obtained confirmation from the French authorities that restrictions on the use and sharing of the data could be lifted for the purpose of investigating other financial crimes.[298] HMRC later met the Serious Fraud Office, the NCA and the FCA to consider the sharing of the data.[299] However, all investigative activities were discontinued.[300] The failure to act against a UK-headquartered bank could be attributed to a plethora of factors.[301] Regardless, this case study reveals that it took five years for the FCA to become aware of allegations of criminality, again demonstrating inherent flaws in the UK's ability to ensure the exchange of information between LEAs to detect and address financial crimes. Unlike in the preceding case studies, the exchange of this information by HMRC would not have prevented money laundering from taking place, but it could have enabled action to be taken in response to this corporate economic crime by appropriate LEAs. Therefore, despite an extensive legislative framework, HMRC are failing to exchange information with other LEAs in respect of a plethora of financial crimes, including terrorism financing and money laundering. Accordingly, the following section makes important recommendations for reform.

The case study highlights how an excess of overlapping AML and PBS has weakened the submission of DAML SARs and related data-sharing mechanisms. A forthcoming HM Treasury review of the Money Laundering Regulations has identified inconsistent oversight, particularly within accountancy and legal sectors. Consequently, the UK Government is weighing four reform models. The fragmented supervisory landscape hampers effective data-sharing, and HMRC is reluctant to disclose tax-related intelligence. To address this, the case study proposes legal amendments to the Commissioners for Revenue and Customs Act 2005. Firstly, mandating HMRC disclosure when employees suspect money laundering or terrorist activity, mirroring SAR obligations under POCA 2002. Secondly, the introduction of a statutory function for HMRC to prevent and detect

[295] ibid.

[296] J Garside, D Leigh, J Ball, D Pegg and R Mason, 'France Says It Did Not Restrict UK From Using HSBC Files To Pursue Bank and Criminals' (13 February 2015), available at www.theguardian.com/business/2015/feb/13/france-says-it-did-not-restrict-uk-from-using-hsbc-files-to-pursue-bank-and-criminals.

[297] Treasury Committee, *Oral Evidence: Financial Conduct Authority* (10 February 2015, HC 2014–15, 1055) Q75 and 76.

[298] HM Revenue & Customs, 'HMRC Confirms HSBC Suisse Bank Data Can Now Be Shared' (25 February 2015), available at www.gov.uk/government/news/hmrc-confirms-hsbc-suisse-bank-data-can-now-be-shared.

[299] ibid.

[300] First reported by M Kleinman, 'FCA Ends Probe Into HSBC Swiss Tax Affair' (4 January 2016), available at https://news.sky.com/story/fca-ends-probe-into-hsbc-swiss-tax-affair-10334024.

[301] See J Fisher, 'HSBC, Tax Evasion and Criminal Prosecution' (2015) *Tax Journal* 1253 6.

financial crimes alongside its revenue-collection role, fostering a culture of proactive enforcement and international intelligence exchange.

IX. Public Private Partnerships

Voluntary data-sharing mechanisms are crucial because they enable financial institutions and LEAs to detect suspicious patterns early, fostering collaboration and adapting to emerging money laundering typologies. An appraisal of these schemes is essential to illustrate their effectiveness, while also identifying barriers that inhibit broader participation. By sharing internal alerts, industry expertise, and flexible frameworks, participants can reduce redundant investigations and improve investigative perspectives. The most important development in financial intelligence and data-sharing, alongside the DAML SARs regime, is the voluntary exchange of information. The success of information-sharing rests on the relationship between LEAs and reporting entities, which in the UK has been 'plagued by mistrust resulting in poor information sharing where vital information possessed by each party has been kept in silos'.[302] In order to address these weaknesses, the Joint Money Laundering Intelligence Taskforce (JMLIT) was established as a private/public partnership between LEAs and the financial sector to tackle high-end money laundering and other economic threats.[303] JMLIT has been described as a 'collaborative partnership between law enforcement agencies and financial sector institutions, focusing on sharing strategic, tactical, and operational intelligence'.[304]

Announcing the creation of JMLIT, the then Home Secretary Teresa May MP stated that the launch of JMLIT 'marks the next stage in this relationship and demonstrates the progress that we have made. It also shows real leadership and commitment from the banks. But we cannot stop there'.[305] Anthony Browne, the then chief executive of the British Bankers Association (now UK Finance) said

> when banks, the government and law enforcement work together we are undoubtedly stronger in our efforts to combat crime. That's why we are playing a leading role in sharing key intelligence to help protect our customers from fraud and catch sophisticated criminals.[306]

The then City of London Police Commander Steve Head, the Police National Coordinator for Economic Crime, said that JMLIT will

[302] Home Office, 'Home Secretary on the Work of the Financial Sector Forum: Theresa May Announces Launch of Joint Money Laundering Intelligence Taskforce' (24 February 2015), available at www.gov.uk/government/speeches/home-secretary-on-the-work-of-the-financial-sector-forum.

[303] NCA, 'National Economic Crime Centre' (n/d), available at www.nationalcrimeagency.gov.uk/what-we-do/national-economic-crime-centre.

[304] Bociga et al (n 279).

[305] See Home Office (n 302).

[306] ibid.

> give us a better understanding of how the banking system is being exploited, enabling us to choke off the flow of illegal funds that are the life-blood of these highly dangerous and destructive criminal enterprises and ensure the financial sector is better protected.[307]

JMLIT is a member of the NECC which is part of the NCA.[308] JMLIT consists of over 200 members, the FCA, the Credit Fraud Avoidance System, the NCA, HMRC, the Serious Fraud Office, the City of London Police and the Metropolitan Police Service.[309] JMLIT has 'made very quick progress in aiding voluntary information sharing … and has quickly demonstrated [its] … benefits',[310] which has enabled the UK to become a global leader in the exchange of information between reporting entities and law enforcement agencies. As of 31 December 2024, JMLIT has assisted in identifying over 10,700 accounts that were not previously known to LEAs, over 8,100 accounts were closed, approximately 400 arrests, 1,230 legislative orders granted in part due to JMLIT+ activity, over £248 million was identified and under restraint and 100 alerts issued to the wider sector.[311] However, the impact of this has been challenged, 'how many of these money laundering arrests resulted in convictions; this information has not been made available'.[312] Therefore, the FATF has concluded that 'JMLIT is an innovative model for public/private information sharing that has generated very positive results since its inception in 2015 and is considered to be an example of best practice'.[313] It is unsurprising that the UK model has been adopted in Australia,[314] Singapore[315] and Hong Kong.[316] Other jurisdictions which had used a similar model include the Netherlands and Kenya.[317] Indeed, the use of these data-sharing mechanisms have been endorsed by the FATF.[318]

The exchange of information has also been facilitated by the Criminal Finances Act 2017, which permits 'voluntary disclosures within the regulated sector' as an

[307] ibid.

[308] NCA (n 303).

[309] ibid.

[310] FCA, 'Effectiveness and Proportionality: Our Financial Crime Priorities – Speech by Rob Gruppetta, Head of Financial Crime Department' (10 November 2016), available at www.fca.org.uk/news/speeches/effectiveness-proportionality-financial-crime-priorities. The voluntary exchange of information sharing was introduced by the Criminal Finances Act 2017, which introduced by the Proceeds of Crime Act 2002, ss 3392B–339ZG and the Terrorism Act 2000, s 21CA–CF.

[311] NCA (n 303).

[312] See B Scott and M McGoldrick, 'Financial Intelligence and Financial Investigation: Opportunities and Challenges' (2018) *Journal of Policing, Intelligence and Counter Terrorism*, 13(3), 301–15 at 303.

[313] FATF 2018 MER (n 32) at 6.

[314] See AUSTRAC, 'Fintel Alliance' (n/d), available at www.austrac.gov.au/about-us/fintel-alliance.

[315] See Monetary Authority of Singapore, 'CAD and MAS Partner Industry Stakeholders to Fight Financial Crimes' (24 April 2017), available at www.mas.gov.sg/regulation/anti-money-laundering/amlcft-industry-partnership-acip.

[316] Hong Kong Monetary Authority, 'Fraud and Money Laundering Intelligence Taskforce Launched' (26 May 2017), available at www.hkma.gov.hk/eng/key-information/press-releases/2017/20170526-3.shtml.

[317] See E den Boer, 'Countering Criminal Facilitation Through Public–Private Cooperation in The Netherlands' in G Jacobs, I Suojanen, K Horton, and P Bayerl (eds), *International Security Management New Solutions to Complexity* (Springer, 2021) at 463–76.

[318] FATF, 'Outcomes Joint FATF/GAFILAT Plenary, 1-3 November 2017' (3 November 2017), available at Outcomes Joint FATF/GAFILAT Plenary, 1-3 November 2017.

additional exchange of information mechanism.[319] The aim of this is to permit reporting entities to share information with each other on a voluntary basis in relation to a suspicion that a person is engaged in money laundering.[320] The provision supports the pre-existing statutory provisions introduced by the Crime and Courts Act 2013, which permits reporting entities to act as information gateways to facilitate the exchange of information between the private sector and law enforcement agencies.[321] The FATF has described this as a 'strong feature of the system … [that] enables any person across the public or private sector to voluntarily share information with the NCA … [enabling] it to act as an information intermediary between law enforcement agencies and reporting entities'.[322] Information provided via such mechanisms is contained within what are known as 'Super SARs'.[323] Two further information sharing pathways – the Financial Crime Information Network (FIN-NET) and the Shared Intelligence Service (SIS), both of which are hosted by the FCA – enable the sharing of information between law enforcement agencies and financial regulatory agencies.[324] However, all of these mechanisms are voluntary and that a reporting entity is permitted to decline an invitation to exchange information. Of course, information-sharing and increased cooperation can result in more comprehensive profiles of particular customers that enable financial investigators to focus on certain financial instruments and transactions.

Notwithstanding the acclaim, the JMLIT has attracted some criticism on account of its composition. For example, the FATF has noted that 'some stakeholders felt disenfranchised by their exclusion from it. Many felt that they could provide more useful intelligence if the membership of JMLIT were expanded or if there was greater dissemination of information, particularly regarding emerging trends in money laundering activity.[325] Another criticism has been that the JMLIT does not engage with reporting entities that are particularly vulnerable to abuse by money launderers. For example, it seemingly focuses exclusively on working with the financial services sector while ignoring other professions, such as accountants,[326] lawyers[327] and estate agents.[328] The Law Commission recommended that the JMLIT's remit should be extended to include a wider range of reporting entities from the entire regulated sector in order to 'provide a better understanding of relevant intelligence through

[319] Criminal Finances Act 2017, s 11. This Act introduced this measure into the Proceeds of Crime Act 2002, s 339ZB–ZG and the Terrorism Act 2000, s 21CA–CF.

[320] Criminal Finances Act 2017, s 11(6).

[321] Crime and Courts Act 2013, s 7.

[322] See FATF 2018 MER (n 32) at 57.

[323] See Law Commission 2019 Report (n 3) at 44.

[324] HM Treasury, 'Call for Information: Anti-Money Laundering Supervisory Regime' (16 March 2017), available at www.gov.uk/government/consultations/call-for-information-anti-money-laundering-supervisory-regime/call-for-information-anti-money-laundering-supervisory-regime.

[325] FATF 2018 MER (n 32) at 165.

[326] HM Treasury and Home Office, *National Risk Assessment of Money Laundering and Terrorist Financing 2017* (HM Treasury and Home Office, 2017).

[327] ibid. See also FATF 2018 MER (n 32).

[328] See HM Government, 'Estate Agents Targeted in Money Laundering Crackdown' (4 March 2019), available at www.gov.uk/government/news/estate-agents-targeted-in-money-laundering-crackdown.

the sharing of information across multiple sectors'.[329] In response, the NCA stated, 'we do not believe that a simple expansion of the current JMLIT would be the most effective mechanism for wide engagement'.[330] Conversely, the City of London Police suggested that the JMLIT could contain a number of 'sub-sets … concentrating on different sectors thereby allowing full access or the ability for the JMLIT to co-opt additional members on a short-term basis to allow for their resources/expertise in connection with a particular piece of work'.[331] Another deficiency of JMLIT is that the 'information sharing process between financial institutions and law enforcement agencies is slow and has multiple frictions that hinder the identification and disruption of financial crime'.[332] Finally, although the creation of the JMLIT and the resultant information-sharing has achieved some notable successes, it now seems necessary for the UK Government to widen the scope of the information-sharing model. In the 2018 Serious Organised Crime strategy, HM Government noted that they were open to increasing the membership of JMLIT to include the legal and accountancy professions.[333]

JMLIT has been a valuable tool in tackling financial crime, but there are always ways to enhance its effectiveness. For example, while JMLIT has improved intelligence-sharing between financial institutions and LEAs expanding the scope of sharing data, especially across international borders, it could strengthen efforts against global money laundering. Furthermore, improvements could be made to the public-private collaboration between financial institutions, regulators, LEAs and the UKFIU to improve coordination and response times when tackling money laundering.[334] The JMLIT could be placed on a permanent footing, thus ensuring a consistent focus and ability to address money laundering over the long term. This would also allow JMLIT to conduct more in-depth analysis of money laundering typologies contributing towards a more targeted approach towards investigations.

X. Reform

In 2014, HM Government published its Anti-Corruption Plan which stated that

> the Home Office will review the Suspicious Activity Reporting (SARs) regime to develop ways of better identifying money laundering and preventing the dissipation

[329] See Law Commission 2019 Report (n 3) at 174.

[330] ibid at 44.

[331] ibid at 166.

[332] R Pontes, N Lewis, P McFarlane and P Craig, 'Anti-Money Laundering in the United Kingdom: New Directions for a More Effective Regime' (2022) *Journal of Money Laundering Control* 25(2), 401–13 at 404.

[333] HM Government, *Serious and Organised Crime Strategy* (HM Government, 2018) at 61.

[334] See Data Protection Act 2018 and Council Regulation (EU) 2016/679 of the European Parliament and of the Council of 27 April 2016 on the protection of natural persons with regard to the processing of personal data and on the free movement of such data (United Kingdom General Data Protection Regulation) [2016] OJ L119/1–88.

of the proceeds of corruption; and will work with the reporting sectors to improve the quality and timeliness of reporting to the National Crime Agency.[335]

Here, HM Treasury and the Home Office agreed 'to produce an Anti-Money Laundering Action Plan to address issues highlighted by the National Risk Assessment on Money Laundering and Terrorist Financing'.[336] The Action Plan outlined how HM Government would liaise with the private sector and supervisors to tackle the threats identified in the National Risk Assessment.[337] The Action Plan seeks to build on the 2013 Serious and Organised Crime Strategy that included several mechanisms to make it more difficult for organised criminals to launder the proceeds of crime.[338] The key areas for the Action Plan included addressing the intelligence gaps through the financial and professional services sector, improving the law enforcement response to most serious threats, reforming the SARs regime, advancing the ability of the NCA and tackling the discrepancies in the supervisory regime.[339] In 2015, the Home Office published a 'call for information' seeking views from the regulated sector on identifying money laundering and terrorist financing, improving information-sharing, the consent regime and examples of international best practice.[340] The Action Plan stated that HM Government wanted to identify new mechanisms for the public and private sectors to work together 'and strip away unnecessary bureaucratic burdens in the process'.[341] Specifically, the Action Plan outlined that the reform of the SARs regime would be built on the success of JMLIT, which would be dependent on information provided by the private sector to law enforcement agencies.[342] In relation to data-sharing, HM Government stated that it would introduce legislation that allows reporting entities to share information on money laundering and terrorist financing.[343] In its response to the Action Plan, HM Government stated that it would initiate reform of the SARs system which would involve modernising its IT and processing systems, introduce legislation to permit the NCA to obtain more information from the reporting entities following the submission and receipt of a SAR, and create a new information-sharing gateway with immunity from civil liability.[344] In 2017 the Government announced a SARs reform programme, led by the Home Office, jointly with the

[335] HM Government, *UK Anti-Corruption Plan* (HM Government, 2014) at 44.

[336] ibid at 14.

[337] HM Treasury and Home Office, *UK National Risk Assessment of Money Laundering and Terrorist Financing* (HM Treasury and Home Office, 2015) at 6 and 12.

[338] HM Government, *Serious and Organised Crime Strategy* (HM Government, 2013).

[339] HM Treasury and Home Office (n 60) at 6–7.

[340] Home Office, 'Call for Information' (n/d), available at https://assets.publishing.service.gov.uk/media/5a80dc1440f0b62302695e83/SARs_Review_Call_for_Information_FINAL.PDF.

[341] HM Treasury and Home Office (n 60).

[342] ibid.

[343] ibid 12.

[344] Home Office, *Action Plan for Anti-Money-Laundering and Counter-Terrorist Finance: Consultation on Legislative Proposals Government Response* (Home Office, 2016) at 5.

NCA, which began in July 2018.[345] The NCA stated that the programme would 'deliver more fundamental change to the regime'.[346]

The next stage in the reform process was the publication of the Economic Crime Plan,[347] that was developed in conjunction with UK Finance. An integral part was the reform of the SARs regime and the NCA which 'as cornerstones of our whole response to economic crime, these must work better to produce richer intelligence and improve operational effectiveness'.[348] The Economic Crime Plan contains seven strategic priorities, of which the second seeks to 'pursue better sharing and usage of information to combat economic crime within and between the public and private sectors across all participants'.[349] HM Government stated that the Economic Crime Plan would 'respond to the Financial Action Taskforce's recommendations'.[350]

Additionally, the Economic Crime Plan included 'Actions' which covered a wide range of financial crime policy areas. Of relevance are Action 6,[351] 7,[352] 8,[353] 9,[354] 30,[355] 31,[356] 32[357] and 51.[358] As part of its Economic Crime Plan Online Tracker, the Royal United Services Institute noted that Actions 6, 7 and 8 had completed, but there was no due date set for Action 9.[359] The Tracker noted that Action 30 was overdue, 31 and 42 had been completed and there was no due date for Action 51.[360] Transparency International criticised the Economic Crime Plan and identified a number of areas that were omitted.[361] In 2019, Economic Crime and Strategic Board determined that 'further momentum was needed' and HM Government published its 'Economic Crime Plan: Statement

[345] NCA, *SARs Annual Report 2018* (NCA, 2018) at 29.

[346] ibid at 30.

[347] HM Government and UK Finance, *Economic Crime Plan 2019-2022* (HM Government and UK Finance, 2019).

[348] ibid at 3.

[349] ibid at 28.

[350] House of Commons Treasury Committee (n 278) at 4.

[351] Action 6 deals with the creation of a public-private partnership to review the existing sharing of information to tackle financial crime.

[352] Action 7 seeks to promote sharing of information in corporate groups.

[353] Action 8 deals with extending and improving the public-private information-sharing through JMLIT.

[354] Action 9 considers improving the information-sharing between AML/CTF supervisors and law enforcement agencies.

[355] HM Government and UK Finance (n 347) at 45–46.

[356] ibid at 46.

[357] ibid at 46.

[358] ibid at 66.

[359] RUSI, 'Economic Crime Plan Online Tracker' (n/d), available at www.rusi.org/ecp.

[360] ibid.

[361] Transparency International, 'Urgent Action Required to Address Gaps in UK Government's Plan to Combat Economic Crime' (12 July 2019), available at www.transparency.org.uk/publications/incentivising-ethics. Also see RUSI, 'Getting the Economic Crime Plan Done: Why Economic Crime Matters for Johnson's "Global Britain"' (13 January 2020), available at www.rusi.org/explore-our-research/publications/commentary/getting-economic-crime-plan-done-why-economic-crime-matters-johnsons-global-britain.

of Progress'.[362] HM Government announced the creation of seven new 'Actions' to further develop those in the Economic Crime Plan, of particular relevance were Actions 2,[363] 3[364] and 4.[365] Subsequently, HM Government published the Economic Crime Plan 2, which included an updated list of Actions that applied to SARs and data-sharing.[366] For example, Action 10 aimed to complete the delivery of the SARs Reform Programme, Action 11 seeks to improve the effectiveness of SARs and their use, and Action 34 seeks to create and implement a Public Private Economic Data Strategy.[367] Nizzero described the Economic Crime Plan 2 as feeling like a 'box-ticking exercise rather than a comprehensive framework that is made to have a lasting impact', but did note that 'of the milestones set out in the plan, the vast majority are either in progress or have been completed'.[368] Spotlight on Corruption broadly welcome the commitment by HM Government but argued that more public funding was needed to tackle financial crime.[369]

The Economic Crime Plan sets out a range of actions to improve the SARs regime, including 'IT transformation', 'a comprehensive regime-wide approach to feedback and guidance to iteratively improve SARs quality and regime processes', and an increase in analytical resource and capabilities for the UK Financial Intelligence Unit and for Regional Organised Crime Units.[370] The Treasury Committee welcomed 'the much-needed investment in new IT systems and the plans for increasing staff and analytical capacity'.[371] The programme also aims to 'address the Financial Action Task Force's criticisms regarding the role and resourcing of the UKFIU'.[372]

In December 2017, the Law Commission were invited by the Home Office to conduct a review of the UKs AML and CTF provisions under POCA 2002 and the Terrorism Act 2000.[373] In particular, the Law Commission was asked to

[362] HM Government and UK Finance, *Economic Crime Plan: Statement of Progress* (HM Government and UK Finance, 2021).

[363] Action two seeks to improve the public private operational action to tackle known vulnerabilities enabling the flow of illicit finance within and out of the UK.

[364] Action three seeks to improve the effectiveness and efficiency of the whole system response to economic crime, increasing high value intelligence to law enforcement.

[365] Action four seeks to continue to deliver SARs reform, including the next stages of the rollout of the new IT infrastructure and the increase in UKFIU staffing.

[366] HM Government and UK Finance (n 138).

[367] ibid at 35 and 72.

[368] M Nizzero, 'The UK's Economic Crime Plan 2: Progress, Pitfalls and Prospects' (26 March 2024), available at www.rusi.org/explore-our-research/publications/commentary/uks-economic-crime-plan-2-progress-pitfalls-and-prospects The UK's Economic Crime Plan 2: Progress, Pitfalls and Prospects | Royal United Services Institute.

[369] S Hawley, D Beizsley and J Bolton-Jones, 'No New Government Investment in the Economic Crime Plan Threatens Delivery' (30 March 2023), available at www.spotlightcorruption.org/no-investment-in-economic-crime-plan-1/.

[370] See HM Government and UK Finance (n 347) at 45.

[371] See House of Commons Treasury Committee (n 20) at 41–42.

[372] See House of Commons Treasury Committee (n 278) at 36.

[373] See Law Commission 2018 Report (n 3).

consider the reform of the 'system of voluntary disclosed known as the consent regime and … the disclosure offences'.[374] Following the announcement, Brennan noted that

> the burden on the agencies responsible for processing reports is also substantial, as is the impact on those who are the subject of the suspicions (whose accounts and transactions may be frozen). It is essential, therefore, that the system functions in a fair, effective and efficient way.[375]

The Law Commission investigation was supplemented by a combined NCA/Home Office review of the SARs regime and an AML enquiry by the Treasury Select Committee into AML.[376] The Law Commission were given the unenviable task of making

> realistic recommendations that balance the competing interests of stakeholders. In other words, to improve the quality of suspicious activity reports sent to law enforcement agencies, thereby maximising opportunities to disrupt and detect criminal activity, while reducing the burdens on those who submit and assess suspicious activity reports.[377]

The Law Commission published a Consultation Paper which has three aims 'to identify the most pressing problems; consult on reforming the consent regime; and to generate and consider ideas for long term reform'.[378] The Law Commission identified several practical problems associated with the SARs regime including the large number of reports submitted to the NCA, the poor quality of reports, confusion of the authorised disclosure regime, abuse of the authorised disclosure exemption, defensive reporting, the regulatory burden on reporting entities and the impact of the suspension of transactions.[379] Additionally, the Law Commission identified several legal complications including the all crime approach, the language used in Part 7 of POCA, the interpretation of suspicion, the mixing of criminal and non-criminal funds, data-sharing between the private sector, the interpretation of criminal property and what constitutes a reasonable excuse within POCA.[380]

Consequently, the Law Commission published its final report in 2019 and made the following 19 recommendations:[381]

i. to keep the consent regime;
ii. more analysis on the quality of SARs should be conducted;

[374] ibid.
[375] H Brennan, 'The Law Commission's Review of Anti-Money Laundering and Counter-Terrorism Financing' (2019) *Archibold Review* 2019, 7, 4–6.
[376] House of Commons Treasury Committee (n 278).
[377] See Brennan (n 375).
[378] See Law Commission 2018 Report (n 3) at 11.
[379] ibid.
[380] ibid.
[381] ibid at 197–202.

iii. the Secretary of State should be obligated to issue guidance on the operation of Part 7 of POCA;
iv. an Advisory Board should be created to assist in the production of the statutory guidance;
v. the all-crimes approach should be preserved;
vi. POCA should not be amended to define suspicion;
vii. POCA is amended to require the Secretary of State to publish guidance on suspicion;
viii. the Secretary of State should introduce a prescribed form pursuant to POCA;
ix. an Advisory Board should undertake a review as to whether to increase the threshold;
x. statutory guidance is published on consent within POCA and TACT;
xi. the regime in respect of low value transactions should be retained;
xii. the Advisory Board should explore including appropriate reporting routes within statutory guidance to assist reporters on complying with their obligations;
xiii. reporting entities should be allowed to submit one SAR for multiple transactions on the same account and for multiple transactions for the same company or individual;
xiv. banks should not have to seek consent to repay funds to a victim of fraud;
xv. the current approach to authorised disclosures on international criminality is maintained;
xvi. amendments should be made to sections 327, 328 and 239 of POCA;
xvii. statutory guidance should be published on the operation of ringfencing;
xviii. POCA should be amended to allow funds to be released by the Crown Court for reasonable living expenses and an extension to the moratorium period is made; and
xix. more research is undertaken into the appropriateness of targeted reporting.

The response was predictable, with the Government accepting or partially accepting 13 out of the 19 Recommendations, whilst rejecting six.[382] In particular, HM Government accepted or partially accepted the retention of the current DAML SARs regime, the creation of an advisory board to oversee SARs guidance and effectiveness, ongoing work to improve SAR quality, including consultation with an Advisory Board, maintaining the 'all-crimes' approach to reporting suspicious activity and amendments to the POCA including defining 'suspicion' and allowing banks to repay fraud victims without seeking consent. The rejected recommendations included statutory guidance on suspicion thresholds and appropriate consent, amendments to POCA

[382] Home Office, 'Policy Paper – Response to Law Commission Review of the SARs Regime' (12 February 2024), available at www.gov.uk/government/publications/response-to-law-commission-review-of-the-sars-regime.

requiring the Secretary of State to issue guidance, and the issuing of statutory guidance on arrangements with prior consent under the Terrorism Act 2000. HM Government's response lacks innovation and bolder ideas and several of the concerns raised by the Law Commission have been disregarded. In particular, the rejection of statutory guidance on suspicion thresholds is a missed opportunity, given ongoing uncertainty in the application of POCA. Additionally, the delay in responding – despite the rapid increase in SARs filings – has raised concerns about the effectiveness of the current system.

XI. Conclusions

The UK faces a significant and evolving threat from money laundering. While DAML SARs serve as a critical tool in identifying and preventing illicit financial activity, the current system lacks efficiency, rapid assessment, and effective information exchange, limiting its overall impact. This chapter has demonstrated how weaknesses in data-sharing practices among key sectors impede the effectiveness of DAML SARs enforcement. The first case study identifies a number of common deficiencies in the application of DAML SARs by the legal profession. A large percentage of the financial penalties imposed by the SRA were for law firms not undertaking a risk assessment, which helps firms develop policies, controls and procedures to mitigate money laundering risks. Failure to conduct a firm-wide risk assessment is problematic and could result in increased exposure to money laundering. If a risk assessment is not undertaken, a firm could unknowingly engage with high-risk clients or transactions, thus making them vulnerable to money laundering. Therefore, the risk assessment is an important mechanism for the legal profession to identify and alleviate money laundering risks. The second case study highlights deficiencies in the internal AML systems of financial institutions, illustrating the important crucial role of compliance with reporting obligations to prevent money laundering. Weak internal monitoring and inadequate risk-based due diligence have led to financial penalties and ineffective DAML SARs, which impede money laundering investigations. While financial institutions have attempted to enhance their AML processes, challenges remain in ensuring meaningful improvements. Strengthening AML frameworks, improving transaction monitoring, and fostering better coordination with regulators are essential to enhancing financial institutions' ability to combat financial crime and protect their reputations.

The third case study has highlighted the fragmentation in the UK's AML supervisory framework, where numerous supervisory bodies hinder effective intelligence-sharing. While recent reforms aim to enhance compliance and coordination, inconsistencies remain, particularly among professional body supervisors. HM Government is exploring models to streamline AML supervision, including consolidation of supervisory bodies or the creation of a single supervisory entity. Additionally, intelligence gaps persist, partly due to HMRC's reluctance to share data. To address this, legal amendments to the Commissioners for Revenue and Customs Act 2005 have been proposed to mandate information disclosure when there are suspicions of money laundering. Such changes would align HMRC's duties with broader crime prevention efforts, enabling improved financial intelligence-sharing. These measures, along with a strengthened crime prevention mandate for HMRC, could enhance the UK's ability to combat financial crime by developing greater coordination, transparency, and enforcement action within the AML regime. However, effective implementation requires sustained commitment to overcoming systemic barriers and improving inter-agency collaboration. The fourth case study illustrated that public-private partnerships have played a pivotal role in improving collaboration, ensuring that banks contribute to AML efforts. The NCA case study serves as a model for best practices, highlighting the need to extend the pilot study and explore the benefits of voluntary data-sharing mechanisms.

The Law Commission made 19 recommendations aimed at improving the SARs regime. Important proposals included maintaining the consent regime, enhancing SARs quality analysis, obligating the Secretary of State to issue operational guidance, and establishing an Advisory Board to oversee statutory guidance. Furthermore, the Law Commission suggested retaining the all-crimes approach, amending POCA to clarify suspicion guidance, streamlining SAR reporting processes for entities, allowing banks to return fraud victims' funds without seeking approval, and exploring appropriate reporting routes. However, HM Government's response was predictable and is cautious rather than transformative, opting for incremental improvements rather than significant reforms. The rejection of statutory guidance on suspicion thresholds is notable, as it leaves unresolved concerns about inconsistent interpretations of POCA 2002. Furthermore, the delayed response, despite the surge in SAR filings, raises doubts about the effectiveness of the current system and the Government's commitment to improving the SARs regime and related data-sharing mechanisms. The lack of bold innovation suggests a preference for 'status quo' adjustments rather than a complete overhaul of the SARs processes. Through an analysis of legal frameworks, institutional cooperation and the four case studies, it is evident that modernising DAML SARs submission, streamlining intelligence dissemination, and enhancing collaboration are crucial to closing existing gaps. The findings reinforce some of the conclusions of the 2018 FATF MER and highlight the need for reforms that improve data-sharing mechanisms, strengthen regulatory oversight, and enable a more proactive approach to combating money laundering. Addressing these deficiencies is essential to ensuring that LEAs, regulatory bodies, the UKFIU and private sector work collectively to mitigate emerging threats and safeguard the integrity of the financial system.

The 2018 FATF MER praised the UK's AML regime as one of the strongest in the world. However, the report also cautioned that the intensity of supervision was uneven across sectors, the UKFIU required greater resources and the SARs regime needed modernisation and reform. Despite this, the chapter has presented evidence that shows failures in firm-wide risk assessments within the legal sector, which the MER identified as a priority for consistent supervision. The SRA's penalties for not conducting risk assessments reveal that supervision intensity is patchy and that formal compliance has not translated into uniform practice across non-financial professional bodies. Financial institutions, too, exhibit critical shortcomings in transaction monitoring and risk-based due diligence. Weak internal AML systems have produced low-quality DAML SARs, delaying investigations and undermining the MER's finding on the effective use of financial intelligence. The fragmented AML supervisory landscape, marked by several overlapping bodies and HMRC's reluctance to share data despite proposed legislative amendments, directly challenges FATF's conclusion that coordination mechanisms were sufficiently strong. The ongoing intelligence gaps and inconsistent inter-agency collaboration demonstrate that, the structural weaknesses flagged in the MER remain unresolved. FATF commended the UK's public–private partnerships as best-practice models, yet our fourth case study shows these pilots are still limited in scope and voluntary data-sharing mechanisms have not been scaled up. The promise of public private partnerships has yet to be fully realised in routine operational settings, suggesting that formal endorsement alone cannot drive meaningful change.

Collectively, this evidence highlights a divergence between FATF's formal assessment and on-the-ground reality. Merely tweaking supervisory frameworks or issuing incremental guidance will not bridge the gaps in data-sharing, oversight and SAR quality. A renewed emphasis on measurable outcomes, rather than box-ticking, alongside bold institutional reforms is essential to align practice with the high standards set out in the 2018 MER.

5

Terrorist Financing

> Retrospective SARs are less helpful in terrorist financing cases given the relatively short time period in which attacks were planned ... historic information is of little value.[1]

I. Introduction

The fight against terrorist financing is a crucial element of national and international security, requiring the coordination of financial intelligence, data-sharing, and information exchange between various entities. However, weaknesses persist in these areas, limiting the effectiveness of counter-terrorist financing (CTF) efforts. This chapter examines these shortcomings, focusing on the exchange of information between reporting entities, the United Kingdom Financial Intelligence Unit (UKFIU), law enforcement agencies (LEAs), anti-money laundering supervisory agencies (AMLSAs) and the Security Intelligence Services (SIS). To contextualise these challenges, the chapter first outlines the evolution of the United Kingdom's (UK) CTF laws, before and in response to the terrorist attacks in the United States of America (US) in September 2001 ('9/11'). The legislative developments following 9/11 reshaped global approaches to combating terrorist financing, leading to stringent regulatory frameworks and enhanced monitoring mechanisms. A key element in this discussion is the Financial Action Task Force (FATF) Mutual Evaluation Report (MER), which assessed the UK's level of compliance with its Recommendations.[2] By summarising the report's conclusions, this section highlights both progress made and gaps that remain in the UK's financial intelligence infrastructure.

Building on this foundation, the chapter focuses on defence against terrorist financing suspicious activity reports (DATF SARs) under the Terrorism Act 2000 (TACT). These are essential for identifying potential threats, yet inefficiencies in their handling and exchange often undermine their intended purpose. Through

[1] Law Commission, *Anti-Money Laundering: The SARs Regime Consultation Paper* (Law Commission, 2018) at 57–58.

[2] See generally Financial Action Task Force (FATF), *Anti-Money Laundering and Counter-Terrorist Financing Measure: United Kingdom Mutual Evaluation Report* (FATF, 2018) (hereinafter 'FATF 2018 MER').

an exploration of case studies, deficiencies and successful mechanisms used in the detection and prevention of terrorist financing are highlighted. These examples underscore the critical need for improved collaboration and communication across financial institutions, intelligence services and LEAs. Moving beyond individual cases, the chapter assesses existing mechanisms for CTF data-sharing and their effectiveness. The analysis presented in this chapter seeks to identify key areas for improvement and provide targeted recommendations for strengthening financial intelligence coordination, enhancing data-sharing practices, and bolstering the UK's overall CTF strategy.

By evaluating the structural weaknesses in financial intelligence and data-sharing systems, this chapter aims to contribute to ongoing discussions on enhancing national security measures against terrorist financing. In doing so, it highlights the necessity of a more integrated, transparent, and responsive approach to information exchange, one that seeks to ensure financial intelligence is leveraged, and used effectively to combat evolving threats in an increasingly complex global landscape. Therefore, in light of these findings, it appears that the HM Revenue and Customs (HMRC) practice is not in line with national, regional and international legal instruments. For example, FATF Recommendation 31 provides that 'when conducting [terrorist financing] investigations … competent authorities should be able to obtain access to all [author's emphasis] necessary documents and information for use in those investigations, and in prosecutions and related actions'.[3] The evidence presented in this chapter illustrates that the UK has not met the requirements of Recommendation 31, yet the 2018 FATF MER concluded that here 'all criteria' are met. Recommendation 31 is rated 'Compliant'.[4] In order to address this weakness, the chapter suggests that HM Government extend the automatic exchange of information model as advocated by the Organisation for Economic Co-operation and Development (OECD), to UK competent authorities.[5]

This chapter seeks to answer this subsidiary question 'how effective the UK's mechanisms are for detecting and disrupting terrorist financing through DATF SARs and CTF data-sharing mechanisms'. Therefore, in order to answer this question, the chapter begins by defining terrorist financing, outlines the impact of the Financial War on Terrorism and then focuses on emerging terrorist financing typologies. It is against this background that the second part of the chapter outlines the reporting process of DATF SARs under TACT 2000 before discussing the use of customer information orders and financial directions. The third part of the chapter adopts the case study methodology to highlight deficiencies and examples of best practice in the use of DATF SARs and exchange of information. The

[3] FATF, *The International Standards on Combating Money Laundering and the Financing of Terrorism & Proliferation – the FATF Recommendations* (FATF, 2025).

[4] See FATF 2018 MER (n 2) at 226.

[5] For a brief discussion of what is a 'competent authority', see N Ryder, *Financial Crime and Policy in the 21st Century – Law and Policy* (Edward Elgar, 2011).

fourth part of the chapter identifies and appraises the CTF data-sharing mechanisms before identifying a set of recommendations.

II. Terrorist Financing

Terrorist financing is defined by the International Convention for the Suppression of the Financing of Terrorism as including 'assets of every kind, whether tangible or intangible, movable or immovable, however acquired, and legal documents or instruments in any form'.[6] It has also been defined as providing 'the financial support, in any form, of terrorism or of those who encourage, plan, or engage in it'.[7] Furthermore, the International Monetary Fund stated that terrorist financing 'involves the solicitation, collection or provision of funds with the intention that they may be used to support terrorist acts or organizations'.[8] Terrorist financing has also been referred to as 'reverse money laundering', which is a practice whereby 'clean' or 'legitimate' money is acquired and then funnelled to support acts of terrorism.[9] Some researchers have argued that terrorist financing can be used as a tool for ideological movements rather than an end in itself.[10] Furthermore, the widespread adoption of FATF Recommendations has led to a more standardised approach to combating terrorist financing.[11] For the purposes of terrorist financing, terrorism in the UK is defined as the use or threat of action which involves serious violence against a person; serious damage to property; endangers a person's life; creates a serious risk to the health or safety of the public; or is designed to seriously interfere or disrupt an electronic system.[12]

A. Financial War on Terrorism

Prior to 9/11, the international community's efforts towards tackling financial crime focused on the prevention of money laundering and the related illegal

[6] International Convention for the Suppression of the Financing of Terrorism, opened for signature 9 December 1999, entered into force 10 April 2002, 2178 UNTS 197, Arti 1, para 1.

[7] World Bank, *Reference Guide to Anti-Money Laundering and Combating the Financing of Terrorism* (World Bank, Washington DC, 2006) at 19.

[8] International Monetary Fund, 'Anti-Money Laundering/Combating the Financing of Terrorism – Topics (n/d), available at www.imf.org/external/np/leg/amlcft/eng/aml1.htm#financingterrorism.

[9] For a more detailed discussion of this process, see S Cassella, 'Reverse Money Laundering' (2003) *Journal of Money Laundering Control* 7(1), 92–94 at 92.

[10] H Trinkunas, 'Financing Terrorism' in E Chenoweth, R English, A Gofas and S Kalycas, *The Oxford Handbook of Terrorism* (Oxford University Press, 2019).

[11] J Zarate and S Watson, 'The Lexicon of Terror Crystallization of the Definition of Terrorism through the Lens of Terrorist Financing and the Financial Action Task Force' (2022) *Harvard National Security Journal* 13, 369.

[12] Terrorism Act 2000 (TACT), s 1.

drugs trade.[13] A direct consequence of these terrorist attacks was a fundamental change in the international communities' attitudes towards addressing the threat of terrorist financing. However, the legislative response by the United Nations (UN), the European Union (EU) and soft law standards of the FATF were incorrectly based on the global anti-money laundering (AML) standards and strategy.[14] The global AML strategy targets attempts by money launderers to conceal the profits of crime that contribute towards their so-called 'champagne lifestyle'.[15] Terrorists and terrorist organisations tend not to make profit to facilitate such a lifestyle, and their financing typologies differ from money launderers.[16] The terrorist attacks resulted in terrorist financing being propelled from political obscurity to the top of the international political agenda. On 24 September 2001, President George Bush declared 'we will starve terrorists of funding, turn them against each other, rout them out of their safe hiding places, and bring them to justice'.[17] This announcement was followed by the freezing of the assets of terrorists and their supporters.[18] These declarations have been referred to as the 'Rose Garden Strategy', which laid the foundations for the Financial War on Terrorism,[19] which has been defined as

> attacking, whether via criminalisation, confiscation, forfeiture, freezing, or sanctioning, the financial assets of known or suspected terrorists. Furthermore … [it] … also contains the use of preventative methods that have previously been used for money laundering and the collection of financial intelligence from suspicious activity reports.[20]

The UK, influenced by the international legislative measures introduced by the UN, the EU and the Recommendations of FATF, has consequentially implemented legislation aimed at combating terrorist financing. Such measures included the Anti-terrorism Crime and Security Act 2001, the Prevention of Terrorism Act 2005, the Counter-Terrorism Act 2008 and the Terrorist Asset Freezing (Temporary Provisions) Act 2010. However, the UK was one of the first countries to introduce CTF measures, due to the historic threat presented by domestic

[13] N Ryder, *Money Laundering an Endless Cycle? A Comparative Analysis of the Anti-Money Laundering Policies in the USA, UK, Australia and Canada* (Routledge, 2012) 8–39.

[14] N Ryder, 'Is it Time to Reform the Counter-Terrorist Financing Reporting Obligations? A Critical and Comparative Assessment of the Counter-Terrorist Financing Reporting Obligations in the European Union and the United Kingdom' (2018) *German Law Review* 19(5), 1169–90.

[15] National Audit Office, *The Asset Recovery Agency* (National Audit Office, 2007).

[16] See S Irwin, A Kim-Kwang, R Choo and L Liu, 'Modelling of Money Laundering and Terrorism Financing Typologies' (2012) *Journal of Money Laundering Control* 15(3), 316–35.

[17] The White House, 'Fact Sheet on Terrorist Financing Executive Order' (24 September 2001), available at https://georgewbush-whitehouse.archives.gov/news/releases/2001/09/20010924-2.html#:~:text=The%20Order%20expands%20the%20Treasury,to%2C%20foreign%20banks%20who%20refuse.

[18] United States Department of State, 'Executive Order, 13,224', available from www.state.gov/executive-order-13224.

[19] R Suskind, *The One Percent Doctrine* (Simon & Schuster, 2006) at 142.

[20] N Ryder, *The Financial War on Terror: A Review of Counter-Terrorist Financing Strategies since 2001* (Routledge, 2015) at 11.

terrorism.[21] Therefore, the UK has a substantial experience of tackling domestic terrorism and the evolution of its terrorist-related measures and policies can be traced back to the start of the twentieth century.[22] In relation to the financing of terrorism, the Prevention of Terrorism (Temporary Provisions) Act 1974 enabled the courts to forfeit assets which were 'controlled by an individual convicted of membership, where such resources were intended for use in Northern Ireland terrorism'.[23] The Prevention of Terrorism (Temporary Provisions) Act 1989 Act criminalised contributions towards acts of terrorism,[24] contributions to resources of proscribed organisations,[25] assisting in retention or control of terrorist funds,[26] disclosure of information about terrorist funds,[27] penalties and forfeiture.[28] These CTF measures were aimed at disrupting financial flows and limiting terrorist activities, yet the success of these measures was limited. For example, the 'Lloyd Inquiry' or 'Inquiry into Legislation Against Terrorism' that was conducted by Lord Lloyd of Berwick to evaluate the need for permanent counter-terrorist legislation in the UK, concluded that the CTF measures had limited impact on terrorist financing.[29] The effectiveness of the Act was questionable and it was amended by TACT,[30] which has become an integral part of the UK's CTF strategy.

TACT extended the scope of its offences to international terrorism,[31] it maintained the concept of proscription,[32] a Proscribed Organisations Appeal Commission was created,[33] new seizure and forfeiture powers were introduced[34] and financial institutions were required to detect accounts that could be relevant to terrorist investigations.[35] Part III of the Act is entitled 'Terrorist Property' and introduced criminal offences relating to terrorist financing. These include: raising,

[21] See Prevention of Terrorism (Temporary Provisions) Act 1989 ss 9–13. See generally J Horgan and M Taylor, 'Playing the "Green Card" – Financing the Provisional IRA: Part 1 (1999) *Terrorism and Political Violence* 11(2), 1–38; J Horgan and M Taylor, 'Playing the "Green Card" – Financing the Provisional IRA: Part 2' (2003) *Terrorism and Political Violence* 15(2), 1–60 and J Adams, 'The Financing of Terror' in P Wilkinson and A Stewart, *Contemporary Research on Terrorism* (Aberdeen University Press, 1989) 393–405. A Silke, 'In Defence of the Realm: Financing Loyalist Terrorism in Northern Ireland – Part One: Extortion and Blackmail' (1998) *Studies in Conflict & Terrorism* 21(4), 331–61 at 349.

[22] L Donohue, *The Cost of Counterterrorism – Power, Politics and Liberty* (Cambridge University Press, 2008) at 129.

[23] Prevention of Terrorism (Temporary Provisions) Act 1974, s 1(7).

[24] Prevention of Terrorism (Temporary Provisions) Act 1989, s 9.

[25] ibid s 10.

[26] ibid s 11.

[27] ibid s 12.

[28] ibid s 13.

[29] Lord Loyd of Berwick, *Inquiry into Legislation Against Terrorism* (Cm 3420, 1996) at 81.

[30] See Home Office, *Legislation against Terrorism – A Consultation Paper* (Home Office, 1998).

[31] See Crown Prosecution Service, 'Terrorism' (n/d), available at www.cps.gov.uk/crime-info/terrorism#:~:text=The%20Terrorism%20Act%202000%20defines,or%20to%20intimidate%20the%20public.

[32] TACT ss 3–13.

[33] ibid sch 3.

[34] ibid ss 23, 23A and 23B.

[35] ibid s 19.

receiving or providing funds for the purpose of terrorism;[36] using or possessing funds for the purpose of terrorism;[37] becoming involved in an arrangement which makes funds available for the purposes of terrorism;[38] and, facilitating the laundering of terrorist property and money.[39] Additional offences include failing to disclose information about the occurrence of terrorist financing[40] and, for those working in the regulated financial sector, the offence of tipping off.[41] If a person does anything outside of the UK which would have been an offence under sections 15–18 of the Act within the UK, they will also be guilty of an offence.[42] An important point to note is that while the terrorist financing offences have been acknowledged for their broadness, the number of terrorist financing convictions are low. For example, at the end of June 2025 there were seven terrorist funding convictions under sections 15–19 of TACT.[43]

B. Terrorist Financing Typologies

Prior to 9/11, terrorists relied on two forms of financial support: state sponsorship and donations from private individuals. State sponsorship of terrorism is where national governments provide support to terrorist organisations. It is impossible to provide an accurate statistical figure for the amount of funding that terrorists receive from nation states, but it has been described as considerable.[44] Prior to 9/11, state sponsored terrorism was an important factor in international conflicts, particularly during the 1970s and 1980s.[45] However, by the 2010s, the prevalence of direct state sponsorship had declined, largely due to the implementation of the 'Financial War on Terrorism'.[46] At the time of writing the US has identified four

[36] ibid s 15.
[37] ibid s 16.
[38] ibid s 17.
[39] ibid s 18.
[40] ibid ss 19 and 21A.
[41] ibid s 21D.
[42] ibid s 63.
[43] See Home Office, 'Operation of Police Powers under the Terrorism Act 2000 and Subsequent Legislation: Arrests, Outcomes, and Stop and Search, Great Britain, Quarterly Update to June 2025' (11 September 2025), available at www.gov.uk/government/statistics/operation-of-police-powers-under-tact-2000-to-june-2025/operation-of-police-powers-under-the-terrorism-act-2000-and-subsequent-legislation-arrests-outcomes-and-stop-and-search-great-britain-quarterly-u#:~:text=Main%20results,-For%20arrests%20and&text=there%20were%20234%20arrests%20for,median%20number%20of%20arrests%20(238).
[44] See A Richard, *Fighting Terrorist Financing: Transatlantic Co-operation and International Institutions* (Centre for Transatlantic Relations, John Hopkins University, 2005) at 6.
[45] See D Bryman and S Kreps, 'Agents of Destruction? Applying Principal-Agent Analysis to State-Sponsored Terrorism' (2010) *International Studies Perspectives* 11(1), 1–18 and D Carlton, 'The 1980s: Encouraging and Sponsoring Terrorism' in D Carlton (eds), *The West's Road to 9/11 Resisting, Appeasing and Encouraging Terrorism Since 1970* (Palgrave, 2005) 172–87.
[46] See S Collins, 'State-Sponsored Terrorism: In Decline, Yet Still a Potent Threat' (2014) *Politics & Policy* 42(1), 131–59.

state sponsors of terrorism: Cuba, Iran, North Korea and Syria.[47] Additionally, it has been suggested that other states have provided terrorists with financial support and assisted in the planning of their operations.[48] Since Russia's invasion of Ukraine on 24 February 2022, concerns about state sponsored terrorism have intensified.[49] While there is no universally agreed definition of state sponsored terrorism, Russia has been accused of using terrorist tactics in Ukraine, including attacks on civilian infrastructure and hospitals.[50] The European Parliament declared Russia a state sponsor of terrorism, citing its deliberate destruction of civilian infrastructure and killings of Ukrainian civilians.[51] This was preceded by the Estonian Parliament adopting a resolution with similar effect.[52] However, this designation is largely symbolic, as the EU lacks a legal framework to formally label a country as a state sponsor of terrorism.[53] Russia has revived Cold War-era tactics, using terrorism as part of its foreign policy strategy.[54] The US Congress has debated adding Russia to its list of state sponsors of terrorism, but the State Department has declined to do so.[55]

The use of private financial benefactors was highlighted by the US Department of Treasury, which conducted an analysis of terrorist financing cases and prosecutions, between 2001 and 2014, determined that approximately one-third of the cases involved financial support from private donors.[56] The FATF stated that, 'wealthy private donors can be an important source of income for some terrorist groups'.[57] For example, the FATF acknowledged that

[47] See Department of State, 'State Sponsors of Terrorism' (n/d), available at www.state.gov/state-sponsors-of-terrorism/.

[48] For a more detailed discussion, see K Jeewon, 'Making State Sponsors of Terrorism Pay: A Separation of Powers Discourse under the Foreign Sovereign Immunities Act' (2004) *Berkeley Journal of International Law* 22, 513–40 and A Chase, 'Legal Mechanisms of the International Community and the United States Concerning State Sponsored Terrorism' (2004) *Virginal Journal of International Law* 45, 41–137.

[49] See K Rekawek, *Russian State Terrorism and State Sponsorship of Terrorism* (International Centre for Counter Terrorism, 2024).

[50] See S Lucas, 'Ukraine War: EU Parliament Names Russia a 'State Sponsor of Terrorism' – but it Won't Stop the Missiles' (24 November 2022), available at https://theconversation.com/ukraine-war-eu-parliament-names-russia-a-state-sponsor-of-terrorism-but-it-wont-stop-the-missiles-195309.

[51] European Parliament, 'Russia's War on Ukraine: Designating a State as a Sponsor of Terrorism' (11 November 2022), available at www.europarl.europa.eu/RegData/etudes/ATAG/2022/738218/EPRS_ATA(2022)738218_EN.pdf.

[52] See T Fielder, 'Estonian Parliament Declares Russia a Terrorist State' (18 October 2022), available at www.politico.eu/article/as-the-third-country-to-estonia-declares-russia-a-terrorist-state/.

[53] See European Parliament (n 51).

[54] C Marsh, 'Putin's Playbook: The Development of Russian Tactics, Operations, and Strategy from Chechnya to Ukraine' in A Farhadi, M Grzegorzewski and A Masys (eds), *The Great Power Competition Volume 5 The Russian Invasion of Ukraine and Implications for the Central Region* (Springer, 2023) at 161–83.

[55] See L Graham, 'Graham, Blumenthal Introduce Bill Designating Russia a State Sponsor of Terrorism' (20 June 2024), available at https://www.lgraham.senate.gov/public/index.cfm/2024/6/graham-blumenthal-introduce-bill-designating-russia-a-state-sponsor-of-terrorism.

[56] United States Department of Treasury, *National Terrorist Financing Risk Assessment 2015* (United States Department of Treasury, 2015).

[57] FATF, *Emerging Terrorist Financing Risk* (FATF, 2015) at 13.

the Islamic State has received some funding from wealthy private donors in the region.[58] In order to understand and identify these common and emerging terrorist financing mechanisms, the international community have used typologies. The FATF adds that 'these typologies provide a contemporary snapshot of the ways in which terrorists raise, move and use funds'.[59] Some of the most commonly used terrorist financing methods include the proceeds of drug trafficking,[60] kidnapping for ransom,[61] counterfeit currencies,[62] oil refining,[63] natural resources,[64] piracy,[65] Hawala,[66] private donations and extortion.[67] The Financial War on Terrorism has been able to limit some of these funding avenues and as a result terrorist financiers have turned towards alternative sources. Therefore, we have seen the emergence of new terrorism funding typologies. For example, low-cost terrorism has become a prominent typology as illustrated by the terrorist attacks in Madrid,[68] London,[69] London,[70] Paris,[71] London,[72] Manchester,[73] and London.[74] Other emerging terrorist financing typologies include fraud. Here, terrorists have obtained funding via passport fraud, immigration fraud, identity fraud, financial fraud, online fraud, public funding and grant fraud, benefit fraud, student loan fraud, non-profit organisation fraud, tax fraud, counterfeiting, insurance fraud, mortgage fraud and

[58] FATF, *Financing of the Terrorist Organisation Islamic State in Iraq and the Levant* (FATF, 2015) at 11.

[59] ibid at 5.

[60] Federal Research Division Library of Congress, *A global Overview of Narcotics-Funded Terrorist and other Extremist Groups* (Library of Congress, 2002).

[61] See FATF, *Emerging Terrorist Financing Risk* (n 57) at 18.

[62] FATF, *Money Laundering and Terrorist Financing Related to Counterfeiting of Currency* (FATF, 2011).

[63] See FATF, *Emerging Terrorist Financing Risk* (n 57).

[64] ibid 39–42.

[65] FATF, *Organised Maritime Piracy and Related Kidnapping for Ransom* (FATF, 2011).

[66] FATF, *The Role of Hawala and other Similar Service Providers in Money Laundering and Terrorist Financing* (FATF, 2013).

[67] See FATF, *Emerging Terrorist Financing Risk* (n 57).

[68] L Nepoleoni, 'Terrorism Financing in Europe' in H Trinkunas and J Giraldo (eds), *Terrorism Financing and State Responses* (Stanford University Press, 2007) at 171–84.

[69] HM Government, *Report of the Official Account of the Bombings in London on 7th July 2005* (House of Commons, 2005).

[70] BBC News, 'Lee Rigby Murder: Adebolajo and Adebowale Jailed' (26 February 2014), available at www.bbc.co.uk/news/uk-26357007.

[71] CNN, 'A Timeline of the Charlie Hebdo Terror Attack' (10 January 2015), available at http://edition.cnn.com/2015/01/08/europe/charlie-hebdo-attack-timeline/.

[72] BBC News, 'London Attack: Who was Khalid Masood?' (26 March 2017), available at www.bbc.co.uk/news/uk-39373766 London attack: Who was Khalid Masood? – BBC News.

[73] T Keatinge, 'Terror on the Cheap: Financing Lone Actor and Small Cell Attacks' (17 August 2015), available at https://rusi.org/commentary/terror-cheap-financing-lone-actor-and-small-cell-attacks.

[74] N Ryder, 'Cryptoassets, Social Media Platforms and Defence against Terrorism Financing Suspicious Activity Reports: A Step into the Regulatory Unknown' (2020) *Journal of Business Law* 8, 668–93.

trade-based fraud.[75] Furthermore, terrorists have been able to obtain funding from cryptoassets and social networking platforms, as the anonymity and speed provided by the internet is an appealing tool for terrorists to solicit financial donors.[76] Finally, the unprecedented scale of Islamic State's finances illustrated the use of the 'corporate' or 'hierarchical' funding model. The unprecedented scale of Islamic State's finances has been underscored by the development of its own currency: an unparalleled development in the financing of terrorism. The Islamic State was a well-funded terrorist group that while reminiscent of Al-Qaeda in its pomp, belittles their achievements and those of other terrorist groups. Assessing the wealth of publicly traded companies is extremely difficult – as evidenced in the 2007 global financial crises – and so it is no surprise that evaluating the wealth of illicit organisations relies at best on educated guesswork. However, if the most accepted estimates are accurate, and Islamic State earned approximately USD$1million per day, then from a financial perspective it has the financial capability to operate for many years. This financial resilience has come about because the Islamic State's financial infrastructure is significantly more advanced than any other known terrorist organisation, therefore it can be reasoned to say that the 'Financial War on Terrorism' is not fit for purpose when it comes to the Islamic State. Not only do all financial institutions need to redouble their efforts to avoid being conduits for Islamic State funding, the regulatory regimes that oversee them also need to be better monitored to ensure the consistency and efficiency of their CTF measures. Even with more consistent implementation of CTF measures, the fact remains that Islamic State's funding model has proved to be extremely flexible and adaptable, and it was only when the territorial reach of Islamic State was defeated that we have seen their funding streams significantly reduced.

As terrorism financing typologies continue to evolve, the CTF measures used remain the same. For instance, the UK continues to pursue terrorism financiers under the offences created by the TACT and the ability of HM Treasury to freeze the assets of terrorists was extended by the Anti-terrorism, Crime and Security Act 2001. Following the Russian invasion of Ukraine in February 2022, the UK Government extended its ability to use sanctions by introducing the Economic Crime (Transparency and Enforcement) Act 2022. The Office of Financial Sanctions Implementation, which was created in 2016, implements and enforces these financial sanctions in the UK.[77] The UK continues to use DATF SARs to

[75] N Ryder, 'To Report or not to Report? An Analysis of the Relationship between Defence against Terrorism Financing Suspicious Activity Reports and Fraud in the United Kingdom' in L de Koker and D Goldbarsht, *Financial Crime, Law and Governance – Navigating Challenges in Different Contexts* (Springer, 2024) 169–202.

[76] See, eg, the convictions of Ali Shukri Amin (2015), Zoobia Shahnaz (2020), Hisham Chaudhary (2021), Victoria Jacobs (2024), Mohammed Azharuddin Chhipa (2024) and Amin Rahman (2024).

[77] See Office of Financial Sanctions Implementation (OFSI), 'About Us' (n/d), available at www.gov.uk/government/organisations/office-of-financial-sanctions-implementation/about.

provide financial intelligence on suspected financiers of terrorism and several data-sharing mechanisms have been introduced by the Criminal Finances Act 2017; the Digital Economy Act 2017 and the Economic Crime and Corporate Transparency Act 2023.

The UK has a long history of using suspicious activity SARs to tackle financial crime. For instance, the AML reporting mechanisms in the Drug Trafficking Offences Act 1986 influenced the CTF provisions in the Prevention of Terrorism Act 1989.[78] Of relevance here, the reporting entities were required to detect accounts that could be relevant to terrorist investigations and submit DATF SARs to the UKFIU.[79] Here, it is a criminal offence for failing to disclose information about the occurrence of terrorist financing,[80] for those working in the regulated financial sector, the offence of tipping off.[81] Additionally, the Anti-terrorism, Crime and Security Act 2001 included CTF mechanisms that permit authorities and LEAs to seize terrorist cash anywhere in the UK,[82] to freeze the funds at the start of a terrorist related investigation,[83] to examine accounts that might be used to support acts of terrorism,[84] to impose CTF reporting obligations on financial institutions that suspect that funds are being used to support acts of terrorism[85] and permit HM Treasury to freeze the accounts of people where they have reasonable grounds to suspect they pose a threat to the UK.[86] The UK's CTF strategy forms a key part of CONTEST strategy,[87] which aims to reduce the threat of terrorist financing by preventing, detecting, deterring, and disrupting the flow of funds to terrorists.[88] This involves reducing the threat of terrorist financing by detecting, preventing, deterring and disrupting the flow of terrorist finance; understanding terrorist finance activity by exploiting financial intelligence to prevent and detect illicit activity; investigating terrorist finance activity to disrupt; and deterring illicit activity and holding terrorist financiers to account.[89] DATF SARs are crucial in tackling terrorist financing because they can provide the UKFIU and LEAs with valuable intelligence on potential illegal activities, helping to identify and

[78] See B Rider, 'Taking Money Launderers to the Cleaners: Part 2' (1996) *Private Client Business*, 3, 201–210, at 205–206.

[79] TACT, s 19.

[80] ibid ss 19 and 21A.

[81] ibid s 21D.

[82] Anti-terrorism, Crime and Security Act 2001, sch 1, part 2, para 2.

[83] ibid, part 2, ss 4–16.

[84] ibid, sch 2, part 1, para 1.

[85] ibid, sch 6A.

[86] ibid s 4.

[87] See HM Government, *CONTEST – The United Kingdom's Strategy for Countering Terrorism 2023* (HM Government, 2023).

[88] See HM Government, 'Guidance Counter-Terrorist Financing' (2 September 2021), available at www.gov.uk/government/publications/countering-terrorist-financing/countering-terrorist-financing#:~:text=HMG%20%27s%20approach%20to%20tackling,hold%20terrorist%20financiers%20to%20account.

[89] ibid.

disrupt terrorist financing schemes. The DATF SARs act as a bridge between reporting entities and LEAs, enabling them to gain insights into suspicious transactions and activities that might otherwise go unnoticed. DATF SARs can identify terrorist financing activities, preventing them from escalating and causing further harm; they can provide LEAs with detailed information about potential criminals, their methods, and the flow of illicit funds, which is crucial for investigations; they can provide support to terrorist related investigations; identify emerging terrorist financing typologies; and play a crucial role in the risk management for reporting entities.

The international AML and CTF legislative provisions from the UN and EU are supported by the Recommendations of the FATF, which was established in 1989,[90] and is the 'world standard setter in the fight against money laundering'.[91] The FATF promotes 'measures for combating money laundering, terrorist financing and other threats', through its Recommendations.[92] Members of the FATF, such as the UK, are subject to a peer-review process, with MERs recording the level of compliance.[93] In its 2018 MER of the UK's compliance with its Recommendations,[94] the FATF rated the UK's AML/CTF regime as the best in the world.[95] One of the FATF's key findings was that 'co-operation and co-ordination between agencies on AML/CTF issues is a strength of the UK system'.[96] Therefore, the UK was rated as in full compliance with Recommendations 2, 30 and 31, which require national coordination and cooperation, including the exchange of information, between LEAs.[97] The UK was also considered to have moderate to high levels of effectiveness to Immediate Outcomes 1 and 6, concerning risk, policy and coordination, and financial intelligence, as well as Immediate Outcomes 7 and 9, concerning effective money laundering and terrorist financing investigations. However, this chapter questions these findings by presenting case studies that will serve to demonstrate inherent flaws in the UK's ability to ensure the exchange of information between LEAs to detect and address financial crimes. This is a significant weakness in the UK's AML/CTF framework, for the FATF, the EU and others, have all stressed the importance of national LEA coordination and cooperation.

[90] G7 Research Group, 'Economic Declaration' (16 July 1989), available at www.g8.utoronto.ca/summit/1989paris/communique/index.html.

[91] A Damais, 'The Financial Action Task Force' in WH Muller, CH Kälin, JG Goldsworth (eds), *Anti-Money Laundering: International Law and Practice* (John Wiley & Sons, 2007) at 71.

[92] FATF, *International Standards on Combating Money Laundering and the Financing of Terrorism & Proliferation: The FATF Recommendations* (FATF, 2012).

[93] See chapter three.

[94] See FATF 2018 MER (n 2).

[95] ibid at 5. Also, see HM Treasury, 'UK Takes Top Spot in Fight against Dirty Money' (7 December 2018), available at www.gov.uk/government/news/uk-takes-top-spot-in-fight-against-dirty-money.

[96] See FATF 2018 MER (n 2) at 37.

[97] ibid.

Since the implementation of the 'Financial War on Terrorism', terrorist financiers have continually adapted their funding typologies, moving away from traditional methods to more opaque networks. They now exploit cryptocurrencies and other virtual assets, leverage informal value transfer systems such as hawala, and hide illicit flows within complex trade-based money-laundering schemes. At the same time, micro-transaction platforms and peer-to-peer fundraising through social media have emerged as channels for small-scale donations that aggregate the funds of terrorist groups. These evolving tactics place new pressures on regulators and LEAs, which must chase an ever-shifting landscape of digital and informal finance. In contrast, the UK's CTF mechanisms have remained largely unchanged since TACT 2000. That static framework struggles to keep pace with emerging terrorist financing typologies that can route funds through dozens of jurisdictions in minutes. To address this gap, the CTF regime needs an update its reporting and related data-sharing mechanisms.

III. Defence against Terrorist Financing Suspicious Activity Reports

This section of the chapter examines how TACT 2000 establishes specific CTF reporting mechanisms and uses Customer Information Orders to serve as a front-line mechanism for LEAs to compel disclosure of client data. Under TACT, reporting entities must file a CTF SAR whenever they suspect funds may be linked to terrorist activity, triggering a confidential flow of intelligence to the UKFIU. Customer Information Orders sit alongside DATF SARs, empowering authorities to demand detailed records, ranging from account opening documents to transaction histories wherever there is a reasonable belief that such information is necessary for an investigation. Building on that framework, the chapter then explores financial directions as a mechanism for freezing or restricting the use of assets tied to terrorism. Once a Customer Information Order reveals suspect funds or a DATF SAR flags an elevated risk, a financial direction under TACT can immediately impose prohibitions on spending, moving, or dealing with specified property.

A. Terrorism Act 2000

This subsection identifies the mandatory reporting requirements for terrorist financing and identifies the number of DATF SARs submitted to the UKFIU. The CTF reporting regime is contained in Part 2 of TACT, which is similar to the AML regime under Part 7 of the Proceeds of Crime Act 2002 (POCA).[98] There

[98] See chapter 4 at 70.

are four key parts that need to be introduced – the reporting obligations of the regulated sector,[99] terrorist financing criminal offences,[100] the exemptions to the terrorist financing offences,[101] and the criminal offence of tipping off.[102] The Anti-terrorism, Crime and Security Act 2001 inserted section 21A into TACT and creates the offence of failing to disclose in the regulated sector.[103] A person commits an offence under this section if three conditions are met: i) the accused knows or suspects, or has reasonable grounds for knowing or suspecting that a person has committed an offence under sections 15–18 of the TACT;[104] ii) the information or other matter upon which the accused has based his knowledge or suspicion, or which gives reasonable grounds for such knowledge of suspicion which came to him in the course of a business that operates within the regulated sector;[105] and iii) the accused does not disclose the information or other matter to a constable or nominated officer (normally a money laundering reporting officer), as soon as practicable after he received the information.[106] A person does not commit an offence if they had a reasonable excuse for not disclosing the information or other matter or he is a professional legal adviser and the information or other matter came to him in privileged circumstances.[107] Furthermore, the Anti-terrorism, Crime and Security Act 2001 amends TACT by inserting a further defence of protected disclosures.[108] In order for this to be utilised, three conditions must be met. The first condition is that the information or other matter disclosed came to the person making the disclosure (the discloser) in the course of a business in the regulated sector.[109] The second condition is that the information or other matter causes the discloser to know or suspect, or gives him reasonable grounds for knowing or suspecting that a person has committed an offence as outlined above under sections 15–18 of TACT.[110] The third and final condition is that the disclosure is made to a constable or a nominated officer as soon as is practicable after the information or other matter comes to the discloser.[111]

The reporting obligations can take two forms. Firstly, there is a required disclosure whereby the reporting entity provides and submits a DATF SAR to the UKFIU where they suspect someone is laundering terrorist property or committing one of the terrorist financing offences. Secondly, an authorised

[99] TACT ss 19 and 21A.
[100] ibid ss 15–18.
[101] ibid s 21.
[102] ibid s 21D.
[103] Anti-terrorism, Crime and Security Act 2001, sch 2, Part III.
[104] TACT, s 21A(2).
[105] ibid s 21A(3).
[106] ibid s 21A(4).
[107] ibid s 21A.
[108] ibid s 21B.
[109] ibid s 21B(2).
[110] ibid s 21B(3).
[111] ibid s 21B(4).

disclosure where an employee of a reporting entity intends to conclude a transaction but becomes 'suspicious or forms the belief that the transaction involves criminal property'.[112] Here, if a disclosure is made to the UKFIU and consent is granted, they will be 'protected from criminal liability in relation to a terrorism financing offence'.[113] DATF SARs are submitted to the National Terrorist Financial Intelligence Unit (NTFIU), within the Special Operations Section 15 (SO15) which is part of the Metropolitan Police Counter Terrorist Command.[114] The UKFIU screens the DATF SARs and the NTFIU analyses DATF SARs and is able to use a wide range of open source and classified materials to build financial profiles that are submitted by the 11 regional counter-terrorism units and SIS.[115] The NTFIU

> has the strategic lead of law enforcement for countering terrorist financing in the UK and is responsible for all investigations of financial matters with possible links to terrorism activities or entities. NTFIU also supports mainstream police counter-terrorism investigations with financial intelligence and financial disruption options.[116]

The Royal United Services Institute described the NTFIU as 'a world-leading terrorist finance investigation capability … this capability has served the UK well'.[117] The NTFIU is 'considered as a world-leader in its field of investigation, the NTFIU have paved the way in disrupting terrorist financial activity by successfully limiting criminals tactics'.[118] The Head of the Metropolitan Police Counter Terrorism Command said

> financial investigation is a crucial part of the counter terrorism effort. Not only is this team stopping money from reaching the hands of terrorists or being used to fund terrorist attacks, but it's also using specific legislation to access a range of financial data. Once pieced together, this information paints a very telling picture about suspects' activities, who they are associated with and who should also be investigated'.[119]

In addition to the NTFIU, the 'NCA's Terrorist Finance Team identifies, assesses and exploits SARs submitted under both TACT and POCA'.[120] The Terrorist Finance Team (TFT) is a specialised unit within the National Crime Agency (NCA) that focuses on CTF by identifying, analysing and disseminating DATF SARs to the

[112] See Law Commission (n 1) at 51.
[113] ibid.
[114] ibid at 51 and FATF 2018 MER (n 2) at 25.
[115] FATF 2018 MER (n 2).
[116] M Normark and M Ranstorp, *Understanding Terrorist Finance. Modus Operandi and National CTF Regimes* (Swedish Defence University, 2015) at 34–35.
[117] Written evidence submitted by the The Royal United Services Institute (RUSI) Centre for Financial Crime and Security Studies (ECR0018) (May 2018), available at https://committees.parliament.uk/writtenevidence/89823/html/.
[118] Counterterrorism Policing, 'Detectives Praised for Financial Investigations' (7 December 2018), available at www.counterterrorism.police.uk/praise-for-detectives-who-stop-terrorist-funding/.
[119] ibid.
[120] HM Treasury and Home Office, *UK National Risk Assessment of Money Laundering and Terrorist Financing* (HM Treasury and Home Office, 2015) at 92.

NTFIU.[121] The TFT plays an important role in disrupting terrorist financing by tracking financial transactions linked to terrorism.

B. Financial Information Orders

In addition to the traditional means of gathering financial intelligence via the use of DATF SAR, the TACT 2000 contains a number of statutory measures that relates to financial information orders. For example, schedule 6 allows a constable or counter terrorism expert to 'require a financial institution to provide customer information for the purposes of the investigation'.[122] An application for an order can be made by a police officer that could 'require a financial institution [to which the order applies] to provide customer information for the purposes of the investigation'.[123] The order could apply to: '(a) all financial institutions, (b) a particular description, or particular descriptions, of financial institutions, or (c) a particular financial institution or particular financial institutions'.[124] If a financial institution fails to comply with the financial information order it is guilty of an offence.[125] However, the financial institution does have a defence to breaching the financial information order if they can illustrate that either the '(a) information required was not in the institution's possession, or (b) that it was not reasonably practicable for the institution to comply with the requirement'.[126] Furthermore, TACT 2000 permits the use of account monitoring orders.[127] They can be granted by a judge if they are satisfied that: '(a) the order is sought for the purposes of a terrorist investigation, (b) the tracing of terrorist property is desirable for the purposes of the investigation, and (c) the order will enhance the effectiveness of the investigation'.[128] There must be reasonable grounds for suspecting that the named person in the application 'has benefitted from criminal conduct in a confiscation investigation [or has] committed a money laundering offence in a money laundering investigation'[129] and reasonable grounds to believe that the account information which is subsequently produced will be of 'substantial value to the investigation'.[130] Under the order, a financial institution is required to provide information on a specified account for a specified period of time, although this cannot be for more than 90 days.[131]

[121] National Crime Agency (NCA), 'UKFIU Operations Teams (n/d), available at www.nationalcrimeagency.gov.uk/careers/ncaroles/ukfiu-careers/ukfiu-operations-teams.

[122] TACT, sch 6 (1).

[123] ibid sch 6, 1(1).

[124] ibid sch 6, 1(1)(a).

[125] ibid sch 6, 1(3).

[126] ibid sch 6, 1(4).

[127] ibid sch 6A.

[128] ibid sch 6A, 2.

[129] Home Office, *Financial Orders under part 8 of the Proceeds of Crime Act 2002* (Home Office, 2015) at 27.

[130] ibid.

[131] ibid.

C. Financial Directions

One of the most controversial pieces of CTF legislation that has been enacted in the UK is the Counter-Terrorism Act 2008, with schedule 7 implementing a regime of financial directions. The Act provides HM Treasury with the ability to give a direction to a country if one or more of three conditions are met. These are:

1) that the FATF has advised that measures against a country are needed because of the risk of terrorist financing or money laundering is occurring either in the country, by the government of the country or by persons resident in the country;
2) that the Treasury reasonably believes that there is a risk that terrorist financing or money laundering is occurring by the same three named entities and that this poses a significant risk to the national interests of the UK; and/or
3) the Treasury reasonably believes that the country is developing or producing nuclear, radiological, chemical or biological weapons or it is doing anything that facilitates the development or production of such weapons, with such activities again posing a significant risk to the national interest of the UK.[132]

Directions can also be given to persons who operate in the financial sector.[133] Part three of schedule 7 provides for the requirements of a direction and the obligations that can be imposed. For example, the obligations can be imposed on transactions, business relationships with a person carrying on business in the country, the government of the country, or a person resident or incorporated in the country. It is highly likely that once a direction has been imposed the recipient will be required to improve their due diligence measures. Part 5 of schedule 7 permits the relevant enforcement agency to obtain information and part 6 permits the use of financial sanctions on those who fail to observe the directions. Due to this extension, the powers of HM Treasury under schedule 7 of the Counter-Terrorism Act 2008 have been challenged. In *Bank Mellat v HM Treasury (No 2)*,[134] the Treasury had made a direction prohibiting UK commercial dealings with Bank Mellat due to the Bank's alleged connection with Iran's nuclear programme. The Supreme Court determined that the directions breached Article 6 of the European Convention on Human Rights and the rules of natural justice. HM Treasury challenged the open judgment of the Supreme Court, and the Court of Appeal determined that HM Treasury should disclose and grant Bank Mellat access to the documents which were used to impose the sanctions.[135]

[132] Counter-Terrorism Act 2008, sch 7, para 1.
[133] ibid sch 7, para 3.
[134] *Bank Mellat v HM Treasury (No 2)* [2013] UKSC 38 and 39, [2013] 3 WLR 179.
[135] *Bank Mellat v HM Treasury* [2015] EWCA Civ 1052.

D. Number of DATF SARs

The process of submitting a DATF SAR is slightly different from defence against money laundering (DAML) SARs because 'it is not always reasonable to expect a reporter to be able to identify a terrorist association with suspicious activity, when that association is only visible through sensitive government and law enforcement databases'.[136] Terrorist financing is often harder to detect than money laundering because it does not always follow the same financial patterns.[137] For example, unlike money laundering, which can involve large sums, terrorist financing can involve small, seemingly insignificant transactions that do not raise concerns by the reporting entity.[138] Terrorist financiers can use legitimate sources such as charities,[139] businesses,[140] or personal donations,[141] thus making them harder to distinguish from regular financial activity. Furthermore, terrorist financiers move money quickly across borders using informal networks,[142] cryptocurrencies,[143] or cash-based transactions,[144] avoiding the financial systems that are subject to the CTF reporting obligations. Finally, terrorist funding is about funding activities and not about disguising the proceeds of crime, this difference makes is more difficult to track financial transactions or patterns.[145] Therefore, the number of DATF SARs is small when compared to DAML SARs. However, the Lander Review noted that

> the proportion of SARs of CTF interest. In 2005, just under 2,100 of the total SARs (1%) were judged by the FIU terrorism team to be of potential interest in a terrorist context, of which about 650 were passed on to the NTFIU for more detailed investigation. There was a slight peak of reports of interest following the events of 7 and 21 July 2005.[146]

[136] HM Treasury and Home Office (n 120) at 93.

[137] See generally S Iwrin, R Choo, and L Liu, 'Modelling of Money Laundering and Terrorism Financing Typologies' (2012) *Journal of Money Laundering Control* 15(3), 316–35.

[138] See generally J Besenyő, 'Low-Cost Attacks, Unnoticeable Plots? Overview on the Economical Character of Current Terrorism' (2017) *Strategic Impact* (63), 83–100.

[139] See generally FATF, *Combating the Terrorist Financing Abuse of Non-Profit Organisations* (FATF, 2023).

[140] See F Lemieux and F Prates, 'Entrepreneurial Terrorism: Financial Strategies, Business Opportunities, and Ethical Issues' (2011) *Police Practice and Research* 12(5), 368–82.

[141] See M Rudner, 'Hizbullah Terrorism Finance: Fund-Raising and Money-Laundering' (2010) *Studies in Conflict & Terrorism* 33(8), 700–15.

[142] See M Basile, 'Going to the Source: Why Al Qaeda's Financial Network is Likely to Withstand the Current War on Terrorist Financing' (2004) *Studies in Conflict & Terrorism* 27(3), 169–85.

[143] See S Wagman, 'Cryptocurrencies and National Security: The Case of Money Laundering and Terrorism Financing' (2022) *Harvard National Security Journal* 14(1), 87–101.

[144] See P Neumann, 'Don't Follow the Money: The Problem with the War on Terrorist Financing' (2017) *Foreign Affairs* 96(4), 93–102.

[145] N Ryder, 'Out with the Old and … in with the Old? A Critical Review of the Financial War on Terrorism on the Islamic State of Iraq and Levant' (2018) *Studies in Conflict and Terrorism* 41(2), 79–95. Conversely, see JA Rosenthal, 'For-Profit Terrorism: The Rise of Armed Entrepreneurs' (2008) *Studies in Conflict & Terrorism* 31(6), 481–98 and T Baumert, 'Do Terrorists Play the Market? Or Can Their Attacks Serve as a Source of Financing for Terrorism?' *Policing: A Journal of Policy and Practice* 2(4), 434–40.

[146] Serious Organised Crime Agency, *The Sars Review; Sir Stephen Lander* (Serious Organised Crime Agency, 2006) at 13.

Table 1 Number of DATF SARs submitted to NCA 2014–2023

YEAR	NUMBER OF DATF SARS SUBMITTED
2014–2015	1,889[147]
2016–2017	422[148]
2017–2018	2,688[149]
2018–2019	1,909[150]
2019–2020	1,897[151]
2020–2021	425[152]
2021–2022	358[153]
2022–2023	342[154]
2023–2024	406[155]

The benefit of DATF SARs is that where the

> outcome is disruption of terrorist activity rather than a prosecution for a terrorism financing offence. For example, a suspected terrorist planning an attack may commit credit card fraud which is flagged and reported as suspicious activity by a bank. Rather than seek further evidence to pursue a prosecution for a terrorism financing offence, the credit card fraud can be prosecuted separately, effectively disrupting any plans for an attack.[156]

The Law Commission stated that the NTFIU noted that

> suspicion is inconsistently applied by reporters. Frequently a very low threshold is adopted by reporters which meant that the intelligence provided is not useful. For example, in the aftermath of recent terror attacks in London in 2017, some banks were submitting DATF SARs to close accounts and pay back customers because they had some fleeting transactional relationship with one of the attackers or had lived in the same street.[157]

Another problem with DATF SARs is

> retrospective SARs are less helpful in terrorism financing cases given the relatively short time period in which attacks were planned. Unsophisticated attacks could be planned and executed in less than six months and often no more than 12 months. Historic information is of little value.[158]

[147] NCA, *The Suspicious Activity Reports Regime Annual Report 2015* (NCA, 2015) at 38.
[148] NCA, *SARs Annual Report 2017* (NCA, 2017) at 6. There was no report for 2015–2016.
[149] NCA, *SARs Annual Report 2018* (NCA, 2018) at 19–20.
[150] NCA, *SARs Annual Report 2019* (NCA, 2019) at 7.
[151] NCA, *SARs Annual Report 2020* (NCA, 2020) at 19.
[152] NCA, *Suspicious Activity Report 2022* (NCA, 2022) at 9.
[153] NCA, *Suspicious Activity Report 2022* (NCA, 2024) at 12.
[154] NCA, *Suspicious Activity Report 2023* (NCA, 2024) at 12.
[155] NCA, *Suspicious Activity Report 2023* (NCA, 2025) at 4.
[156] See Law Commission (n 1) at 57.
[157] ibid.
[158] ibid at 57–58.

The Law Commission noted that the usefulness of DATF SARs is not necessarily replicated in the data on terrorist financing prosecutions and convictions. Successful convictions for terrorism financing offences are low, and the NCTFIU noted that this did not reflect the overall utility of DATF SARs.[159] The Law Commission referred to examples of

> disruption of terrorist activity rather than a prosecution for a terrorism financing offence ... a suspected terrorist planning an attack may commit credit card fraud which is flagged and reported as suspicious activity by a bank. Rather than seek further evidence to pursue a prosecution for a terrorism financing offence, the credit card fraud can be prosecuted separately, effectively disrupting any plans for an attack.[160]

Conversely, the prosecution of terrorist financiers reinforces the rule of law and ensures that suspected terrorists are held accountable for the full scope of their actions. By focusing only on credit card fraud, authorities risk overlooking deeper networks and financial mechanisms that support terrorist activities. The prosecution for a terrorist financing offence may not only punish an individual act but also deter future financing efforts. If suspects are only prosecuted for fraud, they may continue seeking alternative illicit financing routes without being formally recognised as financiers of terrorism. Breaches of TACT carry harsher penalties compared to fraud offences under the Fraud Act 2006. Pursuing charges specifically related to terrorism financing ensures that individuals involved in such activities face the most severe legal repercussions possible, preventing leniency that fraud charges may entail. Investigating terrorism financing offences more thoroughly allows law enforcement and intelligence agencies to gather valuable information on broader networks, associates, and financial transactions linked to terrorist organisations. A simple fraud charge may disrupt one individual's immediate plans but fail to expose larger connections. While disrupting terrorist activity through fraud prosecution may have short-term advantages in preventing an imminent attack, a strategic approach to prosecuting terrorism financing itself could offer longer-term benefits in dismantling financial structures that support terrorism on a wider scale.

The deficiency of DATF SARs is illustrated by the emergence of the micro terrorist financing typology. Terrorism financing in the UK is associated with very small amounts of funding which are often impossible to detect via a DATF SAR. Examples of low-cost acts of terrorism include the London terrorist attacks in July 2005, which, according to the Metropolitan Police cost approximately £7,235 (£4,600 for the deployment of devices and materials; international travel £1,810 and training weekends £825).[161] Another example of cheap terrorism occurred in March 2017 when Khalid Masood killed four people and injured 50 more when he drove a car towards pedestrians on Westminster Bridge.[162] In June 2017, Darren

[159] ibid.
[160] ibid at 57.
[161] See HM Government (n 69) at 23.
[162] Khalid Masood drove a hired car across Westminster Bridge, killing four people and he then murdered a police officer in Parliament Square.

Osborne rented a vehicle, at an estimated cost of £85 per day, and drove the vehicle into a crowd of people outside Finsbury Park Mosque at an estimated cost of £255.[163] In June 2017, eight people were killed by Khuram Shazad Butt, Rachid Redouane and Youssef Zaghba, when they drove a van into pedestrians on London Bridge and launched a knife attack in Borough Market on Saturday, 3 June 2017. The terrorists rented a vehicle that was hired for approximately £30 per day and used salad knives that cost approximately £3 each.[164] In September 2017, Ahmed Hassan was convicted of attempted murder after he planted an improvised explosive device (IED) on the District Line in London. Hassan manufactured the IED using a £20 Amazon voucher.[165] In May 2017, Salman Abedi, who detonated an IED in the Manchester Arena, killing 22 people, acquired funding via two years of student loans (worth approximately £14,000) and misused benefit payments to fund this act of terrorism.[166] Several of these attacks have involved terrorists using a rental vehicle to target pedestrians. Of course, anyone has the financial capability to self-fund the renting of a vehicle, thus providing more evidence that low-cost acts of terrorism exploit the loopholes in the DATF SAR system. If a terrorist or terrorist cell is financially self-sufficient, there is no need for them to be involved in funding activities that could lead to the submission of a DATF SAR by a reporting entity. This problem was acknowledged by the Law Commission which stated that

> stakeholders in the NTFIU told us that in cases where there are concerns relating to terrorist financing or other activity, the amounts involved may be comparatively small. Consequently, the customer may only have a small amount of money in their bank account or they might be in debt. They may present as an undesirable customer from a commercial perspective. As such, even low-level concerns may lead to the termination of the banking relationship before any suspicion is formed. In turn, this may frustrate efforts to investigate as the opportunity to gather evidence may be lost.

Additionally, the Law Commission stated that

> terrorist financing activity in the United Kingdom typically involves small amounts of money, that may be legitimate in origin. These funds are raised by UK-based individuals either to send to terrorist groups abroad, to fund their own travel to join terrorist groups, or to fund their own attacks. In some cases, money can be donated directly to a central organisation, network or charity to fund living expenses, training, travel or equipment. Low-value transactions intended to raise funds for the purposes of terrorism are difficult to detect within the financial system.[167]

[163] See *R v Darren Osborne*, Woolwich Crown Court, 2 February 2018, sentencing remarks of Mrs Justice Cheema-Grubb, available at www.judiciary.uk/wp-content/uploads/2018/02/r-v-osborne-sentencing-remarks.pdf.

[164] BBC, 'London Bridge Inquests: Attacker Bought Pink Knives from Lidl (29 May 2019), available at www.bbc.co.uk/news/uk-48443724.

[165] See *R v Hassan*, sentencing remarks of the Hon Mr Justice Haddon-Cave, 23 March 2018, available at www.judiciary.uk/wp-content/uploads/2018/03/r-vhassan-sentencing.pdf.

[166] R Mendick, 'Manchester Suicide Bomber Used Student Loan and Benefits to Fund Terror Plot' (27 May 2017), available at www.telegraph.co.uk/news/2017/05/26/exclusive-manchester-suicide-bomber-used-student-loan-benefits/.

[167] See Law Commission (n 1) at 49–50.

IV. Case Studies

There are flaws in the UK's ability to obtain and exchange information to detect and address terrorist financing. The first part of the case study on terrorist financing focuses on the link with fraud and questions the suitability of reporting obligations by examining three terrorist attacks: London (7 July 2005), Manchester Arena (22 May 2017) and London Bridge (3 June 2017). Conversely, the case study presents evidence that highlights examples that illustrate how financial intelligence and data-sharing has resulted in the conviction of terrorist financiers Amal El-Wahabi, Oghenochuko Ojiri and Muhammad Choudhary. The evidence presented here illustrates that the UK has not met the requirements of Recommendation 31, yet as previously mentioned, the 2018 FATF MER concluded that here 'all criteria are met. Recommendation 31 is rated "compliant"'.[168]

A. London: 7 July 2005

On 7 July 2005, a coordinated terrorist attack occurred on London's public transport system. Three IEDs were detonated on the London Underground and a fourth on a double-decker bus. As a result of the terrorist attack, 52 people were killed and approximately 800 were injured. The first IED was detonated on a Circle Line train between Liverpool Street and Aldgate, the second on a train departing Edgware Road, the third on the Piccadilly Line and the latter on a bus in Tavistock Square.[169] HM Government estimated that this act of terrorism cost less than £8,000 and noted that the terrorist cell 'appears to have raised the necessary cash by methods that would be extremely difficult to identify as related to terrorism or other serious criminality'.[170] Mohammad Sidique Khan provided most of the funding via credit cards and a personal loan.[171] Collectively, the terrorists were able to fund the attack via legitimate income, including wages, personal savings and small cash withdrawals from their bank accounts.[172] To avoid detection, the terrorists bought the bomb-making components using small cash transactions at pharmacies and hardware stores. The low-value, commonplace nature of these purchases put them beyond the usual scope of CTF reporting obligations, escaping the notice of the NTFIU.[173] The

[168] Organisation for Economic Co-operation and Development (OECD), *Global Forum on Transparency and Exchange of Information for Tax Purposes, Peer Review of the Automatic Exchange of Financial Account Information* (OECD, 2021) at 226.
[169] HM Government (n 69).
[170] ibid at 23.
[171] ibid.
[172] BBC News, 'London Bombs Cost Just Hundreds' (6 January 2006), available at http://news.bbc.co.uk/1/hi/uk/4576346.stm.
[173] ibid.

next section illustrates the siloed approach towards CTF data-sharing, revealing deficiencies in CTF data-sharing mechanisms.

In 1995, HMRC connected several suspected frauds with Shahzad Tanweer, one of the July 2005 terrorists, yet this information was not disclosed to the FIU or the SIS.[174] The group linked to Tanweer gained approximately £8 billion from VAT and benefit frauds, of which it sent '1% of its gains, or £80 million to al-Qaeda'.[175] HMRC officials 'were prevented from sharing intelligence with SIS due to its desire to keep tax records confidential'.[176] However, the Anti-terrorism, Crime and Security Act 2001 permits the disclosure of information held by HMRC and provides that 'no obligation of secrecy … prevents the voluntary disclosure of information … to assist any criminal investigation … the section allows for disclosure to the intelligence services … in support of their functions'.[177] However, the ability of HMRC to disclose information is restricted by the Commissioners for Revenue and Customs Act 2005, which provides that information must not be disclosed to anyone unless the person making the disclosure has the authority to do so.[178] This applies to HMRC providing information to government departments, LEAs, FIUs and other public bodies. This restriction does not apply if the disclosure is 'made for the purposes of a criminal investigation or criminal proceedings relating to a matter in respect of which the Revenue and Customs have functions'.[179] HMRC's duty of confidentiality is also 'subject to any other enactment permitting disclosure',[180] and many legal gateways have been enacted to provide for the exchange of information between HMRC and LEAs. The Counter Terrorism Act 2008 provides that 'a person may disclose information to any of the intelligence services for the purposes of the exercise by that service of any of its functions'.[181] Additionally, the Money Laundering Regulations provide that HMRC as a

> supervisory authority which, in the course of carrying out any of its supervisory functions or otherwise, knows or suspects, or has reasonable grounds for knowing or suspecting, that a person is or has engaged in money laundering or terrorist financing must as soon as practicable inform the NCA.[182]

[174] It has been suggested that HM Revenue & Customs (HMRC) became aware of the tax fraud scheme as early as 1995. See T Harper, and M Macaskill, 'Glaswegian in £300m Fraud Linked to Bin Laden' (14 April 2019), available at www.thetimes.co.uk/article/glaswegian-in-300m-fraud-linked-to-bin-laden-x707d09pk?region=global.

[175] S Williams, '£80m of British Taxpayers' Money "Funnelled to Al-Qaeda" in Decades-Long Scam' (31 March 2019), available at www.telegraph.co.uk/news/2019/03/31/80m-british-taxpayers-money-funnelled-al-qaeda-decades-long/.

[176] ibid.

[177] Anti-terrorism, Crime and Security Act 2001, s 19.

[178] Commissioners for Revenue and Customs Act 2005, s 18(1).

[179] ibid s 18(2)(d).

[180] ibid s 18(3).

[181] Counter Terrorism Act 2008, s 18(1).

[182] Money Laundering, Terrorist Financing and Transfer of Funds (Information on the Payer) Regulations 2017 (SI 2017/692) (hereinafter the 'Money Laundering Regulations'), Reg 46(5).

Between 2021 and 2022 the HMRC Economic Crime Supervision 'continued to submit SARs to the NCA in line with its regulatory obligations in respect of SARs that are relevant to the supervisory activity'.[183] It added that it:

> has also worked to increase its interactions and close working with the NCA … in relation to SAR submissions and has worked with [the FIU] … to look at when reporting is relevant and required to ensure the best use of intelligence sharing within the Regulations … to ensure that intelligence … is not duplicated, creating potential resourcing impacts for any party in the process.[184]

HMRC, in its capacity as a supervisory authority under the Money Laundering Regulations, has potentially breached Regulation 46(5) by not submitting a DATF SAR to the NCA. However, it is unlikely that HMRC will be subjected to a civil penalty for breaching the Money Laundering Regulations because they are imposed by statutory supervisory authorities on the regulated sector, not on statutory supervisory authorities. Furthermore, HMRC will not be exposed to any disciplinary action by the Office for Professional Body AML Supervising which supervises professional body supervisors in the legal and accountancy sectors.[185] Additionally, HMRC also has a 'duty to co-operate' and a duty of 'disclosure' under the Money Laundering Regulations,[186] which provide that 'co-operation may include the sharing of information which the supervisory authority is not prevented from disclosing'.[187] The funding mechanisms of this terrorist attack did not result in a DATF SAR being submitted to the UKFIU or NTFIU. The decision by HMRC not to disclose the information, despite several mechanisms facilitating the exchange of information is problematic for this information would have provided intelligence on the financing of the terrorist attack and could potentially have prevented its commission. The difficulty is not with the legislation or guidance, but the restrictive interpretation of 'taxpayer confidentiality'. HMRC practice is not in line with national, regional and international legal instruments, thus illustrating that the reporting obligations are not suitable and questioning the findings of the 2018 MER. A similar failure deficiency was highlighted when HMRC did not disclose information regarding the conduct of HSBC Suisse, despite several bilateral and multilateral treaties that facilitated the exchange of information. HMRC's overly restrictive interpretation of taxpayer confidentiality is at odds with the FATF Recommendations.

[183] HMRC, 'Corporate Report, HMRC Economic Crime Supervision Annual Assessment Report: 1 April 2021–31 March 2022' (6 October 2022), available at www.gov.uk/government/publications/hmrc-economic-crime-supervision-annual-assessment-report-2021-to-2022.

[184] ibid.

[185] Financial Conduct Authority, 'Office for Professional Body Anti-Money Laundering Supervision (OPBAS)', (23 January 2018), available at www.fca.org.uk/about/how-we-operate/who-work-with/opbas.

[186] Money Laundering Regulations, Regs 50 and 52.

[187] ibid, Reg 50(3).

B. Manchester: 22 May 2017

On 22 May 2017 Salman Abedi detonated an IED in the City Room Foyer of the Manchester Arena following an Ariana Grande concert, killing 22 people and injuring over 1,000.[188] Further investigation revealed that Salman Abedi had enrolled on a degree at Salford University in October 2015 and had dropped out at the start of his second year in 2016. However, he continued to receive his student loan payments for both 2015–2016 and 2016–2017 academic years. It was reported that at the time of the terrorist attacks, Salman Abedi was unemployed and he was claiming Jobseeker's Allowance and received housing benefit and income support, giving him a weekly income of £250 per week. The student loan and benefit payments were used to fund his trips to Libya and to purchase the materials for the IED.[189] The following section illustrates gaps in the UK's data-sharing mechanism architecture. Salman Abedi was able to continue receiving his student loan payments after he had withdrawn from his degree. A student who is withdrawing from study at university is required to submit a 'Change of Circumstances: Withdraw' through the Student Loan Company and if this meets the automated processing criteria it will be actioned within 48 hours. If not, the process can take between 20 and 30 working days. There is no automated system between universities and the Student Loans Company, instead universities must manually notify the Student Loan Company when a student withdraws. Without a statutory obligation or technical integration to share withdrawal, the gap remains open.

The Money Laundering Regulations do not apply to Higher Education Institutions (HEIs) and they are under no obligation to report any suspicions to the NCA, thus illustrating a loophole that has been exploited by terrorist financiers. Student loans are a perfect financial mechanism for terrorists to exploit. Any new full-time student in the UK can apply for a Maintenance Loan, between £7,987 and £10,866, which is paid directly into the student's bank account.[190] For example, Yahya Rashid, who fraudulently obtained a place at Middlesex University, used his student loan to fund travel for himself and associates to Turkey.[191] Rashid was convicted of two counts of preparing acts of terrorism under TACT.[192]

In order to commit the terrorist attack in the Manchester Arena in 2017, Salman Abedi used student loans and his maintenance grant.[193] Abedi received £7,000 from the Student Loans Company after securing a place on a degree at Salford

[188] Intelligence and Security Committee, *The 2017 Attacks: What Needs to Change?* (Intelligence and Security Committee, 2018) at 10.

[189] See Mendick (n 166).

[190] HM Government, 'Student Finance' (n/d), available at www.gov.uk/student-finance/new-fulltime-students.

[191] *R v Yahya Rashid* [2016] EWCA Crim 568.

[192] Terrorism Act 2006, s 5(1(b).

[193] See Mendick (n 166).

University in October 2015. An investigation by the European Commission estimated that Abedi had received up to £18,000 in student loans and other benefit payments.[194] The Student Loan Company paid £1,000 into Abedi's account at the start of January 2017 and a further £2,258 at the end of that month. The money from the student loan was withdrawn in regular amounts of up to £300.[195] It is interesting to note that Abedi continued to receive funds from the Student Loan Company even though he had stopped attending classes at Salford University.[196] The Money Laundering Regulations do not apply to HEIs, only the regulated sector,[197] and HEIs have a limited legal obligation to report any suspicions of fraud or terrorism financing to the NCA.[198] Theoretically, HEIs could be regarded as high value dealers for the reporting obligations to apply. The term is defined as 'a firm or sole trader who by way of business trades in goods … when the trader makes or receives, in respect of any transaction, a payment or payments in cash of at least 10,000 euros in total'.[199] However, a survey of the application of the reporting obligations to the HEIs noted that only two out of 110 respondents considered themselves to be high value dealers.[200] Therefore, the uncertainty surrounding the applicationof the reporting obligations to HEI illustrates further weaknesses in the exchange of information

C. London Bridge: 3 June 2017

On 3 June 2017, three terrorists murdered eight people and wounded 48 other people after driving a van into pedestrians on London Bridge before launching a knife attack in Borough Market.[201] The terrorists, Khuram Shazad Butt, Rachid Redouane and Youssef Zaghba, were armed with 12-inch ceramic-bladed knives and wore fake explosive vests. The voluntary nature of reporting suspected frauds illustrates a deficiency in the use of DATF SARs and claims by HM Government that is uses all methods to disrupt acts of terrorism.

One of the terrorists, Khuram Butt, was investigated and arrested on suspicion of falsely reporting fraudulent activity (£3,300),[202] on three bank accounts

[194] European Commission, *Study on an EU Initiative for a Restriction on Payments in Cash, Final Report* (European Commission, 2017) at 42.

[195] P Stubley, 'Hashem Abedi Trial: Benefits Claimed by Manchester Bomber's Family were Used in Terror Plot Jury Hears' (10 February 2020), available at www.independent.co.uk/news/uk/crime/manchester-arena-bombing-benefits-family-samia-abedi-hashem-trial-a9327816.html.

[196] See European Commission (n 194).

[197] Money Laundering Regulations at Reg 8(2).

[198] N Ryder, S Bourton, H Hillman and D Hall, 'Higher Education Institutions and the Anti-Money Laundering and Counter-Terrorism Financing Regulations' (2023) *Criminal Law Review*, 9, 560–80.

[199] Money Laundering Regulations at Reg 14.

[200] See Ryder et al (n 198).

[201] See Intelligence and Security Committee (n 188) at 10.

[202] M White, 'London Bridge Attack: MI5 Accused of "Damning List" of Failures' (28 June 2019), available at https://news.sky.com/story/london-bridge-attack-mi5-accused-of-damning-list-of-failures-11750204.

in October 2016.[203] It was alleged that Butt had been making 'unauthorised withdrawals from his accounts, with Santander, and then pocketing the refunds'.[204] Indeed, in preparation for the terrorist attack, Butt emptied his two other bank accounts (Nationwide and Lloyds) and had successfully applied for two loans (totalling £14,000).[205] After his arrest, Butt was granted bail and the fraud charges were eventually dropped due to insufficient evidence.[206] The Intelligence and Services Committee (ISC) stated that 'during Butt's arrest … counter-terrorism police had discovered files that it considered 'may be successfully used in a prosecution under the Terrorism Act'; however … the issue was not explored further'.[207] The ISC noted that

> in July 2016, there was a potential disruption opportunity presented by Butt's suspected engagement in bank fraud, and counter terrorist police arrested Butt in October 2016. However, by June 2017 it was decided that no further action could be taken, due to a lack of evidence.[208]

Similarly, Anderson noted that, 'while under investigation by MI5, Khuram Butt was arrested for fraud in October 2016 and granted bail. He had not yet been told by 3 June 2017, the date of the attack that on 1 June the decision had been taken not to prosecute him'.[209] Here, Santander was under no legal obligation to submit a SAR to the NCA concerning attempted fraud.[210] Therefore, the reporting obligations are unfit to track and prevent terrorist financing through fraud. Clearly, the exchange of information mechanisms as they currently stand are therefore unsatisfactory.

Fraud is a well-established funding mechanism for terrorist financing and there are no documented cases in the UK where a planned terrorist attack was disrupted by charging one of the suspects with fraud. The investigation and prosecution of fraud sits within the economic crime units rather than counter-terrorism units which means that information associated with fraud offences might not be systematically shared until after the terrorist attack. It is clear that missed opportunities arose from these three terrorist attacks and the statement by HM Government that all disruptive mechanisms are used must be questioned. While the UK rarely turns fraud cases into pre-emptive counterterrorism investigations, the US model treats most financial crime investigations as potential threats to national security.[211] The three case studies reveal that the UK's CTF data-sharing mechanisms suffer from

[203] See Intelligence and Security Committee above (n 188) at 85.
[204] London Bridge Inquests, *Inquests Concerning the Attackers Day 6A* (9 July 2019), available at londonbridgeinquests.independent.gov.uk/wp-content/uploads/2019/07/LBI-Day-6A.pdf.
[205] ibid at 42, 43, 66 and 67.
[206] ibid at 41.
[207] See Intelligence and Security Committee above (n 188).
[208] ibid at 85.
[209] D Anderson, *Attacks in London and Manchester. March-June 2017: Independent Assessment of MI5 and Police* (Brick Court Chambers, 2017) at 17.
[210] See chapter six.
[211] For a more detailed discussion see chapter six.

several weaknesses. Collectively, the case studies challenge the 2018 MER rating of the UK having a robust CTF regime.

D. Amal El-Wahabi

Financial intelligence and data-sharing was essential in convicting Amal El-Wahabi for funding terrorism. Here, the NTFIU worked with the SIS, the UK Border Force and overseas LEAs to identify the route of the cash transfer.[212] Amal El-Wahabi was convicted under the TACT for 'being involved in an arrangement which makes money or other property available to another with the knowledge or reasonable cause to suspect it may be used for terrorism'.[213] The defendant arranged for €20,000 to be transferred to her husband (Aine Davis), who was fighting for ISIL in Syria, via a cash courier (Nawal Msaad). Consequently, the

> NTFIU was able to intercept the cash courier at the airport and confirm that she had been paid to take money out of the UK for TF purposes using communications evidence to support this. The cash was forfeited as terrorist property under TACT and Wahabi was sentenced to 28 months' imprisonment in 2014.[214]

Amal El-Wahabi's communications and financial records revealed her intent to provide financial support for her husband and the Court concluded that she knowingly supported terrorism, leading to her conviction and 28-month prison sentence. The cash courier was acquitted.

Her arrest also showcases effective collaboration between Border Force, counter-terrorism police, intelligence services, and telecommunications providers. Passenger Name Record (PNR) data supplied by airlines, call-detail records from network operators, and real-time alerts from national intelligence repositories were integrated to flag her as a high-risk traveller. This multi-agency fusion of financial, travel, and communications data enabled a timely interception that disrupted the flow of terrorist financing at a critical juncture.

This case illustrates that when data-sharing mechanisms are properly implemented and resourced, the UK's CTF related provisions are effective. By linking the financial intelligence with travel and communication data, authorities were able to prevent a large cash transfer intended to support ISIL.

E. Oghenochuko Ojiri

The conviction of Oghenochuko Ojiri highlights how financial intelligence is successfully being used to combat terrorist financing. This case focuses on London

[212] See FATF 2018 MER (n 2) at 88.
[213] TACT, s 17.
[214] See FATF 2018 MER (n 2) at 88.

art dealer Oghenochuko Ojiri, who was convicted under TACT and sentenced to prison after failing to report financial transactions with a suspected Hezbollah financier, Nazem Ahmad. Between October 2020 and December 2021, Ojiri sold £140,000 worth of artwork to Ahmad, despite knowing about his alleged ties to terrorism. Under TACT, businesses in regulated sectors must disclose suspicious financial activity, which Ojiri deliberately failed to do.[215] Investigators uncovered WhatsApp messages and altered invoices that showed he tried to conceal Ahmad's identity in financial records. Financial intelligence played a key role in convicting Oghenochuko Ojiri. Authorities used financial records, transaction analysis, and regulatory oversight to track his dealings with Nazem Ahmad, a Lebanese businessman sanctioned for alleged ties to terrorism. His phone contained discussions about money laundering regulations, proving he was aware of the legal requirements but chose to ignore them. His conviction is considered a landmark case, highlighting the importance of financial intelligence in detecting and prosecuting terrorism financing. Commander Dominic Murphy, head of the Met's Counter Terrorism Command, said:

> This prosecution, using specific Terrorism Act legislation, is the first of its kind and should act as a warning to all art dealers that we can, and will, pursue those who knowingly do business with people identified as funders of terrorist groups. Oghenochuko Ojiri wilfully obscured the fact he knew he was selling artwork to Nazem Ahmad, someone who has been sanctioned by the UK and US Treasury and described as a funder of the proscribed terrorist group Hizballah. Financial investigation is a crucial part of the counter-terrorism effort. A team of specialist investigators, analysts and researchers in the National Terrorist Financial Investigation Unit works all year round to prevent money from reaching the hands of terrorists or being used to fund attacks.[216]

This case is the first of its kind and involved the NTFIU, Office of Financial Sanctions Implementation in HM Treasury, HMRC, and the Met's Art and Antiques Unit.[217] The case also underscores the importance of financial regulations in preventing terrorist financing. Since 2020, art market participants have been subject to money laundering and terrorist financing regulations, requiring them to report suspicious transactions. Ojiri's failure to comply led to his conviction, marking a significant legal precedent in enforcing financial transparency in the art world. This prosecution illustrates how financial intelligence units are actively monitoring transactions, enforcing sanctions, and holding individuals accountable for facilitating terrorist financing.

The case studies highlight both the strengths and weaknesses of financial intelligence and data-sharing in the UK. On one hand, the case studies reveal significant challenges, such as HMRC's reluctance to share information with SIS due to taxpayer confidentiality conventions, despite numerous data-sharing mechanisms being in place. This raises concerns about the conclusions drawn by FATF regarding

[215] TACT, s 21A.

[216] Counter Terrorism Policing, 'Art Dealer Jailed for Terrorism Offence' (9 June 2025), available at www.counterterrorism.police.uk/art-dealer-jailed-for-terrorism-offence/.

[217] ibid.

financial intelligence effectiveness. Similarly, a gap within the Money Laundering Regulations leaves UK HEIs without an obligation to report suspicious activities to the UKFIU, exposing vulnerabilities in financial crime detection. Fraud reporting issues are also evident, as the case study illustrates how Santander, like other financial institutions, was under no formal obligation to report suspected fraud to the UKFIU, highlighting a broader concern regarding private sector accountability. On the other hand, successful data-sharing efforts have led to significant prosecutions, such as those of Amal El-Wahabi and Oghenochuko Ojiri, which illustrate how financial intelligence can be effectively harnessed to combat terrorist financing. However, a limitation remains in the retrospective nature of DATF SARs, which means intelligence is often provided only after a terrorist attack has occurred, rather than being used proactively to prevent one. Ultimately, while financial intelligence plays a critical role in tackling financial crimes, regulatory gaps and institutional hesitations continue to pose challenges, making it essential to enhance proactive intelligence mechanisms and close existing loopholes to strengthen financial crime prevention efforts.

V. Conclusion

The case studies have identified deficiencies and gaps in the use of financial intelligence and data-sharing. Despite the 2018 MER, this chapter has illustrated that the UK's legal framework and data-sharing practices do not fully align with international standards. The discrepancies raise important questions about the findings of the 2018 MER, necessitating a reconsideration of the UK's compliance status. Addressing these deficiencies is not merely a technical necessity but an urgent policy imperative to ensure the integrity, effectiveness, and global credibility of the UK's financial crime response mechanisms.

There are flaws in the UK's ability to obtain and exchange information to detect terrorist financing. The chapter has examined the circumstances leading up to three acts of terrorism to illustrate deficiencies in how suspected fraud and terrorist funding is investigated. The chapter challenges the 2018 MER. The findings of this chapter illustrate that the UK is not fully compliant with international standards relating to the reporting and sharing of information. The Fraud Strategy and counter-terrorism laws currently work in isolation, with each not referencing the other. The UK fraud strategy and counter-terrorism laws must therefore be more closely aligned. The key findings of the chapter illustrate that in 1995, HMRC connected several suspected frauds with Shahzad Tanweer, one of the July 2005 terrorists, but this information was not disclosed to the UKFIU. The group linked to Tanweer gained approximately £8bn from VAT and benefit frauds, of which it sent '1% of its gains, or £80m to al-Qaeda'. In order to commit the terrorist attack in the Manchester Arena in 2017, Salman Abedi used student loans and his maintenance grant. The Money Laundering Regulations do not apply to HEIs, only the regulated sector. One of the terrorists involved in the attacks on London

Bridge in June 2017, Khuram Butt, was investigated and arrested on suspicion of falsely reporting fraudulent activity (£3,300) on three bank accounts in October 2016. But a decision was made not to prosecute him for these initial offences, thus illustrating that the UK does not use all disruptive mechanisms to tackle terrorist financing. The scope of the Money Laundering Regulations should be extended to include HEIs and the Commissioners for Revenue and Customs Act 2005, which includes 'requiring' HMRC to disclose rather than 'permit' disclosure where HMRC employees suspect they are in in possession of information that reveals money laundering or terrorism.

6

Fraud

Fraud is massively underreported.[1]

I. Introduction

The United Kingdom (UK) has a strong history of utilising financial intelligence and data- sharing as part of its financial crime strategies. The UK's anti-money laundering and counter-terrorist financing (AML/CTF) reporting obligations predate the international community's efforts to tackle money laundering and terrorist financing as part of the 'War on Drugs' and the 'Financial War on Terrorism'. These reporting mechanisms are associated with intelligence-led policing and have benefited from a statutory infrastructure, a UK Financial Intelligence Unit (UKFIU), internal reporting systems and mandatory reporting. Conversely, the reporting of fraud does not benefit from this approach and when reports are submitted 'little is done with them … the official crime statistics display just the tip of the iceberg and developing a strategic law enforcement response is impossible because the information to target investigations does not exist'.[2] Therefore, this chapter critically analyses and determines the effectiveness of the UK's fraud reporting mechanisms in detecting, investigating and addressing fraudulent activities. It seeks to answer the following subsidiary research question – how does the complexity of the UK's legal framework for data-sharing affect the effectiveness of fraud prevention, and what legal and structural reforms are needed to improve coordination between public and private sector stakeholders? The chapter begins by providing an overview of the extent of fraud, the threat it presents and appraises recent policy developments. The second part highlights the mandatory and voluntary fraud reporting mechanisms and attempts to identify the number of reported frauds. The third part focuses on four case studies to illustrate deficiencies in the reporting of fraud. The chapter builds on the case studies and moves on to appraise the fraud related data-sharing mechanisms and highlights areas of best practice that could address the deficiencies highlighted. The final part of the chapter summarises the key findings and conclusions.

[1] Attorney General's Office, *Fraud Review – Final Report* (Attorney General's Office, 2006) at 7.
[2] ibid.

II. Fraud

The profile of this financial crime has increased in part due to frauds including the Bank of Credit and Commerce International,[3] Barings Bank,[4] Enron,[5] WorldCom,[6] Bernard Madoff,[7] Alan Stanford,[8] FTX,[9] Theranos[10] and its association with the 2007/2008 global financial crisis.[11] The UK has experienced large scale instances of fraud including, Polly Peck,[12] the Mirror Group Pension Scheme,[13] the Guinness share-trading fraud,[14] the collapse of Barlow Clowes,[15] the manipulation of the London Interbank Offered Rate/Foreign Exchange market[16] and fraud associated with the global pandemic.[17] The calculation of fraud is fraught with methodological difficulties.[18] Indeed, the Fraud Review concluded

[3] J Kerry and H Brown, *The BCCI Affair A Report to the Committee on Foreign Relations United States Senate* (1992) 102d Congress 2d Session Senate Print 102-14.

[4] Board of Banking Standards, *Inquiry Report of the Board of Banking Standards Inquiry into the Circumstances of the Collapse of Barings Bank* (Board of Banking Standards, 1995).

[5] Permanent Subcommittee on Investigations of the Committee on Governmental Affairs, *The Role of the Board of Directors in Enron's Collapse* (Permanent Subcommittee on Investigations of the Committee on Governmental Affairs, 2002).

[6] D Beresford, N Katzenbach and C Rogers, *Report of Investigation by the Special Investigative Committee of the Board of Directors of WorldCom* (Securities and Exchange Commission, 2003).

[7] Securities and Exchange Commission Office of Investigations, *Investigation of Failure of the SEC to Uncover Bernard Madoff's Ponzi Scheme* (Securities and Exchange Commission Office of Investigations, 2009).

[8] Securities and Exchange Commission Office, *Investigation of the SEC's Response to Concerns Regarding Robert Allen Stanford's Alleged Ponzi Scheme* (Securities and Exchange Commission Office, 2010).

[9] United States Department of Justice, 'Samuel Bankman-Fried Sentenced to 25 Years for His Orchestration of Multiple Fraudulent Schemes' (28 March 2024), available at www.justice.gov/archives/opa/pr/samuel-bankman-fried-sentenced-25-years-his-orchestration-multiple-fraudulent-schemes.

[10] United States Department of Justice, 'Elizabeth Holmes Sentenced To More Than 11 Years For Defrauding Theranos Investors Of Hundreds Of Millions' (18 November 2022), available at www.justice.gov/usao-ndca/pr/elizabeth-holmes-sentenced-more-11-years-defrauding-theranos-investors-hundreds.

[11] See National Commission on the Causes of the Financial and Economic Crisis in the United States, *The Financial Crisis Inquiry Report* (National Commission on the Causes of the Financial and Economic Crisis in the United States, 2011).

[12] J Gallagher, J Lauchlan and M Steven, 'Polly Peck: The Breaking of an Entrepreneur?' (1996) *Journal of Small Business and Enterprise Development* 3(1), 3–12.

[13] Department for Trade and Industry, *The Maxwell* Report (Department for Trade and Industry, 2001).

[14] Department for Trade and Industry, *Guinness Plc* (Department for Trade and Industry, 1997).

[15] Parliamentary Commissioners for Administration, *The Barlow Clowes Affair* (Parliamentary Commissioners for Administration, 1989).

[16] See generally HM Treasury Select Committee, *Fixing LIBOR: Some Preliminary Findings* (HM Treasury Select Committee, 2012).

[17] See National Audit Office, *Implementing Employment Support Schemes in Response to the COVID-19 Pandemic* (National Audit Office, 2020); Public Accounts Committee, *Covid-19: Bounce Back Loan Scheme* (Public Accounts Committee, 2020); and House of Commons Committee of Public Accounts, *Local Authority Administered COVID Support Schemes in England* (House of Commons Committee of Public Accounts, 2023).

[18] Attorney General's Office (n 1) at 20.

that 'there are no reliable estimates of the cost of fraud'.[19] Nonetheless, estimates of the global losses have been attempted, with Gee and Button approximating that the losses equate to 6.05 per cent of Gross Domestic Product (GDP), equating to USD$5.127trillion or £3.89trillion.[20] This makes the global fraud losses more than 80 per cent of the UK's GDP.[21] In the UK, the cost of fraud has varied. For example, it was estimated to be £13.9billion (2005),[22] £30.5billion (2010),[23] £38.4billion (2011),[24] £73billion (2012),[25] £193billion (2016),[26] £190billion (2017)[27] and £219billion (2023).[28] In 2023, the Office of National Statistics (ONS) reported that fraud had become the most prevalent crime in the UK accounting for over 40 per cent of reported crime.[29] In December 2024 the ONS reported that there were 4.1million reported instances of fraud, representing a 33 per cent increase from December 2023.[30] Therefore, the precise scale of fraud is considerable if unknown.[31]

Fraud is a threat to the UK economy, and it is the funding mechanism of choice for terrorists.[32] It poses a threat to UK businesses,[33] its citizens[34] and it is a mechanism that allows organised criminal gangs (OCGs) to benefit from significant

[19] ibid at 21.

[20] J Gee and M Button, *The Financial Cost of Fraud 2019* (Crowe, 2019).

[21] ibid.

[22] M Levi, J Burrows M Fleming and M Hopkins, *The Nature, Extent and Economic Impact of Fraud in the UK* (Association of Chief Police Officers, 2007).

[23] National Fraud Authority, *National Fraud Authority Annual Fraud Indicator* (National Fraud Authority, 2010) at 7.

[24] National Fraud Authority, *Annual Fraud Indicator 2011* (National Fraud Authority, 2011) at 3.

[25] National Fraud Authority, *Annual Fraud Indicator 2012* (National Fraud Authority, 2012) at 3.

[26] Experian, *Annual Fraud Indicator 2016* (Experian, 2016).

[27] Experian, *Annual Fraud Indicator 2017* (Experian, 2017).

[28] Crowe, *Annual Fraud Indicator 2023* (Crowe, 2024).

[29] Office of National Statistics, 'Crime in England and Wales: Year Ending September 2024' (30 January 2025), available at www.ons.gov.uk/peoplepopulationandcommunity/crimeandjustice/bulletins/crimeinenglandandwales/yearendingseptember2024.

[30] Office of National Statistics, 'Crime in England and Wales: Year Ending December 2024' (24 April 2025), available at www.ons.gov.uk/peoplepopulationandcommunity/crimeandjustice/bulletins/crimeinenglandandwales/yearendingdecember2024.

[31] House of Lords Fraud Act 2006 and Digital Fraud Committee, *Fighting Fraud: Breaking the Chain* (House of Lords Fraud Act 2006 and Digital Fraud Committee, 2022) 11.

[32] See HM Government, *Fraud Strategy: Stopping Scams and Protecting the Public* (HM Government, 2023) and N Ryder, 'To Report or Not to Report? An Analysis of the Relationship between Defence against Terrorism Financing Suspicious Activity Reports and Fraud in the United Kingdom' in L de Koker and D Goldbarsht, *Financial Crime, Law and Governance – Navigating Challenges in Different Contexts* (Springer, 2024) 169–202.

[33] National Crime Agency, 'Fraud' (n/d), available at www.nationalcrimeagency.gov.uk/what-we-do/crime-threats/fraud-and-economic-crime?highlight=WyJuYXRpb24iLCJuYXRpb25hbCIsIm5hdGlvbmFsbHkiLCJuYXRpb25zJyIsIm5hdGlvbmFsaXR5IiwibmF0aW9uYWxzIiwibmF0aW9ucyIsIm5hdGlvbmFsbHknIiwibmF0aW9uYWxpdGllcyJd.

[34] International Public Sector Fraud Forum, *Guide to Understanding the Total Impact of Fraud* (Cabinet Office and Commonwealth Fraud Prevention Centre, 2020) at 9–14.

financial gains.[35] Nonetheless, 86 per cent of fraud in the UK is not reported.[36] Therefore, the threat presented by fraud necessitates a coordinated strategy from HM Government, the foundations of which were the Roskill Report and the creation of the Serious Fraud Office (SFO).[37] However, it was not until the publication of the Fraud Review in 2006 and introduction of the Fraud Act in 2006 that fraud reappeared within the remit of the Home Office. The Fraud Review covered a wide range of areas including fraud prevention, investigation, prosecution and recommendations that were aimed at improving fraud deterrence and penalties.[38] The Fraud Act 2006 covered a range of fraud-related offences including fraud by false representation, fraud by failing to disclose information and fraud by abuse of position.[39] It was a further 13 years until the next set of fraud policy measures were published.

In 2019 HM Government introduced a series of counter-fraud policy measures including the Economic Crime Plan 1,[40] the Beating Crime Plan,[41] the Economic Crime Plan 2,[42] the Fraud Strategy,[43] the extension of failure to prevent model to fraud,[44] the publication of the 'Fighting Fraud' report by the Fraud Act 2006 and Digital Fraud Committee,[45] the Economic Crime and Corporate Transparency Act 2023, and the Home Affairs Select Committee's fraud investigation.[46] Additionally, fraud has been added to the Strategic Policing Requirement which means that police forces are required to treat the threat presented by fraud as a top priority.[47]

Several of these measures have included initiatives aimed at improving the reporting of fraud and related data-sharing. For example, the Economic Crime

[35] It has been estimated that over 60% of UK organised criminal gangs (OCGs) participate in committing fraud. M Levi, 'Organised Fraud' in L Paoli (eds), *The Oxford Handbook of Organised Crime* (Oxford University Press, 2014) 460–81. It has been suggested that there are 4,772 OCGs and 59,000 known serious organised crime suspected in the UK. See The Tony Blair Institute, *A New Approach to Serious and Organised Crime in the UK* (The Tony Blair Institute, 2024) and The Tony Blair Institute, *A New International Approach to Beating Serious and Organised Crime* (The Tony Blair Institute, 2025).

[36] National Crime Agency (n 33).

[37] Roskill, *Fraud Trials Committee Report* (His Majesty's Stationery Office, 1986). See Criminal Justice Act 1987, s 1.

[38] Attorney General's Office (n 1).

[39] Fraud Act 2006, ss 2–4.

[40] HM Government and UK Finance, *Economic Crime Plan 2019-2022* (HM Government and UK Finance, 2019).

[41] HM Government, *Beating Crime Plan – Fewer Victims, Peaceful Neighbourhoods, Safe Country* (HM Government, 2021).

[42] HM Treasury and Home Office, *Economic Crime Plan 2 2023–2026* (HM Treasury and Home Office, 2023).

[43] HM Government, *Fraud Strategy* (n 32).

[44] Economic Crime and Corporate Transparency Act 2023, s 196.

[45] House of Lords Fraud Act 2006 and Digital Fraud Committee (n 31) at 87.

[46] Home Affairs Select Committee, 'Home Affairs Committee Launches Inquiry into Fraud' 14 September 2023), available at https://committees.parliament.uk/work/7913/fraud/news/197427/home-affairs-committee-launches-inquiry-into-fraud/.

[47] Home Office, 'The Strategic Policing Requirement 2023' (23 June 2023), available at www.gov.uk/government/publications/strategic-policing-requirement-2023#:~:text=The%20SPR%20sets%20out%20the,needed%20to%20counter%20those%20threats.

Plan 1 included recommendations aimed at expanding and enhancing the public-private information-sharing through the Joint Money Laundering Intelligence Task Force (JMLIT), to improve the information-sharing between the AML/CTF supervisors and law enforcement agencies (LEAs) and to promote information-sharing in relation to fraud.[48] The Economic Crime and Corporate Transparency Act 2023 allow LEAs to proactively gather information by reinforcing the powers of the UKFIU to acquire information from companies relating to money laundering, permitting businesses to share information and enable information-sharing via a third part intermediary.[49] Therefore, the UK efforts to address fraud is multi-pronged, which involves a combination of HM Government strategies and collaboration with the private sector. However, four decades of neglect has resulted in an uncoordinated and unstructured strategy that can be heavily contrasted with the AML/CTF strategies.[50]

In order to address this failing, HM Government published its 'Fraud Strategy' in May 2023 which focused on reducing fraud by 10 per cent, prevention, strengthening the SFO and National Crime Agency (NCA), collaboration with technology companies, a public awareness campaign and improvements on how fraud is reported.[51] The Fraud Strategy announced the creation of 400 new police officers to tackle fraud as part of the National Fraud Squad (NFS). However, the additional officers will have little impact on fraud when it has been suggested that an additional 20,000 police officers are needed,[52] at an estimated cost of £600million.[53] The Social Market Foundation went further and suggested that 30,000 additional police officers should be focussed on economic crime to redress this imbalance at a cost of £3.5billion per year.[54] The Fraud Strategy developed a voluntary system of engagement with social media companies and the telecommunications sector via the Online Safety Act 2023 and the Online Fraud Charter.[55] The Fraud Strategy stated it would replace Action Fraud with a new 'state-of-the-art national fraud and cybercrime reporting service'.[56] Following the 2024 General Election, HM Government announced that it would publish a new and expanded Fraud Strategy

[48] HM Government and UK Finance (n 40) at 30–31.

[49] Department for Business and Trade, 'Guidance on the Information Sharing Measures in the Economic Crime and Corporate Transparency Act 2023' (20 December 2024), available at www.gov.uk/government/publications/information-sharing-measures-in-the-economic-crime-and-corporate-transparency-act/guidance-on-the-information-sharing-measures-in-the-economic-crime-and-corporate-transparency-act-2023.

[50] For a more detailed discussion see chapters four and five.

[51] HM Government, *Fraud Strategy* (n 32) at 4.

[52] House of Commons Justice Committee, *Fraud and the Justice System* (House of Commons Justice Committee, 2023) at 19.

[53] Institute for Fiscal Studies, *Police Workforce and Funding in England and Wales* (Institute for Fiscal Studies, 2017) at 9.

[54] Social Market Foundation – Written Evidence (FDF0026), 21 April 2022, available at committees.parliament.uk/writtenevidence/108022/html/.

[55] For a detailed discussion and analysis see section IV.C.

[56] HM Government, *Fraud Strategy* (n 32) at 19. For a detailed discussion and analysis see section IV.A.

that focuses on 'combatting tech-enabled fraud, including emerging tech such as AI'.[57]

Successive governments have lacked the political will to create a coordinated, continuous fraud strategy that is capable of meeting the globalisation and industrialisation of fraud, the threat of emerging technology, its link to serious organised crime and terrorism. The lack of political will is illustrated following the publication of HM Government's 'Plan for Change', which does not make any reference to fraud.[58] It is against this background that the next section of the chapter identifies and appraises the fraud reporting mechanisms to illustrate how they have contributed towards an intelligence gap.

III. Reporting Fraud

The fraud reporting mechanisms seek to identify the arrangement used to defraud a person or company of their money or resources. Conversely, the AML reporting system comprises the identification of suspicious transactions of the proceeds of crime that do not meet the financial profile of the customer. The aim of the CTF reporting obligations is to prevent and disrupt the flow of funds to terrorist organisations. These reporting obligations require the regulated sector to identify and report suspicious transactions.[59] The difference between these reporting mechanisms is that only 'successful' frauds are required to be reported to the UKFIU under the Proceeds of Crime Act 2002 (POCA). The reporting of 'unsuccessful' or 'suspected' frauds is voluntary and these reports are submitted to a myriad of counter fraud bodies from both the public and private sector. The next subsection identifies and appraises the compulsory and voluntary fraud reporting mechanisms.

A. Proceeds of Crime Act 2002

The primary statutory obligation for reporting 'successful' frauds is POCA 2002. It is a criminal offence under the Act to fail to disclose via a defence against money laundering suspicious activity report (DAML SAR) where there is knowledge, suspicion or reasonable grounds to know or suspect, that a person is laundering the proceeds of criminal conduct.[60] Successful fraud is defined as money laundering for the purpose of this Act.[61] The Act specifies that members of the regulated

[57] HM Government, 'Lord Hanson Unveils Ambitious New Approach to Tackling Fraud' (27 March 2025), available at www.gov.uk/government/news/lord-hanson-unveils-ambitious-new-approach-to-tackling-fraud.

[58] HM Government, *Plan for Change – Milestones for Mission-Led Government* (HM Government, 2024).

[59] Proceeds of Crime Act 2002 (POCA), sch 9.

[60] ibid s 330.

[61] A successful fraud could be defined as one where the deception goes undetected, allowing the fraudster to achieve their intended gain without facing consequences.

sector are required to report their suspicions as soon as reasonably practical to the UKFIU. There is no legal obligation to report unsuccessful or attempted frauds because any attempted fraud will not give rise to any legal criminal proceedings and therefore fall outside the scope of the mandatory reporting obligations under POCA 2002.[62] The reporting of fraud is a voluntary victim orientated action where individuals of businesses can report the suspected fraud to countless organisations including the Police and Action Fraud. The mandatory reporting for money laundering and terrorist financing, is by contrast, a statutory intelligence-gathering requirement that is designed to disrupt. There is no statutory obligation to compel people or businesses to report suspected fraud and the non-reporting of fraud carries no criminal penalty. The decision to report rests with the victim or witness to the fraud.

B. Voluntary Reporting Mechanisms

This subsection of the chapter identifies the voluntary fraud reporting systems and the total number of suspected frauds reported by each of these mechanisms.

i. Action Fraud

Action Fraud is the reporting centre for victims of fraud in England, Wales and Northern Ireland.[63] If a person believes they have been the victim of a scam, fraud or online crime they are 'encouraged', but not 'mandated', to submit a report to Action Fraud.[64] Action Fraud receives reports in four ways – telephone; an online reporting mechanism, directly from the Police or other LEAs and from companies.[65] It is managed by the City of London Police (COLP) and works in conjunction with the National Fraud Intelligence Bureau (NFIB), which evaluate reports to determine typologies or patterns before referring them to the Police or to Regional Organised Crime Units (ROCUs).[66] Since 2014 'all fraud complaints to the police, unless an immediate response is required for a crime in action', have to be recorded through Action Fraud.[67]

[62] For a more detailed analysis see chapter four.

[63] Her Majesty's Inspectorate of Constabulary and Fire & Rescue Services (HMICFRS), *Fraud: Time to Choose An Inspection of the Police Response to Fraud* (Her Majesty's Inspectorate of Constabulary, 2019) at 66. In Scotland, fraud is reported to Police Scotland. See Police Scotland, 'Online Reporting Form' (n/d), available at www.scotland.police.uk/secureforms/c3/.

[64] House of Commons Treasury Committee, *Economic Crime: Consumer View Third Report of Session 2019* (House of Commons Treasury Committee, 2019) at 21.

[65] HMICFRS (n 63) at 31.

[66] House of Commons Home Affairs Committee, *Policing the Future* (House of Commons Home Affairs Committee, 2018) at 23.

[67] M Levi, A Doig, R Gundur, D Wal and M Williams, 'Cyberfraud and the Implications for Effective Risk-Based Responses: Themes from UK Research' (2017) *Crime Law Social Change*, 67, 77–96, at 80.

Table 1 Action Fraud

YEAR	NUMBER OF FRAUD REPORTS SUBMITTED
2018–2019	310,675[68]
2019–2020	326,554[69]
2020–2021	413,945[70]
2021–2022	481,096[71]
2022–2023	304,730[72]
2023–2024	305,460[73]

ii. Credit Industry Fraud

Cifas is the UK's Fraud Prevention Service, a non-profit membership association created in 1988 that aims to unite hundreds of organisations across the public, private and voluntary sectors to detect, deter and prevent fraud. It provides a secure framework for the exchange of high-grade fraud risk data and intelligence through its two core systems, the National Fraud Database and the Internal Fraud Database, which enables members to flag suspicious applications, share details of insider fraud and protect innocent victims, thereby strengthening collective defences against financial crime.[74]

Table 2 Cifas

YEAR	NUMBER OF REPORTS SUBMITTED
2010–2011	237,000[75]
2011–2012	248,000[76]
2012–2013	221,000[77]
2013–2014	276,993[78]
2014–2015	320,900[79]

(continued)

[68] Office of National Statistics, 'Crime in England and Wales: Year Ending September 2019' (23 January 2000), available at Crime in England and Wales – Office for National Statistics.

[69] Action Fraud, 'Fraud Crime Trends' (n/d), available at https://data.actionfraud.police.uk/cms/wp-content/uploads/2021/07/2020-21-Annual-Assessment-Fraud-Crime-Trends.pdf.

[70] ibid.

[71] J Andrieux, 'Action Fraud: 62% of Reports of Fraud Cyber-Enabled' (24 January 2022), available at www.moneymarketing.co.uk/news/action-fraud-62-of-reports-of-fraud-cyber-enabled/#:~:text=In%20that%20period%2C%20Action%20Fraud,reporting%20losing%20%C2%A31.6bn.

[72] See Office of National Statistics (n 29).

[73] ibid.

[74] Cifas, 'What is Cifas?' (n/d), available at www.cifas.org.uk/about-cifas/what-is-cifas.

[75] Cifas, *Annual Report 2012* (Cifas, 2013) at 22.

[76] ibid.

[77] Cifas, *Annual Report 2013* (Cifas, 2014) at 16.

[78] Cifas, *Annual Report 2014* (Cifas, 2015) at 26.

[79] Cifas, *Annual Report 2015* (Cifas, 2016) at 1.

Table 2 ***(Continued)***

YEAR	NUMBER OF REPORTS SUBMITTED
2015–2016	325,000[80]
2016–2017	305,000[81]
2017–2018	324,000[82]
2018–2019	364,000[83]
2019–2020	310,000[84]
2020–2021	309,849[85]
2021–2022	309,000[86]
2022–2023	409,000[87]
2023–2024	374,000[88]
2024–2025	421,000[89]

iii. UK Finance

UK Finance is the trade association representing around 300 firms across banking, insurance, capital markets and the broader financial services sector. UK Finance provides strategic leadership and promotes collaboration across the banking and finance sector. It leads the sector's fight against fraud and works closely with LEAs to share intelligence. As the designer of the public-private Economic Crime Plan, UK Finance helped develop the first joint strategy with HM Government. It supplies the fraud statistics for the industry and operates a central Information and Intelligence Unit that circulates threat intelligence to member firms.

Table 3 UK Finance

YEAR	NUMBER OF REPORTS SUBMITTED
2018–2019	740,847[90]
2019–2020	2,900,000[91]

(continued)

[80] Cifas, *Annual Report 2016* (Cifas, 2017) at 1.
[81] Cifas, *Annual Report 2017* (Cifas, 2018) at 5.
[82] Cifas, *Annual Report 2018* (Cifas, 2019) at 1.
[83] Cifas, *Annual Report 2019* (Cifas, 2020) at 3.
[84] Cifas, *Annual Report 2020* (Cifas, 2021) at 3.
[85] Cifas, *Fraud Scape 2021 Key Findings* (Cifas, 2022) at 2.
[86] Cifas, 'Fraud Skyrockets as Cost-of-Living and Economic Crises Begin to Deepen' (14 November 2022), available at www.cifas.org.uk/newsroom/fraudscape-9mth-2022.
[87] Cifas, *Fraud Scape 2023* (Cifas, 2024) at 4.
[88] Cifas, *Fraud Scape 2024* (Cifas, 2024) at 4.
[89] Cifas, *Fraud Scape 2025* (Cifas, 2025) at 2.
[90] UK Finance, *Fraud – The Facts 2020* (UK Finance, 2021).
[91] Office of National Statistics, 'Crime in England and Wales: Year Ending December 2020' (13 May 2021), available at Crime in England and Wales – Office for National Statistics.

Table 3 ***(Continued)***

YEAR	NUMBER OF REPORTS SUBMITTED
2020–2021	2,912,467[92]
2021–2022	2,988,705[93]
2022–2023	2,970,000[94]
2023–2024	1,500,000[95]

iv. The Police

The Police serve as the initial point of contact for many victims of fraud, receiving reports via calls for service or direct contact. Police Forces are expected to log these incidents and submit the details to Action Fraud, ensuring each report feeds into the NFIB. Once the report has been logged, the Police will assess emerging trends and if there are indicators of victim vulnerability, they can provide support and/or commence an investigation.

Table 4 The Police

YEAR	NUMBER OF REPORTS SUBMITTED
2016–2017	653,468[96]
2017–2018	638,358[97]
2018–2019	648,214[98]
2019–2020	739,131[99]
2020–2021	912,203[100]
2021–2022	1,100,000[101]

(continued)

[92] UK Finance, *Annual Fraud Report – the Definitive Overview of Payment Industry Fraud in 2021* (UK Finance, 2022).

[93] UK Finance, *Annual Fraud Report – the Definitive Overview of Payment Industry Fraud in 2022* (UK Finance, 2023).

[94] UK Finance, *Annual Fraud Report – the Definitive Overview of Payment Industry Fraud in 2023* (UK Finance, 2024).

[95] UK Finance, *Half Year Fraud Report* (UK Finance, 2024).

[96] Figures were not collected by UK Finance prior to 2015. See UK Finance, *Annual Report 2024* (UK Finance, 2025) at 5.

[97] Office of National Statistics, 'Crime in England and Wales: Year Ending September 2019' (23 January 2000), available at Crime in England and Wales – Office for National Statistics.

[98] Office of National Statistics, 'Crime in England and Wales: Year Ending December 2020' (13 May 2021), available at ibid.

[99] ibid.

[100] Office for National Statistics, 'Crime in England and Wales: Year Ending December 2022', available at www.ons.gov.uk/peoplepopulationandcommunity/crimeandjustice/bulletins/crimeinenglandandwales/yearendingdecember2022#fraud.

[101] ibid.

Table 4 ***(Continued)***

YEAR	NUMBER OF REPORTS SUBMITTED
2022–2023	1,200,000[102]
2023–2024	1,300,000[103]

v. Other Reporting Mechanisms

Frauds relating to counterfeit currency, stolen vehicles, counterfeit medicine or medical devices, tax fraud, benefit fraud, immigration fraud, reports made by whistleblowers and companies are not reported to Action Fraud, Cifas and UK Finance. They are reported to the Police,[104] the Medicines and Healthcare products Regulatory Agency (MHRA),[105] HM Revenue and Customs (HMRC),[106] the Department for Work and Pensions (DWP) Fraud and Error Service,[107] the Home Office,[108] the SFO,[109] the Financial Conduct Authority,[110] Trading Standards[111] and Crime Stoppers.[112] Specific statistics on the number of suspected fraud cases reported to some of these entities are not readily available. Freedom of Information requests reveal that the SFO reported that it has received 8,655 reports of suspected fraud[113] and the MHRA has 208 reports.[114]

There are too many fraud reporting mechanisms that hinder the prevention of fraud, the collection of data that can be shared, thus contributing towards the intelligence gap. This is complicated by the use of a multi-agency approach towards the policing of fraud.[115] This subsection has illustrated that there is no single unified reporting system, no legislative infrastructure, no clear reporting pathway and

[102] Office for National Statistics, 'Crime in England and Wales: Year Ending December 2023', available at www.ons.gov.uk/peoplepopulationandcommunity/crimeandjustice/bulletins/crimeinenglandandwales/yearendingdecember2023#fraud.

[103] Office for National Statistics, 'Crime in England and Wales: Year Ending June 2024', available at www.ons.gov.uk/peoplepopulationandcommunity/crimeandjustice/bulletins/crimeinenglandandwales/yearendingjune2024#fraud.

[104] M Skidmore et al, *More than Just a Number: Improving the Police Response to Victims of Fraud* (Police Foundation, 2018) at 44.

[105] Police.UK, 'Action Fraud' (n/d), available at www.actionfraud.police.uk/.

[106] HM Government, 'Report Tax Fraud or Avoidance to HMRC' (n/d), available at www.gov.uk/report-tax-fraud.

[107] HM Government, 'Report Benefit Fraud' (n/d), available at www.gov.uk/report-benefit-fraud.

[108] Home Office, 'Report an Immigration or Customs Crime' (n/d), available at www.gov.uk/report-immigration-crime.

[109] Serious Fraud Office (SFO), 'Serious or Complex Fraud, Including Bribery and Corruption' (n/d), available at https://sforeporting.egressforms.com/.

[110] Financial Conduct Authority, 'Report a Scam' (n/d), available at www.fca.org.uk/consumers/report-scam.

[111] Skidmore et al (n 104) at 45.

[112] See Crime Stoppers, *Impact Report 2023-2024* (Crime Stoppers, 2024) at 9.

[113] Freedom of Information Request, Reference: 2025-051, Serious Fraud Office, 19 May 2025.

[114] Freedom of Information Request, FOI2025/00409, Medicines and Healthcare products Regulatory Agency, 14 May 2025.

[115] House of Lords Fraud Act 2006 and Digital Fraud Committee (n 31).

there are too many reporting mechanisms. The current system includes multiple agencies, many of which have overlapping responsibilities which causes confusion and inefficiency. This system would benefit from a single counter fraud reporting mechanism, a single fraud reporting entity, a single point of contact for victims and a central fraud database. The reporting of suspected fraud can be contrasted with the reporting of successful fraud, which falls under the AML/CTF reporting regime. Despite the data collected by Action Fraud, Cifas, the Police and UK Finance, the voluntary reporting system remains unmanaged and uncoordinated. Now that we have identified the mandatory and voluntary reporting systems and the number of suspected frauds reported, the next part of the chapter adopts the case study methodology to illustrate deficiencies, highlighting the need for further reform.

IV. Case Studies

The voluntary reporting of fraud in the UK represents a complex and fragmented landscape, where the burden of disclosure falls on individuals and organisations to navigate the reporting systems. To illustrate the problems, four case studies offer distinct yet interconnected perspectives on the limitations of the current reporting systems. The case studies demonstrate how inconsistent practices and technological deficiencies contribute towards ineffective responses. Action Fraud has faced criticism for its limited investigative powers and ineffective communication with victims which leave reports either unresolved or unacknowledged. Police forces across the UK continue to struggle with limited resources leading to an uneven and inconsistent reporting approach. Social media platforms are increasingly exploited for scams and phishing attacks and they lack robust repotting systems whilst the communications sector is a key conduit for the execution of fraud. Collectively, these case studies illustrate the need for a more coordinated and mandatory framework for reporting fraud in the UK.

A. Action Fraud

Action Fraud is the national fraud and cybercrime reporting centre and since its establishment, it has been subjected to criticism and its effectiveness questioned. This subsection identifies weaknesses including high levels of victim dissatisfaction, limited public awareness, the absence of investigative powers, a low success rate, limited resources and technical weaknesses. Action Fraud was heavily criticised following an investigation by *The Times* which illustrated how the organisation's staff were trained to mislead victims of fraud that their cases were being investigated.[116] *The Times* reported that fewer than two per cent of reports

[116] M Morgan-Bentley, 'Action Fraud Scrapped after Times Expose' (28 July 2021), available at www.thetimes.co.uk/article/fraud-line-scrapped-after-times-expose-n2tlkbmrv.

submitted resulted in an arrest and fewer than one per cent of police officers were assigned to fraud investigations. Consequently, the Home Office commissioned a review of how fraud is policed in the UK by Sir Craig Mackey, which concluded that the Police are not adequately prepared to tackle fraud.[117] As a result, HM Government announced in July 2021 that Action Fraud was to be abolished and placed within the NCA in 2024.[118]

i. Victim Dissatisfaction

Fraud is not a victimless crime, it has a detrimental impact not only on the finances of the victim but their confidence and mental health.[119] The financial and emotional impact on the victims of fraud is immeasurable with 'Which?' reporting that it receives between '300–350 fraud reports a week where victims show signs of severe emotional distress'.[120] The victims of fraud are often blamed for the crime being committed against them, they may never get their money back and it is very unlikely that the perpetrator will be arrested, prosecuted and convicted. Victim dissatisfaction of Action Fraud is a common criticism. For instance, the Home Affairs Select Committee noted that 'Action Fraud has irretrievably lost the confidence of the public, and reasonable expectations from victims are not being met'.[121] Similarly, the House of Commons Committee of Public Accounts was critical of how Action Fraud treated and supported the victims of fraud. They stated, 'we are seriously concerned that the failures of Action Fraud … it [has earned] the nickname "Inaction Fraud" … victims feel lost in the system as there is often no response when they make a report'.[122] The Public Accounts Committee concluded that the 'victims of fraud are being failed by Action Fraud, which risks undermining public trust in the police'.[123] Academic studies have illustrated varying levels of dissatisfaction towards Action Fraud. For instance, the Police Foundation noted that 'with the number of victims reporting they were dissatisfied with … Action Fraud … [increased] from 18 per cent in 2016-17 to nearly

117 C Mackey and J Savill, *Fraud: A Review of the National 'Lead Force' Responsibilities of the City of London Police and the Effectiveness of Investigations in the UK* (City of London, 2020).

118 HM Government, *Beating Crime Plan* (n 41) at 2.

119 See generally M Button, C Lewis, and J Tapley, 'Not a Victimless Crime: The Impact of Fraud on Individual Victims and their Families' (2014) *Security Journal* 27(1), 36–54 and M Levi and A Pithouse, 'The Victims of Fraud' in D Downes (eds), *Unravelling Criminal Justice* (Palgrave Macmillan, 1992) 229–46.

120 Which?, 'Devastating Emotional Impact of Online Scams Must Force Government Action' (21 March 2021), available at www.which.co.uk/news/article/devastating-emotional-impact-of-online-scams-must-force-government-action-aRSZo6V8HPaD.

121 HMICFRS (n 63) at 80. For a more detailed discussion, see M Button, C Lewis and J Tapley, *Support for the Victims of Fraud: An Assessment of the Current Infrastructure in England and Wales* (National Fraud Authority, 2009) and F Reynoso-Serna, A Evans, F Smith, E Brown and S Davis, *Online Fraud: What does the Public Think?* (Crest, 2023).

122 House of Commons Committee of Public Accounts, *Progress Combatting Fraud* (House of Commons Committee of Public Accounts, 2023) at 5–6.

123 ibid.

half (49%) in 2019–20'.[124] The Home Office reported that the satisfaction levels was 61 per cent, with 74 per cent of victims satisfied with the response by Action Fraud.[125] Furthermore, Crest reported that 'of those who reported to Action Fraud, the satisfaction rate increased to 80 per cent'.[126] In order to improve the levels of support provided to fraud victims, the National Economic Crime Victim Care Unit (NECVCU) was created by the Metropolitan Police Service and COLP. The NECVCU proved to be successful and after two test cases involving the West Midlands Police and Greater Manchester Police the NECVCU has been successfully rolled out to all police forces,[127] it has supported 440,994 victims of fraud and recovered over £3.85million.[128]

A factor that has contributed towards victim dissatisfaction is the length of time taken by victims to report to Action Fraud. HMICFRS reported that 'the length of time people … wait for their call to be [answered] … and the number of people who hang up before they are answered [is] … still unacceptably high'.[129] This was supported by Alpin who concluded that '44% of people abandoning reporting [to Action Fraud] once started',[130] which suggests that victims are suffering from 'reference' or 'referral' fatigue. In oral evidence to the Fraud Act 2006 and Digital Fraud Committee, Dame Vera Baird, the former Victims Commissioner for England and Wales, stated that 'fatigue which means victims are a bit worn out with this kind of Alphabetti spaghetti … there are a lot of places to go … which makes it very difficult for victims of fraud to know what they are supposed to do to get help'.[131] HMICFRS reported that 'the average call abandonment rate for Action Fraud for the 12 months to March 2018 was 37 percent. This was an increase on the previous year's figure of 34 percent' and for online reports the 'abandonment rate was 44 percent'.[132] Victim dissatisfaction with Action Fraud is a significant issue, with reports highlighting the concerns about the effectiveness of the service of addressing fraud and assisting redress. Action Fraud could be regarded as a 'black hole' where fraud reports disappear, leaving victims without sufficient support or financial recovery. This is problematic for the victims of fraud who have experienced financial losses and emotional distress due to the fraud. However, recent reports have indicated that the levels of dissatisfaction with Action Fraud have reduced but are still at an unacceptably high level.

[124] The Police Foundation, *More than Just a Number: Improving the Police Response to Victims of Fraud* (The Police Foundation, 2018) at 43.

[125] Home Office, *Research and Analysis – Experiences of Victims of Fraud and Cybercrime* (Home Office, 2025).

[126] Reynoso-Serna et al (n 121) at 8.

[127] See Action Fraud, 'The Action Fraud National Economic Crime Victim Care Unit' (n/d), available at www.actionfraud.police.uk/victimcare.

[128] Dan Jarvis MP (15 January 2025), available at https://questions-statements.parliament.uk/.

[129] HMICFRS (n 63) at 3.

[130] R Alpin, 'The Policing, Investigation and Governance of "Rogue Trader" Fraud: Whose Responsibility?' (2022) *Police Journal* 95(4), 617–36.

[131] Fraud Act 2006 and Digital Fraud Committee, Oral evidence: Fraud Act 2006 and Digital Fraud, Dame Vera Baird, 28 April 2022, available at committees.parliament.uk/oralevidence/10178/html/.

[132] HMICFRS (n 63) at 18–19.

ii. Limited Public Awareness

A problem with reporting fraud in the UK is the lack of awareness of where and who the victims should report to. The Police Foundation noted that there 'remains confusion among the public about where to report fraud'.[133] According to Citizen's Advice, the public's awareness of the fraud reporting mechanisms is low, with only five per cent of people specifically referring to Action Fraud.[134] The HMICFRS stated that 'thirteen years [after the Fraud Review 2006] … confusion still exists … the main reason for not reporting fraud was a lack of awareness of Action Fraud'.[135] Blakeborough and Correia concluded that 66 per cent of people who did not report to Action Fraud did not know that the organisation existed.[136] In 2024, the Home Affairs Select Committee concluded that 'many victims find it difficult to know how to report [fraud], and those who do are often passed around between different agencies causing further confusion'.[137] The House of Commons Home Affairs Committee recommended that 'HMG should increase efforts in advertising Action Fraud to raise public awareness of how to report incidents of fraud'.[138] In his evidence to the Justice Committee, the then Minister for Security and Borders Damien Hines MP stated that HM Government were 'totally redesigning and recreating Action Fraud'.[139] In response to the Justice Committee, HM Government noted that Action Fraud had 'developed a calendar of campaign activity to … increase public confidence and [the public's awareness] of Action Fraud'.[140] The 2023 Fraud Strategy included a commitment to launch a 'simple cross-government anti-fraud public awareness campaign to further unite messaging … [to] make it easier for people to avoid fraud, and to know how to respond and recover if they have been scammed'.[141] De Liemia et al highlighted the benefits of fraud awareness campaigns which have reduced revictimisation rates by 8.6 per cent, while multiple mailings reduced it by 22.4 per cent.[142] However, this is not the first fraud awareness campaign and there are several initiatives and campaigns from Action Fraud, Cyber Aware, ScamSmart, Friends

[133] The Police Foundation (n 124) at 43.

[134] X Couture and A Pardoe, *Changing the Story on Scams: Protecting Consumers and Increasing reporting* (Citizens Advice, 2017) at 22.

[135] HMICFRS (n 63) at 18.

[136] L Blakeborough and S Correia, *The Scale and Nature of Fraud: A Review of the Evidence* (Home Office, 2018) at 4. Also see F Smith, M Roberts, S Davis, A Evans and A Murray, *Behind the Screen: Perceptions and Experiences of Online Fraud Victimization* (Crest, 2024) at 24.

[137] Home Affairs Select Committee, 'Letter to the Home Secretary' (23 May 2024), available at committees.parliament.uk/publications/45006/documents/223338/default/.

[138] ibid at 12.

[139] Justice Committee Oral evidence: Fraud and the Justice System, HC 961, Tuesday 22 March 2022, available at committees.parliament.uk/oralevidence/10008/html/.

[140] House of Commons Justice Committee, *Fraud and the Justice System: Government Response to the Committee's Fourth Report of Session 2022–23 Sixth Special Report of Session 2022–23* (House of Commons Justice Committee, 2023) at 3.

[141] HM Government, *Fraud Strategy* (n 32) at 38.

[142] M DeLiema, D Brannock, E Preble and L Langton, 'A Fraud Awareness Mail Campaign Significantly Reduces Revictimisation Among Older Victims' (2024) *Innovation in Aging* 8(1), 114, available at https://academic.oup.com/innovateage/article/8/Supplement_1/114/7936082.

Against Scams and UK Finance. These campaigns have helped raise awareness of the threat but have led to confusion about what to do.[143] Commentators have questioned the effectiveness of these schemes. For example, several studies have concluded that there is less empirical data that supports the use of consumer awareness campaigns to reduce the extent of fraud.[144] The limited public awareness of Action Fraud has hindered efforts to improve the experience and support provided to the victims of fraud. Consequently, many victims have not reported their experiences to Action Fraud, limiting the ability of the Police and counter fraud agencies to ascertain an accurate picture of fraud. This has created and contributed towards an intelligence gap.

iii. Absence of Investigative Powers

Action Fraud does not have any investigative powers and as outlined above, its primary purpose is to collect reports of fraud and cybercrime and forward them to the NFIB, which will assess them and determine if there is a need for an investigation and further dissemination. Victim Support noted that 'the purpose of and remit of Action Fraud is also often unclear to victims who have reported, who often assume their case is being investigated and consequently feel let down when they realise it is not'.[145] There are several reasons why Action Fraud does not have any investigative powers. Firstly, Action Fraud does not have the financial resources or employees to investigate every reported fraud. As illustrated in Table 1, on average Action Fraud receives over 300,000 reports of fraud every year and it only employs 95 people.[146] Therefore, it would be impractical for Action Fraud to undertake any fraud-related investigative measures. Secondly, Action Fraud and the NFIB aim to provide a national picture of fraud and cybercrime by attempting to identify local, regional and national fraud patterns that will assist the Police and ROCUs to identify cases that need to be prioritised. However, Action Fraud receives less than ten per cent of the total fraud reports in the UK, illustrating an intelligence gap that undermines efforts to understand fraud trends. One possible solution would be to position Action Fraud within the UKFIU which would centralise the reporting of fraud, making investigations more efficient and reducing delays in identifying and prosecuting fraudsters. Furthermore, it would also provide the victims of fraud with greater clarity of who to report to.

[143] HM Government, *Fraud Strategy* (n 32).

[144] See C Cross and M Kelly, 'The Problem of "White Noise": Examining Current Prevention Approaches to Online Fraud' (2016) *Journal of Financial Crime* 23(4), 806–18 and T Prenzler, 'What Works in Fraud Prevention: A Review of Real-World Intervention Projects' (2020) *Journal of Criminological Research, Policy and Practice* 6(1), 83–96.

[145] Written evidence submitted by Victim Support, October 2023, available at committees.parliament.uk/writtenevidence/125742/pdf/.

[146] House of Commons Justice Committee (n 140)at 13.

iv. *Low Success Rate*

Action Fraud has a low success rate for several reasons. One factor is the volume of fraud cases reported, making it difficult for law enforcement to investigate each one. Furthermore, fraud is complex and requires extensive coordination between the public and private sector to slow down the process. Many cases are closed without a successful outcome, with research estimating that approximately 96 per cent of reports submitted to Action Fraud do not result in a resolution.[147] Similarly, the Public Accounts Committee noted that 'less than 1% of cases received by Action Fraud result in a criminal justice outcome, where an offender is charged or prosecuted for the crime'.[148] 'Which?' reported several shortcomings following an investigation into Action Fraud.[149] In particular, 'Which?' concluded that reports submitted to Action Fraud were reviewed by artificial intelligence and the COLP has failed to 'guarantee that every report is then read by its crime reviewers'. Additionally, the investigation concluded that the Police branded Action Fraud as 'not fit for purpose' and that local police forces were given 'appallingly' low numbers of detailed fraud cases to investigate.[150] Mackey and Savill noted that 'for fraud to be investigated effectively, Action Fraud and the NFIB need to work seamlessly with the 43 police forces in an assured end to end process'.[151] However, it is unrealistic for every reported fraud to be fully investigated by the Police. This was acknowledged by COLP who stated that 'there is an expectation by some members of the public that most, if not all, frauds should be investigated. Operationally this is not feasible … [therefore] criminal justice outcomes are not always achievable'.[152] Button took the view that budgetary constraints and limited investigative capacity have also contributed towards the low success rate.[153]

v. *Limited Resources*

A connected criticism of Action Fraud are its limited resources, a factor that has impacted broader counter financial crime efforts. Spotlight on Corruption concluded that 'while economic crime costs the UK around 14.5% of GDP at a conservative estimate, the UK spends the equivalent of just 0.042% on

[147] Which?, 'Exclusive: More than 96% of Reported Fraud Cases go Unsolved' (24 September 2018), available at www.which.co.uk/news/article/exclusive-more-than-96-of-reported-fraud-cases-go-unsolved-apfql3E0JxDz.

[148] House of Commons Committee of Public Accounts (n 122) at 5.

[149] F Lipson, 'Scam Victims Ignored by Police Fraud Reporting System' (27 September 2019), available at www.which.co.uk/news/article/exclusive-scam-victims-ignored-by-police-fraud-reporting-system-avxU06T4Hclz.

[150] ibid.

[151] See Mackey and Savill (n 117) at 2.

[152] City of London Police, 'Written Evidence Submitted to the Home Affairs Select Committee' (February 2017), available at https://committees.parliament.uk/writtenevidence/77936/pdf/.

[153] M Button, 'Hiding behind the Veil of Action Fraud: The Police Response to Economic Crime in England and Wales and Evaluating the Case for Regionalization or a National Economic Crime Agency (2021) *Policing: A Journal of Policy and Practice* 15(3), 1758–72.

resourcing core national level economic crime enforcement bodies – £852 million per year'.[154] The disparity in the funding is illustrated when the budgets of the Federal Bureau of Investigation ($USD11.3billion)[155] is compared to the NCA (£869.64million).[156] In relation to Action Fraud, its budget was £5.7 million (2009/2010), £4/9million (2010/11), £6.68 million (2011/2012), £9.4 million (2012/2013), £11.11 million (2013/2014), £10.62million (2014/2015), £11.03million (2015/2016),[157] £7.5million (2018/2019); £7.5million (2019/2020); £7.5million (2020/2021); £7.5million (2021/2022); £7.5million (2022/2023); £9.1million (2023/2024); and £8.9million (2024/2025).[158] These figures illustrate that the budget and resourcing levels for Action Fraud have remained static, at a time when levels of fraud continue to increase. Indeed, the House of Lords Fraud Act 2006 and Digital Fraud Committee reported that a more sustained funding model was needed to prevent Action Fraud to avoid 'cliff-edge' funding patterns.[159] In response, the then Home Secretary Suella Braverman MP, stated that the 'Government is investing £30 million over three years to turn Action Fraud into a state-of-the-art reporting centre, including a simple to use reporting website and upgraded call centre with reduced waiting times'.[160] The House of Commons Home Affairs Committee acknowledged that 'Action Fraud has undergone reform in recent years, with £35m of government funding spent on improvements to the helpline and website, including a new online reporting tool'.[161] HM Government stated that the funding will provide a 'wide range of benefits to victims and other users. The modifications included improved use of technology, increased numbers of staff, sending cases to police forces more quickly, and prioritising cases involving vulnerable victims.[162] The House of Lords Fraud Act 2006 and Digital Fraud Committee noted that in 2020/21, Action Fraud received 413,945 reports of fraud and 'based on this volume of crime and current staffing levels, in a year each member of staff within Action Fraud is expected to record and manage 4,357 cases'.[163] Therefore, 'the volume of reports an individual member of staff is expected to deal with in Action Fraud clearly makes it difficult to provide a high-quality service to

[154] Spotlight on Corruption, *Closing the UK's Economic Crime Enforcement Gap: Proposals for Boosting Resources for UK Law Enforcement to Fight Economic Crime* (Spotlight on Corruption, 2022) at 3.

[155] Federal Bureau of Investigation, 'A Review of the President's Fiscal Year 2025 Budget Request for the Federal Bureau of Investigation' (4 June 2024), available at www.fbi.gov/news/speeches-and-testimony/a-review-of-the-president-s-fiscal-year-2025-budget-request-for-the-federal-bureau-of-investigation.

[156] National Crime Agency, *National Crime Agency Annual Plan 2024-2025* (National Crime Agency, 2025) at 19.

[157] Mike Penning MP, 14 December 2015, available from Written questions and answers – Written questions, answers and statements – UK Parliament.

[158] Freedom of Information Request, Home Office, 19 May 2025.

[159] House of Lords Fraud Act 2006 and Digital Fraud Committee (n 31) at 98.

[160] Suella Braverman, MP, Written Statement of House of Commons, 3 May 2023, available from Written statements – Written questions, answers and statements – UK Parliament.

[161] House of Commons Home Affairs Committee (n 66) at 23.

[162] HM Government, *Fraud Strategy* (n 32)5 at 20.

[163] House of Lords Fraud Act 2006 and Digital Fraud Committee (n 31) at 12.

each individual victim reporting their crime'.[164] The House of Commons Justice Committee recommended that HM Government 'should take steps now to address these issues … sufficient staffing needs to be put in place to ensure Action Fraud and its successor service can provide a high-quality service to victims'.[165] The limited budget presents several challenges – it has contributed towards a reduced capacity at a time when the Office for National Statistics reported a 33 per cent increase in reported fraud in December 2024. This has contributed towards a slower response time and has negatively impacted the public trust in Action Fraud.

vi. Weak Technology

Action Fraud has faced criticism regarding its technical capabilities. Reports have highlighted problems with data recording, intelligence utilisation, and the lack of awareness among investigators and supervisors about relevant resources.[166] Mackey and Savill noted that Action Fraud requires 'adequate resources and a dependable ICT platform to operate effectively'.[167] Police forces have struggled to provide basic data on fraud, including how many reported fraud cases result in further action by the Police.[168] Furthermore, the use of intelligence products provided by the NFIB has proven to be inconsistent.[169] Since the COLP took over the management of Action Fraud, it has been acknowledged that the technology used is not 'fit for purpose'.[170] HMICFRS stated that 'we do not underestimate the … technical complexities that COLP has faced in updating the respective systems … these developments are significantly overdue'.[171] The House of Commons Justice Committee reported that the replacement of Action Fraud will focus on an effective 'IT system that underpins the service, improving the call centre technology and the analytical software that is used to gather reports and consider potential leads and links between crimes'.[172] The Committee concluded that the planned changes 'are focused on the technology underpinning the service, primarily improving the analytical tools applied when a crime is reported rather than improving customer experience'.[173]

In 2023, HM Government announced that Action Fraud would be replaced by 'a state-of-the-art system for victims to report fraud and cybercrimes to the police'[174]

[164] House of Commons Justice Committee (n 52) at 12.
[165] ibid at 19.
[166] HMICFRS (n 63).
[167] See Mackey and Savill (n 117) at 7.
[168] See Blakeborough and Correia (n 136).
[169] HMICFRS (n 63).
[170] ibid.
[171] ibid.
[172] See House of Commons Justice Committee (n 52) at 13.
[173] ibid.
[174] HM Government, *Fraud Strategy* (n 32) at 4.

and that 'the full replacement service will launch within a year [by 2024]'.[175] In his evidence to the Home Affairs Select Committee, Chris Bell, Service Delivery Director for the COLP, stated that 'we recognise that Action Fraud had to be modernised and transformed'.[176] The Home Affairs Select Committee concluded that 'Action Fraud is not fit for purpose, and whilst its replacement is expected to rectify some longstanding issues, it is vital that the new system makes it easier for all victims to report the crime and know how their case is being handled'.[177] In response, HM Government stated that the 'Home Office is continuing to implement the outstanding recommendations from the previous fraud strategy … including … replacing Action Fraud with a more effective fraud reporting system'.[178] The COLP stated that the replacement for Action Fraud, the Fraud and Cyber Crime Reporting and Analysis Service (FCCRAS), would cost £150m.[179] The FCCRAS has five objectives. Firstly, to simplify and speed up the reporting of fraud and cybercrime. Secondly, to inform the victims of fraud what has happened to their report. Thirdly, by providing practical and targeted advice for business and people on how to avoid being the victim of fraud. Fourthly, to improve the quality and speed of the sharing of data with LEAs. Finally, by blocking and disrupting fraudulent websites, activities, and bank accounts which we know are enabling criminal activity.[180] The replacement for Action Fraud was originally planned to launch in 2024 and it has been further delayed until 2025, thus highlighting a limited commitment by successive governments. Action Fraud plays an important role in the UK's counter fraud strategy. It has become the focal point of reporting fraud and online scams and serves as the national fraud reporting centre in the UK. Action Fraud has a number of merits – it is the single point of contact, staff expertise, its availability and its relationship with the NFIB. Action Fraud has faced several challenges – victim dissatisfaction, limited public awareness, no investigation powers, a low success rate, limited resources and technical weaknesses. In order for improvements to be made, the UK's approach towards tackling the reporting of fraud must change. The Government must adapt to the evolving threat of fraud and move away from four decades of implementing a reactive and unstructured strategy with the goal of creating a long term and sustainable fraud strategy.

The case study has illustrated that Action Fraud is hindered by a number of critical weaknesses. Many individuals who report fraud feel ignored and unsupported,

[175] ibid at 20.

[176] Home Affairs Committee Oral Evidence: Fraud, HC 125 Wednesday 28 February 2024, available at committees.parliament.uk/oralevidence/14372/pdf/.

[177] Home Affairs Select Committee (n 137).

[178] Lord Hanson Minister of State, 'Letter to Dame Karen Bradley MP Chair, Home Affairs Select Committee', 31 October 2024, available at committees.parliament.uk/publications/45610/documents/225866/default/.

[179] City of London Police, *National Policing Strategy for Fraud, Economic and Cyber Crime 2023–2028* (City of London Police, 2023) at 10.

[180] ibid.

often receiving little feedback after submitting their report. Another important finding is the limited public awareness of Action Fraud, which, despite its national role, remains relatively unknown to many potential victims. These problems are exacerbated by the absence of any investigative powers and Action Fraud relies on local police forces to investigate and prosecute fraud cases. Limited resources have also constrained Action Fraud's capacity, making it difficult to manage the growing number of fraud cases. The outdated technical system had adversely affected the quality of data collected which impairs the sharing of data with LEAs. In conclusion, while Action Fraud performs an important role in centralising fraud reports, its current structure and limitations prevent it from delivering a robust intelligence system.

B. The Police

The Police play an important part in addressing fraud; however, their role and response has been subjected to criticism.[181] For example, the Police Foundation noted that 'police forces may always struggle to prioritise fraud, due to competing demands and the fact that the nature of fraud offending'.[182] The association between the competing demands and the nature of fraud was also acknowledged by the Fraud Advisory Panel which noted that this 'makes the effective policing of fraud difficult (if not impossible)'.[183] The House of Commons Justice Committee stated that there is a 'disparity between the amount of work fraud creates for the police and the resources allocated to it. Fraud now accounts for more than 40% of all crime, yet only 2% of police resources are allocated to fraud'.[184] Thus, it is not surprising that the approach adopted towards fraud by the 43 police forces is inconsistent.[185] The National Audit Office reported that police forces have 'different approaches to reporting and recording fraud … and lack performance information around reporting and investigating fraud'.[186] The problem is exacerbated because fraud is regarded as a low priority by many police forces and in general the 'police are not interested … in fraud'.[187] The policing of fraud is ineffective for several reasons. For example, the organisation and operational challenges of police force regions; the problems posed by the international nature of fraud; the limited resources provided to the police and low peripheral treatment

[181] House of Lords Fraud Act 2006 and Digital Fraud Committee (n 31) at 90.

[182] Written evidence submitted by The Police Foundation, FRA0011, available at committees.parliament.uk/writtenevidence/125623/pdf/.

[183] Witten Evidence submitted by Fraud Advisory Panel, Written evidence, FDF0048 (n/d), available at committees.parliament.uk/writtenevidence/108063/html/.

[184] House of Commons Justice Committee (n 52) at 19.

[185] HMICFRS (n 63) at 16.

[186] National Audit Office, *Online Fraud* (National Audit Office, 2017) at 31.

[187] FRA0003 1 Written evidence submitted by Professor Mark Button, Co-Director of the Centre for Cybercrime and Economic Crime, University of Portsmouth, available at committees.parliament.uk/writtenevidence/125246/pdf/.

of fraud.[188] HMICFRS reported that the scale of fraud outstrips the resources that are allocated to it.[189] The Home Office acknowledged that despite fraud accounting for 40 per cent of reported crime, the police receive less than one per cent of police resources.[190] It has been estimated that there are 1,000 specialist fraud police officers in the UK spread across 43 different police forces,[191] investigating 4.1million reported instances of fraud, resulting in millions of cases being uninvestigated.[192] Consideration could be given to reinvesting the proceeds of asset recovery, financial penalties or deferred prosecution agreements into tackling fraud.[193] The funding provided to the Police to tackle fraud is miniscule and it remains a considerable challenge. Therefore, it is unsurprising that the Police response to fraud has been criticised, yet the Royal United Services Institute optimistically noted 'it is important that law enforcement continue to aggressively pursue fraudsters'.[194] In order to redress the funding deficiency and insufficient number of appropriately trained police officers, the Fraud Strategy proposes to create a NFS, consisting of 400 new fraud investigators.[195] However, the impact of the new investigators is negligible. It has been suggested that 30,000 additional police officers need to be recruited to tackle economic and associated crimes.[196] The police response to fraud is ineffective. The position is worsened by the lack of a consistent reporting strategy, inconsistent practices and attitudes towards fraud. Therefore, fraud is 'severely underreported … with fewer than a third (32%) reporting the crime to the Police'.[197] The Home Office has advised that the Police should only investigate where there are good grounds to believe that a criminal offence has been committed.[198] These issues need to be addressed to improve the quality of how the Police deal with reports of fraud and provide better support to the victims of fraud.

The COLP is the national lead police force and manages both Action Fraud and the NFIB, which disseminate reports to ROCUs and 43 police forces to investigate. This approach has been criticised for including too many bodies, structural

[188] HMICFRS (n 63) at 3.

[189] ibid.

[190] HM Government, *Fraud Strategy* (n 32) at 16.

[191] House of Commons Justice Committee (n 52) at 19.

[192] City of London Police, Written Evidence Submitted by the Office of the City Remembrancer on behalf of the City of London Police and City of London Police Authority Board, October 2023, available at committees.parliament.uk/writtenevidence/126156/pdf/.

[193] H Wood, 'Five Problems with Economic Crime Policing – and How to Solve Them' (*Royal United Services Institute (RUSI)*, 11 July 2022), available at www.rusi.org/explore-our-research/publications/commentary/five-problems-economic-crime-policing-and-how-solve-them.

[194] RUSI, 'FRA0060 Written Evidence Submitted by the Royal United Services Institute (RUSI)', October 2023, available at committees.parliament.uk/writtenevidence/125871/pdf/.

[195] HM Government, *Fraud Strategy* (n 32) at 1.

[196] Social Market Foundation, Written evidence, FDF0026, available at committees.parliament.uk/writtenevidence/108022/html/#_ftnref7.

[197] National Trading Standards, '19 million Lose Money to Scams but Fewer than a Third Report' (23 October 2023), available at www.nationaltradingstandards.uk/news/19-million-lose-money-to-scams-but-fewer-than-a-third-report/.

[198] Home Office, *Home Office Circular 47/2004: Priorities for the Investigation of Fraud Cases* (Home Office, 2004).

challenges related to the organisation and responsibilities of police force areas, the international nature of fraud, the under-prioritisation of fraud, insufficient resources and lack of specialist police officers.[199] Therefore, it is not surprising that investigations have recommended reform. For example, the Treasury Committee suggested that a single LEA should be created to tackle economic crime.[200] The Police Foundation, Strategic Review of Policing in England and Wales recommended the creation of a new Crime Prevention Agency, the extension of the NCA and that fraud investigations would be undertaken by ROCUs.[201] The Social Market Foundation advocated that local police forces lose their responsibility for economic crime and that the functions of the COLP and SFO should transferred to the NCA.[202] In 2022, Policy Exchange recommended that the Home Office should reorganise the response to fraud by including it in the Strategic Policing Requirement and giving responsibility for investigation.[203] In 2024, the Institute of Economic Affairs recommended that the SFO should be reformed into a Serious Economic Crime Office.[204] Interestingly, these investigations have one common theme, to merge the existing LEAs into one single agency, which was initially suggested in 2010 and dismissed by the Government.[205]

The Police play a central role in the fight against fraud, yet persistent structural and operational shortcomings have inhibited their effectiveness. Competing demands on limited resources mean that fraud receives between one to two per cent of police resources. The fragmented responsibility across 43 police forces, Action Fraud, the NFIB and ROCUs have caused confusion and inconsistent reporting practices. As a result, the system has failed to prioritise, record and prosecute fraudsters. Resource constraints and a lack of specialist officers have exacerbated these challenges. With approximately 1,000 dedicated fraud investigators dispersed across the UK, millions of reported frauds go unexamined. Efforts to improve numbers in the shape of the 400 strong NFS, are dwarfed by calls for tens of thousands of officers focused on tackling fraud. Unless additional funding and training is provided, the Police will continue to lag behind sophisticated and transnational fraud networks. There have been calls for radical reform to the

[199] House of Lords Fraud Act 2006 and Digital Fraud Committee (n 31) at 90.

[200] Treasury Committee, *Economic Crime* (Treasury Committee, 2021). However, this recommendation was rejected by HM Government. See Treasury Committee, *Economic Crime: Responses to the Committee's Eleventh Report* (Eighth Special Report, Session 2021–22, HC 1261).

[201] The Police Foundation, *A New Mode of Protection: Redesigning Policing and Public Safety for the 21st Century* (The Police Foundation, 2022).

[202] Social Market Foundation, *Fraud is Now Britain's Dominant Crime, but Policing has Failed to Keep Up* (Social Market Foundation, 2022).

[203] Policy Exchange, *What Do We Want from the Next Prime Minister? A Series of Policy Proposals for New Leadership: Crime & Policing – A Force Fit for the Future* (Policy Exchange, 2022).

[204] M Button, B Hock and D Shepherd, *Replacing the Serious Fraud Office – the Case for a New Approach to Serious Economic Crime* (Institute of Economic Affairs, 2024).

[205] See, eg, Policy Exchange, *Fighting Fraud and Financial Crime: A New Architecture for the Investigation and Prosecution of Serious Fraud, Corruption and Financial Market Crimes* (Policy Exchange, 2010) and The Fraud Advisory Panel, *Roskill Revisited: Is there a Case for a Unified Fraud Prosecution Office?* (Fraud Advisory Panel, 2010).

efforts to tackle fraud since 2010 – from consolidating functions into a single LEA, to extending the remit of the NCA, to reinvesting the proceeds of asset recovery into front-line fraud fighting. Moving forward, a coherent national fraud strategy must unite the reporting of fraud, intelligence analysis and investigations under one roof. Sustainable funding models are essential to recruit and retain fraud experts.

C. Social Media

Fraudulent content is 'rife across the internet' and 90 per cent of UK adults have encountered such content.[206] Criminals are able to create phishing emails, copycat websites and fake social media profiles in an attempt to defraud victims.[207] Social media can be used to permit fraud by false advertising, the use of online influencers relating to investment scams, the recruitment of money mules, theft of personal information and romance frauds.[208] UK finance social media accounts for the largest number of online fraud cases,[209] a view supported by The Lloyds Banking Group which suggested that a person in the UK becomes a victim of a purchasing fraud from two Meta-owned platforms every seven minutes.[210] Specifically, 68 per cent of these frauds started on Facebook and Instagram, accounting for 40 per cent of total related losses.[211] Additionally, TSB Bank noted that Google made up 20 per cent of investment fraud cases that were reported to them[212] and that Meta accounted for 87 per cent of all investment fraud cases reported to TSB.[213]

The Online Safety Act 2023 imposes an obligation on social media platforms to prevent or limit consumers interacting with fraudulent activity. Specifically, the Act includes provisions to tackle online fraud, requiring online platforms and search services to implement measures to moderate, remove fraudulent content and to create reporting channels.[214] Furthermore, companies are required to undertake risk assessments to understand and appreciate the potential for fraud on their platforms.[215] The Act requires social media platforms to

[206] Which?, 'One in Five Fraud Victims Send Money to Criminals via Cryptocurrency' (21 September 2022), available at www.which.co.uk/news/article/one-in-five-fraud-victims-send-money-to-criminals-via-cryptocurrency-alCPq3K8KPa8.

[207] ibid.

[208] FRA0060 Written evidence submitted by the Royal United Services Institute (RUSI), available from committees.parliament.uk/writtenevidence/125871/pdf/.

[209] ibid.

[210] Lloyds Banking Group, 'Two-Thirds of All Online Shopping Scams Now Start on Facebook and Instagram' (30 March 2023), available at www.lloydsbankinggroup.com/media/press-releases/2023/lloyds-banking-group-2023/two-thirds-of-all-online-shopping-scams-now-start-on-facebook-and-instagram.html.

[211] ibid.

[212] FRA0081 1 Written evidence submitted by TSB, available at committees.parliament.uk/writtenevidence/125982/pdf/.

[213] ibid.

[214] Online Safety Act 2023, ss 38–40.

[215] ibid s 29.

moderate and remove fraudulent content and create mechanisms for users to report suspected fraudulent activity.[216] Failure to comply with these obligations could result in a financial penalty being imposed of up to 10 per cent of the company's global turnover.[217] These provisions are supported by the Online Fraud Charter, a voluntary agreement between HM Government and the technology sector to reduce fraud on their platforms and services.[218] The Online Fraud Charter includes commitments to use measures to create a simple and quick route to report fraudulent material; to take down and remove fraudulent content; to use measures to protect users from fraudulent adverts; to create dedicated liaison officers who will respond to law enforcement requests; to share intelligence quicky, to provide information about fraud risks and what they are doing to address them; to provide information to support users to recognise and avoid online fraud and to try and stay ahead of the threat presented by fraud.[219] Of particular relevance here are the reporting and information- sharing commitments. Here, all firms are required to:

> (a) Have, or adopt, and maintain a simple mechanism to report fraudulent content generated by users, which can be accessed within two clicks of a button. (b) Action user reports as swiftly as possible. (c) Run and maintain a simple and direct process for law enforcement and trusted partners to quickly, and easily, report suspected fraudulent activity occurring on the company's platform or services. (d) Provide information to users on how to report incidents of fraud to law enforcement and their bank, and where to seek support, preferably at the point of reporting or in easily accessible help-centre resources.[220]

The Online Fraud Charter stipulates that social media networks are required to 'provide or develop appropriate warnings where users are contacted by unknown accounts or individuals, through direct messages, who may present a risk of fraud'.[221] Finally, standalone online dating service providers must

> alert and provide education resources to users that have engaged in two-way communications (and have been confirmed to have sent or received contact information), with another user who the platform has positively identified as likely to be involved in financial crimes.[222]

In relation to information-sharing, the Online Fraud Charter provides that firms:

> (a) Contribute to a sector-wide 'gap analysis', to identify blockers for Government to act on. (b) Explore what data, both internal and external, could facilitate the identification and prevention of fraud. (c) Help stakeholders identify mechanisms

216 ibid s 20.
217 ibid sch 13, 1 (4)(b).
218 HM Government, 'Online Fraud Charter' (30 November 2023), available at www.gov.uk/government/publications/online-fraud-charter-2023.
219 ibid.
220 ibid.
221 ibid.
222 ibid.

> and legal frameworks to share data, including mapping any current or potential industry-standard third-party databases. (d) Discuss and agree typologies and taxonomies useful for clarifying data sharing. (e) Share best practice and identify opportunities to work toward sharing data with other sector partners and other industries.[223]

Signatories include Amazon; eBay; Facebook; Google; Instagram; LinkedIn; Match Group; Microsoft; Snap Inc; TikTok; X; YouTube; and techUK.[224] However, the effectiveness of the Online Fraud Charter can be questioned. 'Which?' warned that 'these measures are voluntary and still sector specific'.[225] Similarly, Victim Support stated that the Charter is 'limited by being voluntary, with no ability to hold industry to account for compliance'.[226] Google and Meta were slow to remove fraudulent adverts after they had been reported to them by victims,[227] or fail to identify repeat offenders.[228]

The effectiveness of how social media companies report fraud is complex, with some social media companies actively involved in reporting fraudulent contact. Despite the pledges within the Online Fraud Charter, fraud remains prevalent on many social media platforms. The Online Fraud Charter is no more than any other self-regulatory gesture and it has not resulted in a reduction in the number of reported frauds, with Crest noting that there has been a 19 per cent increase in fraud following the introduction of the Online Fraud Charter.[229] The voluntary nature of the Online Fraud Charter is problematic and it does not incentivise firms to act to reduce fraud on their platforms. The Online Fraud Charter has the potential to improve online safety, but it is not the complete solution. Whilst the increased collaboration is to be welcomed, the ongoing voluntary nature of the reporting of fraud is problematic and is symptomatic of the voluntary nature of the fraud-reporting systems in the UK.

Fraudulent activity on social media is becoming more entrenched, with criminals exploiting platforms to deploy phishing campaigns, fake profiles, romance scams and bogus job adverts. Victims frequently encounter copycat websites, impersonated accounts and misleading promotions on a near constant basis, highlighting how fraud permeates people's online interactions.

[223] ibid.

[224] ibid.

[225] Which?, 'Which? Response to the Government's Online Fraud Charter' (30 November 2023), availableatwww.which.co.uk/policy-and-insight/article/which-response-to-the-governments-online-fraud-charter-aAnKf6h3kXaq.

[226] FRA0026 Written evidence submitted by Victim Support, available at committees.parliament.uk/writtenevidence/125742/pdf/.

[227] Which?, 'Two in Five Victims of Online Scam Adverts don't Report to Host Platforms' 26 April 2021, available at www.which.co.uk/news/article/two-in-five-victims-of-online-scam-adverts-dont-report-to-host-platforms-aFErb6N58pY5.

[228] Which?, 'Facebook Repeatedly Sells Ad Space to Known Scammer' (22 January 2022), available at www.which.co.uk/news/article/facebook-repeatedly-sells-ad-space-to-known-scammer-auNcp5Y20OSR.

[229] F Smith, 'New Fraud Strategy: A Moment for Bold Reform Insights Perspective' (17 April 2025), available at www.crestadvisory.com/post/new-fraud-strategy-a-moment-for-bold-reform.

The Online Safety Act 2023 places clear duties on platforms to moderate, remove and report fraudulent content. This is backed by fines of up to 10 per cent of global turnover for non-compliance. These requirements should limit fraud by compelling companies to conduct risk assessments, create reporting mechanisms and remove harmful content. This is complemented by the Online Fraud Charter that commits its signatories to user-reporting mechanisms, intelligence-sharing with LEAs and proactive user education. However, the non-binding nature and its self-regulation cannot and does not deliver consistent, platform-wide protection. To address this, the UK must introduce mandatory reporting requirements, standardised data-sharing protocols and robust enforcement powers.

D. Telecommunications Sector

Between June and August 2022, three quarters of the UK population said they had received a suspicious message, in the form of either a text, recorded message or live voice call to a landline or mobile. This represents an estimated 40.8million adults in the UK. An estimated 700,000 followed the fraudster's instructions, risking financial loss and significant emotional distress.[230] The most common type of suspicious message were texts, with 65 per cent of people reporting they had received a suspicious text message.[231] In October 2021, HM Government published the Telecommunications Charter, under which providers have agreed to tackle fraud.[232] Here, telecommunication providers have committed to identify and implement techniques to block scam calls and share data on the source of these calls across the sector; identify and implement techniques to block smishing texts and work with banks to strengthen authentication checks at the point a device contract is applied for and at the point a customer requests to move their number to a new provider.[233] Furthermore, the telecommunications sector has introduced firewalls to detect and stop scam texts from reaching customers. In his oral evidence to the Home Affairs Select Committee, Mike Haley from Cifas stated that criminals use the telecommunications network to imitate financial services providers.[234] The appropriateness of the Telecommunications Charter was questioned by Which? that stated 'the Government's approach to tackling fraud must address gaps in

[230] Home Office and Ministry of Justice, *Policy Paper Criminal Justice Bill: Serious Crime* (Home Office and Ministry of Justice, 2024).

[231] Of com, 'Research Supporting Scams Statements 2022', 5–7 August 2022, available at www.ofcom.org.uk/siteassets/resources/documents/phones-telecoms-and-internet/information-for-industry/scams/cli-and-suspicious-calls-and-messages-research/ofcom-cli-and-scams-research-august-2022-slides.pdf?v=328765.

[232] HM Government, 'Fraud Sector Charter' (21 October 2021), available at www.gov.uk/government/publications/joint-fraud-taskforce-telecommunications-charter.

[233] ibid.

[234] Home Affairs Committee, Oral Evidence: Fraud, HC 125, Wednesday 17 January 2024, James Daley, available at https://committees.parliament.uk/oralevidence/14101/html/#:~:text=harvesting%20your%20details.-,Q103,-James%20Daly%3A.

the telcos […] and place legal obligations on them to protect consumers from fraud'.[235] The Telecommunications Security Act 2001 and the Communications Act 2003 seek to ensure greater due diligence on the telecommunications sector. This includes, for example, that public telecommunication providers operate secure and resilient networks for security compromised. However, fraud is not regarded as a security compromise. Short Messaging Service (SMS) messages are a key method used by criminals to commit fraud and the Home Office stated that these are frequently traced back to SIM farms.[236] A SIM farm is a device which can use five or more SIM cards to make phone calls or send SMS text messages through radio frequencies. SIM farms are used by criminals to send out thousands of scam texts.[237] SIM farms are available on popular online marketplaces, at low prices, with limited or no requirement to verify the buyer's identity. This makes them an easy to access, low-cost option to fraudsters who deceive victims into giving sensitive information such as bank details.[238]

The alarming prevalence of suspicious messages, received by 75 per cent of UK adults with some 700,000 individuals following fraudsters' instructions, underscores a national crisis in telecom-enabled fraud. Texts represent the primary vector, affecting an estimated 65 per cent of recipients and exposing millions to financial loss and emotional distress. Government and industry initiatives, notably the October 2021 Telecommunications Charter, signal a collective intent to tackle this threat. Network providers have pledged to deploy call- and SMS-blocking technologies, share data on malicious sources, implement firewalls against smishing attacks, and collaborate with banks on stronger authentication at contract initiation and number-porting stages. However, critical loopholes remain. The voluntary nature of the Telecommunications Charter falls short of binding legal duty, and existing statutes such as the Telecommunications Security Act 2001 and Communications Act 2003 do not categorise fraud as a security compromise. This loophole enables criminals to exploit readily available SIM farms, devices that can cycle through multiple SIM cards to dispatch mass scam texts with minimal buyer vetting, thereby perpetuating the cycle of deception. To close these loopholes, fraud must be reframed as a core network security issue. Legislative reform should impose mandatory due-diligence obligations on providers, enforcing robust identity checks for SIM acquisitions. A legal duty to classify and mitigate fraud alongside cyber-security risks would compel more consistent, proactive protections.

The case studies have revealed a fractured landscape in which fraud reporting in the UK has failed to capture its full scale, complexity and its evolving nature. The analysis across these four domains has highlighted systemic gaps in data quality, interagency collaboration, victim engagement and technological adaption, all of which have undermined effective prevention and enforcement efforts. Since its

[235] FRA0043 Written evidence submitted by Which? Consumers Association Ltd, October 2023, available at committees.parliament.uk/writtenevidence/125794/pdf/.
[236] Home Office and Ministry of Justice (n 230).
[237] ibid.
[238] ibid.

creation, Action Fraud was intended as the single point of contact for victims, yet suffers from under-reporting, long delays in acknowledgement, a cumbersome online interface and lack of tangible follow-up discourages both individuals and corporate victims from submitting detailed intelligence. This erodes the data's reliability, impairs trend analysis and leaves LEAs without the necessary data needed to allocate resources strategically. The Police are limited by resource constraints and the adoption of different approaches towards the reporting of fraud. Many police forces lack trained fraud investigators to triage fraud referrals effectively and this inconsistency has created cold spots where emerging scams can continue to dent the public's confidence in reporting fraud. Social media platforms are the new breeding ground for fraud and the minimal requirements to share intelligence leaves a blind spot in monitoring sophisticated fraud networks. The telecommunications sector illustrates a final piece of the missing reporting puzzle: proactive blocking and data-sharing. Carriers possess vast logs of call origin and messaging patterns that could flag suspicious activity, yet cooperation is often limited by privacy concerns and commercial competition. As a result, many phone-based frauds materialise unchecked, and the lack of near-real-time alerts prevents swift intervention. Collectively, the case studies illustrate that no single agency or industry can shoulder the burden of fraud reporting. Without an integrated reporting framework, underpinned by standardised classification, timely intelligence-sharing, and victim-centric processes, the UK remains ill-equipped to map and collect accurate data on fraud. Addressing these deficiencies demands a unified strategy, harmonising online and offline reporting channels, expanding cross-sector data partnerships, investing in digital forensic expertise, and embedding clear regulatory mandates for platforms and telecom providers.

V. Data-Sharing

This section of the chapter examines the role of data-sharing mechanisms in strengthening fraud detection and response across varied contexts. The analysis of the four case studies has exposed how emerging fraud threats and complex operational environments have outpaced traditional reporting systems. In the established reporting regimes for money laundering and terrorist financing, the regulated sector operates under a clear mandatory reporting requirement. DAML SARs or defence against terrorist financing (DATF) SARs are submitted to the UKFIU, which consolidates insights and disseminates actionable intelligence. The internal reporting obligations compel front-line staff to escalate suspicious transactions creating multiple layers of oversight, which can be contrasted with fraud. The case studies in this chapter have illustrated that the reporting of fraud can be contrasted with the more established reporting systems for money laundering and terrorist financing. The absence of binding reporting mechanisms has resulted in fragmented intelligence, thus underscoring that without proactive data-sharing, information is siloed and action insights can be missed.

The sharing of data is essential in combatting fraud,[239] and it has become a priority in the effort to address fraud in the UK.[240] However, at present, both the public and private sector face significant legal impediments in sharing information to prevent and detect fraud.[241] The next subsection concentrates on the sharing of data between LEAs and other public authorities. The section then moves on to address the sharing of data between the private sector and LEAs, before addressing data-sharing within the private and public sectors.

A. The Sharing of Data between Law Enforcement and Other Public Authorities

i. Legal Gateways

The UK has created several legal gateways that allow LEAs and public authorities to exchange information with one another for the purposes of preventing fraud. Some LEAs, such as the police service, have a common law power to proactively share personal information with third parties if there is a 'pressing social need' to do so,[242] as well as a statutory duty to share information with LEAs, such as the NCA.[243] Other LEAs have been provided with statutory powers to share information, often through the statute establishing the relevant LEA. For instance, the Financial Conduct Authority, SFO, HMRC, and the NCA all have the power to share information with specified bodies for specified purposes, including for criminal investigation and prosecution purposes.[244] Supervisory authorities have the power to disclose information to relevant authorities, including other supervisory authorities and LEAs, connected with the exercise of their functions.[245] Importantly, fraud is included as a predicate offence to money laundering,[246] meaning that these mechanisms could be used by supervisory authorities to share information pertaining to scams. The Financial Crime Information Network and the Shared Intelligence Service, both of which are hosted by the Financial Conduct Authority, enable the sharing of information between LEAs and supervisory authorities.[247] Part 3 of the Data Protection Act 2018 enables competent

[239] HM Government, *Fraud Strategy* (n 32).

[240] ibid at 46.

[241] House of Lords Fraud Act 2006 and Digital Fraud Committee (n 31) at 134.

[242] National Police Chief's Council, *Common Law Police Disclosures Provisions to Supersede the Notifiable Occupations Scheme* (National Police Chief's Council, 2017).

[243] Crime and Courts Act 2013, sch 3, Part 2.

[244] Financial Services and Markets Act 2000, s 349; Financial Services and Markets Act 2000 (Disclosure of Confidential Information) Regulations 2001/2188, Reg 4; Criminal Justice Act 1987, s 3(5); Commissioners for Revenue and Customs Act 2005, ss 18–21; Crime and Courts Act 2013, s 7(4).

[245] The Money Laundering, Terrorist Financing and Transfer of Funds (Information on the Payer) Regulations 2017 (SI 2017/692), Reg 52.

[246] POCA, s 340(2).

[247] HM Treasury, 'Call for Information: Anti-Money Laundering Supervisory Regime' (16 March 2017), available at www.gov.uk/government/consultations/call-for-information-anti-money-laundering-supervisory-regime/call-for-information-anti-money-laundering-supervisory-regime.

authorities to share data for law enforcement purposes.[248] Competent authorities include the Police and LEAs, as well as other authorities with law enforcement functions.[249] The innumerable number of powers and obligations that are permitted by a plethora of different statutory provisions have created an overly complex and confusing set of data-sharing mechanisms across sectors for the prevention of fraud and scams.

These legal gateways deliver several strengths. First, statutory mandates provide each competent agency with the authority to share sensitive information. Second, treating fraud as a predicate offence for money laundering expands the remit of financial crime supervisors to tackle scams. Third, dedicated networked platforms promote rapid, structured data exchange across agencies. Finally, the Data Protection Act's law enforcement provisions harmonise the need for investigative data-sharing with individuals' privacy rights. However, this proliferation of overlapping provisions has led to weaknesses. The number of gateways causes confusion among practitioners, who may struggle to identify the correct legal basis for sharing data. Divergent rules and thresholds across LEAs and supervisory authorities risk inconsistent application and potential legal uncertainty. Smaller agencies in particular might be deterred from exercising their information-sharing powers fully, leaving valuable scam-related intelligence under-utilised.

There are opportunities to improve the landscape. Consolidating the myriad statutory gateways into a single, unified fraud-prevention law would simplify decision-making and reduce legal uncertainties. Establishing a central fraud intelligence hub with oversight responsibility could streamline the triage and dissemination of information, ensuring that critical leads reach the right investigators without unnecessary delay. Nonetheless, risks remain if the fragmentation continues hampering the UK's ability to detect and respond to emerging scam trends swiftly.

ii. Information-Sharing in Practice

As outlined in chapters two and three, the Financial Action Task Force (FATF) promotes 'measures for combating money laundering, terrorist financing and other threats', through its Recommendations.[250] As fraud is included as a predicate offence to money laundering, these measures could be used to prevent and detect fraud. In its 2018 Mutual Evaluation Report (MER) of the UK's compliance with its Recommendations,[251] the FATF rated the UK's AML/CTF regime

[248] As defined in Data Protection Act 2018, s 31.

[249] ibid s 30(1), sch 7.

[250] Financial Action Task Force (FATF), 'The FATF Recommendations: International Standards on Combatting Money Laundering and the Financing of Terrorism & Proliferation', available from at www.fatf-gafi.org/en/publications/Fatfrecommendations/Fatf-recommendations.htm.

[251] FATF, *Anti-Money Laundering and Counter-Terrorist Financing Measures: United Kingdom Mutual Evaluation Report*' (FATF, 2018) (hereinafter 'FATF 2018 MER').

as the best in the world.[252] One of the FATF's key findings was that 'co-operation and co-ordination between agencies on AML/CTF issues is a strength of the UK system',[253] including the sharing of data between LEAs.[254] The UK was also considered to have moderate to high levels of effectiveness for Immediate Outcomes 1 and 6, concerning risk, policy and coordination, and financial intelligence, as well as Immediate Outcomes 7 and 9, concerning effective money laundering and terrorist financing investigations. However, research has questioned these findings by presenting several case studies that demonstrate inherent flaws in the UK's ability to ensure the sharing of data between LEAs and other bodies, both public and private in practice.[255] This is a significant weakness in the UK's counter fraud efforts. Case studies relating to fraud in this chapter illustrates that the sharing of data between LEAs often fails to materialise. This may be because the legal framework often only provides a power, and little incentive rather than an obligation, to disclose information. There is a strong case for these legal gateways to be reformed to compel, rather than simply permit, information exchange. Without such reforms, the UK risks reputational damage and weakened counter-fraud resilience.

B. The Sharing of Data between the Private Sector and LEAs

The obligation to report suspected fraud by the private sector to LEAs is not straightforward. The primary statutory obligation for reporting instances of fraud is contained under POCA 2002.[256] It is a criminal offence under the Act to fail to disclose via a DAML SAR where there is knowledge, suspicion or reasonable grounds to know or suspect, that a person is laundering the proceeds of criminal conduct. Successful fraud is defined as money laundering for the purpose of this Act.[257] If a suspected fraud is committed against an authorised institution, it must be reported to its Money Laundering Reporting Officer (MLRO). Successful frauds are then reported to the NCA. However, there is no legal obligation to report unsuccessful or attempted frauds to the NCA because any attempted frauds will not give rise to any legal criminal proceedings and therefore fall outside the scope of the mandatory reporting obligations.[258] It is important to note that the law in data-sharing is not necessarily clear and the private sector tends to take

[252] ibid at 5. Also see HM Government, 'UK Takes Top Spot in Fight Against Dirty Money' (8 December 2018), available at www.gov.uk/government/news/uk-takes-top-spot-in-fight-against-dirty-money.

[253] FATF 2018 MER (n 251) at 37.

[254] FATF, 'The FATF Recommendations' (n 250).

[255] For a more detailed discussion and analysis see chapter seven.

[256] POCA s 330.

[257] It is important to note that POCA applies to serious crime, which includes fraud.

[258] J Goldstraw-White and M Gill, *The Mandatory Reporting of Fraud: Finding Solutions and Sharing Best Practice*' (Fraud Advisory Panel, 2021).

guidance on what data it is allowed to share and with whom from the public sector. The limited amount of data-sharing between public bodies and the private sector does cast a shadow over the benefits of data-sharing. For example, the Criminal Finances Act 2017 allows data-sharing and in June 2023 it was reported that banks were 'gearing up to share more data with their peers on suspected serious economic crime' but that banks are hesitant to share customer data due to the fear of breaching the data protection and privacy laws.[259]

i. General Data Protection Regulation and the Data Protection Act 2018

Aside from the NCA, the private sector can share information pertaining to fraud with other LEAs under the UK General Data Protection Regulation (GDPR) and the Data Protection Act 2018.[260] To do so, they must identify a lawful basis for the sharing of data, which includes compliance with a legal obligation, or pursuance of a legitimate interest,[261] both of which could potentially encompass fraud disclosures.[262] Special category data or criminal offence data can also be shared if there is also both a lawful basis and condition for processing.[263] The data subject does not have to be informed if information is shared to prevent or detect crime, to apprehend or prosecute offenders, or to assess or collect taxation.[264] Additionally, there are a number of sharing of data mechanisms facilitated by legislation. JMLIT was established as a private/public partnership between LEAs and the financial sector.[265] JMLIT has 'made very quick progress in aiding voluntary information sharing … and has quickly demonstrated [its] … benefits'.[266] JMLIT has enabled the UK to become a global leader in the sharing of data between reporting entities and LEAs; the UK model has been adopted in Australia,[267] Singapore[268] and

[259] I Withers and K Ridley, 'Focus: UK Banks to Ramp up Data Sharing in Dirty Money Crackdown' (22 June 2023), available at www.reuters.com/business/finance/uk-banks-ramp-up-data-sharing-dirty-money-crackdown-2023-06-22/.

[260] Information Commissioner's Office, Sharing Personal Data with Law Enforcement Authorities (Information Commissioner's Office, 2023).

[261] Data Protection Act 2018, s 8; Regulation (EU) 2016/679 of the European Parliament and of the Council of 27 April 2016 on the Protection of Natural Persons with Regard to the Processing of Personal Data and on the Free Movement of such Data (United Kingdom General Data Protection Regulation) (hereinafter 'UK GDPR') (SI 2016/679), Art 6.

[262] Information Commissioner's Office (n 260).

[263] ibid. Data Protection Act 2018, ss 10–11, sch 1; UK GDPR, Arts 9–10.

[264] Data Protection Act 2018, sch 2, Para 2.

[265] National Crime Agency, 'National Economic Crime Centre' (n/d), available at www.nationalcrimeagency.gov.uk/what-we-do/national-economic-crime-centre.

[266] Financial Conduct Authority, 'Effectiveness and Proportionality: Our Financial Crime Priorities – Speech by Rob Gruppetta, Head of Financial Crime Department' (10 November 2016), available at www.fca.org.uk/news/speeches/effectiveness-proportionality-financial-crime-priorities.

[267] AUSTRAC, 'Fintel Alliance' (n/d), available at www.austrac.gov.au/about-us/fintel-alliance.

[268] Monetary Authority of Singapore, 'CAD and MAS Partner Industry Stakeholders to Fight Financial Crimes', 24 April 2017, available at www.mas.gov.sg/News-and-Publications/Media-Releases/2017/CAD-and-MAS-Partner-Industry-Stakeholders-to-Fight-Financial-Crimes.aspx.

Hong Kong.[269] The sharing of data has been facilitated by the Criminal Finances Act 2017, which permits 'voluntary disclosures within the regulated sector'.[270] The Law Commission has concluded that JMLIT's remit should be extended to include a broader range of reporting entities from the entire regulated sector in order to 'provide a better understanding of relevant intelligence through the sharing of information across multiple sectors'.[271] However, the creation of the JMLIT and the resultant information-sharing has achieved some notable successes.[272]

C. Sharing of Data in the Public and Private Sectors

i. Public Sector

There are several legal gateways that enable the public sector to exchange information relating to fraud. The Serious Crime Act 2007 permits public authorities to disclose information for the purposes of preventing fraud in accordance with the Specified Anti-Fraud Organisations.[273] Specifically, the Serious Crime Act 'provides for public authorities to disclose information for the purposes of preventing fraud, or a particular kind of fraud, as a member of a specified anti-fraud organisation or otherwise in accordance with any arrangements made with such an organisation'.[274] An anti-fraud organisation is defined in the Serious Crime Act as

> any unincorporated association, body corporate or other person which enables or facilitates any sharing of information to prevent fraud or a particular kind of fraud or which has any of these functions as its purpose or one of its purposes.[275]

There are 11 anti-fraud agencies – BAE Systems Applied Intelligence Ltd; Callcredit Information Group Ltd; Cifas; Dun and Bradstreet Ltd; Equifax Ltd; Experian Ltd; Insurance Fraud Bureau; Insurance Fraud Investigators Group; N Hunter Ltd; Synectics Solutions Ltd and Telecommunications United Kingdom Fraud Forum Ltd.[276]

[269] Hong Kong Monetary Authority, 'Fraud and Money Laundering Intelligence Taskforce Launched' (26 May 2017), available at www.hkma.gov.hk/eng/key-information/press-releases/2017/20170526-3.shtml.

[270] Criminal Finances Act 2017, s 11. This Act introduced this measure into POCA, ss 339ZB–ZG and the Terrorism Act 2000, ss 21CA–CF.

[271] Law Commission, *Anti-Money Laundering: The SARs Regime Report* (Law Commission, 2019) at 174.

[272] N Ryder, 'Cryptoassets, Social Media Platforms and Defence against Terrorism Financing Suspicious Activity Reports: A Step into the Regulatory Unknown' (2020) 8 *Journal of Business Law* 668, 687–92.

[273] Serious Crime Act 2007, s 68.

[274] Home Office, *Data Sharing for the Prevention of Fraud – Code of Practice for Public Authorities Disclosing Information to a Specified Anti-Fraud Organisations Under Sections 68 to 72 of the Serious Crime Act 2007* (Home Office, 2015).

[275] Serious Crime Act 2007, s 68(8).

[276] Home Office (n 274) at 20.

Additionally, the Digital Economy Act 2017 permits the sharing of information to assist the 'digital delivery' of government services to make them more resourceful and effective.[277] The Act allows for information-sharing between public authorities for public service delivery objectives that have been specified in regulations.[278] The Act also grants specific powers to energy suppliers and water and sewerage undertakers to permit a more efficient delivery of public authority schemes intended to help people living in fuel and water poverty.[279] Importantly, the Act creates specific gateways that allow the sharing of information to manage debt and fraud against the public sector.[280] The public sector can also share data relating to fraud using the Counter Fraud Data Alliance (CFDI), 'which has provided a governance structure for sharing data between specific public bodies and private organisations as a pilot, to test the value of such collaborations'.[281] The public sector also participates in the National Fraud Initiative (NFI), managed by the Public Sector Fraud Authority, which is a 'data matching exercise that helps prevent and detect fraud'.[282] It is available to all government departments and has prevented losses of over £300million by detecting fraud in the public sector.[283] The Cabinet Office stated that the Digital Economy Act has

> mechanisms in place to ensure that robust scrutiny is applied to all data sharing agreements to ensure that data sharing using the DEA is balanced, proportionate, transparent and observes relevant legal and data protection requirements, which was confirmed in a recent review of the DEA powers by the ICO.[284]

The Cabinet Office concluded that 'the DEA has been an effective tool which can be utilised by public bodies to … combat fraud … [and it has] provided value by allowing public bodies to share previously inaccessible data'.[285]

The public sector's ability to combat fraud effectively hinges on a diverse yet cohesive set of legal gateways. The Serious Crime Act 2007 facilitates targeted disclosures through specified anti-fraud organisations, the Digital Economy Act 2017 empowers resource-efficient data-sharing for service delivery and debt

[277] HM Government, 'Guidance Code of Practice for Public Authorities Disclosing Information Under Chapters 1, 3 and 5 under Part 5 of the Digital Economy Act 2017' (12 February 2020), available at www.gov.uk/government/publications/digital-economy-act-2017-part-5-codes-of-practice/code-of-practice-for-public-authorities-disclosing-information-under-chapters-1-3-and-4-public-service-delivery-debt-and-fraud-of-part-5-of-the-di#:~:text=Part%205%20of%20the%20Digital%20Economy%20Act%202017%20introduces%20a,the%20delivery%20of%20public%20services.

[278] Digital Economies Act 2017, s 35.

[279] ibid ss 36–38.

[280] ibid ss 48 and 56.

[281] Cabinet Office, Department for Digital, Culture, Media & Sport, *Tackling Fraud in Government with Data Analytics: Starting the Conversation* (Cabinet Office, Department for Digital, Culture, Media & Sport, 2019) at 11.

[282] Public Sector Fraud Authority (PSFA), 'National Fraud Initiative' (n/d), available at https://www.gov.uk/government/collections/national-fraud-initiative.

[283] Cabinet Office, Department for Digital, Culture, Media & Sport (n 281).

[284] Cabinet Office, *The Statutory Review of the Debt and Fraud Powers of the Digital Economy Act (2017)* (Cabinet Office, 2023) at 4.

[285] ibid at 19.

management, and collaborative pilots like the Counter Fraud Data Alliance and the NFI have demonstrated clear, quantifiable results. These frameworks operate under rigorous governance and data protection scrutiny, ensuring that information exchange remains balanced, proportionate, and transparent. The resulting outcomes speak for themselves: over £300 million in losses prevented and the unlocking of previously inaccessible data that has significantly bolstered the public sector's fraud-fighting capabilities.

ii. Private Sector

Presently, the sharing of data for AML/CTF purposes in the private sector is primarily facilitated by s 339ZB of POCA, inserted by the Criminal Finances Act 2017, which permits 'voluntary disclosures within the regulated sector'.[286] POCA allows the regulated sector to 'share information with each other on a voluntary basis in relation to suspected instances of … money laundering and/or terrorist financing', with fraud specified as a predicate offence.[287] Information-sharing can either be instigated by the regulated sector or the NCA.[288] The provision supports the pre-existing statutory provisions introduced by the Crime and Courts Act 2013, which permits reporting entities to act as information gateways to facilitate the sharing of data between the private sector and LEAs.[289] However, before an institution can make a disclosure, it is required to notify a NCA authorised officer.[290] Regulated institutions are also permitted to submit joint disclosure reports, otherwise known as 'Super SARs', following information exchange.[291] Super SARs were introduced to remedy some of the deficiencies in the SAR regime, which is widely regarded as deficient, especially owing to its serious absence of rapid triage, dissemination, evidential gathering processes, the inability to cope with the large volumes of SARs, compliance costs and inadequate sharing of data mechanisms.[292] Super SARs were intended to provide the NCA with fewer, more valuable, SARs, by capturing comprehensive criminal intelligence from a number of sources. However, a number of factors presently inhibit information-sharing within the regulated sector.

Some of these concerns are addressed by the Economic Crime and Corporate Transparency Act 2023, yet significant weaknesses remain. One of the central objectives of the Act is to enable 'businesses in certain sectors to share information more effectively to prevent and detect economic crime'.[293] Section 188 of the Act relates to direct disclosures where there are no breaches of confidence. Under this section,

[286] Criminal Finances Act 2017, s 11.
[287] Home Office, *Home Office Circular: Criminal Finances Act 2017 Money Laundering: Sharing of Information within the Regulated Sector Sections 339ZB-339ZG* (Home Office, 2018) at 1.
[288] ibid.
[289] Crime and Courts Act 2013, s 7.
[290] POCA s 339ZB(4).
[291] Law Commission (n 271) at 44.
[292] See generally chapter four.
[293] Economic Crime and Corporate Transparency Bill, Explanatory Notes, 9, available at https://publications.parliament.uk/pa/bills/cbill/58-03/0154/en/220154en.pdf.

a disclosure can be made that does not breach an obligation of confidence from person A to person B, if they are carrying out business in the regulated sector if B is also carrying on business in a related sector. This information would pertain to a former or a current customer of A's, that may 'assist' B. The disclosure has to have been made at the request of B or form part of a warning regarding financial crime from A to B.[294] The result of this section is that it will likely encourage business in the regulated sector to disclose information about former/current customers that they suspect of having links to financial crime, such as scams, without feeling constrained by concerns relating to confidentiality and data protection law.

Section 189 of the Act concerns indirect disclosures of information with no breach of confidence. Here, a disclosure by person A to person B does not breach any obligation of confidence if the information relates to a customer/former customer and, due to concerns about economic crime, A has decided to 'terminate relationships' with that customer, refuse them products/services or to restrict their product access. This clause has a narrow reach: it encompasses business that take deposits, electronic money, payment institutions, are a cryptoasset exchange provider or are custodian wallet providers.[295] The result is that section 189 only applies to certain types of business which are likely to handle large sums of money and are particularly likely to encounter fraud.

Section 188 enables information-sharing within the regulated sector either upon request, or spontaneously, the latter following 'safeguarding action' by the transmitting institution. Unlike s 339ZB of POCA, there is no requirement for either institution to notify the NCA before a disclosure is made.[296] This is a welcome development, for the current procedure is complicated and may cause delays, discouraging businesses from exchanging information or exposing them to the risk of legal action.[297] Section 188 enables a business in the regulated sector to exchange information upon request, if supplying the information would assist the requesting institution in carrying out 'relevant actions'. Section 191 identifies relevant actions, all of which must be undertaken for the purposes of 'preventing, detecting or investigating economic crime'.[298]

In taking a broad approach, the Act avoids replicating the unsatisfactory former focus on suspicions of AML/CTF as a condition for information exchange. The benefits of incorporating predicate offences into financial intelligence and information exchange provisions in their own right is demonstrated by the failure to report fraud in the UK. By enabling private sector information exchange for the purposes of 'preventing, detecting or investigating economic crime', section 188 may help to provide additional intelligence relating to predicate offences, such as fraud. At face value, this section ostensibly applies to the entirety of the regulated sector.

[294] Economic Crime and Corporate Transparency Act 2023, s 188(1)(a)-(e).

[295] ibid s 189(1)(a)-(g).

[296] POCA s339ZB(4).

[297] See for instance, *Lonsdale v National Westminster Bank Plc* [2018] EWHC 1843 (QB); *Shah v HSBC Private Bank Ltd* [2012] EWHC 1283, [2013] 1 All ER (Comm) 72.

[298] Economic Crime and Corporate Transparency Act 2023, s 191.

This is a positive development, for previous private sector information exchange initiatives have focused on the financial services sector. However, it will be important to ensure that the terms of the statute are not restricted in practice, as is the case with the current s 339ZB of POCA. Indeed, whilst s 339ZB appears to apply to the whole regulated sector, Home Office Guidance and NCA practice restrict the regime to financial and credit institutions.[299] This significantly restricts the dissemination of intelligence relating to economic crime and limits the availability of Super SARs to enhance the current system. Accordingly, it is recommended that section 188 is applied to the entirety of the regulated sector, as currently drafted. In addition, s 339ZB of POCA should be applied to the entirety of the regulated sector, or, preferably, a clause similar to s 339ZD of POCA should be added to the Act, to facilitate the disclosure of Super SARs.

Section 188 removes the risk of civil liability or breach-of-confidence claims when a member of the regulated sector directly shares customer information with another regulated firm, so long as the recipient either requests the data or the sender intends to take safeguarding action, and both agree the disclosure will aid in preventing, detecting, or investigating economic crime. Section 189 extends that same protection to indirect transfers via third-party intermediaries, widening the pool of participants to include crypto exchanges, custodians, large law and accountancy firms, insolvency practitioners, auditors, and tax advisers. By protecting the regulated sector legal action, these provisions encourage collaboration driving earlier interventions and richer SARs. However, data-sharing still must comply with UK GDPR principles to ensure conditions are properly applied and the liability shield remains intact.

iii. Data Protection

Organisations in both the public and private sectors can exchange information pertaining to fraud with other organisations under Data Protection legislation.[300] As with disclosure to LEAs, this requires the identification of a lawful basis for the sharing of data, which includes compliance with a legal obligation, or pursuance of a legitimate interest,[301] both of which could potentially encompass fraud disclosures.[302] Special category data or criminal offence data can also be shared if there is also both

[299] Home Office, 'Circular 007/2018: Criminal Finances Act: Sharing Information within the Regulated Sector' (1 February 2018), available at www.gov.uk/government/publications/circular-0072018-criminal-finances-act-sharing-information-within-the-regulated-sector.

[300] Information Commissioners Office, 'Data Sharing: A Code of Practice' (n/d), available at https://ico.org.uk/for-organisations/uk-gdpr-guidance-and-resources/data-sharing/data-sharing-a-code-of-practice/.

[301] Data Protection Act 2018, s 8; UK GDPR, Art 6.

[302] Information Commissioner's Office, 'Legitimate Interests' (n/d), available at https://ico.org.uk/for-organisations/uk-gdpr-guidance-and-resources/lawful-basis/a-guide-to-lawful-basis/lawful-basis-for-processing/legitimate-interests/#:~:text=%E2%80%9Cprocessing%20is%20necessary%20for%20the,the%20data%20subject%20is%20a>.

a lawful basis and condition for processing.[303] The data subject does not have to be informed if information is shared to prevent or detect crime, to apprehend or prosecute offenders, or to assess or collect taxation.[304] However, at present, data protection concerns are cited as the primary barrier to the sharing of data within the private sector.[305] The Data Protection and Digital Information (No 2) Bill aims to address some of these concerns,[306] in turn helping to 'facilitate the flow and use of personal data for law enforcement and national security purposes'.[307] To achieve this, the Bill no longer requires data controllers to balance their legitimate interests against the individual's interests, rights and freedoms.[308] Instead, they can share data based on a recognised legitimate interest, which includes 'detecting, investigating or preventing crime, or apprehending or prosecuting offenders'.[309] However, these mechanisms are voluntary and organisations can decline a request to exchange information.[310]

iv. Joint Fraud Taskforce

The Joint Fraud Taskforce (JFTF) is a collaboration between the private sector, the Government and LEAs to collectively tackle fraud and it focuses on 'issues that have been considered too difficult for a single organisation to manage alone'.[311] The then Home Secretary Teresa May MP stated:

> Our economy relies on the financial system and everyone in this country benefits from its global success. But the scale and volume of financial activity also brings serious risks of economic crime and real opportunities for criminals to defraud hardworking taxpayers of their savings and earnings. Fraud shames our financial system. It undermines the credibility of the economy, ruins businesses and causes untold distress to people of all walks of life. For too long, there has been too little understanding of the problem and too great a reluctance to take steps to tackle it. I am delighted to officially launch the Joint Fraud Taskforce, which will bring the collective powers, systems and resources of banks, payment providers, police, wider law enforcement and regulators to bear on this threat.[312]

[303] ibid. Data Protection Act 2018, ss 10–11, sch 1; UK GDPR, Arts 9–10.

[304] Data Protection Act 2018, sch 2, para 2.

[305] The Payments Association, *Data Sharing to Prevent Economic Crime: Why You Can Now Share Data with Confidence* (The Payments Association, 2023) at 9.

[306] Data Protection and Digital Information (No 2) HC Bill (2022–23) para 314.

[307] J Woodhouse, *Data Protection and Digital Information (No. 2) Bill: Commons Stages* (House of Commons Library Research Briefing Paper Number 9803, 2023) at 5.

[308] J Woodhouse, *Data Protection and Digital Information Bill* (House of Commons Library Research Briefing Paper Number 9606, 2022).

[309] Data Protection and Digital Information (No 2) HC Bill (2022–23) para 314, cll 5(2)(b) and 5(4), sch 1.

[310] The Data Protection and Digital Information (No 2) Bill failed to become law because Parliament was dissolved for the July 2024 General Election before it could complete its remaining stages.

[311] HM Government, 'Joint Fraud Task Force' (17 October 2017), available at www.gov.uk/government/collections/joint-fraud-taskforce#:~:text=The%20Joint%20Fraud%20Taskforce%20(%20JFT,single%20organisation%20to%20manage%20alone.

[312] HM Government, 'Home Secretary Launches New Joint Fraud Taskforce' (10 February 2016), available at www.gov.uk/government/news/home-secretary-launches-new-joint-fraud-taskforce#:~:text=It%20undermines%20the%20credibility%20of,processes%2C%20which%20fraudsters%20can%20exploit.

The JFTF has several key roles including presenting a codified response to fraud, providing an oversight into the implementation of the Fraud Strategy, it fosters industry collaboration, conducting strategic threat analysis, public-private action, reducing victimisation and impact of fraud and data-sharing.[313] The public-private partnerships play a key part in improving data-sharing. The JFTF acts as a conduit between government departments, LEAs, the private sector by coordinating efforts and collating information to tackle fraud. The Data Fusion initiative is an example of effective collaboration. This public-private partnership is led by the NCA to combat serious and organised crime through the use of shared banking intelligence. A pilot study with NatWest Bank and Lloyds between October 2021 and February 2022 proved to be beneficial in fusing bank data with organised crime data sets. Several banks voluntarily provided customer and transaction data that was identified for potential criminality and sent compliance officers and financial crime experts to work with NCA investigators. The NCA stated that the 'use of financial intelligence in such a way will better protect the public from serious and organised crime, and protect the integrity of the UK's financial system'.[314] Since its launch in 2024, the platform has produced approximately 90 intelligence packages supporting the NCA and LEA investigations. They have identified eight previously unknown organised crime networks, generated additional information for high-priority cases and assisted banks in upgrading their counter-fraud policies.[315]

This initiative has demonstrated important gains in disrupting fraud and potentially reducing banks' compliance costs. By uniting fragmented data sources under strong governance the fusion model hastens detection and improves investigation precision and enhances investigative precision.[316] In July 2025, the Home Office announced that the Data Fusion project would become a permanent 'operational capability, able to deliver benefits across the public-private economic crime system. This includes the implementation of a permanent public-private Joint Analytical Team, housed within the NCA'.[317] The JFTF brings together the financial services sector, regulators and LEAs to deliver a cohesive approach towards tackling fraud. The Data Fusion initiative is its flagship initiative which breaks down traditional siloed operations into a cohesive public-private ecosystem.

[313] ibid.

[314] NCA, 'Ground Breaking Public Private Partnership Launched to Identify Criminality using Banking Data' (26 July 2024), available at https://nationalcrimeagency.gov.uk/news/ground-breaking-public-private-partnership-launched-to-identify-criminality-using-banking-data.

[315] ibid.

[316] R Gibbon and K Fisher, 'Promising Results from Groundbreaking FinCrime Data Sharing Project Between Seven UK Banks and the National Crime Agency' (16 January 2025), available at https://natlawreview.com/article/promising-results-groundbreaking-fincrime-data-sharing-project-between-seven-uk.

[317] NCA, '10 Year Anniversary of the UK's Public Private Partnerships' (17 July 2025), available at www.nationalcrimeagency.gov.uk/news/10-year-anniversary-of-the-uks-public-private-partnerships.

v. Public Sector Fraud Authority

The Public Sector Fraud Authority (PSFA) is committed to modernising HM Government's response to fraud and error. The PSFA aims to widen access to leading practices, tools and technology to protect tax-payers money by strengthening the public sector's ability to detect, prevent and respond to fraud and error.[318] In order to achieve these goals, the PSFA works closely with government departments and public bodies. It provides expert-led services to ministerial departments and public bodies, and shares practices and standards across the wider public sector. The PSFA leads the Government's Counter Fraud Function, bringing together specialists who work to detect and reduce fraud and error. It also operates the Government Counter Fraud Profession, which builds capability across departments.[319] The PSFA is structured into a number of services and functions. These include Risk, Threat and Prevention; Data Analytics; Enforcement and Intelligence; Performance, Assurance and Evidence; Practice, Standards and Capability; and Policy. Of relevance here is the Data Analytics Service which provides cutting-edge tools such as the NFI and the Single Network Analytics Platform, supporting fraud detection and prevention. The Enforcement and Intelligence Unit is a pilot initiative that investigates fraud cases and works to recover losses in collaboration with government entities.[320] The NFI is a

> key data service of the Public Sector Fraud Authority. The NFI compares datasets to identify inconsistencies that are indicators of potential fraud. The results are released securely through a web-based application to 1,100 public and private sector organisations that provide data for further investigation.[321]

The NFI has enabled organisations to deliver savings of £2.9billion.[322] The NFI delivers recurring financial savings, standardises data-matching practices and seeks to foster transparency between agencies. Public bodies are often required to participate under the Local Audit Accountability Act 2014, which provides HM Government with the power to mandate participation for specific public sector entities to combat fraud and error. The PSFA has established a comprehensive framework to modernise error management across the Government. By integrating the NFI, the PSFA empowers government departments and other public bodies to detect anomalies, recover losses and achieve recurring savings.

[318] PSFA, 'About Us' (n/d), available at www.gov.uk/government/organisations/public-sector-fraud-authority/about#:~:text=public%20sector%20fraud.-,Responsibilities,Risk%2C%20Threat%20and%20Prevention.

[319] ibid.

[320] ibid.

[321] PSFA, 'National Fraud Initiative Strategy' (PSFA, 2025).

[322] ibid. The Public Authorities (Fraud, Error and Recovery) Bill 2024 aims to strengthen powers for the public sector to prevent, identify, and recover money lost to fraud and error. The Bill seeks to introduce new investigative and recovery powers for the PSFA to tackle fraud outside tax and social security and provides the Department for Work and Pensions with tools like eligibility verification to combat fraud in social security payments.

VI. Conclusion

The UK legal framework allows for the sharing of data, yet the complex statutory provisions have resulted in a complicated and often difficult to understand system. Part of the problem is the variety of often conflicting standards, industry guidance and statutory provisions, which has the opposite effect of its assisting the sharing of data. The benefits of data-sharing are not yet fully developed and are immature. This occurs even when the data-sharing statutory provisions are clear. Data-sharing is essential to detect, prevent and address scams,[323] and it has become a priority in the effort to address fraud. Accordingly, the chapter began by providing a brief overview of the threat presented by fraud and the growing recognition of the importance of data-sharing to combat fraud in the UK. The chapter then identified the mandatory and voluntary reporting mechanisms before using four case studies to illustrate the deficiencies in the system. The chapter then examined the sharing of data between LEAs and other public authorities, revealing that there is a plethora of legal gateways that could be used to exchange information between LEAs and other public authorities, including statutes establishing the role and powers of LEAs, as well as data protection legislation. However, this section also identified the fact that the legal framework often only provides a power, rather than an obligation, to disclose information, which hinders data-sharing in practice. Accordingly, it is recommended that these legal gateways are reformed to compel, rather than simply permit, information exchange between LEAs. The following section of the chapter examined the sharing of data between the private sector and LEAs. This section revealed that the regulated sector is only required to report successful, rather than attempted, frauds to the NCA under POCA 2002. Accordingly, the chapter recommends that the reporting of unsuccessful frauds to the NCA should become mandatory. There are advantages to adopting this approach – it will lead to an enhanced understanding of fraud, and result in better intelligence for policing fraud. Further, this section revealed that the investigation of fraud reports from the private sector and general public has been limited to date. While the measures contained in the Fraud Strategy, such as the creation of the National Fraud Squad and the replacement of Action Fraud, are likely to improve the processing of reports and investigation of scams, they do not go far enough to ensure that the law enforcement response is commensurate to the risks posed. Accordingly, it is recommended that additional resources should be invested into investigating reports of fraud and proactively addressing fraud risks. Aside from legal gateways, public-private partnerships, such as JMLIT, have also performed an important role in facilitating information-sharing between the private sector and LEAs, achieving some notable successes.

The final section of the chapter examined data-sharing within the private and public sectors. It revealed that the public sector is able to share information

[323] HM Government, *Fraud Strategy* (n 32).

through several legal gateways including, the Serious Crime Act 2007, the Digital Economy Act 2017 and the Data Protection Act 2018. It also benefits from the governance structure for sharing data provided by the Counter Fraud Data Alliance. Similarly, the private sector is able to share information through POCA 2002 and the Data Protection Act 2018. However, in practice, a number of factors presently inhibit information-sharing within this sector. Some of these concerns have been addressed by the Economic Crime and Corporate Transparency Act 2023. In addition, s 339ZB of POCA should be applied to the entirety of the regulated sector, or, preferably, a clause similar to s 339ZD of POCA should be added to the Act, to facilitate the disclosure of Super SARs. Additional guidance should also be provided to the private sector on making requests and disclosures under the Act. The use of public-private partnerships is a beacon of how data-sharing can effectively be used to tackle financial crime. The JFTF and PSFA are examples of best practice and draw comparisons highlighted in previous chapters for JMLIT.

7

Conclusions and Recommendations

I. Introduction

This book has challenged the prevailing narrative surrounding the United Kingdom's (UK) anti-money laundering and counter-terrorist financial regime (AML/CTF), particularly as endorsed by the Financial Action Task Force (FATF) in its 2018 Mutual Evaluation Report (MER). The UK has been praised for its levels of compliance with the FATF Recommendations and its overall effectiveness in many areas. However, this book has demonstrated through the use of case studies that gaps remain in the application of the customer due diligence (CDD) rules, the use of suspicious activity reports (SARs) and related data- sharing mechanisms. These deficiencies undermine the UK's ability to detect, investigate and prosecute financial crime including money laundering, terrorist financing and fraud. The case studies illustrate that the use of CDD, SARs and related data-sharing mechanisms are not as robust or coordinated as the MER suggests. Identified deficiencies include disjointed communication channels, the inconsistent use of SARs and legal ambiguities that delay effective information-sharing. Nonetheless, the MER concluded that the UK had high levels of compliance with Recommendations 2, 3 and 31 and its moderate to high ratings in Immediate Outcomes 1, 6, 7 and 9. These shortcomings are concerning given the emphasis that is placed on these rules by international bodies such as FATF, the European Union (EU) and the Organisation for Economic Cooperation and Development (OECD).

This book has addressed a gap in the literature by offering an evaluation of the UK's legal framework governing the use of financial intelligence and the sharing of data.[1] Previous literature has generally focused on money laundering, terrorist financing, fraud, bribery, corruption and tax evasion, few have examined the exchange of information between UK law enforcement agencies (LEAs), anti-money laundering supervisory agencies (AMLSAs) and the public and private sectors, especially in light of the 2018 MER. This omission has contributed towards an uncritical acceptance of the UK's AML/CTF review by the FATF. In light of these findings, reform is needed. The UK needs to strengthen and improve its legal gateways and data-sharing protocols to facilitate the information exchange. This would include re-evaluating the role of SARs, improving inter-agency data-sharing and ensuring that the legal provisions are not only compliant on paper, but effective

[1] See chapter one at section V.

in practice. In doing so, the UK could move beyond superficial compliance and create a more resilient and effective data-sharing framework that can tackle the evolving threats posed by money laundering, terrorist financing and fraud.

II. The Financial Action Task Force, its Recommendations and Methodology

Chapter two highlighted the important role that FATF has played in shaping the global response to financial crime. At the centre of FATF's assessment framework is the MER and its methodology which measures technical compliance and effectiveness.[2] The chapter highlighted how in-depth country analyses offer a comprehensive review of legal frameworks, supervisory practice and law enforcement outcomes. The 2018 MER concluded that the UK has the strongest AML/CTF framework and serves as an example of best practice for other countries. The chapter evaluated Recommendations 2, 30 and 31 in conjunction with Immediate Outcomes 1, 6, 7 and concluded that the Recommendations are comprehensive and serve as a blueprint for countries to follow. The Recommendations demand identity verification, the proactive use of SARs and effective data-sharing, yet the challenge is the consistent implementation. In answering the subsidiary research question, the chapter determines that whilst the MER is a robust analytical tool, it must be treated with caution. The technical compliance rating offers a clear checklist, however, the effectiveness component, although more subjective, captures the practical realities that the Recommendations do not guarantee. Developing nations or those with emerging economies face challenges in complying with the Recommendations, not through lack of effort, but due to financial constraints, limited institutional capacity and legal systems which differ from Western norms. The chapter concluded that the FATF methodology's reliance on uniform benchmarks fails to take into consideration informal economies and different financial systems. The FATF has elevated the AML/CTF oversight, yet the methodology's rigid application and unintended consequences illustrate the need for a more nuanced and equitable approach towards evaluations compliance.

III. The UK's Fourth Mutual Evaluation Report – An Alternative View

Chapter three explored the UK's longstanding role in global efforts to tackle money laundering and terrorist financing, through its engagement with FATF.[3]

[2] See chapter two at section III.
[3] See chapter three at section II.

The UK's longstanding commitment to tackling financial crime is illustrated by its proactive legislative and institutional responses that predate the international AML/CTF frameworks and the FATF Recommendations. The historical leadership has been translated into a robust AML/CTF regime that has aligned with and often exceeded the global standards. The UK's dual presidencies of FATF and its active role in developing international norms illustrates its strategic influence. The 2007 and 2018 MERs serve as critical benchmarks for assessing the UK's compliance with the FATF standards.[4] These reports confirm the strength of the UK's legal framework and related infrastructures. While the 2007 and 2018 MER praised the UK's AML/CTF legal framework and leadership, they identified persistent weaknesses in CDD, SARs and the resourcing of the UK Finance Intelligence Unit (UKFIU). The 2007 Money Laundering Regulations[5] marked a turning point by expanding the scope of regulated professions. Later, the adoption of the fourth and fifth EU Money Laundering Directives further strengthened the UK's CDD framework, earning it a 'Largely Compliant' rating in the 2022 Follow-Up Report.[6] However, the Follow-Up Report continued to highlight the UKFIU's struggles with increasing SAR volumes and its lack of an adequate IT infrastructure, prompting FATF to recommend better resourcing and improved cooperation with law enforcement agencies.

The 2018 MER portrays the UK as not only compliant but also innovative in its approach towards tackling financial crime.[7] The responses by HM Government and veracious oversight bodies have reflected a nuanced understanding of these challenges. Official statements have celebrated the UK's levels of compliance with the FATF Recommendations, yet the Treasury Select Committee and Transparency International have both cautioned against complacency. Both MERs identified deficiencies in the operational effectiveness and resources of the UKFIU, as well as weaknesses in the use of SARs. These recurring problems suggest that while the UK is effective in policy development and international cooperation, it faces obstacles in the implementation and tactical execution. The UK's AML/CTF regime is regarded as a model of international leadership and also work in progress. Its adherence to the Recommendations and initiative-taking initiatives position the UK as a global leader. Nevertheless, recurring weaknesses in CDD, SARs and data-sharing illustrate the need for continuous improvement. As the UK prepares for its next MER, the findings of this chapter are a timely reminder that effectiveness is not measured by compliance, but on

[4] See Financial Action Task Force (FATF), *Third Mutual Evaluation Report Anti-Money Laundering and Counter Terrorist Financing The United Kingdom and of Great Britain and Northern Ireland* (FATF, 2007) ('2007 MER') and FATF, *Anti-Money Laundering and Counter-Terrorist Financing Measures: United Kingdom Mutual Evaluation Report* (FATF, 2018) ('2018 MER').

[5] The Money Laundering, Terrorist Financing and Transfer of Funds (Information on the Payer) Regulations 2017 (SI 2017/692).

[6] FATF, *Follow Up Report and Technical Compliance Re-Rating* (FATF, 2022) ('2022 Follow-Up Report').

[7] See FATF 2018 MER (n 4).

the practical impact of legislation and policies. The chapter sets the stage for a critical reassessment of these positive evaluations via the use of case studies in chapters four to six.

IV. Money Laundering

Chapter four presented a critical analysis of the UK's approach towards money laundering and focused on the CDD, the effectiveness of defence against money laundering suspicious activity reports (DAML SARs) and data-sharing between AMLSAs. The current system suffers from inefficiencies and slow assessments, which are compounded by weak data-sharing experiences across key sectors. Despite establishing dedicated know-your-customer rules, the continued increase in SARs filing, resources constrain within the UKFIU and fragmented data-sharing arrangements undermine their effectiveness. As organised criminal gangs adapt to the preventative measures, the existing system has become overwhelmed.[8] The Money Laundering Regulations and the Proceeds of Crime Act 2002 (POCA) have codified the obligations for customer verification, the conduct of risk assessments and SAR submissions. However, translating these legal obligations into a consistent and high-quality compliance process across a diverse range of financial institutions remains a challenge. Evidence illustrates these operational struggles. For example, the number of DAML SARs submitted to the UKFIU has risen over 262 per cent since 2009–2010, creating backlogs and delaying analysis for potentially important cases. The data-sharing mechanism between LEAs, regulators and the private sector often prevent cross-agency collaboration. The 2018 MER highlighted gaps in resource allocation and organisational coordination. Addressing these deficiencies requires a multifaceted reform agenda.

A. The Legal Profession

The first case study exposed how the legal profession struggles to meet its AML obligations and revealed multiple examples where risk assessments have fallen short, CDD is incomplete, and client funds have not been properly verified.[9] These regulatory breaches have resulted in an increase in the number of disciplinary actions undertaken by the Solicitors' Regulation Authority (SRA). Effective internal risk assessments play a key role in detecting suspicious activity, tackling money laundering and provides an opportunity for the legal profession to adhere to regulatory standards. The case study illustrated that gaps could arise from limited awareness, underdeveloped AML policies or negligence. The SRA has increased

[8] See chapter four at section IV.
[9] See chapter four at section VI.A.

its oversight through more frequent inspections and heavier financial penalties for non-compliance. The Economic Crime and Corporate Transparency Act 2023 has improved the SRA powers and allows them to impose unlimited fines for money laundering related breaches. The case study highlighted persistent weaknesses in CDD, which have existed since the 2007 MER, ongoing deficiencies that call into question the progress noted in the 2018 'Partially Compliant' rating being increased to 'Largely Compliant' in the FATF Follow-Up Report in 2022.[10]

B. Financial Services Sector

The second case study illustrates the important role that the financial sector plays in tackling money laundering. With millions of transactions processed every day and more SARs submitted than any other industry, the financial services sector is an indispensable gatekeeper. However, high profile scandals and data illustrate underlying weak AML controls. An analysis of the 17 enforcement actions illustrates a clear pattern of CDD failures, drawing comparisons with the findings of the legal profession case study. Other weaknesses included breakdowns in internal reporting obligations, weaknesses in risk assessments, failures in automated transaction monitoring systems and deficiencies in staff training and risk management. Collectively, the regulator imposed £853.1million in fines, averaging £50.1million per enforcement action. These recurring failings mirror deficiencies referred to in the 2007 MER and 2018 MER, which identified inconsistent application of CDD measures. The 2007 MER concluded that the UK was 'Partially Compliant'.[11] The 2018 MER concluded that larger firms demonstrated strong CDD practices, but smaller financial institutions had failed to make similar improvements.[12] Nonetheless, the case study identified an example that involved the conviction of NatWest Bank Plc and a financial penalty on Barclays Bank Plc. Both actions originated from transactions linked to a Bradford-based gold dealer, Fowler Oldfield, which funnelled over £365million through NatWest accounts despite the bank's own rules against large cash dealing. Even after rating Fowler Oldfield as a high-risk client, NatWest downgraded its risk in 2013, only to re-elevate it in 2015. The case study illustrated that branch staff accepted deposits up to £1.8million without undertaking the required CDD procedures. Similarly, the Barclays transaction-monitoring system failed to identify suspicious transactions from the same network of cash couriers, illustrating weaknesses in both banks.[13] The Criminal Finances Act 2017 introduced voluntary data-sharing mechanisms that permit members of the regulated sector to exchange information on suspected money laundering with each other or the UKFIU. However, the voluntary nature

[10] See FATF 2022 Follow-Up Report (n 6).
[11] See FATF 2007 MER and 2018 MER (n 4).
[12] ibid.
[13] See chapter four at sections VIII.K and VII.Q.

of this regime undermines its effectiveness. Making these channels mandatory and automatic could strengthen the UK's defences against money laundering. These shortcomings challenge the findings of the 2018 MER.

C. Anti-Money Laundering Supervisory Agencies

The third case study reveals that there are too many professional body supervisors, with overlapping responsibilities and that there are deficiencies in how data is shared between the AMLSAs.[14] A review of the Money Laundering Regulations by HM Treasury has illustrated these inconsistencies, particularly within accountancy and legal professions. The review concluded that the fragmented oversight has led to varying standards of compliance and enforcement strategies which has resulted in HM Government considering one of four options aimed at streamlining AML supervision and closing regulatory loopholes. HM Treasury proposed four models for reform: OPBAS+ which would involve strengthening the Office for Professional Body AML Supervision's (OPBAS) powers without altering the existing structure. The second would be to consolidate the 22 professional-body supervisors into a small number of entitles. The third would be the Single Professional Services Supervisor, one regulator for the legal profession and accountancy firms. The final is a single AMLSA, the obvious and logical solution. This would eliminate the fragmentation and the inconsistency of having 25 separate supervisors. A single body would streamline data-sharing and intelligence-led enforcement. The UK could learn lessons from the approaches adopted in the United States of America (USA), the Netherlands and Singapore. The case study has also identified HM Revenue and Customs' (HMRC) reluctance to share tax-related intelligence, which has shown limited effort in tackling financial crime. To remedy this, the Commissioners for Revenue and Customs Act 2005 could be amended to standardise data0sharing between HMRC and the Financial Conduct Authority (FCA). Other legislative changes could include compelling HMRC to disclose any suspicions of money laundering or terrorist financing, aligning its duties with the reporting of SARs under POCA. This would in effect create a statutory function for HMRC to prevent and detect financial crime.

D. Public Private Partnerships

the Joint Money Laundering Intelligence Taskforce (JMLIT) was launched in February 2015 as a 12-month pilot by the Home Office, National Crime Agency, City of London Police, the British Bankers' Association and major financial institutions. Its objective was to improve intelligence-sharing and to disrupt money

[14] See chapter four at section VIII.

laundering networks across the UK. JMLIT has contributed towards an increase in SARs submitted to the UKFIU. Internationally, JMLIT is regarded as a blueprint for public-private cooperation, offering structured working groups that blend typology analysis with tactical operations to respond to emerging financial crime threats. Placing JMLIT on a permanent statutory footing would guarantee sustained focus and resources from HM Government.

E. Recommendations

In response to these challenges, the Law Commission proposed 19 recommendations to improve the SARs regime.[15] However, HM Government's cautions response, favouring incremental change over transformative reform, raises concerns about its commitment to modernising the reporting and data-sharing system.[16] Ultimately, the chapter argues that the UK's AML regime, while praised by the 2018 MER, does not fully reflect operational realities.

i. Place JMLIT on a Statutory Footing

The rationale for placing JMLIT on a statutory footing is that it will provide the regulated sector with a clear, legally sanctioned mechanism to share data. Placing JMLIT within a legislative framework will remove uncertainty regarding confidentiality and protect the regulated sector from civil liability when information is shared in good faith. Legislation could be used to formalise the current voluntary information-sharing mechanisms and enable reporting entities to submit joint super SARs to the UKFIU, presenting a comprehensive picture of suspected illicit transactions to the UKFIU. By codifying the ability to share data on a statutory basis it would improve the flow of intelligence across members of the regulated sector, helping to address the problems illustrated between NatWest Bank, Barclays Bank and Fowler Oldfield. A statutory JMLIT would bolster the private-public partnership model as a permanent feature of the UK's economic crime strategy, thus potentially unlocking additional resources. Since its inception, JMLT has inspired more public-private partnerships in other jurisdictions.

ii. Failure to Prevent Money Laundering

An unrelated recommendation towards financial intelligence is extending the statutory failure to prevent offence to include money laundering. This would build on the lessons of the NatWest and Barclays cases by embedding corporate level

[15] See Law Commission, *Anti-Money Laundering: The SARs Regime* (Law Commission, 2019).
[16] See HM Government, *Response to Law Commission Review of the SARs Regime* (HM Government, 2024).

accountability directly into banks. Under the Money Laundering Regulations, prosecutions like NatWest require proof of specific regulatory breaches and failings over a defined period of time. The failure to prevent model would create an offence for any firm that does not have reasonable systems and controls in place to stop money laundering. This approach would mirror failure to prevent offences under the Bribery Act 2010,[17] the Criminal Finances Act 2017[18] and the Economic Crime and Corporate Transparency Act 2023.[19] The second money laundering case study illustrates how failures and individual lapses in NatWest and Barclays can leave gaps in deterrence when institutions can argue that employees were acting outside of the Money Laundering Regulations. The extension of failure to prevent money laundering offence would create a level playing field across the regulated sector, which would need to illustrate that effective controls have been implemented.

iii. Criminal Finances Act 2017

The Criminal Finances Act 2017 introduced information gateways that allow financial institutions to share suspicions of money laundering, tax evasion and related crimes with LEAs. However, the exchange of information is discretionary. The failure of NatWest and Barclays show the dangers of optional gateways, illustrating a loophole in the data-sharing mechanisms in the UK. Mandatory information gateways could improve the submission of DAML SARs and a statutory duty to report would ensure that the UKFIU and LEAs would receive more intelligence. To close the loopholes highlighted by NatWest and Barclays, the Criminal Finances Act 2017 should be amended from a permissive form of data-sharing to an obligatory mechanism.

iv. Anti-Money Laundering Supervisory Agencies

The current landscape of the AML supervision is complicated. There are three statutory AML supervisors and OPBAS, which oversees 25 Professional Body Supervisors (PBS) in the legal and accountancy sectors, ensuring they apply effective AML supervision. HM Treasury proposed four potential models for reform. Firstly, OPBAS+ which would involve OPBAS gaining enhanced statutory powers with a clear mandate to coordinate, inspect and to improve standards across all PBS. Secondly, the consolidation of the 25 PBS into a smaller number of consolidated entities. Thirdly, a single unified PBS supervisor. Finally, a single AML supervisor that would replace all existing AML supervisors. Of these options, the final would be the most radical, it would eliminate fragmentation, deliver greater consistency

[17] Bribery Act 2010, s 7.
[18] Criminal Finances Act 2017, ss 45–46.
[19] Economic Crime and Corporate Transparency Act 2023, s 199.

and strategic oversight. Given the planned deregulation of the financial services sector, Option 3, the single PBS supervisor, is likely to be the preferred option. HM Government's broader deregulation agenda is about reducing unnecessary red tape and lowering compliance costs, without undermining core protections.[20] This option would streamline the oversight by merging the legal and accountancy supervision and the leaner architecture would align with the deregulatory principles around efficiency.

V. Terrorist Financing

The fight against terrorist financing is dependent on the coordination of financial intelligence, data-sharing and information exchange among many entities. Despite the UK having established a rigorous reporting system, monitoring protocols and dedicated financial intelligence capacities, this chapter has identified gaps in interagency coordination, resource allocation and legislative loopholes that have been exploited by terrorist financiers. Most strikingly, inter-agency coordination is a key part of Recommendation 31, which provides that competent authorities should have access to all necessary documents and information for investigations. Although the UK was rated 'Compliant' with Recommendation 31, HMRC falls short of this requirement. The operational shortcomings of defence against terrorist financing (DATF) SARs are a recurring theme, and the case studies here illustrate both the consequences of these delays. Through a detailed case study of three terrorist attacks, the chapter has highlighted failures in tracking and acting on financial intelligence.[21] It has illustrated how fraud was either overlooked or inadequately addressed. There have been missed opportunities to intercept transactions but pockets of success with collaboration between the financial services sector, the UKFIU and LEAs thwarting terrorist financing networks. The appraisal in chapter five of the CTF data-sharing mechanisms highlights a static legislative framework that has not responded to emerging terrorist financing typologies and presents a fragmented information flow. To address these shortcomings the chapter advocates extending the OECD's model of automatic exchange of information to competent authorities, ensuring compliance with Recommendation 31.

The case studies have presented a mixed picture of financial intelligence and data- sharing in the UK, revealing some examples of good practice but critical shortcomings. While multiple data-sharing frameworks exist, conventions and loopholes have hindered effective collaboration and data-sharing. One specific challenge here is HMRC's adherence to taxpayer confidentiality conventions, which has limited exchange of information with the Security and Intelligence

[20] Labour, *Financing Growth Labour's Plans for Financial Services* (Labour, 2024).

[21] See chapter five at sections IV.A, IV.B and IV.C.

Services despite a plethora of established data-sharing mechanisms. A parallel gap in the application of the CTF reporting obligations leaves UK universities outside of the reporting obligations. The voluntary reporting of fraud also undermines the completeness of intelligence flows. Nonetheless, successful data-sharing has resulted in the convictions of Amal El-Wahabi and Oghenochuko Ojiri, illustrating how harnessed financial intelligence can disrupt terrorist networks.[22] However, the reliance on DATF SARs is questionable because any intelligence provided is retrospective. Despite the positive conclusions in the 2018 MER, the chapter argues that the UK does not fully meet the international standards and it calls into question the MER's conclusion.

A. Recommendations

The following section of the chapter outlines the key research-supported proposals that are aimed at disrupting terrorist financing and enhancing data flows. It covers recommendations including the automatic exchange of information and the use of all disruptive mechanisms to tackle fraud as a terrorist financing mechanism.

i. Automatic Exchange of Information

The UK's adoption of the OECD's Automatic Exchange of Information model, via the Common Reporting Standard (CRS), would address the loopholes identified via the case studies. By participating in this international framework, HMRC can both share and receive financial account data, enhancing its ability to identify undeclared assets and enforce compliance. The move reinforces the UK's leadership in international tax cooperation; it fulfils global obligations and supports domestic efforts to close evasion loopholes. It also marks a shift toward proactive governance, with financial institutions required to conduct due diligence and report relevant accounts. Overall, the CRS strengthens HMRC's enforcement capabilities, promotes voluntary compliance, and safeguards the integrity of the UK's tax system. Therefore, it is recommended that the UK continues to adopt and implement the OECD's Common Reporting Standard for Automatic Exchange of Information. This framework enhances HMRC's ability to detect and deter offshore tax evasion by facilitating the reciprocal exchange of financial account data with other jurisdictions. Aligning with the CRS reinforces the UK's leadership in global tax transparency, strengthens international cooperation, and modernises domestic tax enforcement. By mandating due diligence from financial institutions and enabling proactive data-sharing, the UK can uphold the integrity of its tax system and promote voluntary compliance among taxpayers.

[22] See chapter five at section IV.D and IV.E.

ii. Use All Disruptive Mechanisms to Tackle Terrorist Financing

An important and unanticipated recommendation, given the remit of the book, is that HM Government should not treat fraud as a standalone crime and that it has become the funding model of choice for terrorist groups. The first three case studies in chapter five illustrated that terrorists have been able to use fraud to generate revenue and fund acts of terrorism. Successive HM Governments have largely ignored this connection, resulting in strategic vulnerability, after FATF concluded the UK used all means at its disposal to disrupt terrorist financing as required by Immediate Outcome 9. A change of strategy that targets fraud networks could limit the ability of terrorists to use this funding mechanism and would be assisted by creating a dedicated fraud-disruption pillar within the Government's CONTEST strategy, which would address this policy gap.[23] The UK could adopt the disruptive mechanism adopted in the USA where many terrorist financiers have been convicted of fraud offences. Examples include Ahmad Ajaj and Ramzi Yousef,[24] Colleen LaRose and Jamie Paulin Ramirez,[25] Barry Walter Bujol Jr,[26] Ali Charah Damache,[27] Amer Sinan Alhaggai,[28] Ardit Ferizi,[29] Mahmoud Youssef Kourani,[30] Mohamad Youssef Hammoud,[31] Khalid Abu Al-Dahab,[32] Enrique Marquez Jr,[33]

[23] See HM Government, *CONTEST – The United Kingdom's Strategy for Countering Terrorism 2023* (HM Government, 2023).

[24] *United States v Ajaj*, No. 1:92-cr-993 (E.D.N.Y. Sept. 14, 1992) (noting a 13 January 1993 judgment) and *United States v Yousef*, 327 F.3d 56, 79 (2d Cir. 2003).

[25] United States Department of Justice, 'Federal Judge Sentences "Jihad Jane" To 10 Years In Prison For Role In Plot To Commit Murder Overseas' (6 January 2014), available at www.justice.gov/usao-edpa/pr/federal-judge-sentences-jihad-jane-10-years-prison-role-plot-commit-murder-overseas.

[26] United States Department of Justice, 'Texas Man Gets Max for Attempting to Provide Material Support to Al Qaeda' (24 May 2012), available at www.justice.gov/archive/usao/txs/1News/Releases/2012%20May/120524%20Bujol_print.html#:~:text=HOUSTON%20%E2%80%93%20Barry%20Walter%20Bujol%20Jr,Attorney%20General%20for%20National%20Security.

[27] United Stated Department of Justice, 'Algerian Man is Sentenced to 15 Years Imprisonment for Conspiring with Pennsylvania Woman and others to Provide Material Support to Terrorists' (30 October 2018), available at www.justice.gov/opa/pr/algerian-man-sentenced-15-years-imprisonment-conspiring-pennsylvania-woman-and-others-provide.

[28] United States Department of Justice, 'ISIS Supporter Sentenced to Almost 16 Years for Attempting to Provide Materials Support to Foreign Terrorist Organisation and Identity Theft' (29 February 2019), available at www.justice.gov/opa/pr/isis-supporter-sentenced-almost-16-years-attempting-provide-material-support-foreign.

[29] United States Department of Justice, 'Convicted Hacker Charged With Fraud and Identity Theft Committed while Incarcerated in Federal Prison' (12 January 2021), available at www.justice.gov/usao-ndca/pr/convicted-hacker-charged-fraud-and-identity-theft-committed-while-incarcerated-federal.

[30] *United States v Mahmoud Youssef Kourani* (2006) Case number 03CR81030-1.

[31] United States Immigration and Customs Enforcement, 'Mohamad Youssef Hammoud Sentenced to 30 Years in Terrorism Financing Case' (27 January 2011), available at www.ice.gov/news/releases/mohamad-youssef-hammoud-sentenced-30-years-terrorism-financing-case.

[32] United States Department of Justice, 'Justice Department Secures the Denaturalization of a Senior Jihadist Operative who was Convicted of Terrorism in Egypt' (20 April 2017), available at www.justice.gov/opa/pr/justice-department-secures-denaturalization-senior-jihadist-operative-who-was-convicted.

[33] United Stated Department of Justice, 'Enrique Marquez Jr. Agrees to Plead Guilty to Plotting Violent Attacks and Buying Firearms for Shooter in San Bernardino Terrorist Attack' (14 February 2017), available at www.justice.gov/usao-cdca/pr/enrique-marquez-jr-agrees-plead-guilty-plotting-violent-attacks-and-buying-firearms.

Naif Abdulaziz M Afallaj,[34] Nader Elhuzayel,[35] Khalid Ouazzani,[36] Khalid Awan,[37] Yahya Farooq Mohammad,[38] Zoobia Shahnaz,[39] Pedrouz Sedaghaty and Soliman Hamd Al-Buthe,[40] Emadeddin Muntasser, Muhammed Mubayyid and Samir al-Monla,[41] Johnathan Paul Jimenez,[42] Michael Todd Wolfe,[43] Hossein Lahiji and Najmeh Vahid Dasterjerdi[44] and Houcine Becher Ghoul.[45]

VI. Fraud

The UK's use of financial intelligence and data-sharing has underpinned success in combating money laundering and terrorist financing. The UK has an established statutory framework, a UKFIU and mandated AML/CTF reporting regimes. The intelligence-led policing model has fostered a culture of collaboration between

[34] United States Department of Justice, 'Saudi Citizen Sentenced to More than 12 Years in Prison for Concealing Attendance at Al Qaeda Training Camp and Visa Fraud' (3 October 2019), available at www.justice.gov/opa/pr/saudi-citizen-sentenced-more-12-years-prison-concealing-attendance-al-qaeda-training-camp-and.

[35] United States Department of Justice, 'California Man Sentenced to 30 Years for Conspiring to join ISIL and Engaging in Fraud' (26 September 2016), available at www.justice.gov/opa/pr/california-man-sentenced-30-years-conspiring-join-isil-and-engaging-fraud.

[36] *United States v Khaled Ouazzani*, Case No 10-00025-01-CR-W-HFS (Indictment) (W.D. Mo. February 2010).

[37] United Stated Department of Justice, 'Khalid Awan Re-sentenced to 14 Years Imprisonment for Providing Material Support and Resources to Indian Terrorist Organisation' (3 April 2012), available at https://archives.fbi.gov/archives/newyork/press-releases/2012/khalid-awan-re-sentenced-to-14-years-imprisonment-for-providing-material-support-and-resources-to-indian-terrorist-organization.

[38] United Stated Department of Justice, 'Man Sentenced to Over 27 Years for Conspiring to Provide Material Support to Terrorists and Soliciting the Murder of a Federal Judge' (6 November 2017), available at www.justice.gov/opa/pr/man-sentenced-over-27-years-conspiring-provide-material-support-terrorists-and-soliciting.

[39] United States Department of Justice, 'Long Island Woman Sentenced to 13 Years' Imprisonment for Providing Material Support to ISIS' (13 March 2020), available at www.justice.gov/opa/pr/long-island-woman-sentenced-13-years-imprisonment-providing-material-support-isis#:~:text=Earlier%20today%2C%20in%20federal%20court,(ISIS)%2C%20and%20attempting%20to.

[40] *United States v Mubayyid*, 658 F.3d 35 (1st Cir. 2011).

[41] United States Department of Justice, 'Former Officers of a Muslim Charity, Care International, Inc., Convicted' (11 January 2008), available at www.justice.gov/archive/opa/pr/2008/January/08_nsd_021.html.

[42] Federal Bureau of Investigation, 'Man Sentenced to 10 Years in Federal Prison for Lying in Terrorism Investigation and False Claim Conspiracy' (19 April 2013), available at https://archives.fbi.gov/archives/tampa/press-releases/2013/man-sentenced-to-10-years-in-federal-prison-for-lying-in-terrorism-investigation-and-false-claim-conspiracy.

[43] United States Department of Justice, 'Texas Man Sentenced to 82 Months in Prison for Attempting to Travel to Syria to Join ISIL' (5 June 2015), available at www.justice.gov/opa/pr/texas-man-sentenced-82-months-prison-attempting-travel-syria-join-isil.

[44] United States Department of Justice, 'Texas Couple Sentenced to Prison for Conspiracy to Defraud the U.S. and to Engage in Money Laundering' (27 November 2013), available at www.justice.gov/usao-or/pr/texas-couple-sentenced-prison-conspiracy-defraud-us-and-engage-money-laundering.

[45] Federal Bureau of Investigation, 'North Carolina Man Sentenced for Immigration Fraud and Tax Charges' (8 August 2018), available at www.justice.gov/usao-ednc/pr/north-carolina-man-sentenced-immigration-fraud-and-tax-charges.

regulators, LEAs and the private sector for money laundering and terrorist financing. By contrast, the reporting of fraud remains mired in fragmentation and underuse. Unlike the well-established AML/CTF reporting systems, fraud reports languish without analysis, rendering the official crime statistics a mere reflection of its true scale. Fraud investigators lack the consolidated data needed to identify and target emerging fraud typologies and consequently, large amounts of fraud go undetected.

Since its inception, Action Fraud was envisioned as a single point of contact for victims. Instead, under-reporting persists, delays have frustrated users and the absence of meaningful follow-up actions erodes the public confidence and leaves fraud investigators with incomplete datasets depriving them of LEAs with accurate intelligence to conduct investigations. High-profile inquiries and Select Committee reports have concluded that Action Fraud is 'not-fit-for-purpose' and promises to deliver a revamped report system have slipped into indefinite timetables. The Police have limited resources, adopt divergent approaches towards fraud referrals and many police forces lack trained fraud investigators. This when combined with repeated broken promises from successive governments have hamstrung efforts. Fraud accounts for over 40 per cent of recorded crime in England and Wales, yet only two per cent of police funding is dedicated to tackling the issue.

Social media platforms have become a fertile ground for fraudsters and optional data- sharing obligations have left LEAs in a problematic position. The result is a significant blind spot: intricate fraud schemes recruit victims in plain sight, yet the absence of any proactive monitoring hampers disruption. The telecommunications sector represents another missing puzzle piece. The sector retains extensive logs of call origins, messaging patterns, and metadata that could flag anomalous behaviour. Yet cooperation is stymied by privacy concerns and competitive pressures, allowing phone-based frauds to proliferate. Without near-real-time alerts or mandated data-sharing agreements, carriers and investigators remain unable to interdict schemes in motion. However, the two public-private partnerships under the leadership of the Joint Fraud Task Force and Public Sector Fraud Authority unite government oversight private-sector innovation to close the loopholes that fraudsters exploit; by pooling expertise, data and resources, these alliances enhance detection and strengthen prevention.

Collectively, the case studies have demonstrated that no one single agency or industry is able to bear the burden of fraud reporting alone. The current patchwork of offline and online channels, voluntary and mandatory reporting schemes and isolated stakeholders have left the UK ill-equipped to map and mitigate the threat of fraud. An integrated framework is essential to transform fragmented inputs into actionable intelligence. The case studies have illustrated a fractured fraud-reporting landscape.

The UK has permissive rather than mandatory legal gateways across statutes such as the Serious Crime Act 2007, the Digital Economy Act 2017, and the Data Protection Act 2018 that govern data exchange between LEAs, public authorities, and the private sector, noting that POCA only compels reporting of successful frauds, leaving attempted crimes unreported and investigations under-resourced.

A. Recommendations

To bridge the gap between potential and practice, chapter six recommends both legal and structural reforms. Simplification of reporting obligations, consolidating overlapping reporting mechanisms into the UKFIU, strengthening the Online Fraud Charter and the adoption of the intelligence-led policing model would enhance clarity.

i. Mandatory Reporting of Suspected Fraud

The scale of fraud in the UK outstrips the capacity of the multiple voluntary reporting mechanisms contributing towards an intelligence gap. Introducing a mandatory duty for the regulated sector to report any reasonable suspicion of fraud could transform the fragmented data collection and sharing mechanisms. Currently, individuals and businesses report suspected fraud through channels like Action Fraud or the Police at their own discretion. Reporting rates are low and inconsistent, which hinders the ability of LEAs to detect emerging fraud typologies. Mandatory reporting would create a clear reporting system that could allow LEAs and the National Fraud Intelligence Bureau to allocate resources more efficiently. Aligning the mandatory fraud reporting within the existing SARs reporting system and the UKFIU would prevent duplication and simplify compliance. The remit of the UKFIU would be extended and this would require clear legislative amendments to POCA 2002, the Terrorism Act 2000, the Fraud Act 2006 and additional funding for the UKFIU.

ii. Abolish Action Fraud

Action Fraud is no longer fit for purpose and despite announcements by successive governments that the reporting entity will be replaced or overhauled, nothing has happened.[46] Successive governments have lacked the political will to replace Action Fraud and to improve the fraud-reporting mechanisms. Action Fraud should be placed within the UKFIU. Funnelling all fraud reports into the UKFIU would improve data quality and prevent fraud reports from being handed off multiple times. Under this mode, every submission would go straight to a specialist fraud team within the UKFIU.

[46] See chapter six at section III.B.i.

iii. Extend Scope of UKFIU

The extension of the remit of the UKFIU to include fraud will require additional strategic funding. Since its creation in 2013, the National Crime Agency's (NCA) annual budget has increased from £513.3million to £704million, an annual average of £594.9million, an increase of 37.2 per cent.[47] However, the UKFIU's budget only represents a small percentage of the NCA's annual budget. For example, the UKFIU budget was £2.45million (2021–2022), £2.8million (2022–2023) and £4.7million (2023–2024).[48] Therefore, the UKFIU's annual budget for 2023–2024 is 0.66 per cent of the NCA's annual budget. While the NCA has seen a commendable budgetary increase since its creation in 2013, the UKFIU is a financial afterthought within its broader framework. The disparity between the NCA's overall budget and the UKFIU is symptomatic of a systemic undervaluing of financial intelligence. The figure is not only disproportionately low, but it also raises questions about HM Government's commitment to tackling financial crime. The annual budget of the UKFIU pales in comparison to the budgets of other FIUs, including FinCEN ($125million),[49] AUSTRAC ($104million),[50] FINTRAC ($70million),[51] TRACFIN (€40 million),[52] FIU-NL (€15 million)[53] and UIF (€20 million).[54] This data makes it clear: the UKFIU is operating on a shoestring budget compared to its global peers, despite the UK's position as a major financial centre and the growing threat of fraud and money laundering. The extension of the UKFIU's remit to include fraud is not a minor administrative adjustment; it is a strategic pivot that demands a robust infrastructure, skilled personnel and cross-agency coordination. Yet the funding allocated suggests a lack of seriousness in empowering the UKFIU to meet these demands. The UKFIU is a symbolic entity that has been tasked with an unenviable undertaking but denied the means to execute it. The current funding trajectory undermines the UKFIU's potential and jeopardises the UK's broader

[47] National Crime Agency, *National Crime Agency Annual Report and Accounts* (National Crime Agency, 2024) at 11.

[48] National Crime Agency, Question for Home Office, UIN 25136, tabled on 8 May 2024, available at https://questions-statements.parliament.uk/written-questions/detail/2024-05-08/25136/.

[49] Department of the Treasury, *Financial Crimes Enforcement Network (FinCEN) Congressional Budget Justification and Annual Performance Plan and Report FY 2025* (Department of Treasury, 2025).

[50] Australian Government Department of Home Affairs Portfolio, *Budget Statements 2023–24, Program 2.10 "Australian Transaction Reports and Analysis Centre (AUSTRAC)* (Australian Government Department of Home Affairs, 2024) at 30.

[51] Financial Transactions and Reports Analysis Centre of Canada, 'Financial Transactions and Reports Analysis Centre of Canada 2025–2026 Departmental Plan' (n/d), available at https://fintrac-canafe.canada.ca/publications/dp/2025-2026/dp-pm-eng.

[52] Finance Bill for 2023, Annex 7, 'Fight against Fraud, Corruption and Money Laundering, Mission' (n/d), available at www.legifrance.gouv.fr/jorf/id/JORFTEXT000047702714#JORFARTI000047702716.

[53] Financial Intelligence Unit-Nederland, 'Jaaroverzicht FIU-Nederland 2024' (2 July 2025), available at www.rijksoverheid.nl/documenten/jaarverslagen/2025/07/02/tk-bijlage-opgemaakte-versie-fiu-jaaroverzicht-2024.

[54] Financial Intelligence Unit for Italy, *Annual Report 2024* (Financial Intelligence Unit for Italy, 2024).

efforts to tackle financial crime. If fraud is to be treated as a national security threat, the UKFIU must be resourced. Anything else is not just fiscally negligent, it is strategically self-defeating.

Funding could be provided by HM Treasury via the reallocation of money laundering financial penalties paid by financial institutions to the FCA via the Government's Consolidated Fund. The Consolidated Fund is the UK Government's central bank account at the Bank of England, into which all public revenue is paid and from which all parliamentary-approved expenditures for public services are disbursed.[55] Since 2015, the FCA has imposed 27 financial penalties on banks for money laundering breaches totalling £1.07billion.[56] By redirecting a portion of the £1.07billion in money laundering penalties imposed by the FCA since 2015 into a dedicated UKFIU line, HM Treasury would create a transparent accountable funding stream. An additional sum of £20–30million would be transformative for the UKFIU. The 2007 and 2018 MERs and both follow-up reports concluded that the UKFIU lacked sufficient resources. This research has confirmed that the budget of the UKFIU is too small and the conclusions and rating provided by the FATF must be called into question.

iv. Online Fraud Charter

Fraud represents over 40 per cent of all recorded crime in England and Wales, with over 70 per cent of these facilitated online. The Online Fraud Charter is an example of self-regulation because it relied on voluntary industry commitments rather than statutory mandates. Companies agree to undertake a wide range of fraud-prevention measures, including sharing data on emerging threats and offering guidance to help people identify frauds. The Charter's voluntary nature allows each organisation to meet these commitments according to its size and services offered. By making the Online Fraud Charter mandatory, all digital platforms would be compelled to adopt consistent levels of protection and reporting. The voluntary nature of the Online Fraud Charter has attracted several of the largest technology and social media companies but not all of them. Mandating the charter would close these coverage gaps ensuring the implementation of standardised fraud prevention and reporting measures. Compulsory adoption would also strengthen accountability by imposing clear obligations on all signatories. The UK Government's goal to reduce fraud by 10 per cent by 2025 relies heavily on private-sector cooperation. Embedding the Charter's

[55] See UK Parliament, 'Consolidated Fund' (n/d), available from at www.parliament.uk/site-information/glossary/consolidated-fund/.

[56] N Davies, 'FCA AML Fines 2015-2025: A Decade of Data and What it Means for You' (21 August 2025), available at www.northrow.com/blog/fca-aml-fines-2015-2025-a-decade-of-data-and-what-it-means-for-you.

commitments into a mandatory framework aligns industry action with national targets.

v. Intelligence-Led Policing

The scale and complexity of fraud in the UK have outgrown the capacity of traditional, reactive local policing models. The research has determined that fraud's reach and sophistication challenge local and regional policing structures, with dedicated fraud resources being, at best, patchy and often misaligned with emerging criminal threats.[57] Intelligence-led policing would shift the paradigm from responding to fraud after it happens to using information designed for action. This would involve strategically gathering, analysing and deploying intelligence to predict, prevent and disrupt fraudulent activity. Intelligence-led policing has been defined by Ratcliffe as a

> business model and managerial philosophy where data analysis and crime intelligence are pivotal to an objective, decision making framework that facilitates crime and problem reduction, disruption and prevention through both strategic management and effective enforcement strategies that target prolific and serious offenders.[58]

The rationale for adopting intelligence-led policing in fraud investigation is its emphasis on structured information-sharing across public and private sectors. The intelligence-led policing model is focused on optimising resource allocation in an environment of constrained budgets and it was extended to fraud; it would be the same model of policing as money laundering and terrorist financing.

The Fraud Strategy outlined plans for a fundamental shift towards intelligence-led policing to detect, investigate and disrupt fraud.[59] At the centre of the strategy was the creation of the National Fraud Squad (NFS), a dedicated national unit of 400 fraud investigators. The objective of the NFS is to analyse intelligence on the highest-harm offenders, to coordinate complex investigations across police forces so that the most dangerous fraudsters are pursued. A key part of the proposed reform is the replacement of Action Fraud and the adoption of a proactive stance on investigations that moves away from the reactive case-by-case model. Collaboration and intelligence are key aims of the move towards intelligence-led policing and the strategy seeks to improve links between the NCA and international partners. It must be noted that with a change of government in July 2024, not all of these measures have been fully implemented. The adoption of the intelligence-led policing model for money laundering and

[57] See chapter six at section IV.B.

[58] JH Ratcliffe, *Intelligence-Led Policing* (Willan Publishing, 2008).

[59] HM Government, *Fraud Strategy: Stopping Scams and Protecting the Public* (HM Government, 2023).

terrorist financing begins with the submission of a SAR, which feeds into the UKFIU, which acts as a gateway for receiving, analysing and disseminating intelligence to LEAs. Therefore, if the intelligence-led policing model were extended to fraud, it would require reforms of the reporting of fraud and the remit of the UKFIU.

VII. Conclusion

The 2018 MER commended the UK for having one of the world's most technically compliant AML/CTF regimes. In June 2022, the FATF published its Follow-Up Report and technical compliance re-rating the UK, evaluating its progress since the deficiencies identified in its 2018 MER. The review updated the UK's ratings in light of the new FATF Recommendations that came into effect after the FATF's on-site visit. The Follow-Up Report focuses on Recommendation 13, correspondent banking due diligence, and Recommendation 29, the operation of the FIU. The key findings illustrate that the UK is 'Compliant' with 24 Recommendations, 'Largely Compliant' with 15 and 'Partially Compliant' with Recommendation 29. The Follow-Up Report illustrated that the UK has made progress since the 2018 MER, but further improvement is needed in the functioning and resourcing of the UKFIU. This research supports the findings of the FATF regarding the resourcing of the UKFIU. This is a worrying pattern that was also raised by FATF in the 2007 MER.

A deeper dive into the CDD rules, the SARs regime and data-sharing reveals persistent fissures between technical compliance and practice. While the MER's rating reflects a robust legal framework, FATF underplays a disconnection between the CDD rules, the SARs regime and related data-sharing mechanisms. The case studies in chapter three illustrate the inconsistent implementation and application of these rules. CDD remains the cornerstone of the AML/CTF defences, but its implementation is marred by a patchwork of supervisory bodies. JMLIT remains an example of best international practice and this model has been adopted by numerous jurisdictions. However, it needs to be placed on a statutory basis to provide certainty. The UK has a robust CTF legal framework and extensive legislation that permits data-sharing between relevant stakeholders. However, the case studies illustrate that HMRC did not share data due to concerns about taxpayer confidentiality, universities are not bound by the Money Laundering Regulations and fraud is not used as a disruptive mechanism to tackle terrorist financing. The reporting mechanisms for fraud are unstructured, causing confusion and leaving the victims of fraud unsupported and reluctant to report. This has resulted in 86 per cent of fraud cases going unreported, leading to an intelligence gap. The Police face the unenviable task of potentially investigating over 4.2million reported cases of fraud. The Police are hampered by a limited number of fraud investigators, resources and that a large percentage of fraud that targets the UK originated overseas, making investigations difficult. The Online Fraud Charter is insufficient to deal with online fraud. Therefore, fraud is impossible to police. Taken together, these gaps illustrate a familiar paradox: the UK achieves high marks on technical compliance but struggles on effectiveness. The MERs' narrow focus on legal provisions and high-level outcomes obscures resource constraints, ineffective data-sharing practices and a cautions reform agenda. To bridge this divide, the UK and FATF need to recalibrate its approach and move away from a 'tick box' compliance culture.

BIBLIOGRAPHY

A

Action Fraud, 'Fraud Crime Trends' (n/d).

—— 'The Action Fraud National Economic Crime Victim Care Unit' (n/d).

Adams, J, 'The Financing of Terror' in P Wilkinson and A Stewart, *Contemporary Research on Terrorism* (Aberdeen University Press, 1989) 393–405.

Alexander, R, *Insider Dealing and Money Laundering in the EU: Law and Regulation* (Ashgate, 2007).

Alldridge, P, *Criminal Justice and Taxation* (Oxford University Press, 2017).

—— *Impacts upon Substantive Laundering Law. What Went Wrong With Money Laundering Law?* (Palgrave, 2016).

—— *Money Laundering Law: Forfeiture, Confiscation, Civil Recovery, Criminal Laundering and Taxation of the Proceeds of Crime* (Bloomsbury Publishing, 2003).

—— 'Money Laundering and Globalisation' (2009) *Journal of Law and Society*, 2008, 35(4), 437–63.

Alpin, R, 'The Policing, Investigation and Governance of "Rogue Trader" Fraud: Whose Responsibility?' (2022) *Police Journal* 95(4), 617–36.

Amicelle, A, 'When Finance Met Security: Back to the War on Drugs and the Problem of Dirty Money' (2017) *Finance and Society* 3(2), 106–23.

Anderson, D, *Attacks in London and Manchester. March-June 2017: Independent Assessment of MI5 and Police* (Brick Court Chambers, 2017).

Andrieux, J, 'Action Fraud: 62% of Reports of Fraud Cyber-Enabled' (24 January 2022).

Argyrou, A, 'Making the Case for Case Studies in Empirical Legal Research' (2017) *Utrecht Law Review* 13(3), 95–113.

Artingstall, D, 'Asking the Right Questions: Effective Information Sharing in the FATF Context' (*RUSI*, 13 June 2016).

Ashser, J, *Fraud Markers, De-banking, and Financial Crime: A Legal Analysis of Counter-fraud Practices in the UK and Beyond* (Routledge, 2025).

Attorney General's Office, *Fraud Review – Final Report* (Attorney General's Office, 2006).

AUSTRAC, 'Fintel Alliance' (n/d).

Azinge-Egbiri, N, *Regulating and Combating Money Laundering and Terrorist Financing: The Law in Emerging Economies* (Routledge, 2021).

B

Bagley, B, 'US Foreign Policy and the War on Drugs: Analysis of a Policy Failure' (1988) *Journal of Interamerican Studies and World Affairs* 30(2-3), 189–212.

Bank of England, 'Payment and Settlement Statistics' (n/d).

Bank of International Settlements, 'Basel Committee Membership' (14 May 2024).

Barnes, V and De Pascalis, F, 'R. v NatWest (2021): Another Turning Point in the Regulation of Big Banks?' (2023) *Company Lawyer* 44(5), 143–1513.

Başaranel, B, and Türkşen, U, *Counter-Terrorist Financing Law and Policy: An Analysis of Turkey* (Routledge, 2019).

Basel Committee on Banking Supervision, *The Basel Framework* (Basel Committee on Banking Supervision, 2025).

Basile, M, 'Going to the Source: Why Al Qaeda's Financial Network is Likely to Withstand the Current War on Terrorist Financing' (2004) *Studies in Conflict & Terrorism*, 27(3), 169–85.

Basra, R and Neumann, PR, 'Criminal Pasts, Terrorist Futures: European Jihadists and the New Crime-Terror Nexus' (2016) *Perspectives on Terrorism* 10(6), 25–40.

Baumert, T, 'Do Terrorists Play the Market? Or Can Their Attacks Serve as a Source of Financing for Terrorism?' (2008) *Policing: A Journal of Policy and Practice* 2(4), 434–40.

BBC News, 'HSBC Bank "Helped Clients Dodge Millions in Tax"' (10 February 2015).

——, 'London Bridge Inquests: Attacker Bought Pink Knives from Lidl (29 May 2019).

—— 'Lee Rigby Murder: Adebolajo and Adebowale Jailed' (26 February 2014).

—— 'London Attack: Who was Khalid Masood?' (26 March 2017).

—— 'London Bombs Cost Just Hundreds' (6 January 2006).

Benson, K, *Lawyers and the Proceeds of Crime – the Facilitation of Money Laundering and its Control* (Routledge, 2020).

Benson, M, and Simpson, S, *White-Collar Crime: An Opportunity Perspective* (Routledge, 2009).

Beresford, D, Katzenbach, N and Rogers, C, *Report of Investigation by the Special Investigative Committee of the Board of Directors of WorldCom* (Securities and Exchange Commission, 2003).

Besenyő, J, 'Low-Cost Attacks, Unnoticeable Plots? Overview on the Economical Character of Current Terrorism' (2017) *Strategic Impact* (63), 83–100.

Bhat, P, 'Doctrinal Legal Research as a Means of Synthesizing Facts, Thoughts, and Legal Principles' in P Bhat, *Idea and Methods of Legal Research* (Oxford University Press, 2020).

Biersteker, T, Eckert, S and Biersteker, T, *Countering the Financing of Terrorism* (Routledge, 2008).

Blakeborough, L and Correia, S, *The Scale and Nature of Fraud: A Review of the Evidence* (Home Office, 2018).

Board of Banking Standards, *Inquiry Report of the Board of Banking Standards Inquiry into the Circumstances of the Collapse of Barings Bank* (Board of Banking Standards, 1995).

Bociga, D, Lord, N and Bellotti, E, 'Dare to Share: Information and Intelligence Sharing within the UK's Anti-Money Laundering Regime' (2024) *Policing and Society* 35(6), 812–31.

Booth, R, Farrell, S, Bastable G and Yeo, N, *Money Laundering Law and Regulation* (Oxford University Press, 2010).

Bourton, S, *Tax Evasion and the Law A Comparative Analysis of the UK and USA* (Routledge, 2024).

Bowcott, O, 'HSBC Should Face UK Criminal Charges, Says Former Public Prosecutor' (22 February 2015).

Brennan, H, 'The Law Commission's Review of Anti-Money Laundering and Counter-Terrorism Financing' (2019) *Archibold Review* 7, 4–6.

Bryman, D and Kreps, S, 'Agents of Destruction? Applying Principal-Agent Analysis to State-Sponsored Terrorism' (2010) *International Studies Perspectives* 11(1), 1–18.

Button, M, 'Hiding behind the Veil of Action Fraud: The Police Response to Economic Crime in England and Wales and Evaluating the Case for Regionalization or a National Economic Crime Agency' (2021) *Policing: A Journal of Policy and Practice* 15(3), 1758–72.

Button, M and Gee, J, *Countering Fraud for Competitive Advantage: The Professional Approach to Reducing the Last Great* (Wiley, 2013).

Button, M, Hock, B and Shepherd, D, *Economic Crime from Conception to Response* (Routledge, 2022).

Button, M, Hock, B and Shepherd, D, *Replacing the Serious Fraud Office – the Case for a New Approach to Serious Economic Crime* (Institute of Economic Affairs, 2024).

Button, M, Lewis, C and Tapley, J, 'Not a Victimless Crime: The Impact of Fraud' on Individual Victims and their Families' (2014) *Security Journal* 27(1), 36–54.

—— *Support for the Victims of Fraud: An Assessment of the Current Infrastructure in England and Wales* (National Fraud Authority, 2009).

C

Cabinet Office, Department for Digital, Culture, Media & Sport *Tackling Fraud in Government with Data Analytics: Starting the Conversation* (Cabinet Office, Department for Digital, Culture, Media & Sport, 2019).

—— The Statutory Review of the Debt and Fraud Powers of the Digital Economy Act (2017) (Cabinet Office, 2023).

Carlton, D, 'The 1980s: Encouraging and Sponsoring Terrorism' in D Carlton (ed), *The West's Road to 9/11 Resisting, Appeasing and Encouraging Terrorism Since 1970* (Palgrave, 2005) 172–87.
Cassella, S, 'Reverse Money Laundering' (2003) *Journal of Money Laundering Control* 7(1), 92–94.
Celik, K, 'Impact of the FATF Recommendations and their Implementation on Financial Inclusion' (2021) at 25.
Chakrabarty, I, 'The Financial Action Task Force Entrapped within Hypocrisy and Rhetoric: Using India as a Case Study' (2023) *Asia Pacific Law Review* 31(2), 402–27.
Chase, A, 'Legal Mechanisms of the International Community and the United States Concerning State Sponsored Terrorism' (2004) *Virginal Journal of International Law* 45, 41–137.
Chase, I, van der Valk, J and Keatinge, T, Assessing the Financial Action Task Force's Impact on Digital Financial Inclusion (Royal United Services Institute, 2021).
Chau, D and van Dijck Nemcsik, M, Anti-Money Laundering Transaction Monitoring Systems Implementation: Finding Anomalies (John Wiley & Sons, 2020).
Cifas, *Annual Report 2012* (Cifas, 2013).
—— *Annual Report 2013* (Cifas, 2014).
—— *Annual Report 2014* (Cifas, 2015).
—— *Annual Report 2015* (Cifas, 2016).
—— *Annual Report 2016* (Cifas, 2017).
—— *Annual Report 2017* (Cifas, 2018).
—— *Annual Report 2018* (Cifas, 2019).
—— *Annual Report 2019* (Cifas, 2020).
—— *Annual Report 2020* (Cifas, 2021).
—— *Fraud Scape 2021 Key Findings* (Cifas, 2022).
—— *Fraud Scape 2023* (Cifas, 2024).
—— *Fraud Scape 2024* (Cifas, 2024).
—— *Fraud Scape 2025* (Cifas, 2025).
—— 'Fraud Skyrockets as Cost-of-Living and Economic Crises Begin to Deepen' (14 November 2022).
—— 'What is Cifas?' (n/d).
City of London Police, *National Policing Strategy for Fraud, Economic and Cyber Crime 2023–2028* (City of London Police, 2023).
—— 'Written Evidence Submitted to the Home Affairs Select Committee' (February 2017).
—— Written Evidence Submitted by the Office of the City Remembrancer on Behalf of the City of London Police and City of London Police Authority Board (October 2023).
CNN, 'A Timeline of the Charlie Hebdo Terror Attack' (10 January 2015).
Collins, S, 'State-Sponsored Terrorism: In Decline, Yet Still a Potent Threat' (2014) *Politics & Policy* 42(1), 131–59.
Counter Terrorism Policing, 'Art Dealer Jailed for Terrorism Offence' (9 June 2025).
—— 'Detectives Praised for Financial Investigations' (7 December 2018).
Couture, X and Pardoe, A, *Changing the Story on Scams: Protecting Consumers and Increasing Reporting* (Citizens Advice, 2017).
Creswell, J, *Research Design, Qualitative, Quantitative and Mixed Methods Approaches* (Sage, 2003).
Crime Stoppers, *Impact Report 2023–2024* (Crime Stoppers, 2024).
Cross, C and Kelly, M, 'The Problem of "White Noise": Examining Current Prevention Approaches to Online Fraud' (2016) *Journal of Financial Crime* 23(4), 806–18.
Crowe, *Annual Fraud Indicator 2023* (Crowe, 2024).
Crown Prosecution Service, 'Four People Jailed for One of the Largest Money Laundering Cases in the UK' (7 March 2025).
—— 'Proceeds of Crime Act 2002 Part 7 – Money Laundering Offences'.
—— 'Terrorism' (n/d).

D

Damais, A, 'The Financial Action Task Force' in WH Muller, CH Kälin, JG Goldsworth (eds), *Anti-Money Laundering: International Law and Practice* (John Wiley & Sons, 2007).

Dan Jarvis MP, 15 January 2025.

De Koker, L, 'Aligning Anti-Money Laundering, Combating of Financing of Terror and Financial Inclusion: Questions to Consider when FATF Standards are Clarified' (2011) *Journal of Financial Crime* 18(4), 361–86.

—— 'FATF Grey Listing: Time to Revisit the Approach' (2024) *Journal of Money Laundering Control* 27(4), 621–24.

—— 'The 2012 Revised FATF Recommendations: Assessing and Mitigating Mobile Money Integrity Risks within the New Standards Framework' (2012) *Washington Journal of Law, Technology & Arts* 8(3), 165.

De Koker, L, Howell, J and Morris, N, 'Economic Consequences of Grey Listing by the Financial Action Task Force (2023) *Risks* 11(5), 81.

de la Feria, R and Loutzenhiser, G, *The Dynamics of Taxation: Essays in Honour of Judith Freedman* (Hart, 2020).

DeLeeuw, JG and Pridemore, WA, 'The Threat from Within: A Conjunctive Analysis of Domestic Terrorism Incidents in the United States, United Kingdom, and Ireland' (2018) *Perspectives on Terrorism* 12(4), 26–54.

DeLiema, M, Brannock, D, Preble, E and Langton, L, 'A Fraud Awareness Mail Campaign Significantly Reduces Revictimisation Among Older Victims' (2024) *Innovation in Aging* 8(1), 114.

de Oliveira, I, 'The Governance of the Financial Action Task Force: An Analysis of Power and Influence throughout the Years' (2018) *Crime, Law and Social Change* 69(2), 153–72.

Demetis, D, *Technology and Anti-Money Laundering: A Systems Theory and Risk-Based Approach* (Edward Elgar, 2010).

Department for Business and Trade, 'Guidance on the Information Sharing Measures in the Economic Crime and Corporate Transparency Act 2023' (20 December 2024).

Department for Trade and Industry, *Guinness Plc* (Department for Trade and Industry, 1997).

—— *The Maxwell* Report (Department for Trade and Industry, 2001).

Department of State, 'State Sponsors of Terrorism' (n/d).

Deshmukh, S, 'Universal Procedures? An Analysis of Text (dis)similarities in FATF Mutual Evaluation Reports' (2025) *Journal of Economic Criminology* 8.

Dickson, B, 'The Prevention of Terrorism (Temporary Provisions) Act 1989' (1989) *Northern Ireland Legal Quarterly* 40(3), 250–67.

Dill, A, *Anti-Money Laundering Regulation and Compliance: Key Problems and Practice Areas* (Edward Elgar, 2021).

Doig, A and Levi, M, Frauds and Financial Crimes: Trends, Strategic Responses, and Implementation Issues in England and Wales (Routledge, 2023).

Doing, A, *Fraud* (Routledge, 2006).

Donohue, L, *The Cost of Counterterrorism – Power, Politics and Liberty* (Cambridge, 2008).

Doyle, T, 'Cleaning Up Anti-Money Laundering Strategies: Current FATF Tactics Needlessly Violate International Law' (2002) *Houston Journal of International Law* 24, 279–313.

E

Economic Crime and Corporate Transparency Bill, Explanatory Notes, 9.

Edelman, L and Stryker, R, 'A Sociological Approach to Law and the Economy' in N Smelser and R Swedberg, *The Handbook of Economic Sociology* (Sage, 2005) 527–52.

Edmonds, T, *Money Laundering Law, Briefing Paper no 2593* (House of Commons, 2018).

Eggenberger, K, 'When is Blacklisting Effective? Stigma, Sanctions and Legitimacy: The Reputational and Financial Costs of being Blacklisted' (2018) *Review of International Political Economy* 25(4), 483–504.

European Commission, 'Anti-Money Laundering and Countering the Financing of Terrorism at International Level' (n/d).

—— *Study on an EU Initiative for a Restriction on Payments in Cash, Final Report* (European Commission, 2017).

European Parliament, 'Russia's War on Ukraine: Designating a State as a Sponsor of Terrorism' (11 November 2022).

Experian, *Annual Fraud Indicator 2016* (Experian, 2016).

—— *Annual Fraud Indicator 2017* (Experian, 2017).

F

Favarel-Garrigues, G, Godefroy, T and Lascoumes, P, 'Reluctant Partners? Banks in the Fight Against Money Laundering and Terrorism Financing in France' (2011) 42 *Security Dialogue* 179, 189.

Federal Bureau of Investigation, 'A Review of the President's Fiscal Year 2025 Budget Request for the Federal Bureau of Investigation' (4 June 2024).

Federal Research Division Library of Congress, *A Global Overview of Narcotics-Funded Terrorist and other Extremist Groups* (Library of Congress, 2002).

Ferwerda, J, 'Definitions of Money Laundering in Practice' in B Unger, J Ferweda, M van den Broek and I Deleanu, *The Economic and Legal Effectiveness of the European Union's Anti-Money Laundering Policy* (Edward Elgar, 2014) at 87–96.

Fielder, T, 'Estonian Parliament Declares Russia a Terrorist State' (18 October 2022).

Financial Action Task Force, *Anti-Money Laundering and Counter-Terrorist Financing Measures: United Kingdom Mutual Evaluation Report* (Financial Action Task Force, 2018).

—— *Beneficial Ownership of Legal Persons* (Financial Action Task Force, 2022).

—— *Best Practices – Combating the Abuse of Non-Profit Organisations* (Financial Action Task Force, 2015).

—— 'Black and Grey Lists' (n/d).

—— *Combating the Terrorist Financing Abuse of Non-Profit Organisations* (Financial Action Task Force, 2023).

—— 'Countries' (n/d).

—— *Emerging Terrorist Financing Risk* (Financial Action Task Force, 2015).

—— *FATF 40 Recommendations* (Financial Action Task Force, 1990).

—— *FATF 40 Recommendations* (Financial Action Task Force, 2003).

—— *FATF Annual Report 1993-1994* (Financial Action Task Force, 1994).

—— *FATF Guidance: Private Sector Information Sharing* (Financial Action Task Force, 2017).

—— *FATF IX Special Recommendations* (Financial Action Task Force, 2001).

—— *Financial Action Task Force on Money Laundering: Report 1990–1991* (Financial Action Task Force, 1991).

—— 'FATF Steps up the Fight against Money Laundering and Terrorist Financing' (16 February 2012).

—— 'FATF Updates Standards and Consults on Guidance to Better Promote Financial Inclusion' (25 February 2025).

—— *Financing of the Terrorist Organisation Islamic State in Iraq and the Levant* (Financial Action Task Force, 2015).

—— 'Frequently asked Questions – what is Money Laundering?' (n/d).

—— 'Frequently asked Questions' (n/d).

—— *Follow Up Report and Technical Compliance Re-Rating* (Financial Action Task Force, 2022).

—— *Global Money Laundering Terrorist Financing Threat Assessment* (Financial Action Task Force, 2010).

—— *Guidance for a Risk-Based Approach – Money or Value Transfer Services* (Financial Action Task Force, 2016).

—— *Guidance for a Risk-Based Approach – Securities Sector* (Financial Action Task Force, 2018).

—— *Guidance on Risk-Based Approach – Accountants* (Financial Action Task Force, 2019).

—— *Guidance on Risk-Based Approach – Real Estate Sector* (Financial Action Task Force, 2022).

—— 'High-Risk and other Monitored Jurisdictions' (n/d).

—— 'History of the FATF' (n/d).

—— *International Standards on Combating Money Laundering and the Financing of Terrorism & Proliferation: The FATF Recommendations* (Financial Action Task Force, 2025).

—— *International Standards on Combating Money Laundering and the Financing of Terrorism & Proliferation: The FATF Recommendations* (Financial Action Task Force, 2012).
—— 'Mandate of the FATF' (n/d).
—— *Methodology for Assessing Technical Compliance with the FATF Recommendations and the Effectiveness of AML/CFT Systems* (Financial Action Task Force, 2023).
—— *Methodology for Assessing Technical Compliance with the FATF Recommendations and the Effectiveness of AML/CFT/CPF Systems* (Financial Action Task Force, 2025).
—— 'Membership Process and Criteria' (n/d).
—— *Money Laundering and Terrorist Financing Typologies 2004-2005* (Financial Action Task Force, 2005).
—— *Money Laundering and Terrorist Financing Vulnerabilities of Legal Professionals* (Financial Action Task Force, 2013).
—— *Money Laundering and Terrorist Financing in the Art and Antiquities Market* (Financial Action Task Force, 2023).
—— *Money Laundering and Terrorist Financing in the Securities Sector* (Financial Action Task Force, 2009).
—— *Money Laundering and Terrorist Financing Vulnerabilities of Commercial Websites and Internet Payment Systems* (Financial Action Task Force, 2008).
—— *Money Laundering and Terrorist Financing Typologies 2004–2005* (Financial Action Task Force, 2005).
—— *Money Laundering and Terrorist Financing Vulnerabilities of Legal Professionals* (Financial Action Task Force, 2013).
—— *Money Laundering and Terrorist Financing Related to Counterfeiting of Currency* (Financial Action Task Force, 2011).
—— *Money Laundering from Fentanyl and Synthetic Opioids* (Financial Action Task Force, 2022).
—— *Mutual Evaluation Fourth Follow-Up Report: Anti-Money Laundering and Combating the Financing of Terrorism – The United Kingdom* (Financial Action Task Force, 2009).
—— 'Mutual Evaluation Reports' (n/d).
—— *Organised Maritime Piracy and Related Kidnapping for Ransom* (Financial Action Task Force, 2011).
—— 'Outcomes Joint FATF/GAFILAT Plenary, 1-3 November 2017' (3 November 2017).
—— *Partnering in the Fight against Financial Crime – Data Protection, Technology and Private Sector Information Sharing* (Financial Action Task Force, 2022).
—— *Private Sector Information Sharing* (Financial Action Task Force, 2017).
—— *Report on the State of Effectiveness and Compliance with the FATF* Standards (Financial Action Task Force, 2022).
—— *Terrorist Financing* (Financial Action Task Force, 2008).
—— *The 40 Recommendations* (Financial Action Task Force, 2003).
—— *The FATF Recommendations* (Financial Action Task Force, 2012).
—— 'The FATF Recommendations: International Standards on Combatting Money Laundering and the Financing of Terrorism & Proliferation'.
—— *The Financial War on Terrorism – A Guide by the Financial Action Task Force* (Financial Action Task Force, 2014).
—— *The Forty Recommendations* (Financial Action Task Force, 1990).
—— *The Role of Hawala and other Similar Service Providers in Money Laundering and Terrorist Financing* (Financial Action Task Force, 2013).
—— *Third Mutual Evaluation Report Anti-Money Laundering and Counter Terrorist Financing The United Kingdom and of Great Britain and Northern Ireland (Financial Action Task Force*, 2007).
—— 'The United Kingdom's Measures to Combat Money Laundering and Terrorist Financing' (n/d).
—— 'United Kingdom' (n/d).
—— 'What We Do' (n/d).
Financial Conduct Authority, *Anti-Money Laundering Supervision by the Legal and Accountancy Professional Body Supervisors: Progress and themes from our 2023/2024 supervisory work* (Financial Conduct Authority, 2024).

—— *Assessing and Reducing the Risk of Money Laundering Through the Markets* (Financial Conduct Authority, 2025).
—— 'Effectiveness and Proportionality: Our Financial Crime Priorities – Speech by Rob Gruppetta, Head of Financial Crime Department' (10 November 2016).
——, 'Enforcement' (21 April 2016).
—— 'FCA Fines and Imposes a Restriction on Canara Bank for Anti-Money Laundering Systems Failings' (6 June 2016).
—— 'FCA Fines Barclays £42 million for Poor Handling of Financial Crime Risks' (17 July 2025).
—— 'FCA Fines Commerzbank London £37,805,400 over Anti-Money Laundering Failures' (17 June 2020).
—— 'FCA Fines Deutsche Bank £163 million for Serious Anti-Money Laundering Controls Failings' (31 January 2017).
—— 'FCA Fines EFG Private Bank £4.2m for Failures in its Anti-Money Laundering Controls' (24 April 2013).
—— 'FCA Fines Gatehouse Bank £1.5 million for Poor Anti-Money Laundering Checks' (14 October 2022).
—— 'FCA Fines Ghana International Bank Plc £5.8m for Failings in its Anti-Money Laundering Controls' (23 June 2022).
—— 'FCA Fines Guaranty Trust Bank (UK) Limited £7.6 million for Further Failures in its Anti-Money Laundering Systems and Controls' (10 January 2023).
—— 'FCA Fines HSBC Bank Plc £63.9 million for Deficient Transaction Monitoring Controls' (17 December 2021).
—— 'FCA Fines Metro Bank £16m for Financial Crime Failings' (12 November 2024).
—— 'FCA Fines Monzo £21m for Failings in Financial Crime Controls'.
—— 'FCA Fines Santander UK £107.7 million for Repeated Anti-Money Laundering Failures' (9 December 2022).
—— 'FCA Fines Standard Chartered Bank £102.2 million for Poor AML controls' (9 April 2019).
—— 'FCA Fines Sunrise Brokers LLP £642,400 for Serious Financial Crime Control Failings in Relation to Cum-ex Trading' (12 November 2021).
—— 'FCA Imposes Penalties on Sonali Bank (UK) Limited and its Former Money Laundering Reporting Officer for Serious Anti-Money Laundering Systems Failings' (12 October 2016).
—— 'FCA Penalises Al Rayan Bank PLC for Anti-Money Laundering Failures' (11 January 2023).
—— *Handbook – Money Laundering and Terrorist Financing* (Financial Conduct Authority, 2025).
—— 'NatWest Fined £264.8 million for Anti-Money Laundering Failures' (17 December 2021).
—— 'Office for Professional Body Anti-Money Laundering Supervision (OPBAS)' (23 January 2018).
—— 'Report a Scam' (n/d).
—— 'Standard Bank PLC Fined £7.6m for Failures in its Anti-Money Laundering Controls' (23 January 2014).
—— *The Decision Procedure and Penalties Manual* (Financial Conduct Authority, 2025) at DEPP 6.
—— 'Two Individuals Face Bans and £1.3m Fine for Pension Transfer Advice Failings' (1 September 2023).
—— '2013 Fines'.
—— '2014 Fines'.
—— '2015 Fines'.
—— '2016 Fines'.
—— '2017 Fines'.
—— '2018 Fines'.
—— '2019 Fines'.
—— '2020 Fines'.
Financial Services Authority, 'Delivering Credible Deterrence' (27 April 2009).
—— 'FSA Fines Alpari and its Former Money Laundering Reporting Officer, Sudipto Chattopadhyay for Anti-Money Laundering Failings' (5 May 2010).
—— 'FSA Fines Firm and MLRO for Money Laundering Controls Failings' (29 October 2009).
—— 'FSA Fines Habib Bank AG Zurich £525,000 and Money Laundering Reporting Officer £17,500 for Anti-Money Laundering Control Failings' (15 May 2012).

Financial Services Commission, *Guidance Notes – Systems of Control to Prevent the Financial System from Being Used for Money Laundering or Terrorist Financing Activities* (Financial Services Commission, 2011).

Fisher, J, 'HSBC, Tax Evasion and Criminal Prosecution' (2015) *Tax Journal* 1253, 6.

Forston, R, 'Money Laundering Offences under POCA 2002' in W Blair and R Brent, *Banks and Financial Crime – The International Law of Tainted Money* (Oxford University Press, 2010).

—— 'Money Laundering Offences under POCA 2002' in W Blair, R Brent and T Grant, *Banks and Financial Crime: The International Law of Tainted Money* (Oxford University Press, 2017).

FRA0003 1, Written Evidence Submitted by Professor Mark Button, Co-Director of the Centre for Cybercrime and Economic Crime, University of Portsmouth.

FRA0026, Written Evidence Submitted by Victim Support, 2023.

FRA0043, Written Evidence Submitted by Which? Consumers Association Ltd, October 2023.

FRA0060, Written Evidence Submitted by the Royal United Services Institute (RUSI), 2023.

FRA0081 1, Written Evidence submitted by TSB, 2023.

Fraud Act 2006 and Digital Fraud Committee, Oral evidence: Fraud Act 2006 and Digital Fraud, Dame Vera Baird, 28 April 2022.

Fraud Advisory Panel, *Roskill Revisited: Is there a Case for a Unified Fraud Prosecution Office?* (Fraud Advisory Panel, 2010).

—— Written Evidence, FDF0048 (n/d).

Freeman, M, *Financing Terrorism: Case Studies* (Routledge, 2016).

G

G7 Information Centre, 'Economic Declaration' (16 July 1989).

G7 Research Group, 'Statement of the G7 Finance Ministers and Central Bank Governors' (6 October 2001).

Gallagher, J, Lauchlan, J and Steven, M, 'Polly Peck: The Breaking of an Entrepreneur?' (1996) *Journal of Small Business and Enterprise Development* 3(1), 3–12.

Gallant, M, *Money Laundering and the Proceeds of Crime* (Edward Elgar, 2005).

Gambling Commission, 'Money Laundering' (n/d).

Garside, J, Leigh, D, Ball, J, Pegg, D and Mason, R, 'France Says It Did Not Restrict UK From Using HSBC Files To Pursue Bank and Criminals' (13 February 2015).

Gee, J and Button, M, *The Financial Cost of Fraud 2019* (Crowe, 2019).

Gibbon, R and Fisher, K, 'Promising Results from Groundbreaking FinCrime Data Sharing Project Between Seven UK Banks and the National Crime Agency' (16 January 2025).

Gilbert, G, 'The Roots and Variant Definitions of the Concept of "White-Collar Crime"' in SR Van Slyke, ML Benson and FT Cullen (eds), *The Oxford Handbook of White-Collar Crime* (Oxford University Press, 2016) at 25–38.

Gilmore, W, *Dirty Money – the Evaluation of International Measures to Counter Money Laundering and the Financing of Terrorism* (Council of Europe, 2004).

Goldbarsht, D and Harris, H, 'Enhancing Integrity in the Implementation of FATF Recommendations: Robust Governance Frameworks to Combat Financial Crime in an Age of Intergovernmental Rule-making' in D Goldbarsht and L de Koker (eds), *Financial Crime, Law and Governance: Navigating Challenges in Different Contexts* (Springer, 2024) 141–67.

Goldby, M, 'Anti-Money Laundering Reporting Requirements Imposed by English Law: Measuring Effectiveness and Gauging the Need for Reform' (2013) *Journal of Business Law* 4, 367–97.

—— 'The Impact of Schedule 7 of the Counter-Terrorism Act 2008 on Banks and their Customers' (2010) *Journal of Money Laundering Control* 13(4), 351–71.

Goldstraw-White, J and Gill, M, *The Mandatory Reporting of Fraud: Finding Solutions and Sharing Best Practice*' (Fraud Advisory Panel, 2021).

Graham, L, 'Graham, Blumenthal Introduce Bill Designating Russia a State Sponsor of Terrorism' (20 June 2024).

Green, S, 'The Concept of White-Collar Crime in Law and Legal Theory' (2004) *Buffalo Criminal Law Review* 8(1), 1–34.

Gurulé, J, *Unfunding Terror: The Legal Response to the Financing of Global Terrorism* (Edward Elgar, 2008).

H

Hamin, Z, Rosalili, W, Rosli, W, Omar, N, Armadajaya, A and Mahmud, P, 'Configuring Criminal Proceeds in Money Laundering Cases in the UK' (2014) *Journal of Money Laundering Control* 17(4), 374–84.

Harper, T and Macaskill, M, 'Glaswegian in £300m Fraud Linked to Bin Laden' (14 April 2019).

Harris, D, 'The Development of Socio-Legal Studies in the United Kingdom' (1983) *Legal Studies* 3(3), 315–33.

Harvey, J, 'Compliance and Reporting Issues Arising for Financial Institutions from Money Laundering Regulations: A Preliminary Cost Benefit Study' (2004) *Journal of Money Laundering Control* 7(4), 333–46.

Hatchard, J, *Combating Money Laundering in Africa: Dealing with the Problem of PEPs* (Edward Elgar, 2020).

Hawdon, J, 'The Role of Presidential Rhetoric in the Creation of a Moral Panic: Reagan, Bush, and the War on Drugs' (2001) *Deviant behavior* 22(5), 419–45.

Hawley, S, Beizsley, D and Bolton-Jones, J, 'No New Government Investment in the Economic Crime Plan Threatens Delivery' (30 March 2023).

Heathershaw, J, Cooley, A, Mayne, T, Michel, C, Prelec, T, Sharman, J and Soares de Oliveira, R, *The UK's Kleptocracy Problem How Servicing Post-Soviet Elites Weakens the Rule of Law* (Chatham House, 2021).

Helgesson, K and Mörth, U, 'Client Privilege, Compliance and the Rule of Law: Swedish Lawyers and Money Laundering Prevention' (2018) *Crime, Law and Social Change* 69(2), 227–48.

Henn, M, Weinstein, M and Foard, N, *A Critical Introduction to Social Research* (Sage, 2009).

Her Majesty's Inspectorate of Constabulary and Fire & Rescue Services, *Fraud: Time to Choose An Inspection of the Police Response to Fraud* (Her Majesty's Inspectorate of Constabulary, 2019).

Herlin-Karnell, E, 'The Robustness of EU Financial Crimes Legislation: A Critical Review of the EU and UK Anti-Fraud and Money Laundering Scheme' (2017) *European Business Law Review* 28(4), 427–446.

Heywood, P, *Routledge Handbook of Political Corruption* (Routledge, 2015).

Hillman, H, 'Pass or Play: Should Regulators Address the Money Laundering Risks Posed by Cryptocurrencies Themselves or Await Legislative Reform?' (2024) *Journal of Business Law* 4, 301–28.

HM Government, *Beating Crime Plan – Fewer Victims, Peaceful Neighbourhoods, Safe Country* (HM Government, 2021).

—— *CONTEST – The United Kingdom's Strategy for Countering Terrorism 2023* (HM Government, 2023).

—— 'Estate Agents Targeted in Money Laundering Crackdown' (4 March 2019).

—— 'Fraud Sector Charter' (21 October 2021).

—— *Fraud Strategy: Stopping Scams and Protecting the Public* (HM Government, 2023).

—— 'Guidance Code of Practice for Public Authorities Disclosing Information Under Chapters 1, 3 and 5 under Part 5 of the Digital Economy Act 2017' (12 February 2020).

—— 'Guidance Counter-Terrorist Financing' (2 September 2021).

—— 'Home Secretary Launches New Joint Fraud Taskforce' (10 February 2016).

—— 'Joint Fraud Task Force' (17 October 2017).

—— 'Lord Hanson Unveils Ambitious New Approach to Tackling Fraud' (27 March 2025).

—— *National Security Strategy 2025: Security for the British People in a Dangerous World* (HM Government, 2025).

—— *National Security Strategy and Strategic Defence and Security Review 2015 A Secure and Prosperous United Kingdom* (HM Government, 2015).

—— 'Online Fraud Charter' (30 November 2023).
—— *Plan for Change – Milestones for Mission-Led Government* (HM Government, 2024).
—— *Policy Paper Economic Crime and Corporate Transparency Act: Economic Crime in the UK* (HM Government, 2024).
—— *Report of the Official Account of the Bombings in London on 7th July 2005* (House of Commons, 2005).
—— 'Report Benefit Fraud' (n/d).
—— 'Report Tax Fraud or Avoidance to HMRC' (n/d).
—— *Response to Law Commission Review of the SARs Regime* (HM Government, 2024).
—— *Serious and Organised Crime Strategy* (HM Government, 2013).
—— *Serious and Organised Crime Strategy* (HM Government, 2018).
—— 'Student Finance' (n/d).
—— *The Strategic Defence Review 2025 – Making Britain Safer: Secure at Home, Strong Abroad* (HM Government, 2025).
—— *UK Anti-Corruption Plan* (HM Government, 2014).
—— 'UK Takes Top Spot in Fight against Dirty Money' (7 December 2018).
—— 'Your Responsibilities under Money Laundering Supervision' (23 May 2025).
HM Government and UK Finance, *Economic Crime Plan 2019-2022* (HM Government and UK Finance, 2019).
—— *Economic Crime Plan 2 2023-2026* (HM Government and UK Finance, 2023).
—— *Economic Crime Plan: Statement of Progress* (HM Government and UK Finance, 2021).
HM Revenue & Customs, 'HMRC Confirms HSBC Suisse Bank Data Can Now Be Shared' (25 February 2015).
HM Treasury, *Anti-Money Laundering Strategy* (HM Treasury, 2004).
—— 'Call for Information: Anti-Money Laundering Supervisory Regime' (16 March 2017).
—— *Improving the Effectiveness of the Money Laundering Regulations Consultation Response* (HM Treasury, 2024).
—— *Improving the Effectiveness of the Money Laundering Regulations Consultation Response* (HM Treasury, 2025).
—— *Policy Paper: Anti-Money Laundering and Counter-Terrorist Financing: Supervision Report: 2023-24* (HM Treasury, 2025).
—— *Post-Implementation Review of the Oversight of Professional Body Anti-Money Laundering and Counter Terrorist Financing Supervision Regulations 2017* (HM Treasury, 2022).
—— *Reform of the Anti-Money Laundering and Counter Terrorism Financing Supervisory Regime Consultation* (HM Treasury, 2023).
—— *Review of the UK's AML/CFT Regulatory and Supervisory Regime* (HM Treasury, 2022).
—— 'UK Establishes New Money Laundering Watchdog' (21 December 2017).
HM Treasury and Home Office, *National Risk Assessment of Money Laundering and Terrorist Financing 2017* (HM Treasury and Home Office, 2017).
—— National Risk Assessment of Money Laundering and Terrorist Financing 2025 (HM Treasury and Home Office, 2025).
—— *UK National Risk Assessment of Money Laundering and Terrorist Financing* (HM Treasury and Home Office, 2015).
HM Treasury Select Committee, *Fixing LIBOR: Some Preliminary Findings* (HM Treasury Select Committee, 2012).
Hock, B, *Extraterritoriality and International Bribery: A Collective Action Perspective* (Routledge, 2022).
Home Affairs Committee, Oral Evidence: Fraud, HC 125 Wednesday 28 February 2024.
—— Oral Evidence: Fraud, HC 125, Wednesday 17 January 2024, James Daley.
Home Affairs Select Committee, 'Home Affairs Committee Launches Inquiry into Fraud' (14 September 2023).
—— 'Letter to the Home Secretary' (23 May 2024).
Home Office, *Action Plan for Anti-Money-Laundering and Counter-Terrorist Finance: Consultation on Legislative Proposals Government Response* (Home Office, 2016).

—— 'Call for Information' (n/d).
—— 'Circular 007/2018: Criminal Finances Act: Sharing Information within the Regulated Sector' (1 February 2018).
—— *Data Sharing for the Prevention of Fraud – Code of Practice for Public Authorities Disclosing Information to a Specified Anti-Fraud Organisations Under Sections 68 to 72 of the Serious Crime Act 2007* (Home Office, 2015).
—— *Financial Orders under Part 8 of the Proceeds of Crime Act 2002* (Home Office, 2015).
—— *Home Office Circular 47/2004: Priorities for the Investigation of Fraud Cases* (Home Office, 2004).
—— *Home Office Circular: Criminal Finances Act 2017 Money Laundering: Sharing of Information within the Regulated Sector Sections 339ZB-339ZG* (Home Office, 2018).
—— 'Home Secretary on the Work of the Financial Sector Forum: Theresa May Announces Launch of Joint Money Laundering Intelligence Taskforce' (24 February 2015).
—— *Legislation against Terrorism – A Consultation Paper* (Home Office, 1998).
—— 'Policy Paper – Response to Law Commission Review of the SARs Regime' (12 February 2024).
—— 'Report on Immigration or Customs Crime' (n/d).
—— *Report on the Operation in 2004 of the Terrorism Act 2000* (Home Office, 2004).
—— Research and Analysis – Experiences of Victims of Fraud and Cybercrime (Home Office, 2025).
—— 'The Strategic Policing Requirement 2023' (23 June 2023).
Home Office and HM Treasury, *Action Plan for Anti-Money Laundering and Counter-Terrorist Finance* (Home Office and HM Treasury, 2016).
—— *Joint Home Office and HM Treasury Action Plan for Anti-Money Laundering and Counter-Terrorist Finance* (Home Office and HM Treasury, 2016).
—— *National Risk Assessment of Money Laundering and Terrorist Financing 2025* (Home Office and HM Treasury, 2025).
Home Office and Ministry of Justice, *Policy Paper Criminal Justice Bill: Serious Crime* (Home Office and Ministry of Justice, 2024).
Hong Kong Monetary Authority, 'Fraud and Money Laundering Intelligence Taskforce Launched' (26 May 2017).
Horder, J and Alldridge, P, *Modern Bribery Law: Comparative Perspectives* (Cambridge University Press, 2013).
Horgan, J and Taylor, M, 'Playing the 'Green Card' – Financing the Provisional IRA: Part 1 (1999) *Terrorism and Political Violence* 11(2), 1–38.
Horgan, J and Taylor, M, 'Playing the "Green Card" – Financing the Provisional IRA: Part 2' (2003) *Terrorism and Political Violence* 15(2), 1–60.
House of Commons Committee of Public Accounts, *Local Authority Administered COVID Support Schemes in England* (House of Commons Committee of Public Accounts, 2023).
House of Commons Foreign Affairs Committee, *Moscow's Gold: Russian Corruption in the UK* (House of Commons Foreign Affairs Committee, 2018).
House of Commons Home Affairs Committee, *Policing the Future* (House of Commons Home Affairs Committee, 2018).
House of Commons Intelligence Security Committee, Russia (House of Commons Intelligence Security Committee, 2020).
House of Commons Justice Committee, *Fraud and the Justice System* (House of Commons Justice Committee, 2023).
—— *Fraud and the Justice System: Government Response to the Committee's Fourth Report of Session 2022–23 Sixth Special Report of Session 2022–23* (House of Commons Justice Committee, 2023).
House of Commons Treasury Committee, *Economic Crime – Anti-Money Laundering Supervision and Sanctions Implementation* (House of Commons Treasury Committee, 2019).
—— *Economic Crime – Anti-Money Laundering Supervision and Sanctions Implementation Twenty-Seventh Report of Session 2017–19* (House of Commons Treasury Committee, 2019).
—— *Economic Crime: Consumer View* (House of Commons Treasury Committee: 2019).
—— *Economic Crime Eleventh Report of Session 2021–22* (House of Commons Treasury Committee, 2022).

House of Lords Fraud Act 2006 and Digital Fraud Committee, *Fighting Fraud: Breaking the Chain* (House of Lords Fraud Act 2006 and Digital Fraud Committee, 2022).

Hufngael, S and King, C, 'Anti-Money Laundering Regulation and the Art Market' (2020) *Legal Studies* 40(1), 131–50.

Hulsse, R, 'Creating Demand for Global Governance: The Making of a Global Money-Laundering Problem' (2007) *Global Society* 21(2), 155–78.

Hutchinson, S and O'Malley, P, 'A Crime–Terror Bexus? Thinking on Some of the Links between Terrorism and Criminality' (2007) *Studies in Conflict Terrorism* 30(12), 1095–1107.

Hutchinson, T and Duncan, N, 'Defining and Describing What We Do: Doctrinal Legal Research' (2012) *Deakin Law Review* 17(1), 83–119.

Hyde, J, 'Birmingham Firm Fined More than £27,000 for AML Failings' (7 January 2025).

—— 'Compliance Officers Overwhelmed as SRA Dishes out £77K Fine' (4 June 2025).

—— 'Firm Fined £173,000 for Inadequate Checks on Foreign Client' (25 July 2025).

—— 'Four More Firms Hit with SRA Fines for AML Failings' (4 February 025).

—— 'SDT Fines Firm £120k for 15-year Breaches of AML Regulations' (19 May 2025).

—— 'Yorkshire Firm Fined £36,000 over Money Laundering Failings' (22 April 2025).

Hyde, J and Castro, B, 'Clyde & Co Fined £500,000 after Admitting Due Diligence Failure' (11 January 2024).

I

Information Commissioner's Office, 'Data Sharing: A Code of Practice' (n/d).

—— 'Legitimate Interests' (n/d).

—— *Sharing Personal Data with Law Enforcement Authorities* (Information Commissioner's Office, 2023).

Institute for Fiscal Studies, *Police Workforce and Funding in England and Wales* (Institute for Fiscal Studies, 2017).

Institute of Economic Affairs, *Debanked – The Economic and Social Consequences of Anti-Money Laundering Regulation* (Institute of Economic Affairs, 2024).

Intelligence and Security Committee, *The 2017 Attacks: What Needs to Change?* (Intelligence and Security Committee, 2018).

International Consortium of Investigative Journalists, 'Banking Giant HSBC Sheltered Murky Cash Linked to Dictators and Arms Dealers' (*International Consortium for Investigative Journalists*, 8 February 2015).

International Monetary Fund, 'Anti-Money Laundering/Combating the Financing of Terrorism – Topics (n/d).

—— *Financial System Abuse, Financial Crime and Money Laundering – Background Paper* (International Monetary Fund, February 2001).

—— *International Cooperation in Combating the Financing of Terrorism. Good Practices to Enhance Effectiveness* (International Monetary Fund, 2022).

—— 'Money Laundering: The Importance of International Countermeasures – Address by Michel Camdessus' (10 February 1998).

International Public Sector Fraud Forum, *Guide to Understanding the Total Impact of Fraud* (Cabinet Office and Commonwealth Fraud Prevention Centre, 2020).

Irwin, S, Kim-Kwang, A, Choo, R and Liu, L, 'Modelling of Money Laundering and Terrorism Financing Typologies' (2012) *Journal of Money Laundering Control* 15(3), 316–35.

J

Jarvis, L and Lister, M, *Anti-terrorism, Citizenship and Security* (Manchester University Press, 2015).

Jeewon, K, 'Making State Sponsors of Terrorism Pay: A Separation of Powers Discourse under the Foreign Sovereign Immunities Act' (2004) *Berkeley Journal of International Law* 22, 513–40.

Jensen, N, 'Creating an Environment in Australia Hostile to Money Laundering and Terrorism Financing: A Changing Role for AUSTRAC' (2008) *Macquarie Journal of Business Law* 5, 93–111.

Jensen, N and Png, C, 'Implementation of the FATF 40+ 9 Recommendations: A Perspective from Developing Countries' (2011) *Journal of Money Laundering Control* 14(2), 110–20.

Jeremie, J, 'Known Risk in a World of Unknown Threats: The Character and Implications of Risk in the Context of Economically Motivated Crime' (2012) *Company Lawyer* 33(8), 231–34.

John, J and Garrod, M, 'Legacies of the Troubles: The Links between Organized Crime and Terrorism in Northern Ireland' (2022) *Studies in Conflict & Terrorism* 45(5-6), 389–428.

Johnson, D, *Competition Law and Financial Crime: A Comparative Analysis of International Responses to Market Manipulation* (Routledge, 2025).

Johnson, J, 'Is the Global Financial System AML/CTF Prepared?' (2008) *Journal of Financial Crime* 15(1), 7–21.

Joint Money Laundering Steering Group, *Prevention of Money Laundering/Combating the Financing of Terrorism – Guidance for UK Financial Service Sector Part 1* (Joint Money Laundering Steering Group, 2006).

—— *Prevention of Money Laundering/Combating the Financing of Terrorism – Guidance for UK Financial Service Sector Part II – Sectorial Guidance* (Joint Money Laundering Steering Group, 2006).

—— *Prevention of Money Laundering/Combating Terrorist Financing – Guidance for the UK Financial Sector* (Joint Money Laundering Steering Group, 2023).

Justice Committee Oral Evidence: Fraud and the Justice System, HC 961, Tuesday 22 March 2022.

K

Keatinge, T, 'Terror on the Cheap: Financing Lone Actor and Small Cell Attacks' (17 August 2015).

—— 'What's the Point of the Financial Action Task Force Standards?' (*RUSI*, 7 August 2024).

Keatinge, T, Moiseienko, A, Keen, F, Artingstall, D and Wood, H, *No Rest for the Wicked Driving Change in the UK's Post-FATF Evaluation AML Regime* (RUSI, 2019).

Keatinge, T, Reimer, S and Chase, I, 'Good Intentions: The FATF Faces Its Own Unintended Consequences' (*RUSI*, 5 August 2021).

Kebbell, S, *Anti-Money Laundering Compliance and the Legal Profession* (Routledge, 2022).

Kemal, M, 'Anti-Money Laundering Regulations and its Effectiveness' (2014) *Journal of Money Laundering Control* 17(4), 416–27.

Kempa, M, 'Combating White-Collar Crime in Canada: Serving Victim Needs and Market Integrity' (2010) *Journal of Financial Crime* 17(2), 251–64.

Kerry, J and Brown, H, *The BCCI Affair A Report to the Committee on Foreign Relations United States Senate* (1992) 102d Congress 2d Session Senate Print 102–14.

Khah, Z, *Counter-Terrorism Financing and Iran* (Routledge, 2023).

Khouny, H and Drissi, H, 'Addressing the Challenges of Weak AML Measures in Developing Countries: Key Concerns of FATF and Consequences of Grey Listing' (2025) *Multidisciplinary Science Journal* 7(3).

Kida, M and Paetzold, S, *The Impact of Gray-Listing on Capital Flows: An Analysis using Machine Learning* (International Monetary Fund, 2021).

Killick, M and Parody, D, 'Implementing AML/CFT Measures that Address the Risks and not Tick Boxes' (2007) *Journal of Financial Regulation and Compliance* (2007) 15(2) (2), 210–216.

Kleinman, M, 'FCA Ends Probe Into HSBC Swiss Tax Affair' (4 January 2016).

KPMG, 'Global Anti-Money Laundering Survey' (2014).

Krambia-Kapardis, M, *Corporate Fraud and Corruption: A Holistic Approach to Preventing Financial Crises* (Palgrave MacMillan, 2016).

L

Lander, S, *Review of the Suspicious Activity Reports Regime* (Serious Organised Crime Agency, 2006).

Latimer, P, 'Australia: Australian Transaction Reports and Analysis Centre (AUSTRAC)' (1995) *Journal of Financial Crime* 3(3), 306–307.

Law Commission, *Anti-Money Laundering: The SARs Regime Consultation Paper* (Law Commission, 2018).

——*Anti-Money Laundering: The SARs Regime Report* (Law Commission, 2019) at 174.

Law Society Gazette, 'Revealed: Fines Mount up as SRA Cracks Down on AML Breaches' (n/d).

Lemieux, F and Prates, F, 'Entrepreneurial Terrorism: Financial Strategies, Business Opportunities, and Ethical Issues' (2011) *Police Practice and Research* 12(5), 368–82.

Leong, A, 'Chasing Dirty Money: Domestic and International Measures against Money Laundering' (2007) *Journal of Money Laundering Control* 10(2), 140–56.

Levi, M, 'Following the Criminal and Terrorist Money Trails' in P van Duyne, K Von Lampe and J Newell (eds), *Criminal Finances and Organising Crime in Europe* (Wolf Legal Publishers, 2003) 105–22.

—— 'Lawyers as Money Laundering Enablers? An Evolving and Contentious Relationship' (2022) *Global Crime* 23(2), 126–47.

——'Organised Fraud' in L Paoli (eds), *The Oxford Handbook of Organised Crime* (Oxford University Press, 2014) 460–81.

——*Regulating Fraud White-Collar Crime and the Criminal Process* (Routledge, 2013).

Levi, M, Burrows, J, Fleming, M and Hopkins, M, *The Nature, Extent and Economic Impact of Fraud in the UK* (Association of Chief Police Officers, 2007).

Levi, M, Doig, A, Gundur, R, Wal, D and Williams, M, 'Cyberfraud and the Implications for Effective Risk-Based Responses: Themes from UK Research' (2017) *Crime Law Social Change* 67, 77–96.

Levi, M and Gelemerova, L, 'The Anti-Money Laundering Architecture of the United Kingdom' in B Vogel and J Maillart (eds), *National and International Anti-Money Laundering Law Developing the Architecture of Criminal Justice, Regulation and Data Protection* (Intersentia, 2020) 641–792.

Levi, M and Pithouse, A, 'The Victims of Fraud' in D Downes (eds), *Unravelling Criminal Justice* (Palgrave Macmillan, 1992) 229–46.

Levi, M and Reuter, P, 'Money Laundering' (2006) *Crime and Justice* 34(1), 289–375.

Levi, M, Reuter, P and Halliday, T, 'Can the AML System Be Evaluated without Better Data?' (2018) *Crime, Law and Social Change* 69, 307–28.

Lewis, A, Pretorius, R and Radmore, E, 'Outsourcing in the Financial Services Sector' (2013) *Compliance Officer Bulletin* 106, 1–34.

LexisNexis Risk Solutions, *Cutting the Costs of AML Compliance* (LexisNexis Risk Solutions, 2021).

—— *True Costs of Financial Crime Compliance* (LexisNexis Risk Solutions, 2024).

Lipson, F, 'Scam Victims Ignored by Police Fraud Reporting System' (*Which?* 27 September 2019).

Littrell, C, 'Economic and Demographic Biases in FATF Mutual Evaluation Results' in D Goldbarsht and L de Koker (eds) *Financial Crime and the Law: Identifying and Mitigating Risks* (Springer, 2024) 191–224.

Lloyds Banking Group, 'Two-Thirds of all Online Shopping Scams Now Start on Facebook and Instagram' (30 March 2023).

London Bridge Inquests, *Inquests Concerning the Attackers Day 6A* (9 July 2019).

Lord Colville of Culross, *Review of the Operation of the Prevention of Terrorism (Temporary Provisions) Act 1984* (Cm 264, 1987).

Lord Hanson Minister of State, 'Letter to Dame Karen Bradley MP Chair, Home Affairs Select Committee' (31 October 2024).

Lord Loyd of Berwick, *Inquiry into Legislation Against Terrorism* (Cm 3420, 1996).

Lucas, S, 'Ukraine War: EU Parliament Names Russia a "State Sponsor of Terrorism" – but it Won't Stop the Missiles' (24 November 2022).

M

Mackey, C and Savil J, *Fraud: A Review of the National 'Lead Force' Responsibilities of the City of London Police and the Effectiveness of Investigations in the UK* (City of London, 2020).

Makgothu, T, 'Building Legislative Frameworks: Domestication of the Financial Action Task Force' (2020) *European Journal of Law Reform* 22(2) 209, 210.

Manacorda, S and Grasso, C, *Fighting Fraud and Corruption at the World Bank: A Critical Analysis of the Sanctions* (Springer, 2018).

Marsh, C, 'Putin's Playbook: The Development of Russian Tactics, Operations, and Strategy from Chechnya to Ukraine' in A Farhadi, M Grzegorzewski and A Masys (eds), *The Great Power Competition Volume 5 The Russian Invasion of Ukraine and Implications for the Central Region* (Springer, 2023) at 161–83.

Mbaku, J, 'Counter-Terrorism Laws and Human Rights in African Countries' (2021) *Washington University Global Studies Law Review* 20, 863–1020.

McDermott, T, 'Enforcement and Credible Deterrence in the FCA' (18 June 2013).

Mekpor, E, Aboagye, A and Welbeck, J, 'The Determinants of Anti-Money Laundering Compliance among the Financial Action Task Force (FATF) Member States' (2018) *Journal of Financial Regulation and Compliance* 26(3), 442–59.

Mendick, R, 'Manchester Suicide Bomber Used Student Loan and Benefits to Fund Terror Plot' *The Telegraph* (27 May 2017).

Mike Penning MP, 14 December 2015.

Monetary Authority of Singapore, 'CAD and MAS Partner Industry Stakeholders to Fight Financial Crimes' (24 April 2017).

Morais, H, 'Fighting International Crime and its Financing: The Importance of Following a Coherent Global Strategy Based on the Rule of Law' (2005) *Villanova Law Review* 50(3), 583–644.

Morgan-Bentley, M, 'Action Fraud Scrapped after Times Expose' *The Times* (28 July 2021).

Mugarura, N, 'Customer Due Diligence (CDD) Mandate and the Propensity of its Application as a Global AML Paradigm' (2014) *Journal of Money Laundering Control* 17(1), 76–95.

N

Nance, M, 'Re-thinking FATF: An Experimentalist Interpretation of the Financial Action Task Force' (2018) *Crime, Law and Social Change*, 69, 131–52.

Nanyun, NM and Nasiri, A, 'Role of FATF on Financial Systems of Countries: Successes and Challenges (2021) *Journal of Money Laundering Control* 24(2), 234–45.

National Audit Office, *Implementing Employment Support Schemes in Response to the COVID-19 Pandemic* (National Audit Office, 2020).

—— *Online Fraud* (National Audit Office, 2017).

—— *The Asset Recovery Agency* (National Audit Office, 2007).

National Commission on the Causes of the Financial and Economic Crisis in the United States, *The Financial Crisis Inquiry Report* (National Commission on the Causes of the Financial and Economic Crisis in the United States, 2011).

National Crime Agency, '10 Year Anniversary of the UK's Public Private Partnerships' (17 July 2025).

—— 'Fraud' (n/d).

—— 'Ground Breaking Public Private Partnership Launched to Identify Criminality using Banking Data' (26 July 2024).

—— *National Crime Agency Annual Plan 2024-2025* (National Crime Agency, 2025).

—— 'National Economic Crime Centre' (n/d).

—— *National Strategic Assessment Serious and Organised Crime* (National Crime Agency, 2018).

—— *SARs Annual Report 2017* (National Crime Agency, 2017).

—— *SARs Annual Report 2018* (National Crime Agency, 2018).

—— *SARs Annual Report 2019* (National Crime Agency, 2019).

—— *SARs Annual Report 2020* (National Crime Agency, 2020).

—— *SARs in Action – Issue 1* (National Crime Agency, 2019.

—— 'Suspicious Activity Reports' (n/d).

—— *Suspicious Activity Report 2022* (National Crime Agency, 2023).

—— *Suspicious Activity Report 2024* (National Crime Agency, 2025).

—— *The Suspicious Activity Reports Regime Annual Report 2013* (National Crime Agency, 2013).

—— *The Suspicious Activity Reports Regime Annual Report 2014* (National Crime Agency, 2014).

——, *The Suspicious Activity Reports Regime Annual Report 2015* (National Crime Agency, 2015).

—— 'UKFIU Operations Teams (n/d).

National Fraud Authority, *Annual Fraud Indicator 2011* (National Fraud Authority, 2011).

—— *Annual Fraud Indicator 2012* (National Fraud Authority, 2012).

—— *National Fraud Authority Annual Fraud Indicator* (National Fraud Authority, 2010).

National Police Chief's Council, *Common Law Police Disclosures Provisions to Supersede the Notifiable Occupations Scheme* (National Police Chief's Council, 2017).

National Trading Standards, '19 million Lose Money to Scams but Fewer than a Third Report' (23 October 2023).

Nepoleoni, L, 'Terrorism Financing in Europe' in H Trinkunas and J Giraldo, *Terrorism Financing and State Responses* (Stanford University Press, 2007).

Neumann, P, 'Don't Follow the Money: The Problem with the War on Terrorist Financing' (2017) *Foreign Affairs* 96(4), 93–102.

Nizzero, M, 'The UK's Economic Crime Plan 2: Progress, Pitfalls and Prospects' (26 March 2024).

Normark, M and Ranstorp, M, *Understanding Terrorist Finance. Modus Operandi and National CTF Regimes* (Swedish Defence University, 2015) at 34–35.

O

Ofcom, 'Research Supporting Scams Statements 2022' (5–7 August 2022).

Office for National Statistics, 'Crime in England and Wales: Year Ending September 2019'.

—— 'Crime in England and Wales: Year Ending December 2020'.

—— 'Crime in England and Wales: Year Ending December 2022'.

—— 'Crime in England and Wales: Year Ending December 2023'.

—— 'Crime in England and Wales: Year Ending June 2024'.

—— 'Crime in England and Wales: Year Ending September 2024' (30 January 2025).

—— 'Crime in England and Wales: Year Ending December 2024' (24 April 2025).

Office for Professional Body Anti-Money Laundering Supervision and Financial Conduct Authority, *Sourcebook for Professional Body Anti-Money Laundering Supervisors* (Office for Professional Body Anti-Money Laundering Supervision and Financial Conduct Authority, 2023).

Office of Financial Sanctions Implementation, 'About Us' (n/d).

Organisation for Economic Co-operation and Development (OECD), *Global Forum on Transparency and Exchange of Information for Tax Purposes, Peer Review of the Automatic Exchange of Financial Account Information* (OECD, 2021).

OECD Agreement on Exchange of Information in Tax Matters (Organisation for Economic Co-operation and Development: 2002).

—— 'United Kingdom' (n/d).

Oztas, B, Deniz, C, Festus, A, Marcin, B, Gokhan, A and Huseyin, D, 'Transaction Monitoring in Anti-Money Laundering: A Qualitative Analysis and Points of View from Industry' (2024) *Future Generation Computer Systems* 159, 161–71.

P

Palmer, A, *Countering Economic Crime: A Comparative Analysis* (Routledge, 2017).

Parliamentary Commissioners for Administration, *The Barlow Clowes Affair* (Parliamentary Commissioners for Administration, 1989).

Pasculli, L and Ryder, N, *Corruption in the Global Era: Causes, Sources and Forms of Manifestation* (Routledge, 2019).

Payments Association, *Data Sharing to Prevent Economic Crime: Why You Can Now Share Data with Confidence* (The Payments Association, 2023).

Peat, R and Mason, I, 'Credible Deterrence in Action: The FSA Brings a Series of Cases against Traders' (2009) *Company Lawyer* 30(9), 278–79.

Permanent Subcommittee on Investigations of the Committee on Governmental Affairs, *The Role of the Board of Directors in Enron's Collapse* (Permanent Subcommittee on Investigations of the Committee on Governmental Affairs, 2002).

Pijper, T, 'The Collapse of Polly Peck International' in T Pijper (ed), 'Creative Accounting. Finance and Capital Markets Series' (Palgrave Macmillan, 1996) 141–59.

Pisa, M, *Does the Financial Action Task Force (FATF) Help or Hinder Financial Inclusion? A Study of FATF Mutual Evaluation Reports* (Center for Global Development, 2019).

Pol, R, 'Anti-Money Laundering Effectiveness: Assessing Outcomes or Ticking Boxes?' (2018) *Journal of Money Laundering Control* 21(2), 215–30.

Police Scotland, 'Online Reporting Form' (n/d).

Police.UK, 'Action Fraud' (n/d).

Policy Exchange, *Fighting Fraud and Financial Crime: A New Architecture for the Investigation and Prosecution of Serious Fraud, Corruption and Financial Market Crimes* (Policy Exchange, 2010).

—— *What Do We Want from the Next Prime Minister? A Series of Policy Proposals for New Leadership: Crime & Policing – A Force Fit for the Future* (Policy Exchange, 2022).

Pontes, R, Lewis N, McFarlane P and Craig, P, 'Anti-Money Laundering in the United Kingdom: New Directions for a More Effective Regime' (2022) *Journal of Money Laundering Control* 25(2), 401–13.

Prenzler, T, 'What Works in Fraud Prevention: A Review of Real-World Intervention Projects' (2020) *Journal of Criminological Research, Policy and Practice* 6(1), 83–96.

Public Accounts Committee, *Covid-19: Bounce Back Loan Scheme* (Public Accounts Committee, 2020).

—— *Oral Evidence: Increasing the Effectiveness of Tax Collection: A Stocktake of Progress Since 2010* (11 February 2015, HC 2014-15, 974-I).

—— *Oral Evidence: Tax Avoidance and Evasion: HSBC* (23 March 2015, HC 2014-15 1095-I).

Public Sector Fraud Authority, 'About Us' (n/d).

—— *National Fraud Initiative Strategy* (Public Sector Fraud Authority, 2025).

PwC, *PwC EMEA AML Survey 2024 – UK Insights into Effectiveness* (PwC, 2024).

R

Raphael, M, *Bribery: Law and Practice Paperback* (Oxford University Press, 2016).

Rekawek, K, *Russian State Terrorism and State Sponsorship of Terrorism* (International Centre for Counter Terrorism, 2024).

Reynoso-Serna, F, Evans, A, Smith, F, Brown, E and Davis, S, *Online Fraud: What Does the Public Think?* (Crest, 2023).

Richard, A, *Fighting Terrorist Financing: Transatlantic Co-Operation and International Institutions* (Centre for Transatlantic Relations, John Hopkins University, 2005).

Rider, B, 'Taking Money Launderers to the Cleaners: Part 2' (1996) *Private Client Business* 3, 201–10.

Ridley, N, *Terrorist Financing: The Failure of Counter Measures* (Edward Elgar, 2012).

Robert, K, *Case Study Research and Applications: Design and Methods* (Sage, 2013).

Rose, C, *International Anti-Corruption Norms: Their Creation and Influence on Domestic Legal Systems* (Oxford University Press, 2015) 177–216.

Rose, K, 'De-Risking or Re-Contracting: The Risk Dilemma of EU Money Laundering Regulation' (2020) *The Journal of Risk Finance* 21(4), 445–58.

Rosenthal, J, 'For-Profit Terrorism: The Rise of Armed Entrepreneurs' (2008) *Studies in Conflict & Terrorism* 31(6), 481–49.

Roskill, *Fraud Trials Committee Report* (HMSO, 1986).

Rotman, M, *Regulating Fraud Across Borders: Internationalised Criminal Law Protection of Capital Markets* (Hart, 2021).

Royal United Services Institute, 'Economic Crime Plan Online Tracker' (n/d).

—— 'FRA0060 Written Evidence Submitted by the Royal United Services Institute (RUSI)' (October 2023).

—— 'Getting the Economic Crime Plan Done: Why Economic Crime Matters for Johnson's "Global Britain"' (13 January 2020).

—— *No Rest for the Wicked: Driving Change in the UK's Post-FATF Evaluation of the UK AML Regime* (Royal United Services Institute, 2019).

Royal United Services Institute Centre for Financial Crime and Security Studies (ECR0018) (May 2018).

Rudner, M, 'Hizbullah Terrorism Finance: Fund-Raising and Money-Laundering' (2010) *Studies in Conflict & Terrorism* 33(8), 700–15.

Ryder, N, 'Cryptoassets, Social Media Platforms and Defence against Terrorism Financing Suspicious Activity Reports: a step into the regulatory unknown' (2020) *Journal of Business Law* 8, 668–93.

—— *Financial Crime and Policy in the 21st Century – Law and Policy* (Edward Elgar, 2011).

—— 'Is it Time to Reform the Counter-Terrorist Financing Reporting Obligations? On the EU and the UK System' (2018) *German Law Journal* 19(5), 1169–89.

—— *Money Laundering – An Endless Cycle? A Comparative Analysis of the Anti-Money Laundering Policies in the United States of America, the United Kingdom, Australia and Canada* (Routledge, 2012).

—— 'Out with the Old and … in with the Old? A Critical Review of the Financial War on Terrorism on the Islamic State of Iraq and Levant' (2018) *Studies in Conflict and Terrorism* 41(2), 79–95.

—— *The Financial War on Terror: A Review of Counter-Terrorist Financing Strategies Since 2001* (Routledge, 2015).

—— 'To Report or not to Report? An Analysis of the Relationship between Defence against Terrorism Financing Suspicious Activity Reports and Fraud in the United Kingdom' in L de Koker and D Goldbarsht (eds), *Financial Crime, Law and Governance – Navigating Challenges in Different Contexts* (Springer, 2024) 169–202.

Ryder, N, Bourton, S, Hillman, H and Hall, D, 'Higher Education Institutions and the Anti-Money Laundering and Counter-Terrorism Financing Regulations' (2023) *Criminal Law Review* 9, 560–80.

Ryder, N and Pasculli, L, *Corruption, Integrity and the Law: Global Regulatory Challenges* (Routledge, 2020).

S

Salter, M and Mason, J, *Writing Law Dissertations: An Introduction and Guide to the Conduct of Legal Research* (Pearson, 2007).

Sansonetti, R, 'The Mutual Evaluation Process: A Methodology of Increasing Importance at International Level' (2000) *Journal of Financial Crime* 7(3), 218–26.

Schiavo, G, 'The Single Supervisory Mechanism (SSM) and the EU Anti-Money Laundering Framework Compared: Governance, Rules, Challenges and Opportunities' (2022) *Journal of Banking Regulation* 23(1), 91–105.

Schneider, S, 'Testing the Limits of Solicitor-Client Privilege: Lawyers, Money Laundering, and Suspicious Transaction Reporting' (2006) *Journal of Money Laundering Control* 9(1), 27–47.

Schoch, K, 'Case Study Research. Research Design and Methods: An Applied Guide for the Scholar-Practitioner' 31.1 (2020): 245–58.

Scott, B and McGoldrick, M, 'Financial Intelligence and Financial Investigation: Opportunities and Challenges' (2018) *Journal of Policing, Intelligence and Counter Terrorism* 13(3), 301–15.

Securities and Exchange Commission Office, *Investigation of the SEC's Response to Concerns Regarding Robert Allen Stanford's Alleged Ponzi Scheme* (Securities and Exchange Commission Office, 2010).

Securities and Exchange Commission Office of Investigations, *Investigation of Failure of the SEC to Uncover Bernard Madoff's Ponzi Scheme* (Securities and Exchange Commission Office of Investigations, 2009).

See den Boer, E 'Countering Criminal Facilitation Through Public–Private Cooperation in The Netherlands' in G Jacobs I Suojanen, K Horton and P Bayerl (eds), *International Security Management New Solutions to Complexity* (Springer, 2021) at 463–76.

Serious Fraud Office, 'Serious or Complex Fraud, including Bribery and Corruption' (n/d).

Serious Organised Crime Agency, *The Suspicious Activity Reports Regime Annual Report 2010* (Serious Organised Crime Agency, 2010).

—— *The Suspicious Activity Reports Regime Annual Report 2011* (Serious Organised Crime Agency, 2011).

—— *The Suspicious Activity Reports Regime Annual Report 2012* (Serious Organised Crime Agency, 2012).

Shahin, WN, El-Achkar, E and Shehab, R, 'The Monetary Impact of Regulating Banking and Financial Sectors by FATF on Non-Cooperative Countries and Territories' (2012) *Journal of Banking Regulation* 13(1), 63–72.

Sharman, JC, *The Money Laundry: Regulating Criminal Finance in the Global Economy* (Cornell University Press, 2011).

Shehu, A, 'Promoting Financial Inclusion for Effective Anti-Money Laundering and Counter Financing of Terrorism (AML/CFT)' (2012) *Crime, Law and Social Change* 57(3), 305–23.

Silke, A, 'In Defence of the Realm: Financing Loyalist Terrorism in Northern Ireland – Part One: Extortion and Blackmail' (1998) *Studies in Conflict & Terrorism* 21(4), 331–61.

Simser, J, 'Money Laundering: Emerging Threats and Trends' (2012) *Journal of Money Laundering Control* 16(1), 41–54.

Skidmore, M, Ramm, JU, Goldstraw-White, J, Barrett, C, Barleaza, S, Muir and Gill, M, *More than Just a Number: Improving the Police Response to Victims of Fraud* (Police Foundation, 2018).

Smith, F, 'New Fraud Strategy: A Moment for Bold Reform Insights Perspective' (17 April 2025).

Smith, F, Roberts, M, Davis, S, Evans, A and Murray, A, *Behind the Screen: Perceptions and Experiences of Online Fraud Victimization* (Crest, 2024).

Social Market Foundation, *Fraud is now Britain's Dominant Crime, but Policing has Failed to Keep Up* (Social Market Foundation, 2022).

—— Written Evidence (FDF0026) 21 April 2022.

Solicitors Disciplinary Tribunal, Case No. 12639-2024, *Solicitors Regulation Authority Ltd v Simpson Thacher & Bartlett* (12 March 2025).

—— '*Solicitors Regulation Authority Ltd v Rory Peter Heddle Fordyce*' (25 July 2025).

Solicitors Regulation Authority, 'Amphlett Lissimore Bagshaws LLP' (28 July 2025).

—— 'Annual Report by the Money Laundering Reporting Officer (MLRO) for the Year ended 5 April 2024' (5 June 2024).

—— 'Anti-Money Laundering Annual Report 2023-24' (Solicitors Regulation Authority, 2024)

—— 'Ashfords LLP' (15 December 2023).

—— 'Batchelor Sharp' (29 February 2024).

—— 'Burch Phillips & Co' (14 January 2025).

—— 'Commercial Law Practice' (4 December 2025).

—— 'Duffield Harrison LLP' (28 January 2025).

—— 'Gordons Partnership' (27 May 2025).

—— 'J R Jones Solicitors' (10 July 2025).

—— 'OPBAS Confirms that Conveyancing Work is High-Risk' (12 December 2024).

—— 'Richard Kanani & Co Ltd' (18 July 2025).

—— 'Risk Assessment Sectoral Risk Assessment – Anti-Money Laundering and Terrorist Financing' (5 March 2025).

—— 'SRA Code of Conduct for Firms' (n/d).

—— 'SRA Code of Conduct for Solicitors, RELs, RFLs and RSLs' (n/d).

—— 'Steinbergs Solicitors' (14 January 2025).

—— 'Taylor Vinters LLP' (24 July 2025).

—— 'Tolhurst Fisher LLP' (14 August 2024).

—— 'Tyndallwoods Solicitors Limited' (2 December 2024).

Sood, S, 'Socio-Legal Approach to Research' (2023) *Journal of Legal Studies & Research* 9(5), 5–15.

Spotlight on Corruption, *Closing the UK's Economic Crime Enforcement Gap: Proposals for Boosting Resources for UK Law Enforcement to Fight Economic Crime* (Spotlight on Corruption, 2022).

Stanley, R and Buckley, RP, 'Protecting the West, Excluding the Rest: The Impact of the AML/CTF Regime on Financial Inclusion in the Pacific and Potential Responses' (2016) *Melbourne Journal of International Law* 17(1), 83–106.

Stessens, G, *Money Laundering a New International Law Enforcement Model* (Cambridge University Press, 2000).

Strafer, G, 'Money Laundering: The Crime of the '90s' (1989) *American Criminal Law Review* 27, 149–208.

Stubley, P, 'Hashem Abedi Trial: Benefits Claimed by Manchester Bomber's Family were used in Terror Plot Jury Hears' (10 February 2020).

Suella Braverman, MP, Written Statement of House of Commons, 3 May 2023.

Suskind, R, *The One Percent Doctrine* (Simon & Schuster, 2006).

Sutherland, E, 'The White-Collar Criminal' (1940) *American Sociological Review* 5(1), 1–12.
—— *White Collar Crime* (Dryden, 1949).
Sutton, G, 'The New FATF Standards' (2012) *George Mason Journal of International Commercial Law* 4, 68–136.

T

Takáts, E, 'A Theory of "Crying Wolf": The Economics of Money Laundering Enforcement' (2011) *The Journal of Law, Economics, & Organization* 27(1), 32–78.
Tawfick, E, 'SRA Imposes Fines Exceeding £55,000 for Anti-Money Laundering Breaches', (25 April 2024).
Taylor, H, *Broken Record: Latest Round of Legal Sector AML Reports Shows it is Time for Reform* (Spotlight on Corruption, 2025).
The Maxwell Report (Department for Trade and Industry, 2001).
The Police Foundation, *A New Mode of Protection: Redesigning Policing and Public Safety for the 21st Century* (The Police Foundation, 2022).
—— FRA0011.
—— *More than just a Number: Improving the Police Response to Victims of Fraud* (The Police Foundation, 2018).
The Tony Blair Institute, *A New Approach to Serious and Organised Crime in the UK* (The Tony Blair Institute, 2024).
—— *A New International Approach to Beating Serious and Organised Crime* (The Tony Blair Institute, 2025).
The White House, 'Fact Sheet on Terrorist Financing Executive Order' (24 September 2001).
The World Bank, *Reference Guide to Anti-Money Laundering and Combating the Financing of Terrorism* (World Bank, Washington DC, 2006).
Tiwari, M, Gepp, A and Kumar, K, 'A Review of Money Laundering Literature: The State of Research in Key Areas' (2020) *Pacific Accounting Review* 32(2), 271–303.
Toms, S, 'Financial Scandals: A Historical Overview' (2019) *Accounting and Business Research* 49(5), 477–99.
Tosza, S and Voordeckers, O, 'An Anti-Money Laundering Authority for the European Union: A New Center of Gravity in AML Enforcement' (2024) *ERA Forum* 25(3), 405–24.
Transparency International, *Paradise Lost: Ending the UK's Role as a Safe Haven for Corrupt Individuals, their Allies and Assets* (Transparency International UK, 2016).
—— 'UK's "£100 billion" Dirty Money Problem Must be Confronted Following International Review' (7 December 2018).
—— 'Urgent Action Required to Address Gaps in UK Government's Plan to Combat Economic Crime' (12 July 2019).
Treasury Committee, *Economic Crime* (Treasury Committee, 2021).
—— *Economic Crime: Responses to the Committee's Eleventh Report* (Eighth Special Report, Session 2021–22, HC 1261).
—— Oral Evidence: Economic crime, HC 917, Monday 25 January 2021, Graeme Bigger.
—— *Oral Evidence: Financial Conduct Authority* (10 February 2015, HC 2014-15, 1055) Q75 and 76.
Trinkunas, H, 'Financing Terrorism' in E Chenoweth, R English, A Gofas, and S Kalycas, *The Oxford Handbook of Terrorism* (Oxford University Press, 2019).
Turksen, U, *Countering Tax Crime in the European Union: Benchmarking the OECD's Ten Global Principles* (Hart, 2021).
Turksen, U and Erken, E, *Anti-Money Laundering and the Law: Comparative Approaches to Countering Predicate Crimes* (Routledge, 2024).

U

UK Finance, *Annual Fraud Report – the Definitive Overview of Payment Industry Fraud in 2021* (UK Finance, 2022).

—— *Annual Fraud Report – the Definitive Overview of Payment Industry Fraud in 2022* (UK Finance, 2023).
—— *Annual Fraud Report – the Definitive Overview of Payment Industry Fraud in 2023* (UK Finance, 2024).
—— *Annual Report 2024* (UK Finance, 2025).
—— *Fraud – The Facts 2020* (UK Finance, 2021).
—— *Half Year Fraud Report* (UK Finance, 2024).
—— *UK Payment Market Summary* (UK Finance, 2024).
Unger, B. *The Scale and Impacts of Money Laundering* (Edward Elgar, 2007).
Unger, B and Ferwerda, J, *Money Laundering in the Real Estate Sector – Suspicious Properties* (Edward Elgar, 2011).
United Nations Office on Drugs and Crime, *Estimating Illicit Financial Flows Resulting from Drug Trafficking and other Transnational Organized Crime* (United Nations Office on Drugs and Crime, 2009).
United States Department of Justice, 'Elizabeth Holmes Sentenced To More Than 11 Years For Defrauding Theranos Investors Of Hundreds Of Millions' (18 November 2022).
—— 'Justice Department Announces Deferred Prosecution Agreement with HSBC Private Bank (Suisse) SA' (10 December 2019).
—— 'Samuel Bankman-Fried Sentenced to 25 Years for His Orchestration of Multiple Fraudulent Schemes' (28 March 2024).
United States Department of Treasury, *Action Plan: Progress Report on Combating the Financing of Terrorism* (United States Department of Treasury, 2002).
—— *National Terrorist Financing Risk Assessment 2015* (United Stated Department of Treasury, 2015).

V

Victim Support, October 2023.
Vittori, J, *The Evolution of Terrorism Resourcing* (Palgrave Macmillan, 2011).
Vranken, J, 'Methodology of Legal Doctrinal Research' in M Van Hoecke (eds) *Methodologies of Legal Research. Which Kind of Method for What Kind of Discipline* (Hart, 1939) 111–21.

W

Wagman, S, 'Cryptocurrencies and National Security: The Case of Money Laundering and Terrorism Financing' (2022) *Harvard National Security Journal* 14(1), 87–101.
Walker, C, 'Anti-Terrorism Laws: The United Kingdom's Unfinished History' in A Silke (ed), *Routledge Handbook of Terrorism and Counterterrorism* (Routledge, 2018) 406–15.
—— 'Terrorism Financing and the Governance of Charities' in C King, C Walker and J Gurule, *The Palgrave Handbook of Criminal and Terrorism Financing Law* (Springer, 2018) 1085–1115.
Walker, J, 'Estimates of the Extent of Money Laundering in and through Australia', paper prepared for the Australian Transaction Reports and Analysis Centre, John Walker Consulting Services, Queanbeyan, Australia, September 1995.
Walker, J and Unger, B, 'Measuring Global Money Laundering: The Walker Gravity Model' (2009) *Review of Law and Economics* 5(2), 821–53.
Watkins, D and Burton, M (eds), *Research Methods in Law* (Routledge, 2013).
Webley, L, 'The Why and How to of Conducting a Socio-Legal Empirical Research Project' in N Creutzfeld, M Mason and K McConnachie, *Routledge Handbook of Socio-Legal Theory and Methods* (Routledge, 2015) 58–69.
Welling, S, 'Smurfs, Money Laundering, and the Federal Criminal Law: The Crime of Structuring Transactions' (1989) *Florida Law Review* 41(2), 287–343.
Westmore, K, *Conference Report UK FATF Mutual Evaluation Taskforce First Meeting Report* (RUSI: 2025).
—— 'Policy Briefs – Anti-Money Laundering Supervision of the Professions in the UK: Four Key Challenges and How to Address Them' (24 October 2023).

Which?, 'Devastating Emotional Impact of Online Scams Must Force Government Action' (21 March 2021).
—— 'Exclusive: More than 96% of Reported Fraud Cases go Unsolved' (24 September 2018).
—— 'Facebook Repeatedly Sells Ad Space to Known Scammer' (22 January 2022).
—— 'One in Five Fraud Victims Send Money to Criminals via Cryptocurrency' (21 September 2022).
—— 'Two in Five Victims of Online Scam Adverts don't Report to Host Platforms' (26 April 2021).
—— 'Which? Response to the Government's Online Fraud Charter' (30 November 2023).
White, M, 'London Bridge Attack: MI5 Accused of "Damning List" of Failures' (28 June 2019).
Williams, L; 'Research Methods: Our Approach to Socio-Legal Research' in L William, S Corby and B Pauksztat (eds), *Claiming Disability Discrimination Assessing Barriers to Justice* (Palgrave, 2025) 57–73.
Williams, S, '£80m of British Taxpayers' Money "Funnelled to Al-Qaeda" in Decades-Long Scam' (31 March 2019).
Withers, I and Ridley, K, 'Focus: UK Banks to Ramp Up Data Sharing in Dirty Money Crackdown' (22 June 2023).
Wolfsberg Group, *Wolfsberg Anti-Money Laundering Principles for Private Banking* (Wolfsberg Group, 2012).
Wood, H, 'Five Problems with Economic Crime Policing – and How to Solve Them' (11 July 2022).
—— Treasury Committee, Oral evidence: Economic Crime, HC 145, Thursday 8 July 2021.
Wood, H, Artingstall, D, Campbell, H and Moiseienko, A, *Known Unknowns: Plugging the UK's Intelligence Gaps on Money Laundering Involving Professional Services Providers* (RUSI, 2018).
Woodhouse, J, *Data Protection and Digital Information Bill* (House of Commons Library Research Briefing Paper Number 9606, 2022).
—— *Data Protection and Digital Information (No. 2) Bill: Commons Stages* (House of Commons Library Research Briefing Paper Number 9803, 2023).
World Economic Forum, 'Why Financial Inclusion is the Key to a Thriving Digital Economy' (29 July 2024).

Y

Yeoh, P, 'Banks' Vulnerabilities to Money Laundering Activities' (2020) *Journal of Money Laundering Control* 23(1), 122–35.
Yin, R, *Case Study Research: Design and Methods* (Sage, 2014) 16.

Z

Zagaris, B, *International White-Collar Crime – Cases and Materials* (Cambridge University Press, 2010).
Zarate, J and Watson, S, 'The Lexicon of Terror Crystallization of the Definition of Terrorism through the Lens of Terrorist Financing and the Financial Action Task Force' (2022) *Harvard National Security Journal* 13, 369.
Zavoli, I and King, C, 'The Challenges of Implementing Anti-Money Laundering Regulation: An Empirical Analysis' (2021) *Modern Law Review* 84(4), 740–71.

INDEX

www.ingramcontent.com/pod-product-compliance
Ingram Content Group UK Ltd.
Pitfield, Milton Keynes, MK11 3LW, UK
UKHW020804290926
15470UKWH00003B/944